Women in the Workplace in America, 1900–2021

615 Griswold St., Ste. 520, Detroit, MI 48226

* * *

OMNIGRAPHICS
Pearline Jaikumar, *Managing Editor*
Angela L. Williams, *Editorial Director*
Sue Maniloff, *VP, Business Development*
Kevin Hayes, *VP, Operations*

* * *

ISBN 978-0-7808-1957-3
E-ISBN 978-0-7808-1958-0

Library of Congress Control Number: 2021937007

This book is printed on acid-free paper meeting the ANSI Z39.48 Standard. The infinity symbol that appears above indicates that the paper in this book meets that standard.

Printed in the United States

Women in the Workplace in America, 1900–2021

I don't say women's rights – I say the constitutional principle of the equal citizenship stature of men and women.
–U.S. Supreme Court Justice Ruth Bader Ginsburg

Table of Contents

Foreword

Finally, there's a reference book that tells the story of women in the workplace. It is an epic of struggle and triumph, passion and determination. Each working woman plays a part in this historical narrative, including me.

I was born in the 1950s and raised in the Bronx. My mother was a violinist in an orchestra when she was in her twenties but her career as a musician ended when she married my father, an industrial designer who worked with the esteemed Raymond Loewy, who was known as the "man who shaped America." Our home, which my father had designed, was made of industrial materials which were considered cutting edge for their time. He taught me, at an early age, how to see things beyond what they appeared to be. Through his eyes, I learned what creativity is. Whenever he saw me take an interest in something – a new material or a particular type of tool – he would encourage me to create with it. Ultimately, my father taught me that design is about solving problems for humanity.

When I applied to colleges, I told him I wanted to follow in his footsteps and attend a design school. Imagine my shock when he said, "Oh, Ivy, marry someone rich, be a schoolteacher and have your summers off." I recall thinking, "How dare you rob me of my dreams!" My mother would later tell me that she saw my determination to become the designer he inspired me to be. Hearing this from her resonated deeply. I can remember that after she and my dad would fight, when I was growing up, she would retreat to her closet, where she cried over yellowed newspaper articles about the violin recitals she gave as a young woman, and tearfully regret never following her dream to be a professional musician. I felt her sadness then and determined to live a life of no regrets.

Over my career, I have been fortunate to be a design leader in a variety of consumer categories, ranging from apparel and accessories to toys and technology. Some of my designs have been collected by museums and I've received many honors, most recently being named in Fast Company's One Hundred Most Creative People in Business. But what I find most rewarding about my work is enabling each of my team members to realize their full potential.

Today I am a vice president at Google, heading the hardware design team. It was a long hard climb to get there, battling discrimination, overcoming preconceived notions about what women are capable of. Too often I have been the only woman in the room where decisions are made. I wish *Women in the Workplace in America, 1900–2021* had come out forty years ago when I was beginning my own career. I wouldn't have felt so alone but seen myself as part of a continuum of progress as I read about the experiences and achievements of trailblazing women like Mary Jackson, the first Black female engineer at NASA; and Frances Perkins, the "Architect of the New Deal;" and Margaret Chase Smith, the first woman to serve in both houses of Congress; and more than a hundred others profiled in these pages.

Women in the Workplace in America, 1900–2021 is a trailblazer in its own right. In these pages, you will be inspired as I have been by the stories of women you know and many you may not have heard of, from the "Radium Girls," young factory workers who ingested radioactive radium causing them to glow in the dark, to the "Guerrilla Girls," a group of female artists challenging sexism in the art world. All of them deserve our attention. To read about the myriad things they had to battle in every field is to realize how far we have come but also how much further we have to go. This book reminds us that women in every generation have been called to show up as themselves, speak their truth, and expand the consciousness of the workplace. This is necessary now more than ever. If we continue this legacy, we will help solve some of the most complex problems of our time. Whether you are entering the workforce or have been part of it for decades, I hope you will find *Women in the Workplace* informative and motivating. It's on the shoulders of the women you are about to meet that you and I stand tall.

Ivy Ross
Vice President of Design for Hardware Products
Google

Author's Note

In Colonial America, the English common-law concept of *coverture* defined women as the property of men, as chattel, with no legal identity except through him. These women did not exist as far as the law was concerned.

The "hidden figures" who spent their careers calculating trajectories and mathematical formulas for NASA very nearly didn't exist either, at least not in a way that acknowledged the important contributions they made to our nation's space program. We know their names, contributions, and stories today because a woman whose father told her about these trail-blazing mathematicians was curious enough to research them and the segregated building where they made their calculations.

Would these "human computers" have received public recognition if she hadn't written that popular book? Would a building be named after one of them, as one is now?

After all these years of so many women's contributions not being valued or recorded, we have to wonder.

The official American narrative provides us with the names and faces of America's official heroes, but contributions from too many women and people from marginalized populations often remain below the surface, require mining.

That's why you'll find so many previously "invisible" women featured in these pages. We amplify their names and the contributions they made, in part, because women have always worked in this country, but have not always received credit for that work.

Yet we all need role models; we all need to learn the full story.

And these trailblazers deserve to have their inspirational stories heard.

This book includes anonymous millworkers captured in grainy photographs, suffragists who understood that women required representation before they could gain autonomy, woman warriors whose names appear in war documents, a trailblazing new vice president – so many working women are represented here through the years. We hope you find these women and their stories as compelling as the workplace data we offer to help you contextualize women's experiences in the American workplace over time.

Angela Williams
Editorial Director
Omnigraphics

PART ONE

New Century, New Visions, 1900–1929

Milestones for Women Prior to 1900

In Colonial America, England's common law defined women as the property of men. And while both sexes worked during colonial times in order to survive, White men held all the power, made all the laws, and banned women from voting, holding public office, pursuing rights on their own behalf, owning property in their own names, or keeping their own earnings.

A few educated colonial women worked as doctors, lawyers, or teachers and a few worked as "deputy husbands" in their husbands' trade – assisting in a print shop, for example. A few others worked as nurses, and unmarried or widowed women typically ran a boardinghouse or worked as a seamstress in order to earn a living. For the most part though, colonial women worked in their homes and bore and nursed children throughout their reproductive years while their husbands performed agricultural labor.

A colonial code of ethics defined some women as "good wives" and those who fit this definition sometimes enjoyed freedoms that were unavailable even to nineteenth-century women. A good wife, for example, was encouraged to cast a vote for her family when her husband was unavailable to do so.

Mostly though, these good women worked with no formal pay: Making soap and changing diapers, washing children and spinning thread, weaving cloth and sewing clothes, washing clothes and milking cows, minding yard animals and making butter, butchering fowl for dinner, and all other tasks necessary to maintain her home and care for her children. These women also worked in the fields alongside the men come harvest time and were expected to teach their children how to read the Bible and be good Christians (a lesson that included telling these children that the Christian god created women for the benefit of men and that women were designed to be subjugated by them).

We know little else about most colonial women, although the American narrative tells us much about our pilgrim forefathers.

The race- and gender-based subjugation that colonists carried to their New World restricted the freedoms of all women, but the enslaved Black women brought to these shores to toil primarily in the southern states were the most disenfranchised of all.

Northern states, with the exception of Massachusetts, outlawed slavery. Progressive citizens, along with Quakers and Puritans (who considered slavery to be a sin) joined Black abolitionists Phillis Wheatley, Sojourner Truth, and others to canvas for the abolition of slavery, advocate for an end to the systemic oppression of women and obtain a universal right to vote.

Three years after enslaved people were liberated by the Emancipation Proclamation, a petition signed by Elizabeth Cady Stanton, Susan B. Anthony, and others called for a national constitutional amendment to "prohibit the several states from disenfranchising any of their citizens on the ground of sex." In 1878, Senator A. A. Sargent of California introduced the "Anthony Amendment" to Congress.

And so began long decades of constant strategizing, canvassing, marching, lobbying, and enduring imprisonment and beatings in an effort to gain woman's suffrage, which the suffragists understood would be a first step toward allowing working women the opportunity to elect representatives who supported their interests and causes.

CHAPTER ONE

Early Twentieth-Century Trailblazers, 1900–1909

CHAPTER CONTENTS

Section 1.1 • **OVERVIEW**

"Overview: Women in the Workplace in America, 1900–1909," • © 2021 Omnigraphics.

In 1900, the U.S. workforce was comprised of 24 million people. There were no child-labor regulations at this time and many children as young as 10 years of age were actively working. According to U.S. Census data for that year, there were 1.75 million "gainful workers" between the ages of 10 and 15 working. Many families relied on this additional income and child laborers accounted for 6 percent of the working population.

Moreover, the overwhelming majority of the labor force was male. Though women were entering the workplace in larger numbers, their options and opportunities were limited. Between 1880 and 1910, the number of working women tripled. Still, just 19 percent of all working-age women were employed. Accordingly, 80 percent of American children had a working father and a stay-at-home mother. 60 percent of working women were domestic servants, and female representation was abysmal in many industries and fields. Indeed, the Bureau of Labor Statistics reports that just 1 percent of lawyers and 6 percent of physicians were women in 1900. Still, by 1900, every state had passed legislation that granted married women the right to keep their own wages and to own property in their own names. And by 1903, a coalition of workers had formed the National Women's Trade Union League.

In terms of racial diversity, people of color accounted for 3.8 million, or 14 percent, of the labor force that year, with African Americans being the largest underrepresented racial group. Immigration also was on the rise in 1900, a trend that would continue for another two decades and bolster the nation's economic development. That year, immigration authorities recorded 488,572 arrivals, a number that would grow exponentially before the close of the decade.

Typical work hours varied between industries; however, a factory worker would likely labor for 53 hours a week, on average. The per-capita income was $4,200 per year and the unemployment rate was approximately 5 percent.

Workplace injuries were a legitimate risk for many industrial employees, yet there were no protective policies or programs in place at the time. In the absence of disability payments or workers' compensation, injured employees had no option but to take legal action. At the time, however, lawsuits against employers were largely unsuccessful. It is estimated that just 15 percent of lawsuits resulted in compensation for the injured party.

By 1896, Colorado, Idaho, Utah, and Wyoming had extended voting rights to women. By 1900, women had substantial control over their property in every state, as well as legal recognition as the joint guardians of their children. Notably, these political victories were primarily applicable to White women. Since slavery was ongoing, neither Black women or men had property rights, and Indigenous people were routinely denied these rights through the machinery of colonization (e.g., treaty violations on the part of the government). Still, the socioeconomic and political advancements made by some women provided hope that more women could follow. The century prior had shown that equal rights were not beyond reach, and this belief underscored the social-reform efforts witnessed among women and women's organizations in the next century.

Section 1.2 • WOMAN WARRIORS

This section includes text excerpted from "Dr. Anita Newcomb McGee" (National Library of Science at the National Institutes of Health); "Army Nurse Corps Formed," "Navy Nurse Corps Formed," •

ARMY NURSES CORPS FORMED

In 1898, during the Spanish-American War, Dr. Anita Newcomb (McGee) was named acting assistant surgeon general of the U.S. Army, making her the only woman permitted to wear an officer's uniform. She was instrumental in organizing the 1,600 nurses who served during the conflict and wrote the Army Reorganization Act of 1901, which established the Army Nurse Corps as a permanent unit.

Anita Newcomb's childhood and her family's social status afforded her a multitude of educational and professional opportunities. Her parents were both respected intellectuals and academics and her mother, in particular, encouraged her daughter to pursue diverse academic subjects. Educated at home and in elite private schools in the nation's capital, she was later able to travel to Cambridge, England, and the University of Geneva, Switzerland, to take special courses. She pursued interests in history and genealogy, even writing and delivering lectures on these topics.

In 1888, she married William John McGee, who supported her decision to attend medical school soon after they were married. After earning her Doctor of Medicine degree from Columbia University (later George Washington University) in 1892, and gaining experience in political organization, she completed an internship at the Women's Clinic in Washington, D.C., and studied gynecology at Johns Hopkins University School of Medicine. For the next few years, Dr. McGee operated a private practice before withdrawing from clinical work around 1895 to pursue other interests.

Anita McGee's talent for political organization served her during her early career in medicine. During her senior year in medical school at Columbia, a group of male students reportedly used "debased" gestures involving cadavers in an attempt to insult their female peers. In response, the medical staff used the incident as a pretext for ending the school's coeducation policy. Rallying her fellow women students, McGee served on the committee to prevent their removal from the school. Revealing herself a capable organizer and strategist, McGee used every argument she could muster – asserting that friends of women's higher education would denounce the faculty board, that medical standards in Washington would decline as women were forced to attend lesser institutions, and appealing to school pride, noting that rival Georgetown University would soon surpass Columbia as a result of unprogressive policies. Despite a politically savvy campaign, the petition drive failed.

Taking advantage of her social position and her talent for organization, Dr. McGee became involved in the American Association for the Advancement of Science, the Women's Anthropological Society of America, and Daughters of the American Revolution. In 1898 with the outbreak of the Spanish-American War, Dr. McGee discovered through friends that Army Surgeon General George M. Sternberg intended to use nurses at base hospitals for the first time since the Civil War. She petitioned Sternberg to permit only fully qualified nurses to serve. Dr. McGee created a special committee of the Daughters of the American Revolution to screen nurses and then offered their services to Sternberg. After assembling approximately

1,600 highly qualified nurses, Dr. McGee was appointed Acting Assistant Surgeon General of the Army for the duration of the war. At the end of the war, she drafted the legislation that established the U.S. Army Nurse Corps.

NAVY NURSE CORPS FORMED

Dr. Anita Newcomb McGee helped establish the Navy Nursing Corps two years after forming the Army Nurse Corps, and in 1899 wrote a manual on nursing for the military. She also helped found the Society of Spanish-American War Nurses in 1900 to look after the interests of the Army Nurse Corps and served as the organization's president for the next six years. In 1904 during the Russo-Japanese War, Dr. McGee offered the Society's services to the Japanese government. Spending six months in Japan working beside nurses in that country, McGee was designated "superior of nurses" with the rank of an Army officer. For her services, the Japanese government honored her with the Imperial Order of the Sacred Crown. She later briefly lectured on hygiene at the University of California, Berkeley, then for the rest of her life, she divided her time between several homes and oversaw her son's education.

Section 1.3 • SHIRTWAIST WORKERS STRIKE OF 1909

In 1909, 20,000 shirtwaist workers in New York City's garment district went on strike in late November. The strikers, almost all of whom were young immigrants, primarily worked for the three largest manufacturers of shirtwaists: The Leiserson Company, the Rosen Brothers, and the Triangle Shirtwaist Company. These strikers braved a New York winter to demand decent wages, reasonable hours, improved workplace safety, and an end to "workplace indignities," such as invasion of privacy and sexual harassment.

The "Uprising of 20,000," as the strike became known, lasted 11 weeks. The Rosen Brothers factory settled with their workers after five weeks, but Leiserson and Triangle hired thugs who joined with New York police officers in harassing, beating, and otherwise abusing these strikers from the needle trade.

The three main organizers of the strike were Rose Schneiderman, Pauline Newman, and Clara Lemlich, who was arrested 17 times and suffered six broken ribs. When she and other strikers appeared before one magistrate, he told them that they were "striking against God and nature." The Uprising of 20,000 was the largest demonstration of women to date and one that inspired the Great Revolt of 1910, when women cloak makers walked off the job. Although not all of their demands were met – note the horrific Triangle Shirtwaist Factory fire just two years later – the Uprising of 20,000 demonstrated the capabilities of women union organizers.

Section 1.4 • **TRAILBLAZERS**

This section includes text excerpted from "Marie Louise Bottineau Baldwin," "Ida B. Wells," and "Zitkala-Ša" (National Park Service); "Mary Church Turrell," "Madam C. J. Walker," and Maggie L. Walker," • © 2021 Omnigraphics.

MARIE LOUISE BOTTINEAU BALDWIN

Marie Louise Bottineau Baldwin of the Metis tribe of the Anishinaabe (Turtle Mountain Chippewa) Nation was born in Pembina, North Dakota. Her father, J. B. Bottineau, was a lawyer who worked as an advocate for the Anishinaabe Nation in Minnesota and North Dakota. While a teenager, her family lived in Minneapolis and Marie attended school there as well as in nearby St. Paul. She spent some time across the border at St. John's Ladies College in Winnipeg, Manitoba (Canada), and returned to Minneapolis to work as a clerk in her father's law office. She and her father moved to Washington, D.C. in the early 1890s to defend the treaty rights of the Anishinaabe Nation. There, they became part of an established community of professional Native Americans who lived and worked in the capital.

In 1904, President Theodore Roosevelt appointed Baldwin as a clerk in the Office of Indian Affairs (OIA), an agency now called the Bureau of Indian Affairs (BIA) that is within the Department of the Interior. She was hired at $900 per year and received a raise to $1,000 before she had served a full year in the position. While this pay was low compared to what other clerks were making ($1,000 to $1,800 per year), she was the agency's highest-paid Indigenous woman.

Early in her career, Baldwin believed that Native Americans needed to assimilate into European-American society in order to survive, but over time, as she became involved with the suffrage movement and the Society for American Indians (SAI), her views began to change. Instead of assimilation, Baldwin emphasized the value of traditional Native cultures while asserting her own (and therefore others') place in the modern world as an Indian woman.

This shift is evident in a ca. 1911 photo of Baldwin. In this photo taken for her government personnel file, she chose to wear Native dress and to braid her hair. This was a radical act as a federal employee working for the OIA because, at the time, the agency was pushing for Native Americans to assimilate into White American culture and used Indian employees as examples of assimilation. Yet, this radical choice appears to have passed unnoticed at the time, except for by journalists, who often paired this federal service photo with one of her dressed in "modern American dress."

In 1911, Baldwin's father died, and his death proved to be a turning point in her life. That year, she gave a speech at the first meeting of the SAI and became increasingly involved in their work to celebrate and advocate for Native identity. And she went on to become a nationally known spokesperson for modern Indian women, testifying before Congress, meeting with women from across the country. She also was a member of the contingent who met with President Woodrow Wilson in the Oval Office in 1914. While at the SAI, she was colleagues with Zitkala-Ša, another Native American woman who worked to advance the cause of Indian suffrage.

In 1912, at the age of 49, Baldwin enrolled at the Washington College of Law – a college that Ellen Spencer Mussey and Emma Gillet started in Mussey's law offices after a group of

Despite pressure to assimilate to White culture, Marie Louise Bottineau Baldwin braided her hair and wore tribal clothing for her government ID photo.

women asked to study with them because most existing law schools refused to admit women. Mussey and Gillet are, themselves, trailblazers, as is their college, since the Washington College of Law was the first law school in America founded by women, the first with a woman serving as dean, and the first to graduate a class comprised solely of women.

Two years after Baldwin enrolled – and then proceeded to take night classes after working all day – she graduated as an attorney, making Baldwin the first woman of color to graduate from the school.

Baldwin became active with the suffrage movement and marched with a group of female lawyers in the 1913 Woman Suffragist Procession that was organized by Alice Paul. Interviewed in newspapers who were covering the suffrage movement, Baldwin educated people about the traditional political roles of women in Native society.

Changing politics and priorities within the OAI led Baldwin to disengage from the group in 1918 or 1919 – although she continued to work for the Indian Office in Washington, D.C. until 1932, when she retired because of declining health. In 1949, she moved from D.C. to Los Angeles, where she died from a cerebral hemorrhage in 1952. She is buried at Forest Lawn Memorial Park, Glendale, in Los Angeles, California.

MARY CHURCH TURRELL

Mary Church was born on September 23, 1863, in Memphis, Tennessee, to formerly enslaved parents. Her father, Robert Reed Church, was a prominent businessman and among the first Black millionaires in the South. Her mother, Louisa, was also a business owner and ran a popular hair salon. Though they divorced when their children were young, they maintained a shared value for education and saw Mary through an extensive academic career.

In 1884 Mary enrolled at the Antioch College Laboratory School in Ohio. This was one of the only integrated colleges in the nation at the time. Notably, she opted to take the "gentleman's course," which was longer and more challenging than the program the institution offered to women. At Antioch she also met and befriended Anna Julia Cooper and Ida Gibbs Hunt, who became notable intellectuals and civil-rights figures. Antioch was followed by Oberlin College, from which she received both her bachelor's and master's degrees. Mary then completed a two-year stint as an instructor before moving to Washington, D.C., for another teaching position at the M Street Colored High School (one of the nation's first African American high schools). It was there that she met fellow educator Heberton Terrell, whom she married in 1891.

Mary's activism was engendered by tragedy. Her friend, Thomas Moss, had started a grocery business back in Memphis with two partners, also Black men. As the business grew, the White owners of a store nearby saw their profits shrinking and sought to eliminate the threat. In 1892, Moss and his partners were shot and killed by an angry White mob in an incident that became known as the "People's Grocery Lynchings." This loss prompted Mary to partner with Ida B. Wells in her anti-lynching activism. Wells would go on to become one of the foremost anti-lynching activists in the country.

Herself a woman of means and relative privilege, Mary's very existence was a testament to possibility. This likely informed her political perspectives, which were grounded in the notion of racial uplift. Mary believed that Black people could advance themselves through upward mobility (education, employment, activism, and community). Her thoughts on the mechanisms of collective progress are perhaps best explained by her famous phrase, "Lifting as We Climb." From this perspective, the success of each person contributed to the gradual elevation of the race.

This phrase later became the motto of the National Association of Colored Women (NACW), which Mary cofounded in 1896. She led the organization until 1901, when she was memorialized as honorary president for life. This initiative was, in part, inspired by past experiences of exclusion from White women's social organizations. In response, Mary resolved to enhance the presence and influence of organizations that prioritized both gender and racial inequality.

Significantly, she did not lose faith in allyship and cross-cultural collaboration. As NACW president, she partnered with Black and White organizations in support of woman's suffrage and racial justice, believing the former was crucial to the latter. More specifically, Mary believed that to empower Black women was to empower the Black community. To that end, she became an active and vocal suffragist, supporting the movement through her writing and speaking engagements.

A gifted orator, she had worked as a lecturer in the 1890s, befriending eminent Black intellectuals like W.E.B Du Bois during this time. She also became the first Black female member of the Washington, D.C., school board, a position she held twice in two decades, for a total of 11 years. In that capacity, she visited schools, supported fundraising campaigns, and drummed up support for Frederick Douglass Day: A commemoration that laid the foundation for Black History Month. Her experiences in this role also helped inform the NAWC's educational initiatives, and her own support for childcare for working mothers.

In 1909, she became a part of history, as one of the founders and charter members of the National Association for the Advancement of Colored People (NAACP). The following year, she cofounded the College Alumnae Club, later called the National Association of University Women. A decade later, she joined the National Woman's Party as it famously picketed the White House, demanding President Wilson's support for women's voting rights.

Today, Mary would be called an intersectionalist, because her politics were framed by the understanding that various forms of discrimination work to support and amplify each other. Indeed, she noted that she fought for suffrage because she belonged "to the only group in this country that has two such huge obstacles to surmount ... both sex and race." Accordingly, her activism was comprehensive: When one battle was won, she joined another, recognizing that there was always more to be done.

Once the 19th Amendment passed, she turned her attention to other social-justice pursuits, specifically the battle for civil rights. In 1940, she published a memoir, *A Colored Woman in a White World*, though she was far from retired from public life. Indeed, she remained an active political figure into her eighties. Her later years were largely focused on dismantling segregation in schools, workplaces, and other public facilities.

In 1946, the American Association of University Women denied Mary's request that they reinstate her membership, which had lapsed some years before. Upon learning of the refusal, she sued for discrimination, and a two-year legal battle ensued. The subsequent reinstatement was a minor victory compared to the racially inclusive policy changes the organization made in the aftermath. This had been her intention all along, and the latter outcome was the one she truly desired. Mary was later noted as saying it would have been cowardly for her not to take up the fight and potentially pave the way for other women of color.

In 1949, the African American community in Washington, D.C. came together to commemorate Mary's ninetieth birthday. Over 700 people attended the lunch, during which the newly formed Mary Church Terrell Fund was announced. The fund was a charity to support efforts to abolish Jim Crow legislation in Washington, D.C.

Unfortunately, Mary did not live to see the landmark achievements that changed the face of America in the late Civil Rights era. She passed away in July 1954, before *Brown v. Board of Education* helped to desegregate schools, and the Civil Rights Act of 1964 desegregated public facilities. Both had been chief among her political priorities in her later years. Still, she is recognized for her lifelong service to these causes (and countless others), her formidable intellect, and her passion for inclusion and collaboration.

MADAM C. J. WALKER

Sarah Breedlove was born in 1867 on the same Louisiana cotton plantation where her parents had been enslaved. She was orphaned at age seven, widowed at age 20, and worked for more than 10 years as a washerwoman who could barely make ends meet.

At the turn of the century, most Americans lacked indoor plumbing and a combination of poor diet and sub-optimal hygiene practices caused many to develop scalp infections and other ailments that damaged their hair and caused some to experience hair loss or baldness. Breedlove's brothers, who were barbers, taught her how barbers treat such ailments and she began experimenting with her own formulas for a product that would treat these ailments.

In 1905, Breedlove moved to Denver and was hired as a cook. The pharmacist who employed her taught her basic chemistry and what she learned from him allowed her to perfect her formula. In 1906, she both married Charles Joseph Walker and experienced local success selling her new hair-ointment product and method for hair regrowth – a method that became known as the "Walker System of Beauty Culture," or the "Walker Method." And hence her name change to Madam C. J. Walker.

For the next several years Walker traveled the nation training "Walker agents" to sell her product and hair-recovery method, and in so doing provided economic independence and a new career path to thousands of African American women who, like her, would otherwise have been limited to low-paying work as cooks, farmworkers, maids, or washers. A few years later, she opened a beauty college in Pittsburgh and then a manufacturing and distribution company in Indianapolis, a city that already boasted a prosperous Black business community. And then Madam C. J. Walker went international and expanded her business to Central America and the Caribbean – and, by 1919, she boasted 25,000 active Walker sales agents.

Madam C. J. Walker was not only a businesswoman, but also a philanthropist, and one of the first Black female millionaires in the country.

MAGGIE L. WALKER

Maggie L. Walker, daughter of an enslaved parent, was the first woman to open a bank in the United States, and she founded that bank in the former capital of the Confederacy. Walker opened St. Luke's Penny Savings in Richmond, Virginia, to ensure that Black business owners and residents received fair loans. She also wanted to keep funneling profits back into the Black community.

Top image: Maggie L. Walker, whose parents were enslaved, was the first woman in the country to open a bank, c. 1910. • Lower image: Ida B. Wells was an African American civil-rights advocate, journalist, feminist, and American hero, c. 1900.

"Let us put our moneys together," Walker said. "Let us use our moneys; let us put our money out as usury among ourselves, and reap the benefit ourselves. Let us have a bank that will take the nickels and turn them into dollars." Walker also launched a newspaper and an emporium where Black people could walk through the front doors instead of a colored side door to shop or sell their wares.

Walker "wasn't just raising the bar for her community. She was working to create opportunities," said Maryland sculptor Antonio "Toby" Mendez, who created a bronze statue of Walker that is memorialized in the place where she accomplished so much. Richmond resident Gary Flowers helped lead the effort to honor Walker, whose accomplishments could have easily been consigned to a historical footnote. "Children and adults alike need to see the missing pieces of history," Flowers said. And that's why it is crucially important that we "add statues of African Americans who have been left out of the history books."

Washington Post columnist Michael S. Rosenwald points out that Walker's "accomplishments in the face of racial oppression and segregation," make it all the more important that she be memorialized in a city that features row upon row of monuments memorializing slavery-supporting Confederates who were defeated in the U.S. Civil War.

IDA B. WELLS

Ida B. Wells was an African American civil-rights advocate, journalist, feminist, and American hero who worked to guarantee access to the vote and representation for her people.

Wells was born enslaved in Holly Springs, Mississippi, in 1862. She was the oldest daughter of James and Lizzie Wells. During Reconstruction, her parents were active in the Republican Party. Mr. Wells was involved with the Freedman's Aid Society and helped start Rust College. Rust is a historically Black liberal arts college (HBCU) affiliated with the United Methodist Church and one of ten Historic Black Colleges and Universities founded before 1869 that are still operating.

Wells attended Rust College to receive her early education but was forced to drop out. At 16, Wells lost both parents and one of her siblings in a yellow fever outbreak. She convinced a nearby school administrator that she was 18 and landed a job as a teacher to take care of her siblings.

In 1882, Wells moved with her sisters to Memphis, Tennessee, to live with their aunt. Her brothers found work as carpentry apprentices, and for a time Wells continued her education at Fisk University in Nashville.

While on a train ride from Memphis to Nashville in May 1884, Wells reached a turning point. She had bought a first-class ticket, but the train crew forced her to move to the racially segregated car. Wells refused on principle, before being forcibly removed from the train. As she was being removed, she bit one of the crew members. Wells sued the railroad and won a $500 settlement in a circuit-case court. The decision was overturned by the Tennessee Supreme Court.

Following this incident, Wells began writing about issues of race and politics in the South. Using the name Iola, Wells had a number of her articles published in Black newspapers and periodicals. She later became an owner of two newspapers: *The Memphis Free Speech and Headlight* and *Free Speech*. In addition to working as a journalist and publisher, Wells worked as a teacher in a segregated public school in Memphis. She was a vocal critic of the condition of segregated schools in the city and was fired from her job in 1891 because of her criticism.

In 1892, Wells turned her attention to anti-lynching advocacy after a friend and two of his business associates were murdered. Tom Moss, Calvin McDowell, and Will Stewart opened a grocery store that drew customers away from a White-owned store in the neighborhood. The

White store owner and his supporters clashed with Moss, McDowell, and Stewart on multiple occasions. One night the three Black store owners had to guard their store against an attack and ended up shooting several of the White men. They were arrested and taken to jail.

Unfortunately, they did not have a chance to defend themselves. A lynch mob took them from their cells and murdered them. Wells wrote articles decrying the lynching and risked her own life traveling the South to gather information on other lynchings. One of her editorials pushed some of the city's White people over the edge. A mob stormed her newspaper office and destroyed all of her equipment. Wells was in New York at the time of the incident, which likely saved her life. She stayed in the North after her life was threatened and wrote an in-depth report on lynching in America for the *New York Age*. This newspaper was run by T. Thomas Fortune, a former slave.

In 1898, Well brought her anti-lynching campaign to the White House and called for President McKinley to make reforms. In 1895, Wells married Ferdinand Barnett, with whom she had four children. Despite being married, Wells was one of the first American women to keep her maiden name. In 1896, Wells formed several civil-rights organizations, including the National Association of Colored Women. After brutal attacks on the Black community in Springfield, Illinois, in 1908, Wells took action and, in 1909, attended a conference for an organization that would later become the National Association for the Advancement of Colored People (NAACP). Though she is considered a founder of the NAACP, Wells cut ties with the organization because she felt it that in its infancy it lacked action-based initiatives.

Wells was an active fighter for woman suffrage, particularly for Black women. On January 30th, 1913, Wells founded the Alpha Suffrage Club in Chicago. The club organized women in the city to elect candidates who would best serve the Black community. As president of the club, Wells was invited to march in the 1913 Suffrage Parade in Washington, D.C., along with dozens of other club members. Organizers, afraid of offending southern White suffragists, asked women of color to march at the back of the parade. Wells refused and stood on the parade sidelines until the Chicago contingent of White women passed, at which point she joined the march. The rest of the Suffrage Club contingent marched at the back of the parade. Work done by Wells and the Alpha Suffrage Club played a crucial role in the victory of woman suffrage in Illinois with the passage of the Illinois Equal Suffrage Act of 1913 on June 25th.

Wells died of kidney disease on March 25th, 1931, in Chicago, leaving behind a legacy of social and political activism. In 2020, Ida B. Wells was awarded a Pulitzer Prize "for her outstanding and courageous reporting on the horrific and vicious violence against African Americans during the era of lynching."

ZITKALA-ŠA

Zitkala-Ša (Red Bird / Gertrude Simmons Bonnin) was a writer, teacher, intellectual, musician, and political activist who worked with Marie Louise Bottineau Baldwin in the Office of Indian Affairs to advance the cause of Indian suffrage. She was committed to maintaining a public voice for the concerns of diverse women and was a strong advocate for women's rights.

Zitkala-Ša was born on the Yanton Indian Reservation in South Dakota and raised by her mother after her father abandoned the family. When she was eight years old, Quaker missionaries visited the Reservation and took several of the children, including Zitkala-Ša, to Wabash, Indiana, to attend White's Indiana Manual Labor Institute. Zitkala-Ša left despite her mother's disapproval. At this residential school, Zitkala-Ša was given the missionary name Gertrude Simmons. She attended the Institute until 1887.

Zitkala-Ša was conflicted about her experiences at the Institute and wrote about both her great joy in learning to read, write, and play the violin, as well as about the deep grief and pain she felt from losing her heritage by being forced to pray as a Quaker. The missionaries also forced her to cut her hair.

Zitkala-Ša returned to live with her mother on the Yankton Reservation in 1887 but left three years later. She felt that she did not fit in after her experiences at the Institute. At fifteen years old, she returned to the Institute to further her education. Her study of piano and violin led the Institute to hire her as a music teacher. She graduated in 1895 and, when she received her diploma, Zitkala-Ša gave a speech advocating for women's rights. Then, instead of returning home, Zitkala-Ša accepted a scholarship to Earlham College – a Quaker institute of higher learning in Richmond, Indiana. While attending Earlham, she began to collect stories from Native tribes and translated these stories into Latin and English.

Tragically, in 1897, just six weeks before she was to graduate, Zitkala-Ša had to leave Earlham because of financial and health issues. Again, she chose not to return to the Reservation, but instead moved to Boston and pursued studies in violin at the New England Conservatory of Music. In 1899, she accepted a job as music teacher at the Carlisle Indian Industrial School in Pennsylvania. From 1879 until 1918, this school was the flagship Indian boarding school in the United States, and it was used as a model for many others. In 1900, the school sent Zitkala-Ša back to the Yankton Reservation to gather more students. When she returned, she was shocked to find her family home in disrepair and her community living in a state of extreme poverty. She also learned that White settlers were occupying land given to the Yankton Dakota people by the federal government.

Zitkala-Ša returned to Carlisle and began writing about Native American life. Her autobiographical and Lakota stories presented her people as generous and loving and defied the common racist stereotypes that portrayed Native Americans as ignorant savages. These stereotypes were being used as arguments for why Native Americans needed to be assimilated into White American society. Her writing, which was deeply critical of the boarding-school system, were published in national English magazines, including *Atlantic Monthly* and *Harper's Monthly*. In 1901, she wrote for *Harper's Monthly* a piece that described the profound loss of identity felt by a student at the Carlisle Indian School. She was subsequently fired.

Afterward, she spent some time back at the Reservation caring for her mother and collecting stories for her book *Old Indian Legends*. She also worked as a clerk at the Bureau of Indian Affairs (BIA) office at Standing Rock Indian Reservation. And, in 1902, she married Captain Raymond Talefase Bonnin. They were assigned to the Uintah-Ouray Reservation in Utah and lived and worked there for the next fourteen years. While there, they had a son, Raymond Ohiya Bonnin.

In 1910, Zitkala-Ša met William F. Hanson, a professor at Brigham Young University in Utah. Together they collaborated on an opera. *The Sun Dance Opera* was completed in 1913. Based on the sacred Sioux ritual that the federal government had prohibited, Zitkala-Ša wrote the libretto and songs for this first American Indian opera ever written. It is a symbol of how Zitkala-Ša lived in and bridged both her traditional Native American world and the world of White America in which she was raised.

While on the Uintah-Ouray Reservation, Zitkala-Ša joined the Society of American Indians, a group founded in 1911 to preserve traditional Native American culture while lobbying for full American citizenship. Beginning in 1916, Zitkala-Ša served as the Society's secretary. In this position, she corresponded with the BIA but became increasingly vocal in her criticism of the Bureau's assimilationist policies and practice. She also reported abuse of children when they, for example, refused to pray as Christians. Her husband Raymond was fired from the BIA office in 1916.

The family then moved to Washington, D.C., where Zitkala-Ša continued her work with the Society of American Indians, where she was colleagues with Marie Louise Bottineau Baldwin. From 1918 to 1919, Zitkala-Ša edited the society's journal *American Indian Magazine*. She lectured across the country promoting the preservation of Native American cultural and tribal identities (though she was adamantly against the traditional use of peyote and likened it to the destructive effects of alcohol in Native communities). While sharply critical of assimilation, she remained firm in her conviction that Indigenous people in the United States should be citizens, and that, as citizens, they should have the right to vote: "In the land that was once his own – America … there was never a time more opportune than now for America to enfranchise the Red man!" As original occupants of the land, she argued, Native Americans needed to be represented in the current system of government.

The federal Indian Citizenship Act of 1924 granted U.S. citizenship rights to all Native Americans. However, this did not guarantee the right to vote. States retained the authority to decide who could and could not vote. In 1926, Zitkala-Ša and her husband founded the National Council of American Indians. Until her death in 1938, Zitkala-Ša served as president, fundraiser, and speaker. The Council worked to unite the tribes across the United States to gain suffrage for all Indians. She also worked with White suffrage groups and was active in the General Federation of Women's Clubs beginning in 1921. This group worked to maintain a public voice for the concerns of diverse women, including working women. Zitkala-Ša created the Indian Welfare Committee of the Federation in 1924. That year, she ran a voter-registration drive among Native Americans, encouraging those who could to engage in the democratic process and support legislation that would be good for Native Americans. Published that year was a piece co-authored by Zitkala-Ša: "Oklahoma's Poor Rich Indians: An Orgy of Graft and Exploitation of the Five Civilized Tribes – Legalized Robbery." This article was instrumental in convincing the government to investigate the exploitation and defrauding of Native Americans by outsiders for access to oil-rich lands and in the passage of the Indian Reorganization Act of 1934.

Zitkala-Ša worked in a wide range of settings – from teacher to writer to fundraiser to journal editor – and scraped together enough to get by. Until her death in 1928, Zitkala-Ša continued to work for improvements in education, healthcare, and legal recognition of Native Americans, as well as the preservation of Native American culture. She died in Washington, D.C. and is buried at Arlington National Cemetery with her husband. They share a headstone and she is memorialized as "His Wife / Gertrude Simmons Bonnin / Zitkala-Ša of the Sioux Indians / 1876–1936."

CHAPTER TWO

Mobilizing for Inclusion, Enfranchisement, and War, 1910–1919

CHAPTER CONTENTS

Section 2.1 • OVERVIEW

"Overview: Women in the Workplace in America, 1910–1919," • © 2021 Omnigraphics.

The early twentieth century brought the largest wave of European immigration that the United States had ever seen. From the early 1900s until 1914 – the start of World War I – this influx of foreign nationals provided a much-needed boost to the local economy and helped expand American cities. This urbanization was in large part due to the Industrial Revolution: A period marked by technological advancements that changed the labor landscape and sparked a surge in city-dwelling populations.

Meanwhile, organizers in the Woman's Suffrage Movement that began in the 1800s continued to strategize, lobby, and protest for representation, and were cognizant of the fact that women would never have a seat at the table, or autonomy, or a voice in the home, public sphere, or the workplace until they could vote for representation that reflects their priorities and values.

In 1915, when the United States joined the war, nearly half of the nation's 100 million residents lived in rural areas with populations of 2,500 or less. After all, prior to the Industrial Revolution, much of the labor force in both Europe and America was agricultural. The development and availability of sophisticated machinery ushered in an era of mass production – a far cry from the painstaking crafting and sorting processes of yore. As the war increased demand for manufactured goods, more employment opportunities emerged. In the early days of the war, the nation was still reeling from a two-year recession that ended in 1914. By 1916, unemployment had declined to 4.8 percent, reaching an ultimate low of 1.4 percent in 1918. Much of this was thanks to the industrial labor taking place in factories making textiles, iron, glass, and other materials.

Section 2.2 • LONG JOURNEY TO ENFRANCHISEMENT

This section includes text excerpted from "Woman Suffrage and the 19th Amendment" (U.S. National Archives and Records Administration); "Symbols of the Women's Suffrage Movement," "The National Woman's Party and Role of Political Dissent during Wartime" and "Suffrage 'Prison Special' Tour of 1919" (National Park Service); "The Silent Sentinels and Voting Rights," and "Woman's Suffrage: The Early Years,"• © 2021 Omnigraphics.

WOMAN'S SUFFRAGE: THE EARLY YEARS

Beginning in the mid-nineteenth century, several generations of woman's suffrage supporters lectured, wrote, marched, lobbied, and practiced civil disobedience to achieve what many Americans considered to be a radical change to the Constitution – the guarantee of a woman's right to vote. These women recognized that women would never be able to live autonomous lives or have representation in the workplace if they lacked a seat at the table. Some suffragists lobbied politicians and some used more confrontational tactics such as hunger strikes, picketing, and silent vigils to highlight their cause.

In July 1848, Elizabeth Cady Stanton and Lucretia Mott organized the first women's rights convention in Seneca Falls, New York. The Seneca Falls Convention produced a list of demands called the Declaration of Sentiments. Modeled after the Declaration of Independence, it called for broader educational and professional opportunities for women and the right of married women to control their wages and property. After this historic

African American women like Nannie Burroughs (far left, holding banner) were very involved in the suffrage movement with both mainstream and Black suffragist organizations, c. 1905.

gathering, women's voting rights became a central issue in the emerging debate about women's rights in the United States.

Many of the attendees at the convention were also abolitionists whose goals included universal suffrage – the right to vote for all adults. In 1870, this goal was partially realized with the passing of the 15th Amendment, which granted Black men the right to vote. Woman suffragists' impassioned disagreement over supporting the 15th Amendment, however, resulted in a division that split the woman's suffrage movement into two new suffrage organizations that focused on different strategies for winning voting rights for women.

The National Woman Suffrage Association (NWSA) was formed by Elizabeth Cady Stanton and Susan B. Anthony in May of 1869. They opposed the 15th Amendment because it excluded women. In the year following the ratification of the 15th Amendment, the NWSA sent a petition to the Senate and House of Representatives requesting that suffrage rights be extended to include women and that all women have the right to be heard on the floor of Congress.

The second national suffrage organization was the American Woman Suffrage Association (AWSA), founded by Lucy Stone, Julia Ward Howe, and Thomas Wentworth Higginson in 1869. The AWSA supported the 15th Amendment and protested the confrontational tactics of the NWSA. The AWSA concentrated on gaining women access to the polls both at state and local levels, believing that victories there would gradually build support for national action on the issue. While a federal Women's Suffrage Amendment was not their priority, the AWSA did send a petition to Congress in 1871 asking that women in the District of Columbia and the territories be allowed to vote and hold office.

In 1890, the NWSA and AWSA merged into the National American Woman Suffrage Association (NAWSA). It became the largest Woman's Suffrage organization in the country and led much of the struggle for the right to vote through 1920, when the 19th Amendment was ratified. Stanton became president, Anthony became vice president, and Stone became chair of the executive committee. In 1919, one year before women gained the right to vote with the adoption of the 19th Amendment, the NAWSA reorganized into the League of Women Voters.

The tactics used by suffragists went beyond petitions and memorials. Testing another strategy, Susan B. Anthony registered and voted in the 1872 election in Rochester, New York. As planned, she was arrested for "knowingly, wrongfully and unlawfully voting for a representative to the Congress of the United States." She was convicted by the State of New York and fined $100, which she insisted she would never pay. On January 12th, 1874, Anthony petitioned Congress, requesting that "the fine imposed upon your petitioner be remitted, as an expression of the sense of this high tribunal that her conviction was unjust."

It is important to recognize that White women were not the only supporters of woman's suffrage. Frederick Douglass, a formerly enslaved leader of the abolition movement, was also an advocate. He attended the Seneca Falls Convention in 1848. In an editorial published that year in *The North Star*, an anti-slavery newspaper, he wrote, "...in respect to political rights ... there can be no reason in the world for denying to woman the elective franchise..." By 1877, when he was a U.S. marshal for the District of Columbia, Douglass's family was also involved in the movement. His son, Frederick Douglass Jr., daughter, Rosetta Douglass, and son-in-law, Nathan Sprague all signed a Petition to Congress for Woman's Suffrage "... to prohibit the several States from Disfranchising United States Citizens on account of Sex."

A growing number of Black women actively supported Women's Suffrage during this period as well. They organized women's clubs across the country to advocate for suffrage, among other reforms. Prominent African American suffragists included Ida B. Wells-Barnett of Chicago, a leading crusader against lynching; Mary Church Terrell, an educator and the first president of the National Association of Colored Women (NACW); and Adella Hunt Logan, a Tuskegee Institute faculty member, who insisted in articles in *The Crisis*, a publication of the National Association for the Advancement of Colored People (NAACP), that if White women needed the vote to protect their rights, then Black women – victims of racism as well as sexism – needed the ballot even more.

In the second decade of the twentieth century, suffragists began staging large and dramatic parades to draw attention to their cause. One of the most consequential demonstrations was a march held in Washington, D.C., on March 3, 1913. Though controversial because of the organizers' attempt to exclude, then segregate, women of color, more than 5,000 suffragists from around the country paraded down Pennsylvania Avenue from the U.S. Capitol to the Treasury Building.

Many of the women who had been active in the suffrage movement in the 1860s and 1870s continued their involvement more than 50 years later. In 1917, Mary O. Stevens, secretary and press correspondent of the Association of Army Nurses of the Civil War, asked the chair of the House Judiciary Committee to help the cause by explaining, "My father trained me in my childhood days to expect this right. I have given my help to the agitation, and work[ed] for its coming a good many years."

The Declaration of Sentiments is a document signed by 100 attendees of the Seneca Falls (Women's Rights) Convention of 1848. Suffragist Elizabeth Cady Stanton et al. modeled the document after the U.S. Declaration of Independence and used language common to the antislavery movement to demand full rights of citizenship for women, including access to education and the right for married women to keep the wages they earn.

Declaration of Sentiments

When, in the course of human events, it becomes necessary for one portion of the family of man to assume among the people of the earth a position different from that which they have hitherto occupied, but one to which the laws of nature and of nature's God entitle them, a decent respect to the opinions of mankind requires that they should declare the causes that impel them to such a course.

We hold these truths to be self-evident; that all men and women are created equal; that they are endowed by their Creator with certain inalienable rights; that among these are life, liberty, and the pursuit of happiness; that to secure these rights governments are instituted, deriving their just powers from the consent of the governed. Whenever any form of government becomes destructive of these ends, it is the right of those who suffer from it to refuse allegiance to it, and to insist upon the institution of a new government, laying its foundation on such principles, and organizing its powers in such form, as to them shall seem most likely to effect their safety and happiness. Prudence, indeed, will dictate that governments long established should not be changed for light and transient causes; and, accordingly, all experience hath shown that mankind are more disposed to suffer, while evils are sufferable, than to right themselves by abolishing the forms to which they were accustomed. But when a long train of abuses and usurpations, pursuing invariably the same object, evinces a design to reduce them under absolute despotism, it is their duty to throw off such government, and to provide new guards for their future security. Such has been the patient sufferance of the women under this government, and such is now the necessity which constrains them to demand the equal station to which they are entitled.

The history of mankind is a history of repeated injuries and usurpations on the part of man toward woman, having in direct object the establishment of an absolute tyranny over her. To prove this, let facts be submitted to a candid world.

He has never permitted her to exercise her inalienable right to the elective franchise.

He has compelled her to submit to laws, in the formation of which she had no voice.

He has withheld from her rights which are given to the most ignorant and degraded men – both natives and foreigners.

Having deprived her of this first right as a citizen, the elective franchise, thereby leaving her without representation in the halls of legislation, he has oppressed her on all sides.

He has made her, if married, in the eye of the law, civilly dead.

He has taken from her all right in property, even to the wages she earns.

He has made her morally, an irresponsible being, as she can commit many crimes with impunity, provided they be done in the presence of her husband. In the covenant of marriage, she is compelled to promise obedience to her husband, he becoming, to all intents and purposes, her master – the law giving him power to deprive her of her liberty, and to administer chastisement.

He has so framed the laws of divorce, as to what shall be the proper causes of divorce, in case of separation, to whom the guardianship of the children shall be given; as to be wholly regardless of the happiness of the women – the law, in all cases, going upon a false supposition of the supremacy of man, and giving all power into his hands.

After depriving her of all rights as a married woman, if single and the owner of property, he has taxed her to support a government which recognizes her only when her property can be made profitable to it.

He has monopolized nearly all the profitable employments, and from those she is permitted to follow, she receives but a scanty remuneration.

He closes against her all the avenues to wealth and distinction, which he considers most honorable to himself. As a teacher of theology, medicine, or law, she is not known.

He has denied her the facilities for obtaining a thorough education – all colleges being closed against her.

He allows her in church, as well as State, but a subordinate position, claiming Apostolic authority for her exclusion from the ministry, and, with some exceptions, from any public participation in the affairs of the Church.

He has created a false public sentiment by giving to the world a different code of morals for men and women, by which moral delinquencies which exclude women from society, are not only tolerated but deemed of little account in man.

He has usurped the prerogative of Jehovah himself, claiming it as his right to assign for her a sphere of action, when that belongs to her conscience and her God.

He has endeavored, in every way that he could to destroy her confidence in her own powers, to lessen her self-respect, and to make her willing to lead a dependent and abject life.

Now, in view of this entire disfranchisement of one-half the people of this country, their social and religious degradation – in view of the unjust laws above mentioned, and because women do feel themselves aggrieved, oppressed, and fraudulently deprived of their most sacred rights, we insist that they have immediate admission to all the rights and privileges which belong to them as citizens of these United States.

In entering upon the great work before us, we anticipate no small amount of misconception, misrepresentation, and ridicule; but we shall use every instrumentality within our power to effect our object. We shall employ agents, circulate tracts, petition the State and national Legislatures, and endeavor to enlist the pulpit and the press in our behalf. We hope this Convention will be followed by a series of Conventions, embracing every part of the country.

Firmly relying upon the final triumph of the Right and the True, we do this day affix our signatures to this declaration.

THE 1913 WOMAN SUFFRAGIST PROCESSION

The elaborate Woman Suffrage Procession of 1913, which suffragist Alice Paul planned in painstaking detail, was designed to demonstrate the contributions women had made in the U.S. and abroad. The rationale was that emphasizing the accomplishments of women made a clear case for women's competency to fully participate in all aspects of civic life. Thus, they marched in various delegations, some representing their home states, others their academic institutions, and others their professions. Over 5,000 participants joined the procession, and they were met with hostility. The far greater crowd of spectators (approximately 250,000) began to enter the streets and block the parade. Attempts to clear the procession route were unsuccessful, bringing progress to a halt.

> In an account of that day, the National Park Service describes a complex and volatile situation colored by sexism and misogyny. Still, many women forged ahead despite the risk:
>
> The marchers found themselves trapped in a sea of hostile, jeering men who yelled vile insults and sexual propositions at them. They were manhandled and spat upon. The women reported that they received no assistance from nearby police officers, who looked on bemusedly or admonished the women that they wouldn't be in this predicament if they had stayed home. Although a few women fled the terrifying scene, most were determined to continue. They locked arms and faced the ambush, some through tears. When they could, they ignored the taunts. Some brandished banner poles, flags, and hatpins to ward off attack. They held their ground until the U.S. Army troops arrived about an hour later to clear the street so that the procession could continue.

For Black women, the battle began even before the procession, from which they were initially excluded. A publication from the National Association for the Advancement of Colored People (NAACP) indicated that the woman's suffrage party subtly discouraged Black supporters from registering to participate. When that did not work, instructions were given to allow segregated participation, until a flood of objections and telegrams prompted a final order to allow Black women to participate equally.

One such woman was journalist, anti-lynching activist, educator, and suffragist Ida B Wells. Wells had long begun the career of service that would ultimately memorialize her as an early civil-rights leader and an American hero. Yet, White suffrage leaders asked her to join the back of the procession rather than march with delegates from her home state of Illinois. She refused and, accompanied by White allies, marched in the procession with them.

Although there are some reports that some Black women were relegated to the rear of the group, there also is some indication that others held equal, and sometimes even prominent, roles in the procession. *The Crisis*, for example, reported that more than forty Black women processed in their state delegations or with their respective professions and that two carried the lead banners for their sections. Twenty-five students from the Delta Sigma Theta sorority of Howard University marched in caps and gowns with the university women, as did six graduates of other universities, including activist and NAACP cofounder Mary Church Terrell.

Also noted in *The Crisis*:

> In spite of the apparent reluctance of the local suffrage committee to encourage the colored women to participate ... and in spite of the conflicting rumors that were circulated and which disheartened many of the colored women from taking part, they are to be congratulated that so many of them had the courage of their convictions and that they made such an admirable showing in the first great national parade.

Unfortunately, other women of color were tokenized, exoticized, and sexualized in the media. As part of a publicity ploy, the Great National Railroad created the character Dawn Mist, the supposed daughter of a Native American chief, and then hired Indigenous women to perform as her at events such as this one. Informed that she was coming, newspapers reported that Mist and her friends would attend the procession on "their Indian ponies," wearing "buckskin dresses," and "represent[ing] the wildest type of American womanhood."

Perhaps most outrageous were the reports that the delegation would bring their teepees along and camp out on the national mall. Conversely, prominent White participants such as Inez Milholland (who famously led the procession in a white gown and riding a white horse), were said to represent the "highest type of cultured womanhood." Federal worker and advocate for the Ojibwa/Chippewa Nation Marie Louise Bottineau Baldwin was, however, Indigenous and was in attendance. She marched with the lawyers' section on that day and soon become the first native woman to become a lawyer.

Impact

The Woman Suffrage Procession made national headlines the following day, with coverage exceeding that of the presidential inauguration. The discord that day also prompted a congressional investigation into the lack of appropriate crowd control, and those proceedings kept the issue of women's rights in the national consciousness. Though it was not the first nor even the largest demonstration for woman's suffrage, it created a spotlight that inspired a new wave of support that would see the movement through to the passing of the 19th Amendment.

THE SILENT SENTINELS AND VOTING RIGHTS

On January 10th, 1917, a dozen women met in Lafayette Square, the District of Columbia park directly across the street from the White House, to silently protest and advocate for voting rights for women. These women, who became known as the "silent sentinels," continued their daily protest for nearly three years until voting rights were ushered in for women.

The women, all members of the National Women's Party (NWP), organized this "grand pickett" to face the north lawn of the White House, and the sentinels braved the freezing cold and all kinds of adverse weather to continue standing outside with their signs that spoke loudly in support of woman's suffrage, even as the women did not speak a word.

Over the next three years, the sentinels and over 500 women across the nation were arrested for their efforts. The sentinels also faced arrest on charges of obstructing traffic and many went on hunger strikes while they were imprisoned. And Alice Paul, cofounder of the National Women's Party and the protest leader, was arrested and jailed for seven months – and, during her prison hunger strike, endured violent forced feeding.

Top image: Woman suffragists marched in white clothing. Although they were assaulted by angry and violent crowds, they continued to march in an effort to achieve enfranchisement and broader legal standing and freedom for women. • Lower image: The Silent Sentinels protested in Lafayette Square – which is directly across the street from the White House – for nearly three years.

Neither sleet nor sun nor rainy inaugurations nor threats of abuse deterred the Silent Sentinels from picketing for enfranchisement, and equal rights for women. In this image, the Sentinels are picketing President Wilson's second inauguration.

On March 4th, more than 1,000 women joined the sentinels to protest during the presidential inauguration of President Woodrow Wilson despite the rain, but Wilson himself drove past these women without acknowledging them. The sentinels were undeterred, however, and used their banners to directly address the president as their protests continued.

One major critique President Wilson faced was the irony that, as the country was fighting for freedom abroad, its own female citizens lacked it at home.

Famously remembered for such biting lines as "Democracy Should Begin at Home," these protesters lit bonfires using the President's own speeches.

Another of their jabs likened the president to the German emperor during World War I. This comparison escalated tensions between the sentinels and anti-suffragists, who physically attacked the women. And yet, the silent sentinels continued their picket throughout that first summer.

What Is the Role of Political Dissent during Wartime?

MR PRESIDENT,
IT IS UNJUST TO DENY WOMEN A VOICE IN THEIR GOVERNMENT
WHEN THE GOVERNMENT IS CONSCRIPTING THEIR SONS.
–National Woman's Party Draft Day Picket Banner, September 4, 1917

On June 20, 1917, National Women's Party cofounder Lucy Burns took up her position on the sidewalk in front of the White House entry gate. Burns and National Women's Party member Dora Lewis held between them a large banner addressed "To the Envoys of Russia." The banner accused President Woodrow Wilson of deceiving the Russians when he claimed that the two countries were fighting to preserve democracy. "We, the Women of America, tell you that America is not a democracy," the banner read. "Twenty million American Women are denied the right to vote. President Wilson is the chief opponent of their national enfranchisement." The Russian delegation saw the banner as their car passed through the White House gate on their way to meet with the president.

The National Women's Party had organized pickets of the White House for six days a week, in all kinds of weather, since January 10, 1917. The silent sentinels showed up each day except Sunday holding banners demanding the right to vote for American women. Rather than pursue enfranchisement state by state as the National American Women's Suffrage Association (NAWSA) was doing, the NWP focused their efforts on the passage of an amendment to the U.S. Constitution. The amendment, named for Susan B. Anthony and first introduced in 1878, stated that "The right of citizens of the United States to vote shall not be denied or abridged by the United States or by any State on account of sex" – and ensuring the vote would lay the groundwork for greater representation in the work-place and in labor unions.

Silent Sentinels often addressed the president directly on their signage.

The National Women's Party strategy to promote passage of the Anthony Amendment included pressuring President Wilson to support it. Presidents have no role in amending the Constitution, but National Women's Party leader Alice Paul believed that Wilson's endorsement would sway members of Congress from the Democratic Party to vote for the amendment's passage. Their efforts had only managed to push Wilson to offer tepid support for woman's suffrage eventually, although he asked for patience, chiding American women that "you can afford a little while to wait."

During their months of picketing, the women often held banners echoing Wilson's own words, such as

> MR. PRESIDENT, YOU SAY LIBERTY IS THE FUNDAMENTAL DEMAND OF THE HUMAN SPIRIT.

and

> MR. PRESIDENT, HOW LONG MUST WOMEN WAIT FOR LIBERTY?

Once the United States entered the war in Europe, many in the women's suffrage movement believed that their lobbying and activism should be put on hold. The leaders of the National Woman's Party, however, decided to continue the demonstrations. Public opinion turned against the Silent Sentinels, who were now seen as unpatriotic.

Rather than back down, the NWP decided to become more confrontational. Onlookers became increasingly more hostile to the picketers. On that June day when Lucy and Dora raised the provocative banner addressing the Russians, the anger boiled over. Crowds ripped the banner out of the hands of the picketers and off its poles. The next day, picketers returned, this time with a banner quoting Wilson:

> WE SHALL FIGHT FOR THE THINGS WE HAVE ALWAYS HELD NEAREST TO OUR HEARTS.

This time, the police tried to confiscate the banner. When the women refused, they were arrested.

Over the next several months, women continued to take up positions in front of the White House. They faced violence and arrest. More than 150 women were convicted of obstructing traffic for their protest. They served jail time rather than pay what they considered to be unjust fines for exercising their constitutional rights. As picketing and arrests continued, the sentences increased from a few days in the District Jail to several months in the Occoquan Workhouse in Virginia. The women, many of whom came from prominent and politically connected families, demanded to be treated as political prisoners.

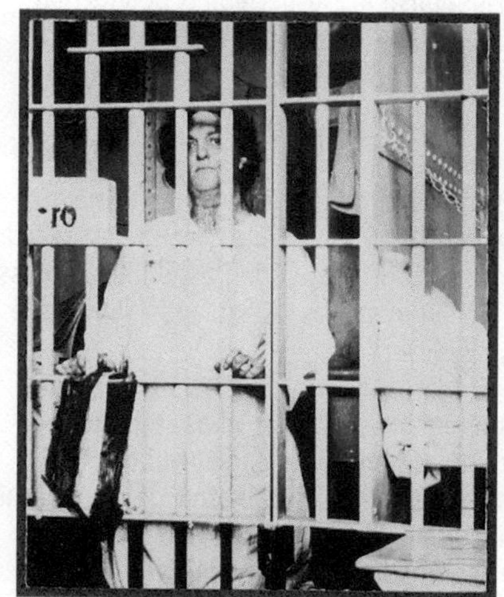

Silent Sentinel Helena Hill in her Occoquan workhouse jail cell.

Among the hunger strikers was National Women's Party leader Alice Paul, arrested on October 20, 1917 carrying a banner that read:

> THE TIME HAS COME TO CONQUER OR SUBMIT. FOR US, THERE IS BUT ONE CHOICE. WE HAVE MADE IT.

The slogan, adapted from Woodrow Wilson's own words, was used throughout the country on posters supporting the war effort. Alice Paul declared her own war against injustice by co-opting the battle cry for the cause of women's suffrage. As she declared in 1919:

> WHEN MEN ARE DENIED JUSTICE, THEY GO TO WAR. THIS IS OUR WAR, ONLY WE ARE FIGHTING WITH BANNERS INSTEAD OF GUNS.

(Source: National Park Service)

Time spent in the Occoquan workhouse took its toll on even the strongest suffragists, as seen in this image of Dora Lewis upon her release.

Still, the National Women's Party received support from people who championed their cause. Famous socialite, suffragist, and multimillionaire Alva Belmont was both cofounder and president of the National Women's Association and famously said, "Just pray to God. She will help you." Belmont provided bail money for the arrested protesters, funded a major woman's rights rally in New York City, and helped pay for the National Women's Party headquarters on Capitol Hill. A larger-than-life figure during her time – and certainly a woman ahead of her time – Belmont, who also famously said, "Marry first for money, and then for love," dedicated much of her time and money to furthering the cause of women's rights.

Of course, the suffragists were subject to gendered critiques, just as the progressive women before them had faced. Some of their more brazen methods even met with disapproval from more moderate suffrage organizations championing the same cause. Indeed, members of the National Women Suffrage Association described the more radical methods of the

National Women's Party as "unladylike," a demonstration of the respectability politics that governed women's lives both then and now.

Impact

The first sign of impending victory came on January 9th, 1918, when President Wilson publicly proclaimed his support for the woman's suffrage movement and began to push Congress to follow suit. An amendment to grant women the right to vote nevertheless failed in the Senate that same year, just as it had for 42 consecutive years. Congress did finally pass the amendment on June 4th, 1919 and the 19th Amendment was ratified and finally made its way into the U.S. Constitution on August 18th, 1920.

Over a century later, the sacrifices of the silent sentinels and suffragists whose tenacious and ongoing advocacy and organizing over four decades were key to passage of the 19th Amendment, continue to be recognized and admired for the trail they blazed for all American women. Their refusal to give up this fight for full inclusion despite assaults and taunts and arrests ushered in one of many giant steps in the ongoing fight for the full recognition and inclusion of women in voting booths, workplaces, and beyond.

On March 4th, more than 1,000 women joined the sentinels to protest during the presidential inauguration of President Woodrow Wilson despite the rain, but Wilson himself drove

Symbols Associated with the Suffrage Movement

Many symbols were used during the campaign for women's suffrage, and many were derogatory of women. Some reappear later during the hostile years when the president and soldiers returning from World War I worked to force women workers back into the home.

Here you will find some of the meanings behind colors, animals, flowers, and other symbols that suffragists and anti-suffragists used.

Dogs and Cats

In the popular mainstream culture of the suffrage era, women – still second-class citizens in a country founded on equality – were associated with animals perceived as passive, such as cats. Middle class, White women were expected to stay in the home rather than enter the workforce, and mainstream women and men perceived women moving beyond these strictures as "unnatural" – and some of these so-called unnatural women were physically assaulted for stepping outside the role men with power and popular culture set for them. Women marching in the 1913 Suffragist Parade experienced such violence in the public sphere, which was largely considered to be a male-only space.

Men, on the other hand, were expected to be outdoors. Men played sports or did other forms of physical exercise. Men were often associated with physically active animals, such as dogs. Anti-suffrage artists used these animals symbolically in their cartoons.

(Meanwhile, anti-suffrage organizations in Britain used cats to try to make the point that women were simple and delicate. The cartoons implied that women's suffrage was just as absurd as cat suffrage because women (and cats) were incapable of voting … or of working outside the home.)

Cats were also used symbolically in some American anti-suffrage ads. A number of American cartoons showed men at home with a cat, taking care of the children. The cat symbolized a loss of the man's masculinity. Some people believed that if women participated in politics, men would be left at home to raise the children.

That's how powerfully mainstream culture opposed women gaining rights or going to work outside of the home.

In England, suffragists reclaimed the cat. Postcards, posters, and cartoons showed cats in purple, green, and gold demanding access to the ballot. In the United States, there was also some reclaiming of the cat as a symbol of suffrage. In April of 1916, Nell Richardson and Alice Burke started a cross-country road trip. Setting out from New York City, these two women stopped in cities and towns across America, speaking on street corners, in people's homes, and other meeting places to talk about the importance of women's suffrage. Along the way, the women were given a little black cat. Named Saxon after the brand of car that they were driving, the cat became their unofficial mascot. Saxon's trials and tribulations were part of the stories the women published in newspapers across the country about their travels.

The Color White

Suffragists were often portrayed as masculine and ugly. To help counter that (homophobic) anti-suffrage media image, suffragists wore dresses in parades. These were often all white, with suffrage sashes. These white dresses symbolized the femininity and purity of the suffrage cause.

Roses (Yellow and Red)

In 1920, suffragists and anti-suffragists met in Nashville, Tennessee, lobby the state legislature for and against ratifying the Nineteenth Amendment. Arguments on both sides were intense – Tennessee was poised to either be the needed 36th state to ratify the amendment for it to become law or to reject ratification and ensure the fight continued. Both sides wore rose-shaped pins to indicate which side of the battle they were on: suffragists work yellow roses, and anti-suffragists wore red roses.

Jail-Cell Door

When the U.S. entered World War I, the public's tolerance for protest diminished. More than 90 of the Silent Sentinels were arrested on charged of obstructing traffic and were sent to prison both in Washington, D.C. and at Occoquan in Virginia. While imprisoned, these women were beaten, force-fed, and endured other indignities. Publicity of their mistreatment was instrumental in changing opinions of the public and of Congress regarding woman suffrage.

Silver pins shaped like a jail-cell door with a heart-shaped padlock were given by the National Woman's Party to each of the women "jailed for freedom." The National Woman's Party "Jailed for Freedom" pin was based on the Holloway Prison pin that English suffragist Sylvia Pankhurst gave to members of the Women's Social and Political Union who had been imprisoned.

Stars

On the flag of the United States, each state in the union is represented by a star. In 1919, the National Woman's Party, led by Alice Paul, began sewing stars on a giant purple, white, and gold flag. Each time a state ratified the Nineteenth Amendment, a new star would be sewn on the flag. There was room on the National Woman's Party flag for 36 stars, symbolizing the number of state ratifications required for the amendment to become law.

(Source: National Park Service)

past these women without acknowledging them. The sentinels were undeterred, however, and used their banners to directly address the president as their protests continued.

THE SUFFRAGE "PRISON SPECIAL" TOUR OF 1919

Introduction

> If particular care and attention is not paid to the ladies, we are determined to foment a rebellion, and will not hold ourselves bound by any laws in which we have no voice or representation.
> –future First Lady Abigail Adams, 1776

In the early spring of 1919, 26 women boarded a train leaving Union Station in Washington, D.C., and heading south. Their goal: To share the story of the horror they had endured in prison. This section explores how and why the "Prison Special" aided the cause of woman's suffrage and how it helped secure the ratification of the 19th Amendment the following year.

These women and their prison stays were notable because of their standing in society. They were White, educated, and well-connected. In a society with deeply ingrained racial and class prejudice, women of their stature were expected to stay home to care for their families. Men occupied the more active "public sphere" of business, trade, and politics. As wives and mothers, women were expected to occupy the "domestic sphere" – cooking, cleaning, and taking care of the home and children. They were not expected to work outside the home. They were excluded from politics. And they certainly did not go to prison.

Except when they did. By 1919, several hundred women had been arrested for picketing the White House and protesting for the right to vote. Women of all ages, races, and socioeconomic classes were prohibited from voting. While there were two Western states that did allow women to vote, in most states, women were banned from voting. In the few states where women could vote, in most cases they were limited to local and state elections.

> The militancy of men, through all the centuries, has drenched the world with blood. The militancy of women has harmed no human life save the lives of those who fought the battle of righteousness.
> –British Suffragist Emmeline Pankhurst

As mentioned earlier, public opinion began to turn against the silent sentinels when the United States entered the war in April 1917 and many Americans felt that criticism of the government during wartime was unpatriotic and even treasonous. But the Nation Women's Party refused to stop picketing.

In November of 1917, 41 silent sentinels, including Lucy Burns, Dorothy Day, Dora Lewis, and Mary Nolan, were arrested for protesting and sentenced to jail for periods ranging from six days to six months at the Occoquan Workhouse in Lorton, Virginia. The Workhouse was a minimum-security prison, but that did not mean that the mostly poor and working-class women there were well treated. They experienced brutality from the guards, poor food, and dirty conditions. The middle-class White suffragists who arrived at Occoquan quickly got a window into this world.

The suffragists' second night in Occoquan became known as the "Night of Terror." Guards attacked the women, threw them around, hung them by their arms, and denied them food and medical care.

The Politics of Respectability

> Nay, be not alarmed. They are perfectly gentle, lovable, delightful women are more or less known throughout the nation by reason of their social position and prominence in families in the money marts of the world, yet who, nevertheless, wear upon their breasts the badge of the prison gate with its dangling chain.
> –*Oakland Tribune*, January 30, 1919, on the Prison Special Tour

What Are Respectability Politics?

"Respectability" is a set of social guidelines dictating acceptable behavior, from clothing to the way someone interacts with those around them. "Respectability politics" refers to the way that people attempting to make social change present their demands in ways that are acceptable to the dominant standards of their society.

Top image: Woman Suffrage Headquarters, Ohio. • Lower image: Headquarters of the National Association Opposed to Woman Suffrage.

During the suffrage movement of the early twentieth century, women argued for increased political rights for themselves to a government run by men with little incentive to agree. Cartoons and caricatures in the press at the time demonstrate the ways in which women were mocked and dismissed for stepping out of their traditional role as wives and mothers. Women had to show that what they were fighting for was respectable for women.

How Did Respectability Politics Affect the Suffrage Movement?

The question of respectability affected the suffragists in ways that made many feel out of place in the movement. Part of the conflict between the National American Woman Suffrage

Association (NAWSA), the largest suffrage organization under Elizabeth Cady Stanton and Carrie Chapman Catt, and Alice Paul and Lucy Burns' National Women's Party (NWP) was disagreement over how best to frame their cause. Stanton and Catt were sure that the best way to gain support for women's right to vote was through careful fundraising and influential members. This meant recruiting women who could convince their rich fathers and political husbands to join the effort for woman's suffrage. All of these women were White. The attention-getting tactics the NWP proposed were rejected as violation of the reserved ways in which society expected women to act. The violence that occurred at the 1913 Suffrage Procession demonstrated why it was so dangerous to violate society's rules.

The suffragists who followed Alice Paul and risked their freedom and lives for the cause but also struggled with presenting themselves in a "respectable" manner. The NWP invited women from different social classes to join and work with their organization. Rallying the many women who worked outside their homes was one of their key strategies gained some much-needed numbers. The NWP continued to fail in building a multiracial movement for woman's suffrage, however. The Suffrage Procession of 1913 demonstrated underlying racism in the White woman's suffrage movement. Organized and led by the forward-thinking Alice Paul, it was intended to be a demonstration of unity in protest of the exclusion of women from the country's government. Yet the NWP initially attempted to exclude Black women from the parade and even after conceding, told Black women suffragists that they must march in the back of the procession. Often excluded from NAWSA and the NWP, Black women suffragists often formed their own organizations where they would not have to face racism from White women activists. Paul and others believed that marginalizing Black women would make their cause palatable and respectable to White southerners who were opposed to suffrage rights for Black Americans. The mainstream suffrage movement's dismissal of Black women's voting rights damaged the movement's claim that they were fighting for all women. Many Black women, particularly in the South, would not gain full voting rights until the passage of the Voting Rights Act of 1965.

What Role Did Respectability Politics Play in the Prison Special?

The six women on the Prison Special tour were aware of the standards of respectability of the time and presenting the imprisoned suffragists as respectable and abused women was intended to garner sympathy from influential male politicians. Some of the women were wives and mothers, sisters of politicians, and granddaughters of America's Founders. These were the women who were already highly regarded in society and treated better than other women. At the time, tales of the imprisonment and abuse of poor White women and women of color would have been less shocking to the suffragists' target audience. The significance of the Prison Special specifically was that respectable women were treated very poorly.

Depictions of these women as abused criminals was considered outrageous to many who attended the tour. Social standards decreed that these privileged women had sensitive natures and should be kept safe from harm. Anti-suffragists often argued that politics were too dirty for women and that men needed to protect them. Yet these suffragists' accounts of their time in prison showed that they had dealt with literal filth as they were forced to scrub toilets and live in unsatisfactory hygienic facilities. They also had lived with incarcerated individuals whom respectable society considered "dirty." And it was the men and the state, who were meant to protect these women, who had put them into that situation. What the suffragists described only had the impact it did because of who was speaking. Alice Paul and the suffragists she led leveraged their societal "respectability" for the cause of woman's suffrage. At the same time, wealthy White suffragists' use of respectability politics meant that they neglected other populations of women, particularly Black and Native American women. Paul justified their exclusion with the argument that, once women could vote, the movement would be able to address the issues of women who had been left out. Yet it took decades more for the promise of the 19th Amendment to be realized.

"Looking Backward" artwork by Laura E. Foster, c. 1912, published in *Life* magazine (August 22, 1912). This exemplary anti-suffrage artwork depicts a woman leaving behind love, marriage, children, and home for suffrage and loneliness. The message that women who had the vote would be miserable was common in anti-suffrage propaganda.

(Source: National Park Service)

What Inspired the Prison Special?

In both the Occoquan Workhouse and the jails in the District of Columbia, suffragists were denied contact with the outside world. They were rarely allowed visitors and not allowed to write letters. Protesting their treatment in jail, several suffragists, including Alice Paul and Lucy Burns, began hunger strikes. In response, prison guards restrained and force fed them.

Those on the outside learned of this treatment through notes smuggled out of prison. Once the public heard about the treatment of the suffragists, many Americans who were not sympathetic to the cause of woman's suffrage were horrified at how these women were being treated. It wasn't long before action was taken. Public outrage and the efforts of several well-connected women forced the government to act. Alice Paul's seven-month sentence was commuted and she was freed after five weeks. The women of the National Women's Party decided to use the public outrage about their treatment in prison to further their mission. They created the Prison Special to spread their firsthand accounts of what they had suffered in prison. By sharing their stories with the public, they gained a new platform for arguing for women's voting rights and full autonomy.

> We do not like to do this, but it seems to be the only way to rouse the Nation and awaken the consciousness of the people to the justice of our cause.
> –Louisine Waldron Elder Havemeyer

"From Prison to the People": The Prison Special Tour

By the end of 1918, picketers expected to be arrested and almost all leaders of the National Women's Party had been in jail for some amount of time. Alice Paul's 7-month sentence was the longest of any suffragist, followed closely by her second-in-command, Lucy Burns' sentence of 6 months. During their prison stays, the women faced emotional and physical abuse. During the early spring of 1919, 26 of the women who had been imprisoned at Occoquan Workhouse and in District of Columbia jails traveled the country by train to share their stories. They called their train the "Democracy Limited" and their tour the "Prison Special." These politically savvy women used their experience as part of their reasoning for why women should get the vote – but also showed that women had a right to speak in the public sphere and do more than just remain in their homes (which surely inspired budding feminists as well). The suffragists reminded their audiences that they had been mistreated in a system in which women are not allowed to participate because they lack a vote or say in government or seats of power.

The suffragists planned the tour to reach the areas where support was most needed for their movement. Over three weeks, they traveled to 15 major cities around the United States. The 26 women took the Democracy Limited train to San Antonio, Texas, and San Francisco, California, then on to Denver, Colorado, and Jacksonville, Florida. Knowing that the most outspoken opponents to woman suffrage tended to represent more conservative southern states, the organizers of the Prison Special tried to visit southern cities. On February 10th, the woman's suffrage amendment had failed in the Senate by one vote.

Suffragists believed that southern support would be important in securing woman's suffrage nationwide.

Impassioned speeches were a highlight of the Prison Special tour, which drew huge crowds like this one in San Francisco, California.

The Politics of Dress

> Fashion is part of the daily air and it changes all the time, with all the events. You can even see the approaching of a revolution in clothes. You can see and feel everything in clothes.
>
> –Diana Vreeland

Suffragists who had been imprisoned did not let the uniforms they were forced to wear stifle their message. In fact, they used the politics of dress in new ways. When suffragists appeared in public on the Prison Special, they wore replicas of the clothes they'd been forced to wear in prison. Though still dresses, the prison uniform violated the idea of appropriate clothing for middle-class White women in the early twentieth century. The dresses were thin and straight-cut in a way that would have been scandalous had the women chosen them for themselves. Audiences watching the suffragists wear their prison uniforms generally viewed the fact that the prisons had put the women in such clothing as reflecting negatively on the political system. How could women put their trust in a government that would disgrace them in such a way? The message of the Prison Special was that women needed the right to vote to protect their dignity from government abuses.

During the Prison Special tour, suffragists reenacted scenes from their time in the Occoquan prison workhouse. Here Pauline Adams demonstrates protests, such as hunger strikes, that she and her fellow inmates staged during meals.

Why Were the Prison Special's Clothing Choices Impactful?

The fashion choices of these suffrage activists were effective because they spoke to the public in a way that they would understand. Highlighting their loyalty combatted the belief that all women in the suffrage movement wanted to overthrow the United States government or force men to take on feminine roles. These suffragists were constantly careful about how they presented themselves and tried to make sure the attention they received was in favor of their cause. The Prison Special highlighted how the government without women's votes was harmful to women by showing how it violated social rules of female modesty. The success of the Prison Special relied on the unofficial politics of dress to make the argument that women not only deserved the right to vote but actually needed it in order to be virtuous women.

(Source: National Park Service)

Suffragists in prison uniforms reenact scenes from their time imprisoned in the Occoquan workhouse. The uniforms the suffragists were made to wear were rough and considered degrading to someone of their social standing.

There Is a Difference between a Suffragist and a Suffragette

Although we often see "suffragist" and "suffragette" used as though they mean the same thing, their historical meanings are quite different. The terms "suffrage" and "enfranchisement "mean having the right to vote. Suffragists are people who advocate for enfranchisement. After African American men got the vote in 1870 with the passage of the 15th Amendment to the United States Constitution, "suffrage" referred primarily to woman's suffrage (though there were many other groups who did not have access to the ballot).

The battle for woman's suffrage was in full force in both Britain and the United States in the early 1900s. Reporters took sides, and in 1906, a British reporter used the word "suffragette" to mock those fighting for a woman's right to vote. The suffix "-ette" is used to refer to something small or diminutive, and the reporter used it to minimize the work of the British suffragists. Some women in Britain embraced the term "suffragette" as a way of reclaiming it from its original derogatory use. In the United States, however, the term "suffragette" was seen as an offensive term and not embraced by the suffrage movement. Instead, it was wielded by anti-suffragists in their fight to deny women in America the right to vote. *(Source: National Park Service)*

Who Participated in the Prison Special Tour?

The women who went on tour were all well-educated and well-connected White women who were working to pave the way for all women to have more rights, freedom, and autonomy. Among these women were Lucy Burns, Pauline Adams, Vida Milholland, Louisine Havemeyer, and others who had lived through the Night of Terror. Wearing recreated versions of the uniforms they had worn in jail, the women told stories, gave speeches, and reenacted scenes from prison life. Each woman demonstrated how women were mistreated by the government when they had no say in it.

Who Attended the Tour?

In the cities that the tour visited, the Prison Special drew large crowds eager to see the performance and hear the women's tales. The suffragists on the tour raised money and made connections that helped grow public support for the movement. Even in less sympathetic cities, the suffragists had an impact. Though their stories may not have suddenly changed anti-suffragists' opinions, they still encouraged anti-suffragists to question their arguments. The Prison Special helped make the conversation about women's rights and voting laws unavoidable.

What Did the Tour Achieve?

By the time of the tour, arrests of picketing suffragists had ended due to public outrage and Paul's and the other women's sentences were overturned. Although we cannot measure the tour's exact impact, it helped contribute to increasing public support for the woman's suffrage amendment and for expanded rights and autonomy for women in general. The following spring, the 19th Amendment was finally passed in both houses of Congress and sent to the states for ratification.

Section 2.3 • **WOMAN WARRIORS**

This section includes text excerpted from "Women in World War I," (National Park Service); "Lenah H. Sutcliffe Higbee: The U.S. Navy's First Living Female Navy Cross Recipient," (U.S. Navy); "The Story of the Female Yeomen during the First World War," (National Archives); "Women Marines," • © 2021 Omnigraphics.

INTRODUCTION

Five million men were mobilized for service in the Great War.

And over nine million women mobilized themselves.

The contributions made by American women during the Great War continue to be largely overlooked, when the reality is that women played a crucial and defining role in the nation's victory. Without the efforts of women, tens of thousands of men who were needed at the front, would have been tied to jobs in agriculture, industry, and home-front military operations instead of being available for wartime service, and the success of United States' military effort may have been in the balance.

1917 was a watershed year for America. Militarily and economically, the U.S. was cementing its position as a world power, American industry was prospering in the run-up to the war, and American agriculture was shipping vast amounts of food to our allies in Europe. Also, in 1917 the woman's suffrage movement was on the verge of a breakthrough in attaining the right of full citizenship, through the vote, of twenty million American Women. Though by no means assured, enfranchisement of women seemed nearer than ever before.

The two primary powers in the suffrage movement were taking very different and distinct approaches to attaining the vote; the National American Woman Suffrage Association (NAWSA), led by Carrie Chapman Catt, wholeheartedly supported the war effort and saw the full participation by women as a patriotic demonstration of citizenship which might tip the balance toward woman's suffrage. Alice Paul, founder of the National Women's Party (NWP), was less concerned with the war effort; her primary focus was suffrage and suffrage alone. If patriotic participation would lead to suffrage, she'd support it; if not, so be it. Her focus – her priority – was getting women the vote by any means necessary, including picketing the White House.

With America's entry into the fight, wartime production reached a fever pitch. Hundreds of new warships were being built and outfitted. Factories were converting to war work for the manufacture of airplanes, tanks, rifles and machine guns, uniforms, and all other military hardware with which to equip the exponentially expanding armed forces. American agriculture was also in full production, now with a vast Army and Navy to feed. The treat looming over all of this ramped-up and crucial production however was the loss of manpower as men were leaving the factories, farms, and offices for military service.

Then came America's women, answering the nation's call.

Women Mobilize for War

Upon the United States' entry in the war in April of 1917, former NAWSA president Anna Howard Shaw became a driving force in mobilizing American women for the war effort. Shaw founded the Women's Committee of the Council of National Defense as a clearinghouse and organizing method for the millions of women who wanted to serve, matching women with the specific need.

It must be remembered that in those days the timeworn axiom was "A Woman's Place Is in the Home," and whether World War I–era women were already in the workforce or were just joining the military in a paid or voluntary capacity, or were emerging from their homes to work in manufacturing jobs, both these women and these workplaces were transformed.

Meanwhile, organizations like Shaw's, as well as other organizations that employed women, went to great lengths to assure the nation that women would not become "masculinized" by stepping outside of their traditional roles and into jobs traditionally held by men. Newspaper and magazine publishers, especially women's magazines, stressed the importance of women entering the war effort. Graphic depictions of women serving invariably depicted determined though still utterly attractive and unquestionably "feminine" women taking to the factory, the plow, the munitions plant, and even the military.

"All over America today suffragists are leading a back to the land movement ... they have put their hand to the plow and are not turning back," read a headline in the publication *The Woman's Journal*. Tens of thousands of women joined The Women's Land Army to work the soil, fields, and orchards to free men for military service. Women took to the land gladly and brought in the harvest during the war years to supply food to the nation, the military, and our allies.

Eight million women volunteered as American Red Cross workers in a variety of capacities, from making surgical dressings, masks, and gowns, operating servicemen's canteens to provide wholesome entertainment for soldiers and sailors, volunteering as nurses' aides in veterans' hospitals, and providing recreational services to convalescing servicemen. The Red Cross also trained and provided nearly twenty thousand nurses to the Army, Navy, and U.S. Health Service.

The Red Cross organized the Motor Service comprised almost entirely of women drivers, most of whom owned their own vehicles and many were trained as auto mechanics. They provided transportation to canteens, hospitals, and camps. They were motorcycle messengers – and, by war's end, over twelve-thousand drivers logged over 3.5 million miles.

The Salvation Army "lassies" were a welcome sight to allied forces both at home and abroad. Operating close to the battlefront the Salvation Army women provided coffee, donuts, letter writing, clothes mending, and a variety of other services to soldiers and sailors at embarkation and debarkation ports and canteens.

America's librarians joined the war effort too with 1,100 library workers at home and abroad supplying books and periodicals to American service members. Our nation's librarians erected 36 camp libraries and distributed nearly ten million books and magazines and raised over five million dollars from public donations to support their efforts.

Perhaps the most emblematic symbol of the nation's attitude toward women helping out for the emergency was the admission of women into the ultimate domain of men at the time:

The military. Seven thousand women applied to become one of the so-called Hello Girls – switchboard operators working for the U.S. Army Signal Corps. Two hundred and twenty-three were sent recruited and sent overseas, and some served very near the front lines. These patriotic women took the same oath of allegiance as enlisted soldiers, received the same pay as soldiers, and wore the insignia of the Signal Corps. Serving with distinction, seven of these women were awarded the Distinguished Service Medal. It should be noted that upon their discharge, the Hello Girls did not receive veteran status or any of the benefits that go along with that designation. What was seen widely as a betrayal by the War Department wasn't rectified until 1979 when only a handful of these women were still living.

As more and more warships were being built and sent into war, the Navy needed ever-increasing numbers of sailors to keep the ships operational and enlistments and the draft were not sufficient to keep up with the need.

Thousands of sailors were involved in shore-duty positions as clerks, truck drivers, armorers, instructors, medical technicians, radio operators, and other positions (which made these men unavailable for the fleet) and something had to be done.

Enter Josephus Daniels, Secretary of the Navy.

Daniels, desperate for sailors to participate in combat operations, found a loophole in the Naval Act of 1916. This legislation determined who could be enlisted into the Navy, and nowhere in the regulations did it stipulate that only men could be enlisted. Daniels seized upon this opportunity to start actively recruiting women into the ranks and the response was overwhelming. Patriotic young women, many if not most of them suffragists, flocked to the recruiting offices.

Daniels recognized that nation's involvement overseas was imminent and so was actively recruiting women to serve as Yeoman (F) even before the United States officially entered the Great War. These recruits served as clerks, cryptographers, mechanics, messengers, ordnance workers, radio operators, stenographers, truck drivers, and in all other non-combat shore-duty roles, which freed thousands of sailors to join the fleet.

All told, 11,272 women joined the U.S. Navy for the duration of the war, and when they left the service Daniels made sure that all of them received veteran status and were first in line for civil-service jobs.

The Army and Navy Nurse Corps contributed 22,804 nurses to the war effort, and served abroad, on the home front, and on hospital and troop ships. Lenah Sutcliffe Higbee, chief of the Navy Nurse Corps, was the first woman to be awarded the Navy Cross, which is second only to the Medal of Honor.

Army nurses served at home as well as overseas in Belgium, England, France, and even Siberia. Of the Army nurses, many were wounded and more than two hundred died in service; among the ranks of the Navy Nurse Corps, thirty-six women lost their lives. The service of these women was not merely an inconvenience but involved the supreme sacrifice.

The Battle for Suffrage

The service of American women at war cost them more than just the burden of putting their lives on hold or deferring marriage, children, or higher education. All told, more than 600 of these patriotic women lost their lives in service to their country. The question was, how would the nation return that debt?

Suffragists at war and at home were pointing out the inequity of women fighting for freedom when they didn't have that right at home. Meanwhile, millions of American women were demonstrating, through service and sacrifice, their claim to full citizenship.

Finally, President Wilson, who was at best a reluctant supporter of suffrage, threw his support behind the issue. On September 30th, 1918, with the end of war just weeks away, the President addressed Congress:

> We have made partners of women in this war.... Shall we admit them only to a partnership of suffering and sacrifice and toil and not to a partnership of privilege?

With the support of the president the die was cast, and on August 18th, 1920, twenty-million women won the right to vote. These U.S. citizens were not given the right to vote. They were not given anything. The decades-long battle for full inclusion and equality was still in its salad years, but suffragists moved American women one step closer to autonomy and gave women representation and a voice by relentlessly organizing and pursuing enfranchisement. In Lafayette Park and in the battles involving service, sacrifice, protest, imprisonment, and unflinching commitment to a global war, these women won. They won victory in war, and a victory that remains with all of us.

NAVY YEOMEN (F): "THE FIRST, THE FEW, THE FORGOTTEN"

The Navy formed its Nurse Corps reserves in 1907 to avoid potential shortages during a war, but the U.S. military did not officially accommodate women who wished to serve in its ranks until World War I. But even when women did enlist, as Jean Ebbert and Marie-Beth Hall point out in their 2002 book *The First, the Few, the Forgotten*, the military failed to recognize these female reservists, who sometimes "had to dress like men to fight in the field [or] risk their lives as frontline nurses," (Patch, 1) for their brave service.

World War I was both the first world war and the first industrial war, and the Industrial Revolution ushered in entirely new weapons capable of mass destruction that could be manufactured in then-modern factories.

By the turn of the century, multiple navies had submarines, but these subs stuck close to the shoreline. Then Germany began unrestricted submarine warfare on the open seas and in January 2017 alone, sunk 540,000 tons of shipping – which soared to 900,000 tons by April (ibid.). Some of those vessels were American, and the United States joined the war after Germany refused to cease these attacks.

The Naval Act of 1916 declared that a U.S. Navy reserve force would be assembled and would include people with prior naval or merchant marines experience, crewmembers on civilian ships commissioned for naval service during a time of war, or "all persons who may be capable of performing special useful service for coastal defense" (ibid.). And

A U.S. Navy Yeoman (F) on submarine K-5 gazes through her binoculars.

that last description provided the loophole needed to allow women to enlist in the reserves.

In March of 1917, the Bureau of Navigation confirmed that naval districts could and should recruit women into the Naval Coast Defense Reserve and stated that these women should be "utilized as radio operators, stenographers, nurses, messengers, chauffeurs, etc. and in many other capacities in the industrial line."

Translation: The Navy recruited and enlisted women to serve as "electricians" to complete radio operators, recruited a large number of Yeomen (F) – the "F" is for "female"– to fill skilled administrator and clerk positions previous filled by enlisted men, or as unskilled industrial workers (who worked

...al Victor Blue (left, center), chief of the Bureau of Navigation, inspects U.S. Navy Yeomen ...unds of the Washington Monument in Washington, D.C., in 1918.

alongside male workers), and in other capacities deemed necessary for naval district operations. Recruiters also "borrowed" female nurses from naval hospitals to conduct examinations (ibid.) and relied heavily on nurses in the female Naval Nurse Corps reserves.

All 11,272 women who joined the U.S. Navy and survived served for the duration of the war (National Park Service, "Women in World War I"). But these women warriors had been largely overlooked until researchers – sometimes women in search of role models – and historians, writers, and publishers began amplifying the important role they played during the Great War.

Yeomen (F) Reservists Serving in Clerical and Industrial Capacities

Yeomen (F) reservists were primarily educated young women. Many came from large immigrant families. To qualify, the clerical-level Yeomen (F) were required to complete four years of high school. Many had also attended college-level secretarial schools. These women had to pass not just a physical examination, but a skills test as well. Upon acceptance, their designation was typically listed as "stenographer." Technically proficient in shorthand, stenographers rapidly wrote dictations using abbreviations and symbols. In reality, though, these Yeoman (F) stenographers were also responsible for typing, bookkeeping, filing, and payroll, which required copious paperwork. Some even branched out to become radio and telephone operators, electricians, and draftsmen. As Ebbert and Hall put it: "The women were enlisted just as men were, doing many of the same jobs, receiving the same pay, subject to the same military regulations, wearing similar uniforms, and required to meet the same standards of performance, and they received naval benefits."

Despite these significant changes, though, only White women could enter this new program, as Black women were excluded by the Naval Act of 1916, and the armed forces as a whole remained segregated.

During America's participation in World War I, over 10,000 women served as Yeomen (F) across the country and over 1,000 worked in the First Naval District, which encompassed Boston and the Boston Naval Shipyard (today's Charlestown Navy Yard). As the Navy increased production to meet the needs of World War I, they also hired unskilled workers to build, repair, and supply ships. One hundred and fifty unskilled female yeomen were hired to work as civilians in the Navy Yard ropewalk section but were outnumbered by male workers by roughly 10 to 1. Nevertheless, adding them to the workforce allowed rope and cable production teams to work 6-day, 60-hour workweeks in order to meet Navy demand. The service of the Yeomen (F) at the Boston Naval Shipyard also enabled more men – who would otherwise be performing these shipyard duties – to enlist and fight overseas.

The law stated that these unskilled women would be paid at the same rate as their male counterparts: $2.24 per day, which increased to $4.32 in late 1918.

Yeomen (F) in the Charlestown Navy Yard

Yeomen (F) enlistments ended on October 24, 1920, although many had been discharged after the war ended in November 1918. Some of these women, however, continued to work at the shipyard as civilian employees through their veterans' preference on civil-service exams. At a time when less than 25 percent of American women worked outside the home, the Yeomen (F) stepped out of traditional female roles and joined an emerging trend of women becoming clerical workers. By 1920, almost half the clerical workers and 92 percent of stenographers in the national workforce were women.

World War I and Yeoman status provided these female military pioneers the opportunity to showcase their skills and education in support of the war effort. These women also were unique in another way: They were part of the first generation of female voters. In August 1920, the 19th Amendment to the United States Constitution took effect, recognizing that women 21 years of age and older had the right to vote. The 19th Amendment of the U.S. Constitution states:

> The right of citizens of the United States to vote shall not be denied or abridged by the United States or by any State on account of sex. Congress shat have power to enforce this article by appropriate legislation.

Before the passage of the 19th Amendment, 15 states had granted full voting rights to women and twelve states had permitted women to vote in presidential elections. Massachusetts was not among them, having turned down an Amendment to the state constitution for woman's suffrage as recently as 1915 (although the Massachusetts legislature granted women the right to vote for their local school committee members in 1879). Some women did register to vote from 1880–1920, knowing that they could only vote for that one office alone.

What follows are short biographies of 20 Yeomen (F) who registered to vote between 1917 and 1921: Nineteen from Boston and one from a small town nearby. Eight married after the war, while 11 never married and one was a widow when she enlisted and did not remarry. For women who remained single, being a Yeomen (F) enabled them to gain experience and an income during and after World War I. They mostly spent their careers doing clerical work and lived much of their lives with family members. They represent some of the first career women and female white-collar wage earners. However, it should be noted that whereas men could use clerical work as a springboard to management positions, these women performed the same tasks, namely stenography, typing and bookkeeping, throughout their working lives.

Blanche Billington

Blanche Billington registered to vote prior to the passage of the 19th Amendment. While her motivations for registering are unknown, she may have had a desire to vote for school committee members or wished to celebrate adulthood with this new privilege. Billington enlisted in the Naval Reserves in 1918 as a Yeoman (F) 2nd Class when she was 24 years old. She married in 1921 and had three children. In both the 1930 and 1940 Censuses, she was not listed as working outside the home. In 1940, her husband was listed as a chauffeur for the City of Boston. Her 1960 obituary listed her as past president of the Kennedy Foundation, and requested donations to it in her name.

Driscoll

Census listed Driscoll as a "Cashier Bookkeeper" at the Navy Yard. Like Blanche he also registered to vote in 1917 when she turned 21. In the register of voters, the official listed Driscoll's occupation as "yeoman" in the Navy Yard, misspelling the position. Driscoll married John Murphy in 1922, and by 1940 she was listed as the mother of four children, ages 6–16. Driscoll is the only known instance of someone registering to vote as a "yoeman," even if it was spelled incorrectly.

Abigail Collins

Abigail Collins had deep roots in Charlestown. She lived with her family on Monument Square. Collins was the daughter of former state representative Michael W. Collins, who remained active in Democratic politics until his death in 1956. Abigail Collins joined the Naval Reserves at the age of 18 in 1917 as Yeoman (F) 1st Class and later was promoted to Chief. The *Boston Globe* stated that both she and her sister were "active in social affairs." Not surprisingly, Collins, her mother, and a sister registered to vote in 1920 at the earliest opportunity. Voter records often showed women, including the Yeomen (F), registering with family members and neighbors, accounting for many new voters in their 60s, 70s, and even in their 80s.Collins married Frederic Crehan, a World War I Army veteran, in 1920 and soon after moved to Maplewood, New Jersey, where she spent the rest of her life. Frederic was an educator while Abigail Crehan remained at home and raised two children. Most of the former Yeomen (F) remained very near to where they started out, some even living in the same house for all or most of their lives. Collins was an exception; she was the only one of the married women to leave Massachusetts after marriage. She and her husband are both buried in Arlington National Cemetery. Her headstone identifies her as a Chief Yeoman, United Stated Naval Reserve Forces, World War I. Rather than burial in Arlington by virtue of her husband, the headstone makes it clear that she is buried there of her own right.

Mildred Curtis

Curtis registered to vote on August 20, 1920, at the age of 23. In 1923, she married Edward P. Ryan, who for many years served as chief deputy sheriff of Suffolk Superior Court. Mildred Curtis Ryan was not listed in the 1930 or in the 1940 Census as employed outside the home, but her obituary stated that she had worked as a medical aide in the Boston School System. She was the mother of four children and was extremely active in the American Legion Bessie Edwards Post, made up exclusively of women veterans; she even served as leader of the Post. This was a departure from most women prominent in American Legion Posts, who largely remained unmarried.

Esther McCall

McCall enlisted as a Yeoman (F) at the age of 21 in May 1917, soon after the United States' entry into World War I. She previously worked as a stenographer in a downtown Boston department store. In appreciation, the office employees presented her with a pearl and cameo pendant when she left. She served as a Chief Yeoman (F). Even before the passage of the 19th Amendment, McCall entered the political arena when she appeared before the State Legislature in 1919 as part of the lobbying group to secure inclusion of Yeomen (F) into the Bonus Bill that would give veterans a $100 bonus.

She was an active member of Roxbury Post 44 of the American Legion. In 1936, McCall signed the petition to the U.S. Congress for a national charter and incorporation of the National Yeomen (F), an organization founded in 1924 to preserve the legacy and history of their unique service. In 1922, she resigned as private secretary to Commander Ward K. Wortman, assistant commandant of the First Naval District. That same year she married Francis X. McLaughlin, a veteran who had served with the Medical Corps in France. The couple and their three children made their home at the Norfolk (Settlement) House Center in Roxbury, where Francis served as physical director for many years. McCall registered to vote on August 20, 1920, following in the footsteps of her sister who registered in 1917 at the age of 29.

Helen Beecher

Beecher registered to vote in 1920 at the age of 21. She enlisted on November 7, 1918 at the age of 19 and served for only five days as a landsman, a trainee status prior to the Yeoman (F) rate, before the war ended on November 11. However, she still worked as a stenographer in the Navy Yard in the 1920 Census as a civilian. In 1930, Beecher was employed as a stenographer at the State Street Trust Company until her marriage to John Bride on June 14th. She lived into her nineties and was survived by three children and 13 grandchildren. She was a life-long member of St. Patrick's Parish in Roxbury and attended school there.

Marion T. McEachern

McEachern came from a large family that saw service in World War I. She was one of four sisters who served as Yeoman (F) while her three brothers joined the Army. McEachern was a Chief Yeoman (F). In the 1920 Census, she was listed as a stenographer in a bank living at home with her mother and all her siblings. After her marriage to Edmund G. White about 1923, she no longer appeared on Census lists as employed. In the 1930 Census, Marion McEachern White was living with her husband, who worked in real-estate sales. By 1940, she and Edmund were joined by a son, George, their only child. McEachern registered to vote in 1920 at age 22 in time to cast her vote in the first presidential race in which Massachusetts women could participate. Other than Census records and city directories, she then disappeared from public life until 1967 when she reappeared in a *Boston Globe* article about the "Yeomenettes" 41st reunion. She moved to Cape Cod in the 1980s and died in 1993 at the age of 100. Two of her siblings survived her.

Frances Glover

Glover is the only representative of the Yeomen (F) who registered to vote in 1920 who did not live in the City of Boston. The 1920 voting records of women who lived outside of Boston have thus far been unexplored. Yeomen (F) lived in many towns near Boston including Cambridge, Brookline, Somerville, Winthrop, Malden, as well as Wakefield, Salem, and Framingham. Undoubtedly, a search in their hometowns would yield more 1920 voters and more unique stories. Glover was born in Boston and grew up in comfortable circumstances in the small semi-rural town of Wayland, about 16 miles west of Boston. Her family had inherited a farm and had a live-in housekeeper. Records indicate that Glover attended college before enlisting as a Yeoman (F) 1st Class in July 1918 at age 26. In 1920, she was listed as working as a clerk for the Red Cross and later at Harvard University. Glover was an active er of Wayland's American Legion. She also was an organizer of the Little Theatre Group nd's Vokes Theatre in 1937. That same year, Glover married a prominent Boston attor- founder of the Greater Boston Community Fund, Charles Rogerson. Glover devoted time to charitable endeavors. She is the only known Yeoman (F) from Wayland.

Patricia P. Gleason

Patricia Gleason was 35 years old when she registered to vote in 1920. Before and after her enlistment in April 1917 (one of the first to do so), she worked for the City of Boston. Gleason was appointed postmaster at the Navy Yard, serving in the postal station in Building 24. She was the only woman voter from 1920 in our survey who can be tied to a political party. Gleason was an active member of the Women's Democratic Club of Massachusetts, as was her sister Minnie. She was also active in the Bessie Edwards Post of the American Legion. Gleason signed the Congressional petition in 1936 to incorporate and grant a charter to the National Yeomen (F), which had been founded in 1924. She is a clear example of an independent career woman, an activist and a proud Yeoman (F) who dedicated her life to service.

Helen Regan

Regan enlisted in the Naval Reserves on May 1917 at the age of 33. She served as Yeoman (F) 1st Class and was promoted to Chief. She registered to vote in 1920 along with her 59-year-old mother, Johanna. Regan was a member of the initial 1919 delegation to the Massachusetts State Legislature to lobby for inclusion of Yeomen (F) in the Bonus Bill. She was an active member of the Flaherty American Legion Post in East Boston, and later in the all-woman Bessie Edwards Post. Helen spent her working career in the employ of the federal government, mainly in the Veterans Bureau. Her 1975 obituary listed her as living in Winthrop and made note of the fact that she was a "late veteran of World War I." Most obituaries of Yeomen (F) did not mention their naval service.

Helen Harney

Harney was 21 years old when she registered to vote in 1920; her younger sister, Doris, who also served as a Yeoman (F), registered when she turned 21 years old in 1922. Helen Harney served as a Yeoman (F) 3rd Class, enlisting at the age of 19 in August 1918. She worked in civilian government positions, mostly as a telephone operator for the City of Boston, into the 1940s. During World War II, Harney was back on duty at the Navy Yard, this time as a civilian specialist on property and supply with the United States Army. In 1950, Harney returned to her roots in the Navy and enlisted as a WAVE (Women Accepted for Volunteer Emergency Service) during the Korean Conflict. That made her the oldest WAVE in the Navy. She was delighted to pass the physical, saying "When you've hit 50 and go through a physical that lots of boys and girls can't pass, it makes you feel pretty proud." Harney stayed in the Navy, serving as master-at-arms at the women's barracks in Newport, Rhode Island, and Bainbridge, Maryland. In 1961, she joined about 250 other women veterans marching in President John F. Kennedy's inaugural parade.

Daisy M. Pratt Erd

One young widow with children was among the former Yeomen (F) who registered to vote in 1920. Erd was born in Nova Scotia in 1888; her family immigrated to the United States when she was an infant. She was raised in Chicago and became a naturalized American citizen. Erd registered to vote in 1920 at the age of 32 and is considered one of the most distinguished Yeomen (F). While widowed by the time she enlisted in April 1917 and mother of two young daughters, Erd was known for her considerable musical talents and leadership abilities. According to Lettie Gavin's *American Women in World War I: They Also Served*, "Erd was awarded the Gold Medal for Merit 'War Service,' not an official Navy award but a personal token of esteem from Captain W. R. Rush, USN, commandant." At the time of writing, Erd also stands out as being the only Yeoman (F) with a Wikipedia entry, featuring her musical compositions. After the war ended, Erd was the first woman to join the American Legion in July of 1919. She soon organized the first women's post of the American Legion with Mrs. Lila Woodbury Lane, who was a known suffragist. Erd served as Post Commander. Known as New England Post 29, with a charter membership of 200, enrollment was open to all women of Greater Boston who had served in the military. By September 1919, membership was about 800. Her American Legion Post was dedicated to finding employment for women, and to obtaining sick benefits for them. But first, the location of the clubhouse needed to be resolved. Erd and New England Post 29 were apparently caught up in a turf war between the Bunker Hill Post of the American Legion and the Abraham Lincoln Post of the Veterans of Foreign Wars (VFW) in Charlestown. The Bunker Hill Post asserted that the VFW Post was trying to become an American Legion Post through its association with Erd's Post and "maintained that there was not room in Charlestown for two posts and that Post 29 was there under false pretences [sic]." After six months of acrimonious fighting with the State and National American Legion Executive Committees and a trip to Washington, D.C. to plead her case, Erd's Post had its charter revoked in June 1921. The last mention of Erd and her Post appeared in December 1921 in regard to a Christmas party by the now rogue New England Post with her as commander. But Erd had an even bigger fight to wage. She was fighting for her life. During 1922, she was being treated for tuberculosis and, by 1923, Erd was in California in a hospital for disabled veterans. She was later transferred to Asheville, North Carolina, where she died on October 24th, 1925, at the age of 37. The cause of death was "Tuberculosis contracted during military service." This dynamic and talented woman was a casualty of the War.

Conclusion

The women featured in this section were not radicals, and to the best of our knowledge they were not active in the suffrage movement. Yet, on at least three counts, they stand out as pioneers. Foremost, in becoming the first women to enlist in the United States military. Second, in registering to vote as soon as the opportunity presented itself. And third, by becoming some of the first women to work in full-time, white-collar jobs.

Many of these Yeomen (F) came from the poor and lower-middle classes, often with immigrant parents and many siblings. Other Yeomen (F) came from means that were more middling but needed to work as single women. They all enlisted in service to their country in a time of war. After their service, most remained in the same neighborhoods they grew up in. Their willingness to venture into the world and expand their skills and knowledge surely followed them throughout their lives. For those who married and raised families, their experiences undoubtedly enriched the lives of their children and grandchildren and offered them encouragement in new endeavors. For those who remained unmarried, their experiences as Yeomen (F) created new avenues for women to pursue earning wages to help their families and themselves.

Career women, many spending their lives in government jobs, provided a much larger and diverse world for themselves than the traditional paths of factory or domestic work available in the 19th and early 20th centuries. Regardless of their marriage status, many of the women made time for charitable endeavors, and many remained dedicated advocates for veterans throughout their lives. The courage and persistence of the Yeomen (F) in pushing the

Highly skilled bilingual switchboard operators in the U.S. Army Signal Corps Unit were recruited by the Army and served in Chaumont, France, near the front lines – and sometimes in the trenches – during World War II.

boundaries of women's achievements, often in the face of adversity, remain an inspiration for all of us. (And, as mentioned earlier, the women reservists in the U.S. Navy Nurse Corps were also active in the war.)

ARMY SIGNAL CORPS FEMALE UNIT, ON THE FRONT LINES

During the first world war, the Army recruited a group of women, handpicked its top recruits based on their loyalty and skill, then tasked them with serving the interests of their nation abroad. These women served on the Western Front, but most people still lack even a basic knowledge of them or the service they provided to their country during wartime.

The first group of women selected for inclusion in the U.S. Army Signal Corps Female Telephone Operators Unit joined the war effort in January 1918, at the request of General John "Black Jack" Pershing, commander of the American Expeditionary Forces. The telephone was a new invention back then, and this technology had revolutionized communication on the battlefield. For precisely this purpose, the U.S. Army placed over 20,000 miles of phone cable and provided 8,000 receivers at the warfront. But they hit snags in the switchboard-operation process.

Because very few French switchboard operators spoke English, it took them nearly a minute to connect calls. Every second matters in a war zone though and a minute may as well be an eternity in some scenarios. In a telegram to Washington, General Pershing said that male U.S. soldiers had likewise proven to be "hopelessly inadequate" for the task. Meanwhile, the average experienced American switchboard operator could complete this same task in just 12 seconds. And the average experienced switchboard operator was female.

Grace Banker, chief operator for the first unit of the U.S. Army Signal Corps telephone operators to arrive in France in March 1918. The operators translated classified information about troop movements, logistics, and ammunition between major allied commanders and often worked on the front lines and sometimes in the trenches of the Western Front. She was awarded the Army Distinguished Service Medal.

On November 8, 1917, Pershing requested a unit of American operators who spoke both English and French proficiently. These francophones were recruited and trained locally before traveling to France.

Journalist–editor Clément Thiery notes that these women warriors were not treated with the respect and admiration described by the American media:

> The press compared the U.S. Army's first female recruits to Joan of Arc, fearlessly leaving to fight and save France. Propaganda posters depicted them in the style of the Statue of Liberty holding a telephone set instead of the Declaration of Independence. But the Army was not ready to welcome women into its ranks. Certain members of the Department of War believed enrolling female soldiers was contrary to nature. As a result, the operators were housed away from the military bases and obliged to buy their own uniforms.

Even Pershing's initial decision to hire women was met with objections from the Army, although its switchboard operations were in dire straits. The resistance they faced was ironic, given the rigorous criteria they had met.

In a blog for the Department of Veterans Affairs, Kenneth Holiday notes:

> Those that were accepted into the program underwent a tough selection process and had to agree to serve for the duration of the war. The women were evaluated on tests similar to those given to Army officer candidates. Then they were individually investigated by the Secret Service. Because the nature of the work required them to handle highly confidential information, their loyalty and motivations for serving were investigated more thoroughly than the average soldier.

In addition to their competence as telephone operators and skilled translators, these recruits completed training that included daily military drills. And beyond this, there was an educational component, as the women had to quickly learn military jargon as well as the history and traditions of the U.S. Army.

In every way, these recruits were the first female soldiers in the U.S. Army – women who received rank assignments, donned uniforms, underwent daily inspections, performed daily military drills, and worked in the trenches of the Western Front. And they achieved results.

Working 12-hour switchboard shifts, the "Hello Girls," as the soldiers nicknamed them, raised the number of successful daily connections from 13,000 to 36,000 in the first six months of their assignment. They were so successful, in fact, that Pershing requested more and more units. In the end, 233 women served in this capacity.

Even after the war was over, many remained in Europe to help coordinate the German occupation, the repatriation of American soldiers, and the Paris Peace Conference. The last of them departed France in January 1920, a full two years after the operation began.

During their service, two operators also succumbed to the 1919 flu pandemic and were given a military burial in Suresnes American Cemetery and Memorial, where they are buried alongside thousands of other U.S. service members who died defending their country overseas.

The fate of the Hello Girls after the war only extended the tensions they experienced during their service, however. While these women were recognized for serving their country, they were denied most of the benefits that came with such recognition. For instance, the women's leader, Grace Banker, was one of just a few citizens of either sex to receive the Distinguished Service Medal. There is also evidence that General Pershing gave the women medals shortly after the war. Yet the Army initially refused them veteran status or benefits, and stated that they had served as civilian contractors, not soldiers.

A Sixty-Year Battle for Recognition

Although the U.S. Navy allowed women to enlist during the war, Army regulations at the time stated that soldiers had to be male. Thus, they neither accommodated nor provided for the very women they actively recruited. This allowed the Hello Girls to fall through the cracks and reportedly receive notices of dismissal instead of honorable discharges.

Led by Merle Egan Anderson, the women petitioned president after president with their request to be recognized for their services. From Franklin Delano Roosevelt to Jimmy Carter. Testifying before Congress, Enid Pooley described the ordeal as an injustice done to herself and others who had served their nation with honor. The women were finally recognized as veterans in 1977, thanks to allowances made by the G.I. Improvement Bill. Nearly all of the Signal Corps women had passed away by the time President Carter signed the act into law, however.

Each of the 18 survivors was visited by a military officer, who presented them with honorable-discharge papers and solidified their veteran status. But none of the women who died before this had the opportunity to enjoy their veterans' bonus or benefits. The former was not an insignificant amount, being described as a sum large enough to purchase a car.

Upon her recognition, Egan – one of the last surviving soldiers – reportedly remarked, "I deserve this medal not just for serving in France, but for fighting the U.S. Army for 60 years and winning."

In 1948, passage of the Women's Armed Services Integration Act allowed women to become a permanent part of the Corps, but women were banned from certain military occupation specialties until 2016, when all military occupations were opened to women. Today, women make up about 8 percent of all active Marines and 7.5 percent of active officers.

Egan, and the women who lived to see this recognition, were given military burials and some received their due long after they passed. When Marguerite M. Lovera died two decades before the bill was passed, her tombstone described her as wife to a sergeant, despite being a veteran herself. Decades later, her grandson gathered proof of her service and contacted the cemetery where she lay. In 2018, she received a new headstone commemorating her veteran status.

As mentioned earlier, women reservists in the U.S. Army Nurse Corps were already active in the war.

WOMEN MARINES

Thirty-nine-year-old Opha May Johnson was the first woman to answer the call to become a U.S. Marine. She joined on August 13, 1918, during World War I. Her first duties at Marine Corps Headquarters included managing the records of other female reservists. Her quick promotion to sergeant in September made her the highest-ranking woman in the Corps during World War I.

At the end of the war, 305 women were enlisted as Marine Corps reserves and almost a third of them worked with Johnson at Marine Corps Headquarters. Like the Yeomen (F) of the Navy, World War I Marines performed administrative duties while the men who had filled those roles previously served overseas.

When the war ended all branches of the military disenrolled women, including Johnson, from active service. She returned as a clerk at the War Department, however, and continued working for the Marines Corps as a civil servant until her retirement.

Section 2.4 • TRAILBLAZERS

This section includes text excerpted from "Dr. Susan La Flesche Picotte." National Institutes of Health; "Bessie Coleman," "Jeanette Rankin," "Margaret Sanger," • © 2021 Omnigraphics.

BESSIE COLEMAN

Bessie Coleman grew up on Chicago's South Side and developed a fascination with flying when her brother returned from the war and told her about the female French pilots he encountered across the pond. He also pointed out that Europe was far less segregated than the United States and offered women and people of color more opportunities and freedoms than they had at home.

Coleman applied to multiple U.S. flight schools and was rejected each time based on her race.

So she started teaching herself French, applied to the prestigious Caudron Brother's School of Aviation in Le Crotoy, and was soon enrolled as the sole non-White student in the program.

Top image: Pilot Bessie Coleman, c. 1922 and 1923. • Lower image: Pilot Bessie Coleman and her plane,1922

Over the course of seven months, Coleman learned to fly and perform tailspins, loops, barrel rolls, and other stunts using just a long wooden stick to control the biplane plane. (Later planes featured steering wheels and brakes, but this one did not include these features.)

She graduated and received her international pilot's license in 1921 and was already gaining fame at home and abroad. When she returned to the U.S., the Associated Press ran a feature that referred to her as "a full-fledged aviatrix, said to be the first of her race," and others reported that Coleman had piloted a 220-horsepower Benz-LFB plane – the largest plane ever flown by a woman – while overseas without receiving any instruction particular to that plane.

By 1922, Coleman was barnstorming and wowing American crowds with her stunts and daring. She walked out onto the wings of her plane and performed all kinds of stunts that earned her the nicknames "Queen Bess" and "Brave Bessie." By this time, Coleman was also considering opening her own flight school so that she could offer to others opportunities that were not extended to her.

In 1923, Coleman crash landed after her plane failed midflight. She suffered multiple broken bones that took time to heal, but the *New York Times* reported that Coleman sent a telegram to her fans that said, "Tell them all that as soon as I can walk I'm going to fly!" And she did.

In 1926, Coleman and her publicity agent and mechanic William Wills were conducting a test flight over an airfield in Jacksonville, Florida, in preparation for an air show, when the plane experienced engine trouble. Wills, who was piloting the plane, tried to control it, but the plane nosedived and flipped over. This happened in the days before planes had seatbelts and Coleman fell from the cockpit at 3,000 feet and lost her life at just 34 years of age.

Three years later, Lieutenant William J. Power founded the Bessie Coleman Aero Club and promoted aviation in the Black community. And two years after that, this aviation club sponsored the nation's first all-Black air show, which was attended by 15,000 spectators. The club also started the annual tradition of Black pilots flying over Coleman's grave and dropping flowers from their cockpits in her honor.

Dr. Susan La Flesche Picotte, the first Native American woman in the United States to receive a medical degree, circa 1910.

DR. SUSAN LA FLESCHE PICOTTE

In 1889, Susan La Flesche Picotte was the first person to receive federal aid for professional education and then she became the first American Indian woman in the United States to receive a medical degree. Over the course of her remarkable career she served more than 1,300 people over 450 square miles, giving financial advice and resolving family disputes as well as providing medical care at all hours of the day and night.

Susan La Flesche was born to Chief Joseph La Flesche (Iron Eyes) and his wife, Mary (One Woman) on the Omaha Reservation in northeastern Nebraska. She attended school there until age 14. Her father encouraged his people to seek education and build relationships with White reform groups. After being home-schooled for several years, La Flesche was sent to the Elizabeth Institute for Young Ladies in New Jersey and returned home at age 17 to teach at the Quaker Mission School on the Omaha Reservation for two years.

As a child, she had watched a sick Indian woman die because the local White doctor would not give her care. La Flesche later credited this tragedy as her inspiration to train as a physician, so she could provide care for the people she lived with on the reservation.

While working at the Quaker school, La Flesche attended to the health of ethnologist Alice Fletcher, who was working there. With Fletcher's urging, she went back East to complete her education and earn a medical degree. She enrolled at Hampton Institute, one of the nation's first and finest schools of higher education for non-White students. The resident physician there, Martha Waldron, was a graduate of the Woman's Medical College of Pennsylvania (WMCP) and encouraged La Flesche to apply to there. Once again, Alice Fletcher helped her by securing scholarship funds from the U.S. Office of Indian Affairs and the Connecticut Indian Association, a branch of the Women's National Indian Association. After only two years in a three-year program at WMCP, Susan La Flesche graduated in 1889 at the top of her class. She remained in Philadelphia to complete a year's internship, and then returned home to provide health care to the Omaha people at the government boarding school, where she was responsible for some twelve hundred people.

Dr. La Flesche married Henry Picotte in 1894 and the couple moved to Bancroft, Nebraska, where she set up a private practice, serving both White and non-White patients. Along with her busy practice, Picotte also raised two sons and nursed her husband through a terminal illness. In 1906 she led a delegation to Washington, D.C., to lobby for prohibition of alcohol on the reservation. In 1913, two years before her death, she saw her life's dream fulfilled when she opened a hospital in the reservation town of Walthill, Nebraska. Today the hospital houses a museum dedicated to the work of Dr. Susan La Flesche Picotte and the history of the Omaha and Winnebago tribes.

JEANETTE RANKIN

Jeanette Pickering Rankin, a pacifist, was elected as the first female member of the U.S. House of Representatives in 1916. She spent the six years prior to serving in Congress advocating for women's rights and lobbying for woman's suffrage. Rankin served as an officer for the Women's International League for Peace and Freedom and is known for another historic first: She is the only member of Congress who voted against the nation participating in either world war. While in office, Rankin advocated for regular hours and wages for women workers. She also campaigned for healthcare for expectant mothers and children. Years later, Rankin and other pacifists formed a collective known as the Jeannette Rankin Brigade to protest U.S. involvement in the Vietnam War.

MARGARET SANGER

Margaret Sanger was a nurse, sex educator, and birth-control activist, who came of age during the Progressive Era. She coined the term "birth control."

Sanger was an active participant in women's labor protests, including the labor strikes in Massachusetts in 1912 and in New Jersey in 1913, and one of the progressive New York intellectuals with socialist leanings whose actions increased worker and consumer safety. Emma Goldman and muckraker Upton Sinclair were among her circle of friends. (Sinclair's book *The Jungle* exposed dangerously unsafe practices common in the meat-processing industry, and his findings led Congress to pass the Pure Food and Drug Act of 1905 and the Meat Inspection Act of 1906.)

As a visiting nurse, Sanger visited the homes of poor immigrants and saw firsthand how the health of mothers of large families had been compromised by too many pregnancies, miscarriages and, in some cases, botched abortions. These experiences influenced her belief that controlling family size was necessary in order to decrease impoverishment and increase the independence and autonomy of women. Sanger resolved to share birth-control information with women but recognized that she first had to work to repeal the federal Comstack laws, which banned the mailing and distribution of so-called obscene materials, including all information about birth control.

Sanger described contraceptive techniques in pamphlets and began handing them out. She advocated for birth control in the pages of her feminist publication *The Woman Rebel*. When she used the U.S. Postal Service to mail issues to her subscribers, she was charged in 1915 with violating the Comstock laws. Sanger's conviction was reversed on appeal, however,

The original Section 211 (enacted in 1873) of the Federal Criminal Code (considered to be the "parent" of all the **Comstock Laws** reads

> Every obscene, lewd, or lascivious, and every filthy book, pamphlet, picture, paper, letter, writing, print, or other publication of an indecent character, and every article or thing designed, adapted, or intended for preventing conception or producing abortion, or for any indecent or immoral use; and every article, instrument, substance, drug, medicine, or thing which is advertised or described in a manner calculated to lead another to use or apply it for preventing conception or producing abortion, or for any indecent or immoral purpose and every written or printed card, letter, circular, book, pamphlet advertisement, or notice of any kind giving information directly or indirectly, where, or how, or of whom, or by what means any of the hereinbefore-mentioned matters, articles or things may be obtained or made, or where or by whom any act or operation of any kind for the procuring or producing of abortion will be done or performed or how or by what means conception may be prevented or abortion may be produced, whether sealed or unsealed; and every letter, packet, or package, or other mail matter containing any filthy, vile, or indecent thing, device or substance and every paper, writing, advertisement or representation that any article, instrument, substance, drug, medicine, or thing may, or can be, used or applied, for preventing conception or producing abortion, or for any indecent or immoral purpose; and every description calculated to induce or incite a person to so use or apply any such article, instrument, substance, drug, medicine, or thing, is hereby declared to be a non-mailable matter and shall not be conveyed in the mails or delivered from any post office or by any letter carrier. Whoever shall knowingly deposit or cause to be deposited for mailing or delivery, anything declared by this section to be non-mailable, or shall knowingly take, or cause the same to be taken, from the mails for the purpose of circulating or disposing thereof, or of aiding in the circulation or disposition thereof, shall be fined not more than five thousand dollars, or imprisoned not more than five years, or both.

because contraceptive devices could be legally used to promoted cures for or prevention of disease (Michals, 31). Nevertheless, the prohibition of devices advertised specifically for birth control would not be overturned for another 18 years.

In 1916, Sanger opened the first birth-control clinic in the United States, only to have it raided and shut down one week later. She was jailed for 30 days for that offense but gained significant support as a result. And although she lost her appeal, the courts ruled that doctors could prescribe contraceptives to women for medical reasons. That ruling was the loophole Sanger needed to open a second birth-control clinic in 1923 that was staffed by social workers and female doctors. She continued opening clinics using this model, which eventually led to the creation of the modern-day Planned Parenthood Federation of America.

In 1932, Sanger ordered a shipment of diaphragms to be sent to a sympathetic doctor in New York City from Japan. U.S. Customs identified the contraceptive devices as illegal and confiscated them, at which point Sanger filed suit against the U.S. government. Four years later, a federal appeals court ruled in *United States v. One Package of Japanese Pessaries* that the federal government could not interfere with medical doctors providing contraception to their patients.

The "pill" was approved by the Food and Drug Administration (FDA) in 1960. The 1965 case *Griswold v. Connecticut* struck down a Comstock law that banned contraception for married couples in Connecticut and Massachusetts. The Griswold finding did not apply to unmarried people, however. Comstock laws finally ended in 1971 – almost a century after their passage – when the *Eisenstadt v. Baird* decision applied the same contraception access to unmarried people.

Section 2.5 • WOMEN IN FACTORIES

This section includes text excerpted from Victoria Byerly's *"Hard Times Cotton Mill Girls: Personal Histories of Womanhood and Poverty in the South;"* other sections include text excerpted from "Women in Factories," "Triangle Shirtwaist Factory Fire of 1911," "Bread and Roses Strike of 1912," "Paterson Silk Strike of 1913," "Cotton Mill Girls," • © 2021 Omnigraphics.

The government initially did not regulate factory work during the Industrial Revolution. This oversight made it possible for companies to both exploit their labor forces and keep them in squalor. Thus, women involved in factory work often endured hazardous and unsanitary conditions. Many female laborers worked in mill towns, which were planned and constructed by the company and build around the mill. There, women's lives "were tightly controlled" by the ruling business, which also paid them substantially smaller wages than men. Even the textile factories, where most women worked, were plagued with issues of safety and overcrowding. Although these positions were not as dangerous as coal mining or other industrial jobs emerging during this time, many historians note that the factories were in deplorable states. This was certainly made worse by just how much time was typically spent in those buildings. Some factories ran for 24 hours a day and shifts ranged from 10 to 14 hours, operating spinning and weaving equipment nonstop. The automated equipment posed a high risk, particularly with its moving parts, yet injured workers were typically not compensated. The majority of factory workers were women below the age of 20. Thus, these conditions had a significant impact on working women's quality of life during this time.

TRIANGLE SHIRTWAIST FACTORY FIRE OF 1911

On March 25th, 1911, at New York City's Asch Building, 146 employees of the Triangle Waist Company, which was nearly a third of its workforce, lost their lives. Significantly, the overwhelming majority (123) of the deceased were women and girls, some as young as fourteen years old. Most were immigrants who had only recently come to the U.S. in search of upward mobility. Language barriers and other socioeconomic vulnerabilities came together to make these female immigrants prime targets for exploitative labor in harsh conditions.

The Triangle Shirtwaist Factory Fire was a testament to the potentially disastrous outcome of such environmental hazards. Indeed, many of the fatalities would likely have been avoided if not for the Triangle Factory's neglectful practices and policies. For instance, the company kept the outer doors of the building locked, believing this would keep productivity high. Yet, the practice of essentially locking workers inside made it difficult for them to escape when disaster struck. A common safety practice among garment factories during this time was to keep buckets of water on hand in the event of a fire. Yet, on the day of the tragedy, the Triangle Factory's buckets stood empty.

A survivor recalled noticing that the buckets were empty that morning. However, since workers were not permitted to use the building's bathrooms (which were also locked), filling the buckets themselves was generally not an option. Thus, workers were not only locked inside when the fire broke out, but they also had no extinguishers available. As the blaze advanced, attempts to flee were stifled by clutter that limited workers' mobility. Survivor Cecilia Walker Friedman recalled watching many women succumb to the flames after falling over chairs and baskets in the building's already narrow hallways.

Survivors of the Triangle Shirtwaist Factory fire.

Friedman herself survived only by entering an elevator shaft as the car descended. She grabbed a cable, and used it to slide to the bottom, where the impact was so severe it broke two of her bones. Those who could make it there used the fire escape, which eventually bent under the weight of all those bodies. Others watched as firefighters arrived, only to discover that their ladders were too short to reach the eighth floor. Trapped and hopeless, many jumped to their deaths – sometimes in pairs and groups – rather than burn alive.

The *New York Tribune* reported that firefighters later discovered a pile of bodies six feet high against a door to a back stairway that was barred. Moreover, the building itself had been constructed with fewer stairways than appropriate for a structure of its type. Journalist Patrick J. Kiger notes for *History.com*:

> Young women became trapped by tables, bulky equipment and doors that locked or opened the wrong way as flames enveloped the eighth, ninth and 10th floors of the Asch Building in New York City's Greenwich Village on March 25, 1911. As people struggled to escape, several fell into the flames, their bodies piling by blocked exits. Others leapt – in twos and threes – out the burning building's high windows.

This disregard for individual safety was just a symptom of a company culture that did not value its labor force. Women at the Triangle Factory worked 12.5-hour daily shifts and earned only $6 per week. From these meagre earnings, they were also expected to pay for their own equipment (irons, needles, thread), and sometimes even sewing machines. Moreover, historians note that the Triangle was among the most resistant companies to the growing call for improved labor conditions and compensation during this time. In response to a strike two years prior, the company responded to union demands with notable hostility, and hired thugs to assault and intimidate both strikers and journalists.

Impact

Despite a massive public outcry following the tragedy, many felt that justice was not done. Factory owners Isaac Harris and Max Blanck faced a manslaughter trial in which the jury was given instructions that made conviction both difficult and unlikely. They were not convicted, and journalists at the time reported that they had to be escorted away from the courthouse where an angry mob awaited. The victims' families ultimately received lawsuit settlements of $75 per death, which was barely a quarter of the $400 per death that the factory owners received from their insurer.

Still, the Triangle Shirtwaist Factory Fire alerted the public to the awful conditions that many factory workers endured and prompted demands for reform. A funeral procession for the victims drew a crowd of approximately 350,000 mourners and inspired civic leaders such as Frances Perkins (who went on to become the first U.S. Secretary of Labor, 1933–1945) to strengthen their advocacy for workplace safety. Under Perkins' leadership, the Committee on Public Safety recommended new safety laws to the New York State legislature, 60 of which were passed between 1911 and 1913. While these changes came at a great cost, they ultimately helped to protect other vulnerable workers from facing a similar fate.

Reflecting on the legacy of the loss five years later, Perkins said:

> Out of that terrible episode came a self-examination of stricken conscience in which the people of this state saw for the first time the individual worth and value of each of those 146 people who fell or were burned in that great fire.... We all felt that we had been wrong, that something was wrong with that building which we had accepted, or the tragedy never would have happened. Moved by this sense of stricken guilt, we banded ourselves together to find a way by law to prevent this kind of disaster.... It was the beginning of a new and important drive to bring the humanities to the life of the brothers and sisters we all had in the working groups of these United States.

BREAD AND ROSES STRIKE OF 1912

In 1912, Lawrence, Massachusetts was a mill town ruled by the textile industry. Much like other factories during this time, the people employed by this mill were mostly recent immigrants, many of whom did not possess skills that may have availed better employment. Women and children accounted for nearly half of the labor force, and the worker death rate was alarmingly high. Indeed, a study by Dr. Elizabeth Shapleigh found that 36 of every 100 employees were dead by the age of 25. Beyond workplace risk, financial security was hard to come by. Some workers lived in company housing, where rental costs did not decrease when companies reduced their pay.

Despite these realities, employees were not unionizing. Prior to 1912, those who did unionize were largely skilled laborers, most of whom were native to the United States. That all changed when mill owners at the American Wool Company in Lawrence reduced the pay of their female mill workers. This decision was made in response to a new state law that reduced women's weekly working limit to 54 hours. Since workers only made an average of $8.76 each week, the 32-cent reduction was not insignificant, and likely had genuine implications for workers' ability to feed and care for themselves.

Word of the strike at Everett Mill soon spread to other mills in the area, culminating in massive walkouts the next day. Women's History writer Jone J. Lewis elaborates on the beginning of the strike described as a landmark victory for workers in the U.S.:

On January 11, a few Polish women at the mills went on strike when they saw that their pay envelopes had been shorted; a few other women at other mills in Lawrence also walked off the job in protest. The next day, on January 12, ten thousand textile workers walked off the job, most of them women, and the city of Lawrence rang its riot bells as an alarm. Eventually, the number striking rose to 25,000.

Workers in the Bread and Roses Strike, 1912

Many of the strikers met the afternoon of January 12th and invited an organizer with the Industrial Workers of the World (IWW) to come to Lawrence and help with the strike. The strikers' demands included a 15-percent pay increase, a 54-hour work week, overtime pay at double the normal rate of pay, and elimination of bonus pay (which rewarded only a few and encouraged all to work longer hours).

The movement was notable for its cross-cultural collaboration. Joseph Ettor, an experienced organizer, spoke several of the workers' languages. With peers and union leaders Arturo Giovannitti, Elizabeth Gurley Flynn, and Vincent St. John, he helped to ensure representation for all the nationalities that comprised the workforce, including Syrian, Portuguese, Hungarian, Italian, Slavic, and French-Canadian. The city responded harshly and implemented militia patrols at night and turned fire hoses on and imprisoned strikers. In response, community groups, many of which were socialist organizations, mobilized resources for strikers, including medical care, food, and payments to help relieve their families.

Indeed, the strike was bolstered by structures and principles of community. Local fixtures such as ethnic organizations and community halls provided space for people to come together and organize. When striking parents decided to send nearly 200 children to New York (to protect them from the erupting violence) they were received by supporters, mostly women, who secured foster homes for them. In other demonstrations of solidarity, socialist organizations also joined demonstrations, turning out in numbers as high as 5,000 on February 10th.

As news of the strike spread through the nation, American workers also provided monetary donations and farmers near Lawrence donated food.

The death of Italian immigrant and striker Anna LoPizzo, who was shot by a police officer as she stood in a picket line, was one of many watershed moments that drew national outrage. On March 2nd, Congress began a hearing on the strike under orders from President Taft. The proceedings revealed the perilous and exploitative conditions faced by workers, many of whom were children as young as fourteen who had dropped out of school to earn a living.

Historian Christopher Klein elaborates:

> Striking workers, including children who dropped out of school at age 14 or younger to work in the factories, described the brutal working conditions and poor pay inside the

> Lawrence mills. A third of mill workers, whose life expectancy was less than 40 years, died within a decade of taking their jobs. If death didn't come slowly through respiratory infections such as pneumonia or tuberculosis from inhaling dust and lint, it could come swiftly in workplace accidents that took lives and limbs. Fourteen-year-old Carmela Teoli shocked lawmakers by recounting how a mill machine had torn off her scalp and left her hospitalized for seven months.

After the children's testimony, public tide turned in favor of the strikers for good. The mill owners were ready for a deal and agreed to many of the workers' demands. The two sides agreed to a 15-percent wage hike, a bump in overtime compensation, and a promise not to retaliate against strikers. On March 14th, the nine-week strike ended as 15,000 workers gathered on Lawrence Common shouted their agreement to accept the offer. Only five sounded their dissents.

Impact
Significantly, the strike did not just benefit workers in Lawrence. Within weeks, 275,000 New England textile workers received similar raises. This trend was seen in other industries, too. Moreover, the efforts of workers and organizers shone a national spotlight on workplace safety, unfair distribution of profit, and the problematic but prevalent use of child labor. Over 100 years later, the strike is remembered as a testament to the power of marginalized communities, and the importance of allyship in the quest for socioeconomic justice.

PATERSON SILK STRIKE OF 1913
The Paterson silk strike was one in a series of industrial strikes in the garment and textile industries on America's East Coast from 1900 to 1913. The success of the Bread and Roses Strike gave union organizers hope that they could improve working conditions and wages for the silk weavers of Paterson, New Jersey as well.

Industrial Workers of the World (IWW) leader and prominent feminist Elizabeth Gurley Flynn was one of two main strike organizers.

This five-month work stoppage occurred after workers had endured a sharp decline in wages, unsafe working conditions, and long workdays. Workers were also concerned because new technology in silk mills in three nearby states ran more efficiently, increased profits and reduced the need for skilled silk weavers.

The strike began in February 1913 and ended on July 28th.

All told approximately 1,850 strikers were arrested, including Elizabeth Gurley Flynn, who was arrested for giving a speech encouraging strikers to unite across racial lines. She was charged with inciting violence through radical speech. Bystander Valentino Modestino was fatally shot by a private guard in April and striking worker Vincenzo Madonna was fatally shot by a strikebreaker in June.

Impact
The workers successfully shut down the Paterson factory and defended themselves against American Federation of Labor efforts to undercut the strike but failed to extend the strike to annex mills in other states. Ultimately, the strike failed and the UWW never fully recovered along the East Coast.

COTTON MILL GIRLS

The manufacturing of cotton cloth was a major industry in New England in the years leading up to the U.S. Civil War and innovative merchant Francis Cabot Lowell of Massachusetts opened the first U.S. cotton mill capable of completing all steps involved in the manufacturing process of cloth, from processing to spinning to weaving to dyeing to cutting, under one factory roof.

Unlike mill owners in England and most other New England states, Lowell hired young "mill girls" in the mill that he built and paid them decent wages. But American mill owners eventually abandoned the "Lowell System" and cut worker wages and hours. And when these actions led to numerous labor protests and strikes, the mill owners of New England largely replaced the mill girls with Irish immigrants and their children, who were willing to work longer hours for lower wages.

The Confederate Army's embargo of cotton during the U.S. Civil War stopped the flow of southern cotton to these New England cotton mills and, by the beginning of the twentieth century, many of these mills were in danger of becoming obsolete.

Southern gentry led a successful Cotton Mill Campaign and soon textile mills peppered the South's Piedmont region. But White male sharecroppers who were eager to leave their fields behind soon learned that the mill owners were just as eager to hire the cheapest labor available to them. That meant hiring as many women and children as possible.

Meanwhile, these factories had Whites-only policies, which left Black workers with few opportunities.

The Shift from Farm to Factory

The transition of American workers from farms to factories was in full swing across the U.S. South by the early years of the 20th century. And the new millworkers and their families considered their relocation as moving up in the world. After all, mill owners offered low-cost housing to mill employees (complete with new-fangled electricity, and often indoor plumbing), and a steady and predictable salary provided more economic security than farming.

Victoria Byerly describes the early mill villages that southern workers moved into as "one big white family closed off to the external world."

And they were. Workers soon learned that the mill-village system sought to control "all aspects of workers' lives" – from church (with its steady stream of "y'all-keep-working-hard" sermons) to when mill village lights were turned off to education and social welfare. And working families never seemed to earn much more than the cost of renting one of those company mill houses, despite working eleven-, twelve-, and sometimes even sixteen-hour shifts. The remote locations of these hydro-powered mill villages also ensured that workers would return even more of their earnings to the mill owner each time they made a purchase from the mill-owned general store.

Byerly reports that women comprised 40 percent of mill employees in those years and children 10 to 15 years of age comprised 25 percent.

"We work in *his* mill. We live in *his* houses. Our children go to *his* school. And on Sunday we go to hear *his* preacher." This is the pathetic plaint of the cotton mill workers of North Carolina, spoken more than once to our agent in North Carolina. It is refreshing to observe that at least the system of feudalism is recognized by the workers themselves.

The expression we have quoted might be amplified with regard to some twenty to twenty-five mills in the South that are invariably advertised for their betterment work, with a significant silence as to the 700 other cotton mills that merely bask in the reflected glory of the "show mills."

We also go to *his* Y.M.C.A. when he has built one. We spend our leisure time, after the eleven-hour day, those of us who can read, in *his* reading room. Our children play in *his* streets. Our cows sleep in *his* stable. We are sent to *his* store to buy our goods. When we are sick, or hurt in the mill, we go to *his* hospital. We are arrested by *his* constable, and tried by *his* magistrate. And when we die we are buried in *his* cemetery." –Opening paragraph of the 12-page National Child Labor Committee's pamphlet *Child Wages in the Cotton Mills: Our Modern Feudalism*, prepared by National Secretary A. J. McKelway (May 1913).

Mr. R. M. Miller, Jr., of Charlotte, N. C., who recently appeared before the Ways and Means Committee of the House of Representatives to plead for protection against the competition of the "pauper labor of Europe" in the manufacture of cotton goods, once went into print to say, in opposition to a child labor bill which proposed the raising of the age-limit for girls only, from twelve to fourteen years of age, that 75 percent of the spinners of North Carolina were fourteen years old or under. It is one of the traditions of the cotton mill in the South, that spinning is work for girls, not for boys or women. And that tradition of the industry is directly in the face of all the teachings of medical science, as to the necessity or the special care and protection of young girls at that period of life. Think of your own girls, fathers and mothers, standing at a spinning frame for eleven hours a day, or sometimes a night! Of 295 spinners found under 12 in Southern mills, 246 were girls.

The Federal Bureau of Labor found in 1908–9 that in the Southern mills they investigated and in which agents were required to prove the ages of the children, 17 children 7 years of age, 48 of eight years of age, 107 of nine years of age, 283 of ten years of age, and 494 of eleven years of age.

In a representative South Carolina cotton mill,

- doffers of 12 years were paid $3.54 per week
- doffers of 13 years were paid $3.92 per week
- doffers of 14 years were paid $5.04 per week
- doffers of 15 years were paid $4.75 per week
- and doffers of 20 years and over were paid $2,52 per week, while the earnings of the spinners in 151 Southern mills were $4.54 a week and scrubbers and sweepers $2.96 a week. These are actual wages paid, not the wages computed for full-time, which was an average of 62.7 hours per week. (McKelway, 1913)

Meanwhile, a seventy-hour workweek earned southern mill workers less than $2.50 in 1895, despite profits being "phenomenal" at the turn of the century and it not being "unusual … in those years to make 30 to 70 percent profit' (Broadus Mitchell, as quoted by Byerly, 44).

Byerly also notes that the South permitted White girls as young as seven to work in these cotton mills and "these children who might have worked a sixty-four-hour work week, were allowed to keep maybe twenty-five cents of their wages, if any, after household expenses were taken care of" (Byerly, 44). And working children was the cultural norm at a time when birth control was not available as an option for women workers and most of them had no idea how reproduction worked anyway.

Women work at their stations as supervisors monitor their productivity, c. 1915.

Meanwhile, southern Black girls were "put in the fields as soon as they were able to hoe or pick cotton, usually around the age of five," and worked in these fields until around age twelve, when they were hired out as domestics and lived in the homes of white families, where they were responsible for housework, cooking, and child care" (ibid., 45).

"The working-class southern girl of the early twentieth century was born in severe poverty and raised without protection. She survived overcrowded living conditions, poor nutrition and in some cases starvation, little if any education, and often hostile and violent environments, and a life overwhelmingly centered around work," Byerly explains – and familial and cultural expectations were that she married young and commenced to "birthing as many children as her body could produce" (75).

But that being said, it is important to note that millwork "gave the white southern woman her first taste of economic independence" and, for the first time, an American woman "had a way out of a mentally or physically abusive marriage, because the mill provided a way for her to be financially independent of her husband" (75–76).

Byerly continues:

> This did not mean that the single mill woman lived a more comfortable life than before except perhaps for the peace of mind she found in coming home from work and being boss in her own home. The early-twentieth-century mill woman still worked a sixteen-hour day in the mill and maintained her home, at least until her oldest children were of age to enter the mill. Then she left the mill and the family lived on the wages of the children while the mother worked in the home. This pattern, in which the mill woman received some reprieve from overwork, changed when child labor laws prohibited children from working in the mills.

Oral Histories: The Farm-to-Factory Transition

Byerly collected the following two excerpted oral histories as part of her efforts to preserve the history of hard-working southern cotton mill girls and the impact of the textile industry on the South.

Annie Viola Fries of High Point, North Carolina, was born in 1921 and raised as the youngest child in a farming family that included ten living children.

"When I got old enough I quit school and I went in the mill to help my mother," Fries explained, because her mother was sick and could no longer work.

After a rocky start, Fries adjusted to working the third shift and slept during the day in between helping her mother out.

Fries' mother had been orphaned at a young age and also worked in a cotton mill before getting married, but Fries had "no idea how old [her mother was at the time because] back then you could go to work in the mill around eight or nine."

"Parents would work in the factories and raise what food they eat," she told Byerly. "And a lot of 'em worked in the mills. What didn't work in the cotton mills worked in the shops, the furniture factory [, and some] just farmed and didn't work out nowhere. Like my daddy."

"I remember I made twelve dollars a week," Fries shared (17–25).

Fellow North Carolinian Katie Geneva Cannon, of nearby Kannapolis, described how the introduction of textile mills affected the lives of Black southerners in those early years of the twentieth century.

"All the black people lived together," she told Byerly.

"It was always assumed that we would work. Work was a given in my life, almost like breathing and sleeping. I'm always surprised when I hear people talking about somebody taking care of them, because we always knew we were going to work."

Cannon said, "The first work I did was as a domestic, cleaning people's houses. The interesting thing was that all the white people we worked for were mill workers. Black women were not allowed to work in the mill then, so the only jobs available to black women were as domestics or teachers, and there was only one black school in Kannapolis ... so that [work] was very limited." She also said that all the Black women in her town worked in domestic roles while "all the black men I knew worked in Cannon Mills in the low-paying menial jobs."

Cannon told Byerly that, as a domestic worker, she earned two dollars for two hours of work, "but you had a list of things to do and if it took you longer than that, that was your business [but] the work they wanted you to do, you could never do in two hours."

Her tasks included washing the floors, cleaning and organizing the refrigerator and cabinets, and washing and ironing the clothes. The work Fries performed is counted in official U.S. Department of Labor workforce data, but the work that Cannon and her mother and sisters performed is not (26–39).

A Radical Enough Progression

Byerly asked second-generation mill women, most of whom began work as young children and as a result received little if any education, why so many women of that generation remained in the same jobs at the mills rather than insisting that they be part of mill management and retired mill woman Blan Kilpatrick of Kannapolis, North Carolina, put it this way:

"We felt lucky to have any kind of job at all in the mill. Back then if we had demanded to be supervisors or anything like that, we would have been laughed out of there."

In other words, Byerly says, "entry into the mill itself marked what was thought to be a radical enough progression for southern white women."

In closing, Byerly also notes that,

> except for family size, this way of life continues today for the southern mill woman. Working at some of the same jobs as [Byerly's own] grandmother and ... great-grandmother, mill women are still stuck in the most menial positions at the mill, and they are still earning among the lowest wages in the country (76).

CHAPTER THREE

Uncredited Trailblazers in a Decade of Contradictions, 1920–1929

CHAPTER CONTENTS

Section 3.1 • **OVERVIEW**

"Overview: Women in the Workplace in America, 1920–1929," • © 2021 Omnigraphics.

The 1920s launched with passage of the 19th Amendment, which legalized the right for women to vote. And shortly after the start of the new decade, the U.S. came under a new presidency. In 1921, Warren G. Harding took office and faced the first waves of economic crisis that would ultimately plague the 1920s. The war was finally over, but it left many challenges in its wake. With the fighting over, the demand for manufactured goods decreased, as did the need for employment. Moreover, returning soldiers attempted to re-enter the job market, which then became saturated. These were the circumstances Harding sought to rectify as he established a program to boost the economy.

The president believed in a collaborative relationship between government and business and handpicked leaders such as Herbert Hoover and Andrew Mellon, whose opinions on capitalism and taxes mirrored the president's own ambitions. Industry and business were thus expanded under the new administration and, from 1922 to 1927, the economy grew at a remarkable rate of 7 percent per year. As prosperity increased, so did consumerism, though that would all change when the Great Depression hit at the end of the decade.

The agricultural sector was already feeling the pinch, foreshadowing the downturn to come. The rural–urban migration trend seen in the previous decade continued through the 1920s; however, the nation still rested on an agricultural economy. Approximately one-third of the population still lived and labored on 400 million acres of farmland spread across the country. This meant the U.S. was producing more crops than ever at the start of the decade – exceeding the country's need.

Farmers were also turning out a surplus while paying high prices for the materials they needed to keep their farms running. Thus, laborers in this sector saw minimal profits and took on significant debt. Unsurprisingly, the rural-dwelling, agrarian women of this era had significantly different experiences of the "Roaring 20s" than urban flappers did and often lived in dire poverty while facing foreclosure. To help themselves and their families survive the agricultural depression, many women had to find creative ways to supplement their income, demonstrating remarkable skill and gumption to weather the storm. Dan Bryan elaborates for *American History USA*:

> The women in these areas were not buying the latest rayon undergarments, nor were they trimming their hair and their dresses short, or enjoying the newfound glitz of the Jazz Age. They were still sewing their own clothes, patching holes in their husband's shirts, and making dresses stretch from one daughter to the next. They still slaughtered their own meat, grew and canned their own vegetables, and in many places bartered for what they could not produce. Survival skills took precedence over cultural sophistication. The social safety net was the kindness of relatives, neighbors, and the church. It was not uncommon for more than one family to share the same house, or to take in boarders as times got hard.

The 1920s reflected a new landscape for Americans, 51 percent of whom now lived in cities instead or rural areas for the first time in our nation's history. Only 10 percent of women continued working after marriage during much of 1920s, and the ones who did were primarily working-class women whose families relied on their earnings for survival. Yet real liberation and equality for women, despite the media's portrayal of liberated flappers as unfazed by social taboos of previous decades – were mostly realized in later generations from the social changes that the 1920s set into motion.

The new decade brought on tough times for immigrants, too. Not long before, the U.S. had been known as a refuge for immigrants seeking a better life. However, sentiments of inclusion began to change. The Harding administration also championed new immigration restrictions during this time. Notably, this new resistance came when the immigrant population was becoming more ethnically, religiously, and sociopolitically diverse. The U.S. population, now around 106 million, had grown by 15 percent since 1910, and much of this was due to immigration. The 1920s were marked by more stringent immigration laws and increasing xenophobia. As noted by *Encylcopedia.com*:

> Early waves of immigrants had been dominated by people from northern European countries like England and the Netherlands, whose values and habits were similar to those of most native-born U.S. residents. But the early years of the nineteenth century had seen a big increase in immigrants from southern Europe, especially Italy, and eastern Europe, such as Poland and Yugoslavia. Whereas the United States had historically been dominated by Protestants – such as Baptists, Methodists, and Presbyterians – many of the newcomers were Catholic or Jewish. They came from unfamiliar cultures. Importantly, many of these immigrants did not share mainstream citizens' disapproval of liquor.... Native-born people worried that their beloved U.S. culture was under attack by outsiders with unsavory habits and radical political views [communism]. The result was a movement toward ... favoring native-born citizens over immigrants and new laws to curb the influx of immigrants from places seen as undesirable. In 1921 Congress passed an emergency law that limited immigration to 355,000 immigrants per year (those from Asia had already been severely restricted).

Meanwhile, by 1927, almost two-thirds of American homes had electricity, many had radios, and marketing firms were encouraging post-war Americans to find a greater sense of freedom and possibility through the purchase of their own automobile.

By 1929, more than half the single women in the United States and more than a quarter of all women in the United States were working in jobs associated with the "feminized professions," which later became known as "pink-collar" jobs. The total number of women in the workplace for 1920 was 8,179,017(52.8%). One-third of these women worked as "domestic servants," and the remaining were most commonly employed as store clerks, clerical workers, or factory workers.

In 1927, the average weekly wage for men was $29.35 compared to $17.34 for women.

Section 3.2 • **TWO STEPS FORWARD IN THE JOURNEY TO FULL INCLUSION**

The fight for equality did not end when the 19th Amendment was ratified. As National Women's Party leader Alice Paul famously said, the fight had just begun. After all, this single victory did not change the fact that the Constitution had not been drafted with much consideration for the needs or rights of women, who were still largely consigned to the domestic sphere. Indeed, it is only in the 19th Amendment that the document addresses sex at all, and only in relation to voting rights. Moreover, the provision for woman's suffrage did not always translate to reality. Jim Crow was still alive and well in the South, and voter-suppression tactics successfully barred Black women from voting for decades. Likewise, Native Americans of both sexes only gained the right to vote in federal elections in 1924, at which point all women in the United States, with the exception of residents of the District of Columbia, were guaranteed the right to vote in federal elections. Officially anyway.

To address the gender gaps in the Constitution, the National Women's Party drafted the Equal Rights Amendment (ERA) and proposed it to Congress in 1923. Written by Alice Paul and Crystal Eastman, the amendment sought to address the issue of women's liberties more comprehensively. Specifically, the ERA was designed to eliminate legal distinctions between the genders when it came to employment and other areas in which disparities existed.

Support for the ERA was initially underwhelming, partly due to class divisions among women. Some believed that workplace protections for women and children were the more urgent political priority, while others feared that the amendment could impact existing laws that worked to their benefit (e.g., legislation that capped the number of hours women could work).

The ERA did not receive widespread support at the congressional level either and was promptly buried in committees in of both Houses of Congress.

Alice Paul worked to ensure that the amendment was introduced in each session of Congress – and it was, from 1923 until 1970 – but it languished in committees for years. Still, there were some victories won along the way, such as the Voting Rights Act of 1965, which finally codified the right of all women to vote.

In 1970, members of the newly formed feminist group the National Organization for Women (NOW) disrupted hearings of the Senate Subcommittee on Constitutional Amendments and demanded that the ERA be heard by the full Congress. In response, the Subcommittee began hearings, and the ERA finally left the House Judiciary Committee in June after Rep. Martha Griffiths filed a discharge petition.

The original draft of the ERA proposed by Alice Paul was an affirmative statement:

> Men and women shall have equal rights throughout the U.S. and every place subject to its jurisdiction.

But the version that Congress passed in 1972 was a 1943 revision:

> Equality of rights under the law shall not be denied or abridged by the U.S. or by any State on account of sex."

At any rate, Congress passed the ERA with a two-thirds majority. But before it could be added to the Constitution, it had to be ratified by 38 states within the next 10 years – an arbitrary deadline set by Sen. Sam Nunn, who did not support the amendment.

This goal was complicated by differing ideologies, with many conservatives believing and arguing that the ERA was not beneficial to women and conservative evangelicals in the burgeoning Religious New Right Movement arguing that working women belonged in the domestic sphere and should not be granted new rights. Anti-feminist leader Phyllis Schlafley from the Religious New Right formed Defeat the ERA in 1972 as well, which further highlighted the battlelines in a deeply divided culture. The amendment ultimately gained support from just 35 of the required 38 states.

In the next decade, the notion of feminism came under significant popular and political fire, and support for the amendment began to wane. Progress was stagnant. However, a fresh generation of advocates breathed new life into the process after 2010, despite the long-passed deadline. In January 2020, Virginia became the 38th state to ratify the ERA – nearly 100 years after it was written by the suffragists of this decade.

Section 3.3 • **LEGACIES OF WOMAN SUFFRAGE**

This section includes text excerpted from "Beyond 1920: The Legacies of Woman Suffrage." (National Park Service)

On a sweltering August afternoon in 1920, the struggle of generations to enfranchise women on the same terms as men seemed to come to a triumphant end. Seventy-two years earlier, Elizabeth Cady Stanton, Lucretia Mott, and their intrepid peers had shocked polite society by demanding the right to vote and a raft of other rights for women; now, every signer of their bold "Declaration of Sentiments," save one, was dead. Woman suffragists had persisted through countless trials and humiliations to get to this moment; not only had they spoken out, organized, petitioned, traveled, marched, and raised funds; some also had endured assault, jail, and starvation to advance the cause. When the Tennessee legislature voted to ratify the Nineteenth Amendment, that right was finally won.

The 19th Amendment officially eliminated sex as a barrier to voting throughout the United States. It expanded voting rights to more people than any other single measure in American history. And yet, the legacy of the 19th Amendment, in the short term and over the next century, turned out to be complicated. The amendment advanced equality between the sexes but left intersecting inequalities of class, race, and ethnicity intact. It stimulated important policy changes but left many reform goals unachieved. It helped women, above all White women, find new footing in government agencies, political parties, and elected offices – and, in time, even a run for president on a primary ticket – yet left most outside the halls of power. Hardly the end of the struggle for diverse women's

One argument for woman suffrage, made popular by the song "She's Good Enough to Be Your Baby's Mother and She's Good Enough to Vote with You," was that it would improve women's ability to fulfill their socially acceptable roles as mothers and homemakers.

equality, the 19th Amendment became a crucial step, but only a step, in the continuing quest for more representative democracy.

Once ratification had been achieved, neither the general public nor professional politicians knew quite what to expect when election season arrived in fall 1920. Both suffragists and "Antis" had promised big changes if the 19th Amendment became law. Any prediction was bound to be exaggerated, if only because women in fifteen states already enjoyed full suffrage by state action before the federal amendment had passed. Suffragists had promised that women voters would clean up politics and enact a sweeping agenda of Progressive reforms; Antis worried that the dirty business of politics would compromise women's moral standing, or that women who took part in public affairs might abandon their traditional responsibilities at home. And how would polling places handle the influx of new voters? Election officials in Jersey City, New Jersey, took no chances; they ordered containers "the size of flour barrels" to hold all the votes. Nor was it clear how new women voters would change the balance of political power. Republicans prognosticated that new women voters would choose the party of Lincoln to express their "gratitude for passage of [the] suffrage amendment" (*Detroit Free Press*, 1920).

Democrats countered that new women voters would choose them instead, and perhaps even "rescue the League of Nations" from political death (*New York Times*, October 31, 1920). Perhaps women would reject both major parties and organize into a party of their own, maximizing their power by voting as a bloc. New York City's political bosses at Tammany Hall worried that "wild women" voters might send the "great machine wobbling" if they elected to vote independently rather than toe the party line (*New York Times*, October 17, 1920). Still others predicted that woman suffrage would make no difference at all, believing that women – intimidated by the complexities of voting or uninterested in politics altogether – would simply stay home.

When the election returns were tallied, the impact of new women voters on the results defied simple description. Overall, fewer women voted than men, with female turnout averaging two-thirds the rate of men, and yet the big picture obscured a great deal of variation at the

Top image: Suffragists formed the National League of Women Voters and concentrated their efforts on focused "get out the vote" campaigns ahead of elections. In this image, women from the League hold up signs that read "VOTE" on September 17, 1924. Millions of women did vote in 1920 and in 1924, but in a lower proportion than men. • Lower image: Suffragists hold political placards with political-activist slogans in 1920. Signs read: Know Your Courts–Study Our Politicians, Liberty in Law, Law Makers Must Not Be Law Breakers, and Character in Candidates.

state and local levels. Women's turnout varied from a high of 57 percent in Kentucky to a low of 6 percent in Virginia, and the gap in turnout between the sexes ranged from 28 percent in Missouri and Kentucky to 40 percent in Connecticut. Everywhere the particular political and legal context influenced the turnout rate. For all voters, turnout tended to be higher in states with competitive races or in localities with well-organized parties; in areas with lopsided contests or layers of voting restrictions, turnout generally lagged.

Apart from the election tallies, full suffrage expanded the opportunities for women to seek elected office and shape public policy. Many women had run for political office before the 19th Amendment, yet full enfranchisement spurred a number of female firsts. In Yoncalla, Oregon, temperance-minded voters replaced the entire city council with women backed by the Woman's Christian Temperance Union. ("Sex Uprising in Yoncalla," blared the *New York Times.*) At least twenty-two women between 1920 and 1923 were elected mayor in small towns including Langley, Washington; Salina, Utah; Red Cloud, Nebraska; Goodhue, Minnesota; Fairport, Ohio; and Duluth, Georgia. Iowa City, home to more than ten thousand residents, became the biggest city yet to elect a female mayor when it voted in Emma Harvat in 1923. Bertha Landes became the first female big-city mayor when, in 1926, she filled in as acting mayor of Seattle for a stretch. Two years later, Seattleites elected her to her own term.

Women enjoyed new success in state government elections as well. In 1920 teacher Eva Hamilton became the first woman elected to the Michigan senate. Four years later, Cora Belle Reynolds Anderson won election to the Michigan house, the first Native American woman in the nation to win a state legislative seat. New Mexico elected the first woman to a high-ranking statewide office in 1923 when it elected Soledad Chacon as secretary of state, and at least five other states – South Dakota, Texas, Kentucky, New York, and Delaware – elected women to the same office in the 1920s. Indiana elected the first female state treasurer, Grace B. Urbahns, in 1926.

At the federal level, too, women ran standout races; occasionally they even won. Minnie Fisher Cunningham led Texas's successful campaign for woman suffrage in primary elections in 1918; in 1927, the future New Dealer ran for the U.S. Senate. She lost the primary but threw her support to another candidate who squeaked out a win against the incumbent Democrat, who was in the pocket of the Ku Klux Klan. And in 1928, in a remarkable development, the daughters of two of the nation's most powerful men of the previous generation – men who worked on opposing sides in the storied presidential race of 1896 – both won election to the US House of Representatives. Ruth Hanna McCormick, the daughter of William McKinley's campaign manager Marc Hanna, won election from Illinois as a Republican and advocated for Prohibition, farmers' interests, and isolationism during her single term of service. Ruth Bryan Owen, daughter of "Cross of Gold" orator William Jennings Bryan, won election from Florida as a Democrat and earned praise for her advocacy of child welfare as well as Florida's agricultural interests. Owen's father, the three-time Democratic nominee (and three-time loser) for the presidency, might have smiled from beyond the grave at his daughter's accomplishment. Owen joked about her win: "There! I am the first Bryan who ran for anything and got it!"

Political parties also found new places for women with interests in politics. Of course, women had participated in political parties well before enfranchisement, but in 1920s both the

The Women's Bureau was an offshoot of the Women in Industrial Service Bureau established in 1918 with social activist Mary van Kleeck at the helm. Van Kleeck wrote a number of reports regarding women who were brought into the workforce during the war and noted how the war represented a "new freedom" for women: "Freedom to serve their country through their industry not as women but as workers judged by the same standards and rewarded by the same recompense as men." Van Kleeck also headed the Department of Industrial Studies at the Russell Sage Foundation. Since its founding, the Women's Bureau has always been directed by a woman.

Republican and Democratic organizations created new positions for women. They showcased women at their national conventions; they placed women on party committees; and they created new Women's Divisions for the purpose of integrating new women voters into the party. A few exceptional women such as Harriet Taylor Upton, Emily Newell Blair, and Eleanor Roosevelt exerted unusual influence in political parties. Political advertising expert Belle Moskowitz became Al Smith's closest political advisor, helping him win the governorship of New York and guiding his 1928 presidential bid.

Empowered by full suffrage, women likewise made greater inroads into the executive branch. In the summer of 1920, President Woodrow Wilson established a new Women's Bureau in the U.S. Department of Labor and appointed union organizer Mary Anderson to lead it. Anderson held that leadership post through Republican and Democratic administrations until 1944, building the agency into a powerful advocate for female workers.

Newly enfranchised women also left their mark on public policy. After ratification, suffrage leaders forged an alliance to bring their collective political muscle to bear on the legislative process. Soon twenty organizations, including the League of Women Voters, the General Federation of Women's Clubs, the National Consumers' League, the National Women's Trade Union League, and the Woman's Christian Temperance Union, had banded together to form the Women's Joint Congressional Committee (WJCC). Claiming to represent a combined membership of twenty million women, the WJCC advanced a legislative agenda that put women and children first. The WJCC's efforts produced real legislative gains. The first of these, in 1921, was the Sheppard-Towner Maternity and Infancy Act. Sheppard-Towner addressed the shocking rates of infant mortality uncovered in studies by Julia Lathrop and the Children's Bureau and provided about $1 million per year to states to fund maternal and child health clinics. The Children's Bureau administered Sheppard-Towner and added a new division to do so, thereby expanding women's foothold in the executive branch. Sheppard-Towner created a model for federal–state partnerships that the architects of the New Deal would adopt in the next decade to address the deprivations of the Depression.

Women's lobbyists also succeeded in 1922 in winning congressional passage of the Cable Act. The Cable Act provided a path back to the voting booth for women who had lost their U.S. citizenship by marrying a foreign national after 1907. Women activists enjoyed additional legislative successes at the state and local level. At the federal level, they tried, without success, to win reforms on other important issues, including the international peace movement, child labor, and lynching.

In these ways the 19th Amendment expanded opportunities for women to participate in governance and changed the trajectory of social-welfare policy. And yet, both suffragists and Antis had promised that ratification would do so much more. Where was the Progressive juggernaut that would solve the nation's vast social problems? Where was the chaos caused by voting women abandoning their family responsibilities? Where, in short, was the dramatic change, for good or ill, that both supporters and opponents had promised?

If full suffrage produced less change than suffragists had hoped and Antis had feared perhaps that was partly because women did not vote as a bloc and, indeed, sometimes did not vote at all. Establishment politicians soon learned that, for the most part, they did not need to worry about women voting because there was no such thing as "the women's vote," meaning that ballots cast by women increased the total but rarely changed the outcome. And, local variations aside, the overall turnout numbers for women voters were indisputably lower than those of men. This fact appalled former suffragists and seemed to validate the Antis' claims that women never wanted the vote in the first place. Determined that woman suffrage would not be proved a flop, in 1924 the League of Women Voters began massive campaigns of advertising and education to "Get Out the Vote," a program that, by the end of the decade, would evolve into the organization's main mission.

Critics blamed nonvoting women for shirking their civic duty, but one could fairly ask just which women were enfranchised by the 19th Amendment. States retained the ability to set conditions on access to the ballot, and, bowing to party interests or racial or class bias, many states kept other barriers to voting, for men and women alike, intact or raised them higher still. By the end of the 1920s voters in forty-six states had to contend with complicated registration requirements. Residency requirements were likewise common; at the extreme, Rhode Island required citizens to live not just in the state, but in the locality, for two years before they were eligible to vote. southern states, plus twelve more states outside the South, required literacy or educational tests. These barriers may have proved more difficult for novice women voters to navigate than for men with voting experience. Poll taxes certainly burdened women disproportionately; in many families the male head of household controlled the family finances, and not every husband or father was willing to pay the poll tax on behalf of his wife or daughter.

Women's citizenship status, often complicated by their marital status, confounded access to the ballot further still. Thirty-one states had once permitted immigrants who had started the lengthy naturalization process to vote, but by the early 1920s, every state had abandoned the practice of "alien suffrage." Women from some immigrant communities, especially Italians and Cubans, were far less likely to naturalize than men of the same background, and immigrants from Asia, whether male or female, could not become citizens at all. Remarkably, the ranks of noncitizens included even some US-born women, for American women who had married a foreign national after 1907 lost their American citizenship; unless they naturalized – and many did not pursue that lengthy legal process – they could not vote. Many Native Americans, including women, also lacked US citizenship, at least until Congress passed the Indian Citizenship Act of 1924, but even after that many Indigenous people effectively rejected the US citizenship they had never asked for, preferring to be identified with their tribal communities instead. Some states continued to bar Native Americans from the ballot; in 1962, Utah was the last state to extend them the franchise. None of these barriers to voting violated the 19th Amendment, but they all made voting more difficult, and some of them made voting particularly difficult for women.

Perhaps no community was subjected to more extensive disfranchisement efforts than Black women in the Jim Crow South. Interest in voting by southern African Americans surged in the fall of 1920; not only did many Black women seek to use their new right, but many Black men, honorably discharged from service in the Great War or wishing to accompany female family members, seized the moment to try to return to the polls themselves after decades of disfranchisement. In some locations, Black women succeeded in registering and voting, and those successes, even though few in number, inspired fresh efforts to suppress Black voters. Elsewhere, they were blocked by fraud, intimidation, or violence. And when disfranchised Black women asked the League of Women Voters and the National Women's Party to help, the main organizations of former suffragists turned them down. National Women's Party head Alice Paul insisted in 1921 that Black women's disfranchisement was a "race issue," not a "woman's issue," and thus no business of the National Women's Party. The failure of White suffragists at that moment to address the disfranchisement of southern Black women reverberated for decades to come and undercut efforts of women of both races to make progress on issues of shared concern.

The impact of women's votes was also limited because the coalition that had supported suffrage splintered under the pressures of the troubled postwar political climate and competing political interests. Amid national tensions fueled by widespread labor unrest, bloody race riots, anti-immigrant animus, and anarchist violence, conservative women organized in the Daughters of the American Revolution and the Women's Auxiliary of the American Legion and accused many Progressive women of harboring communist sympathies. Their red-baiting tactics soon brought the Sheppard-Towner Act (created to address infant mortality) to an end; opposed from the beginning by organized medicine, the American Medical Association attacked it as an "imported socialistic scheme" and got Congress to defund it by 1929. Progressive suffragists also divided among themselves, primarily over the possibility of an equal rights amendment. Alice Paul insisted that a blanket amendment to ensure sex equality in broad areas of life must be the next item on the women's agenda, but women who had labored for decades to secure wages and hours protections for working women could not risk the possibility that an equal rights amendment would undo their hard-won gains.

Nor did women find that full suffrage necessarily gave them greater access to the levers of power. The Democratic and Republican Parties had welcomed women with great fanfare in 1920, but the Women's Divisions into which they were shunted lacked real power. The same was frequently true at the state level; a female member of the New Jersey Republican State Committee in 1924 noted ruefully that the state committee on which she sat met rarely and passed "a few resolutions of no importance. ... Then the men met privately and transacted the real business." In the executive branch in the 1920s women found that they exercised considerable power in select agencies, above all the Children's Bureau and Women's Bureau, but had few opportunities to influence policy outside this narrow "female dominion."

The 19th Amendment did not fulfill all its supporters' hopes, but it was no failure. It brought the nation closer to universal suffrage and made the injustice of ongoing disfranchisement even less defensible. It expanded opportunities for women to govern and it changed the direction of public policy. It accorded women the status of decision makers in the public sphere and recognized that they had the authority to help make decisions that others – men – would have to abide. If these changes fell short of expectations, perhaps that was because expectations had been so great. Suffragist Maud Wood Park, the first leader of the League of Women Voters, remarked that it was hardly reasonable to expect women voters "over-night to straighten out tangles over which generations of men had worked in vain."

Despite its limitations, the 19th Amendment over the next century helped women assume a role in public affairs that would be hard to imagine without it. Women gradually closed the turnout gap between the sexes, and in every presidential year since 1984, they have exceeded men in voter turnout. In 2016 the Democrats nominated Hillary Clinton to run for president, the first major party to nominate a woman as its standard-bearer. In 2019 women occupied 9 governorships, 24 seats in the U.S. Senate, and 102 seats in the U.S. House of Representatives. A century after ratification, it is clear that though the 19th Amendment did not perfect American democracy, it advanced gender equality in important ways.

Section 3.4 • **WOMEN IN FACTORIES**

"1925 Labor Developments" and "The Plight of the Radium Girls," • © Omnigraphics.

1925 LABOR DEVELOPMENTS

U.S. Labor Movement

The labor movement in the United States had been steadily growing since the end of World War I and the collapse of the Great Steel Strike of 1919 and the Seattle General Strike. The growth of labor unions and left-wing organizations led many people to support workers' demands when they went on strike. Consequently, the suppression of these strikes was criticized widely by public opinion and generated growing support for labor unions. As people's support for organized labor grew, suppression of strike action became increasingly more difficult. As strikes continued and the crisis deepened, some progressives saw socialism as the solution. As socialist and communist groups became popular, many allied themselves with labor unions. This caused many citizens to view socialism as capable of fulfilling workers' demands and answer to the call of the labor movement.

Progressives and the American Left

In 1924, during his run for presidency, Robert M. La Follette Sr. recreated the Progressive Party. While he lost the election, many left-wing liberals in the Democratic Party began to abandon the party and joined the Progressives or established their own groups. The Progressives prevented any one of the Democratic and Republican presidential candidates from receiving a clear majority, which led to Calvin Coolidge becoming president.

The party remained cohesive after the election and largely grew its support. It continually increased the popularity of left-wing politics, which inadvertently improved the public's view of left-wing organizations, such as the Socialist Party of America, in general. In 1924, the Farmer–Labor Party was absorbed into the Progressive Party and the Proletarian Party was absorbed into the Socialist Labor Party. By the end of the year, the Progressive, Socialist, and

Socialist Labor Parties formed an electoral alliance: The Progressive-Socialist-Labor Alliance. This alliance became the forerunner of the American Workers' Association in 1928.

THE PLIGHT OF THE RADIUM GIRLS

Though the tragedy of the so-called Radium Girls unfolded in the twentieth century, the circumstances that preceded it began the century prior. In 1898, two influential radioactivity researchers, Marie and Pierre Curie, discovered an element that became known as radium. Chief among its notable traits was the fact that radium glowed in the dark. Novel, mystic, and enchanting, it became a cultural phenomenon, sparking a craze which assigned the element with an array of properties it simply did not have. Though radium did have some merit as a treatment for cancer, there was a false belief that it could mitigate other conditions. It became known as something of a miracle cure. Radium was widely available pharmacies, and present in toothpaste and anti-aging cosmetics. Some places even sold radium water.

Inventor William J. Hammer soon used the element to create glow-in-the-dark paint, which the U.S. Radium Corporation (USRC) then used to manufacture novelty watches and military dials for the war. Dozens of women were recruited to work in the factories that made them. After each day of painting watch dials, they were covered in radium from head to toe – quite literally glowing in the dark. As they returned to their locales each evening, they were a sight to behold, and onlookers christened them "the Ghost Girls."

The radium particles seemed to make their way to every surface, even covering the women's undergarments at the end of a long day. A physiologist would later study the dust samples of various factories and find the element on equipment the workers did not even use. It was everywhere. And it was deadly.

The human body mistakes ingested radium for calcium. As a result, the element is incorporated into the bones, radiating them from the inside. This radiation made teeth decay and bored holes in the bones of the poisoned host in a phenomenon known as "honeycombing." In advanced cases, the bones shortened, broke, and spontaneously fractured; cancerous tumors developed; and entire spines began to crumble. Eerily, radium also made the damaged bones glow. There are reports that some women learned of their poisoning through chance events, like catching a glimpse of themselves in the dark, appearing to emit a light from within. As more and more women began to lose their lives, this incandescence became known as "the light that does not die."

The health risks of radium were not unknown to manufacturers. Even Marie Currie had incurred radiation burns simply from handling the substance. And her co-researcher Pierre noted his own fears concerning the inherently dangerous element. Moreover, people had been lost to radium poisoning even before the first woman entered a USRC factory. However, an entire industry had been built around the falsehood that small quantities were safe, and this was the dominant narrative among those who did not know any better. Meanwhile, corporations in this niche had a financial motivation to ignore the evidence to the contrary.

One factory worker, Mae Cubberly, recalled explicitly asking her manager is if the substance could harm her. She was assured it would not. Employers' quiet knowledge of the health risks may have been why the job was so well-paid – at a rate three times greater than the average factory gig. Indeed, dial painting was a surefire vehicle to upward mobility: Upon taking the job, young women joined the top 5 percent of female earners in the country. For women from impoverished families, this was a potential saving grace. Accordingly, dial painting was known as "the elite job for poor working girls" – but, ultimately, it was just another example of the industrial exploitation of vulnerable populations.

Information about the risks of radium was not shared with the Radium Girls. In fact, USRC assured them that the substance was safe. Accordingly, they were not given any protective equipment. Perhaps most alarmingly, the women were even encouraged to lick the tips of their brushes. This practice created neater brushstrokes by keeping the bristles pointed. Yet, each time they did this, they ingested more and more of the substance that caused their painful deaths.

The Death of the First Ghost Girl

In a powerful feature for *Buzzfeed*, author Kate Moore chronicles the demise of the first Radium Girl, and the nature of the sickness that befell them all. The following is an excerpt:

> In 1922, one of Grace's colleagues, Mollie Maggia, had to quit the studio because she was sick. She didn't know what was wrong with her. Her trouble had started with an aching tooth: Her dentist pulled it, but then the next tooth started hurting and also had to be extracted. In the place of the missing teeth, agonizing ulcers sprouted as dark flowers, blooming red and yellow with blood and pus. They seeped constantly and made her breath foul. Then she suffered aching pains in her limbs that were so agonizing they eventually left her unable to walk. The doctor thought it was rheumatism and sent her home with aspirin.
>
> By May 1922, Mollie was desperate. At that point, she had lost most of her teeth and the mysterious infection had spread: Her entire lower jaw, the roof of her mouth, and even some of the bones of her ears were said to be "one large abscess." But worse was to come. When her dentist prodded delicately at her jawbone in her mouth, to his horror and shock, it broke against his fingers. He removed it, "not by an operation, but merely by putting his fingers in her mouth and lifting it out." Only days later, her entire lower jaw was removed in the same way.
>
> On September 12, 1922, the strange infection that had plagued Mollie Maggia for less than a year spread to the tissues of her throat. The disease slowly ate its way through her jugular vein. At 5 p.m. that day, her mouth was flooded with blood as she hemorrhaged so fast that her nurse could not staunch it. She died at the age of 24. With her doctors flummoxed as to the cause of death, her death certificate erroneously said that she had died of syphilis, something her former company would later use against her. As if by clockwork, one by one, Mollie's former colleagues soon followed her to the grave.

Early attempts to receive compensation from USRC were unsuccessful. The corporation was a wealthy entity and government contractor. This prestige afforded them a team of defense attorneys, while the Radium Girls could barely manage their healthcare and legal expenses. As their bodies disintegrated from the inside, the women raced against time to prove that radium exposure was to blame. Finally, in 1925, Dr Harrison Martland created a set of tests that conclusively proved this to be true.

Smear campaigns sought to frame the victims and opportunists and to discredit Dr Martland, but the tide had already begun to turn. As the news of their ordeal spread through the nation, the corporations to blame came under more public scrutiny. Led by Grace Fryer, a group of five women sued USRC for damages to the tune of $250,000. By this time, medical professionals had estimated that the women had just months left to live. Conversely, it was in the company's interests to prolong the proceedings, and historians remark that it did just that. Facing dire financial circumstances and imminent death, the women ultimately settled for just $10,000 each as an upfront payment, and annual installments of $600 for life. Within two years, all of them had died.

Impact

During her years-long court battle, Grace Fryer proclaimed that she and the other women persevered for the sake of those who faced the same fate. Ultimately, they accomplished what they set out to do. Though it came at a magnificent price, much-needed light was shed on the dangers of radiation exposure. Moreover, the case of the ghost girls encouraged scientists to explore the potential risks of the substances they engaged with. Indeed, knowledge of that case inspired nuclear chemist and Nobel Prize winner Glenn Seaborg to investigate the potential risks associated with handling plutonium. His team of researchers also adopted protective measures and regulations that would later help safeguard the government's first nuclear development effort, the Manhattan Project.

The radium-dial factories significantly improved their safety procedures as well, using protective gear and tests that detected surface contamination. The Radium Girls tragedy also led to improved worker-compensation policies. In 1949, Congress passed a law that gave employees the right to be compensated for occupational illnesses.

Ultimately, it is estimated that 4,000 people worked with radium as dial painters across North America. In Illinois, another set of Radium Girls won a legal victory against their employer, RadiumDial. This was one of the first few cases in which an employer was found to be liable for the health of its workers. The case prompted stronger regulations in the 1930s and helped establish the Occupational Safety and Health Administration (OSHA), now a sector of the Department of Labor.

Significantly, before OSHA was formed, there were approximately 14,000 work-related deaths every year. After its creation and enforcement, this number declined by nearly two-thirds. In the end, the case of the ghost girls not only had implications for the lives of radium workers, but for workers throughout the nation, even to this day.

Section 3.5 • UNCREDITED TRAILBLAZERS

EMMY NOETHER: INVISIBLE GENIUS

Amalie "Emmy" Noether was born in German on March 23rd, 1882. Her mother was from a family of financial means, and her father was a mathematics professor. Despite enjoying economic privilege, she was subject to the gender conventions of her time. As an upper-middle-class girl, her early education focused on the arts. Later, she attended a finishing school, since young women were barred from attending college preparatory institutions. By the time she completed her education, she was 18 years old and a certified French and English instructor.

Though she reportedly had every intention of pursuing a teaching career, Noether later decided she wanted to be a mathematician. The former was a conventional path for working

Despite giants in her field acknowledging Dr. Emmy Noether as the most significant female in the history of mathematics – Albert Einstein called her a "mathematical genius" – widespread gender discrimination at universities resulted in her only finding paid employment in the final few years of her life.

women at the time, while the latter was somewhat of a pipe dream. She managed to audit math classes at the University of Erlangen in 1901, where she was one of just two women amidst thousands of men, but neither of the women was allowed to speak or otherwise participate in these classes. With faculty permission, Noether then took the entrance exam and passed, yet the institution would not permit her to become a registered student.

In 1903 she audited classes yet again, this time at the University of Gottingen, which ultimately denied her permission to register as well. In 1904, the University of Erlangen finally approved female enrollment, which prompted Noether's return. Just four years later, she received a Ph.D. in Mathematics, earning *summa cum laude* distinction for her dissertation on algebraic math. However, there were more obstacles ahead. Despite her promise and accomplishments, she could not find a paid position as an instructor.

Dr. Noether remained at Erlangen, where she worked without pay for seven years. Occasionally, she was permitted to serve as a substitute instructor for her father when he was unwell. In 1908 she was invited to join the Mathematical Circle of Palermo, which would soon become the leading mathematical society in the world. In 1909, the German Mathematical Society extended an invitation to her. Yet, despite growing recognition of her expertise, she remained unable to secure a paid position at a German university.

Dr. Noether did some of her most important work in the ensuing decade, but credit was still hard to come by. At the Mathematical Institute in Göttingen, where she was again working without pay, she completed a landmark achievement that "confirmed key parts of the general theory of relativity." One of her mentors, David Hilbert, advocated for her hiring but could not get around policies and biases that excluded female academics.

Her only available option was to lecture classes under Hilbert's name, during which she was acknowledged only as a "participant" rather than the guest instructor. Her paper "Invariante Varlationsprobleme" (Invariant Variation problems) – which would have a profound influence on twentieth-century physics – was first formally presented by another male mentor, Felix Klein, on July 16th, 1918. Scholars presume that this was because the author herself was not permitted to present her own work, and it is unclear whether she was even in attendance during this momentous occasion.

In 1919, Dr. Noether won a small victory and was finally permitted to instruct students who then paid her directly, – an arrangement that may be likened to tutoring. In 1922, Dr. Noether finally was granted a formal position as an adjunct professor and paid a small salary but – despite her publishing recognition, the reality that her unpaid work in the intellectual-labor workforce is now recognized as the foundation for abstract algebra, the fact that she was well-liked by her students, who described her as both amiable and engaged, and her known tendency to champion participation and collaborative problem-solving in her classes – she was not offered a tenure-track position.

Dr. Noether worked on abstract algebra and ring theory, in particular, during the 1920s. By the turn of the decade, Dr. Noether also had served as a visiting lecturer at the universities of Moscow and Frankfurt. In 1933, however, she became one of many Jewish instructors expelled by the Nazis.

Fortunately, an American aid committee helped Dr. Noether attain a professorship at Bryn Mawr College in Pennsylvania, where she was finally recognized and compensated as a professor after 25 years of no or scant recognition or compensation.

Albert Einstein, the German-born, Nobel Prize–winning mathematician and theoretical physicist who developed the special and general theories of relativity, noted that Dr. Noether "found in America up to the day of her death not only colleagues who esteemed her friendship but grateful pupils whose enthusiasm made her last years the happiest and perhaps the most fruitful of her entire career." Unfortunately, this period of her life did not last very long. In 1935, Noether underwent surgery to remove a uterine tumor, but developed postoperative complications and died from an infection on April 14 at the age of 53.

Her ashes were laid to rest near the Bryn Mawr library, where they remain.

Markers of Dr. Noether's influence began to emerge in her homeland after World War II. The University of Erlangen, which had denied her entrance just a few decades earlier, named a co-ed math gymnasium in her honor. Moreover, Dr. Noether was heralded as a pioneer by the giants in her field. Albert Einstein, Jean Dieudonné, Hermann Weyl, and Norbert Wiener all described her as the most significant female figure in the history of mathematics, and Einstein called her a "mathematical genius."

Today, Dr. Noether is one of many female geniuses of the last century who were not duly recognized for their accomplishments. Yet Dr. Noether's name quite literally lives on through her scholarly publications and contributions. The former were found to have implications even in areas far beyond her own professional focus, such as algebraic topology. And the latter is perhaps best evidenced by "Noether's theorem," a physics theory that elucidates the relationship between symmetry and conservation laws.

As journalist Michael Cavna notes in the *Washington Post*, "after a lifetime of being discouraged and disallowed, underpaid and unpaid, doubted and ousted, Emmy Noether [finally] reached the pinnacle of peer respect among her fellow giants of mathematical science."

Mathematician and space scientist Katherine G. Johnson was one of the three students who first integrated West Virginia University. She was hired by NACA in 1953 and worked in the racially segregated West Area Computing Unit of the Langley Research Center until 1958, when NASA took the reins and abolished racial segregation. Johnson overcame the cultural barriers of race and gender to progress from mathematical calculations to computing experimental flight and ground-test data. This photo is taken of her working at the Research Center in 1962. Johnson is featured in the 2016 nonfiction book *Hidden Figures: The American Dream and the Untold Story of the Black Women Who Helped Win the Space Race* and as one of three protagonists in the film adaptation *Hidden Figures.* Young people interested in science, technology, engineering, and mathematics (STEM) consider her a role model.

In the twentieth- and early twenty-first centuries, female physicists and mathematicians truly were [and are] standing on the shoulders of this mathematical giant.

HIDDEN WOMEN OF NACA AND NASA

In 2010, Margot Lee Shetterly began work on a book that would tell the untold story of the trailblazing African American women mathematicians whom the U.S. government began hiring during the war years, and then the Cold War years, to work as "human computers." The calculations these women made were essential to the aeronautical innovations that helped bring an end to World War II. And the contributions they made after the war literally helped send American astronauts to the moon. The groundbreaking work performed by these women remained largely hidden from view for six decades, however.

Shetterly knew about these trailblazers because her father worked at the Langley Memorial Aeronautical Laboratory in Virginia during World War II. The machinery of war created a

Dorothy Vaughan was the first Black female supervisor at NACA and she worked on an IBM machine. She supervised Black human computers who were sequestered in the segregated West Area Computing Unit at the Langley Research Center from 1943 to 1958, when NASA took the reins and abolished racial segregation. Vaughan is featured in the 2016 nonfiction book *Hidden Figures: The American Dream and the Untold Story of the Black Women Who Helped Win the Space Race* and as one of three protagonists in the film adaptation *Hidden Figures.* She was inducted into the Langley Hall of Honor on June 1, 2017.

Mathematician and aerospace engineer Mary Jackson, a former math teacher, was hired as a research mathematician, or human computer, for NACA in 1951. She was the first African American engineer at NASA and is featured in the 2016 nonfiction book *Hidden Figures: The American Dream and the Untold Story of the Black Women Who Helped Win the Space Race* and as one of three protagonists in the film adaptation *Hidden Figures.* She worked in the segregated West Area Computer Unit until 1958, when she transitioned to the Transonic Aerodynamic Branch, where this photo was taken on June 2, 1977. Jackson retired from NASA in 1985 and was posthumously awarded the Congressional Gold Medal. In 2021, NASA also named its D.C. Headquarters after her.

demand for aeronautical research and, when President Roosevelt's Executive Order 8802 desegregated the defense industry, a new career path for these African American mathematicians emerged. Langley Lab hired hundreds of scientists, engineers, and mathematicians to conduct aeronautical research and otherwise assist in the war effort for the National Advisory Committee for Aeronautics (NACA), which later became NASA.

Shetterly's book *Hidden Figures: The American Dream and the Untold Story of the Black Women Who Helped Win the Space Race* – which was made into a popular film – tells the story of some of the early African American "human computers" who lived and worked in the racially segregated Jim Crow South. Employment opportunities for African Americans were unequal at best throughout the country, but were even more restrictive in the southern states, but the work these women performed in their racially segregated computing unit provided them with economic stability, if not recognition.

Mathematician, space scientist, and diversity advocate Jeanette Scissum joined NASA's Marshall Space Flight Center in Alabama in 1964 after earning bachelor's and master's degrees in mathematics from Alabama A&M University. She was the first African American mathematician to be hired by the Marshall Center. Scissum published the NASA report "Survey of Solar Cycle Prediction Models" in 1967. This report put forward techniques for improved forecasting of the sunspot cycle. She worked as a space scientist in the Marshall Space Environment Branch in the mid-1970s, and later led activities in the Marshall Atmospheric, Magnetospheric, and Plasmas in Space project. Over the course of her 39-year career at NASA, Scissum held positions across the agency, including stints at the Goddard Space Flight Center in Maryland, at NASA Headquarters in Washington, D.C. and with the Space Shuttle Program.

Human computers calculating test data from the Ames 16-foot wind tunnel, Ames Research Center, Moffett Field, California, at the southernmost end of San Francisco Bay. The human computers were responsible for making aerodynamic calculations that were critical to NASA's research and mission success.

Young women workers at the Bureau of Aeronautics in a typing contest, April 15, 1926.

The Early Years

The National Women's History Museum the 2017 exhibit The Women of NASA helped amplify the work of these trailblazers and further honored their accomplishments.

Pearl Young and Kitty O'Brien Joyner were two of these early trailblazers.

Young, who triple-majored in physics, mathematics, and chemistry, was hired by NACA as a physicist in 1922. She was the first woman hired to perform technical work at the lab. Young "designed, constructed, calibrated, and repaired virtually all instrumentation carried on aircraft."

Joyner was the first woman to graduate from the University of Virginia engineering program. She also was the first female engineer hired by NACA. Joyner performed supersonic flight research and managed wind tunnels.

Electrical engineer Kitty Joyner is believed to be the first female NACA engineer as well as the first female engineer to graduate from the University of Virginia – but she had to sue the University before they agreed to admit her to its formerly all-male engineering school. Joyner rose to the level of a NASA branch head.

In 1935, many of NACA's male employees were fighting overseas, and NACA was in need of competent mathematicians to serve as "human computers." Few women had served in this role previously, but World War II changed that as women were brought on board to perform mathematical computations by hand. By 1942, a NACA memo noted that "the engineers admit … that the girl computers do the work more rapidly and accurately than they could."

Vera Huckel was hired as one of those human computers in 1939 and was the section head in charge of 17 female human computers by 1945. She also worked as an aerospace engineer. Huckel worked with the mathematicians who tested sonic booms in supersonic flight and sometimes traveled to deserts in the Western United States to compute equations during test flights. Other times, the researchers sent these numbers and test results to her at the Langley Lab because she was the computer most trusted to always calculate accurately. Huckel is also credited with writing the first program for the first electronic computer at NASA. Talk about trailblazing!

Dorothy Vaughn, a former math teacher, was one of the first Black women hired by NACA. Her mathematical computation work focused on wind-tunnel experiments. When Vaughn was named section head of the West Area Computing Unit in 1949, she earned the distinction of being the first Black woman promoted to a managerial role at the lab. The West Area Computing Unit is where women of color performed their work because Jim Crow laws mandated that the races be segregated. This unit was showcased in the 2016 film adaptation of the book, which was also called Hidden Figures.

During the Cold War, aeronautics research was prioritized and NACA was replaced with the National Aeronautics and Space Administration (NASA) in 1958. NASA oversaw all U.S. science and technology associated with airplanes or space. Vaughan joined NASA's Integrated Analysis and Computational Division and had the foresight to recognize that actual computers could eliminate the need for human computers. Two years later she taught herself the early computing language FORTRAN and became the programming expert who taught the engineers how to use their computers. She also contributed to the SCOUT Launch Vehicle Program. Vaughn, along with mathematicians Mary Jackson and Katherine Johnson, performed the calculations and plotted data for the mission that sent astronaut John Glenn into orbit.

Number-cruncher Mary Jackson joined NACA in 1951 and also worked in the West Area Computing Unit until NACA was replaced by NASA. Two years after her arrival, she joined a group of researchers working on the Supersonic Pressure Tunnel. Team members recognized her aptitude for the work and encouraged Jackson to enter the University of Virginia advanced training program for engineers. She encountered a Jim Crow roadblock before she could officially register, however, and was required to obtain permission from the City of Hampton, Virginia, to participate in the coursework. After completing her advanced training, Jackson became NASA's first African American female engineer.

Katherine Johnson joined NACA in 1953 and also worked for the West Area Computing group before joining the Maneuver Loads Branch of the Flight Research Division under NASA. In this role she, like Vera Huckel, analyzed data from flight tests. Johnson was highly skilled at analytic geometry and was the first woman in her division to receive author credit on a research paper. All told, she co-published 26 research papers.

Johnson analyzed flight trajectory and landings for numerous flights for the space program, including those for Alan Shepard's Friendship 7 flight. In those early days of electronic computing, she always double-checked the equations to ensure their accuracy. Her calculations included those for the lunar landing and for the rendezvous of the command module and lunar module.

John Glenn was one of the astronauts who relied on Johnson to provide correct calculations for orbital equations and he specifically requested that she confirm that all equations were accurate.

She calculated the trajectory for the 1969 Apollo 11 flight to the moon and synched the Lunar Lander with the Command and Service Module.

Later, she worked in the Space Shuttle program, in planning for the mission to mars, and with satellites.

Of her work, Johnson said,

> "You tell me when you want it and where you want it and where you want to land, and I'll do it backwards and tell you where to take off." That was my forte.

Jackson was later awarded the Presidential Medal of Freedom for her groundbreaking work.

Jim Crow Laws

This sidebar contains text excerpted from the following sources: Text in this section begins with excerpts from "Jim Crow and Segregation," U.S. Library of Congress (LOC), February 13, 2015; Text beginning with the heading "Sampling of Laws from Various States" is excerpted from "Jim Crow Laws," U.S. Department of the Interior (DOI), April 17, 2018.

For more than a century after the Civil War, a system of laws and practices denied full freedom and citizenship to African Americans and segregated nearly all aspects of public life based on race.

Historical Background

In 1863, the Emancipation Proclamation symbolically established a national intent to eradicate slavery in the United States. Decades of state and federal legislation around civil rights followed. In January of 1865, the 13th Amendment to the Constitution officially abolished slavery in this country, while the 14th Amendment, passed in 1866, set forth three principles:

- All persons born or naturalized in the U.S. were citizens of the nation and no state could make or enforce any law that would diminish their rights of citizenship.
- No state could deny any person of life, liberty, or property without due process of law.
- No state could deny any person equal protection of the laws.

Finally, the 15th Amendment, which passed in 1869, outlawed the denial of voting rights due to race, color, or past servitude. However, immediately after the Civil War ended, some states began imposing restrictions on the daily lives of African Americans, whether they were survivors of slavery or had always been free. By the end of the 19th century, laws or informal practices that required African Americans to be segregated from Whites were often called "Jim Crow" practices, believed to be a reference to the minstrel-show song, "Jump Jim Crow."

With the Compromise of 1877, political power was returned to southern Whites in nearly every state of the former Confederacy and the federal government abandoned attempts to enforce the 14th and

15th Amendments in many parts of the country. By 1890, when Mississippi added a disfranchisement provision to its state constitution, the legalization of Jim Crow oppression had begun.

Jim Crow laws were not enacted as a universal, written law of the land. Instead, a patchwork of state and local laws, codes, and agreements enforced racial segregation to different degrees and in different ways across the nation. In many towns and cities, ordinances designated White and Black neighborhoods, while in others, covenants and unwritten agreements among real-estate interests maintained residential segregation. African Americans were also denied the right to vote when states imposed poll taxes, which essentially required them to pay a voting fee before casting a ballot. And that was just one of the unjust barriers. The signage we associate today with the Jim Crow South, like "Whites Only" and "Colored," appeared at bus stations, water fountains, and restrooms, as well as at the entrances and exits to public buildings. Hotels, movie theaters, arenas, nightclubs, restaurants, churches, hospitals, and schools were racially segregated, and interracial marriages were outlawed. It is important to note that segregation was not limited to African Americans and often applied to other non-White Americans, as well.

Racial segregation was often maintained by uniformed law enforcement. In other instances, it was enforced by armed White mobs and violent attacks by anonymous vigilantes. African Americans resisted these pervasive restrictions using many different strategies, from public advocacy and political activism to individual self-defense and efforts to escape to a better life. In the century following the end of Reconstruction, millions of African Americans moved away from the South in what became known as the Great Migration, only to discover that they faced discrimination in northern states, too.

In the middle of the twentieth century, generations of resistance to racial segregation culminated in the U.S. Civil-Rights movement, in which African Americans launched widespread demonstrations and other public protests to demand the rights and protections provided by the Constitution. As a result, a series of landmark court cases and new legislation was passed in the 1950s and 1960s, including the Civil Rights Act of 1964 and the Voting Rights Act of 1965. These acts nullified many of the Jim Crow laws and practices of the previous century. However, their impact can still be felt today. Although the specific racial-segregation policies of the 19th and 20th centuries have been discredited, voices calling for equal rights and protection for all can still be heard to this day.

A Small Sampling of Jim Crow Laws from Various States

Barbers

Georgia • No colored barber shall serve as a barber [to] White women or girls.

Bathroom Facilities, Male

Alabama • Every employer of White or Negro males shall provide for such White or negro males reasonably accessible ad separate toilet facilities.

Nurses

Alabama • No person or corporation shall require any White female nurse to nurse in wards or rooms in hospitals, either public or private, in which Negro men are placed.

Promotion of Equality

Mississippi • Any person... who shall be guilty of printing, publishing or circulating printed, typewritten or written matter urging or presenting for public acceptance or general information, arguments or suggestions in favor of social equality or of intermarriage between whites and Negroes, shall be guilty of a misdemeanor and subject to a fine not exceeding five hundred ($500.00) dollars or imprisonment not exceeding six (6) months or both.

Section 3.6 • **TRAILBLAZERS**

This section includes text excerpted from "Five Facts about Edith Clarke" (Department of Energy); "Edith Clarke," "Annie Oakley: A Different Way to Earn a Living," "Edith Wilson: America's First (Unofficial) President," • © 2021 Omnigraphics.

EDITH CLARKE

Edith Clarke was the first professionally employed female electrical engineer in the country and the first full-time female professor of electrical engineering in the country. This pioneer in electrical engineering used math to improve our understanding of power transmission. Clarke began her career as a "human computer," or "human calculator," supporting the engineers working to build the first transcontinental phone line.

Her most famous contribution was the Clarke Calculator, which she invented in 1921. This graphical device simplified the equations that electrical engineers used to understand power lines. Clarke patented it in 1925.

Clarke helped build the Hoover Dam, contributing her electrical expertise to the development and installation of the turbines that generate hydropower there to this day. She also used analyzers to gather data about the electric grid, an innovative idea at the time that can be seen as the first step toward "smart grid" technology. In 2015, Clarke was posthumously inducted into the Inventors Hall of Fame, where she joined the likes of Thomas Edison and Nikola Tesla for her invention of the Clarke Calculator.

ANNIE OAKLEY: A DIFFERENT WAY TO EARN A LIVING

The story of Annie Oakley, the public figure, dates back to the late 1800s, when tales of her marksmanship enchanted the nation. Known as America's "shooting sweetheart," she is remembered not just for her skill, but for her defiance of the gender-role expectations of her time. Long before this, however, she showed similar, if not greater tenacity, having overcome a traumatic childhood marked by desperate poverty, starvation, and abuse. It is perhaps this time when Annie developed the spirit of endurance that ultimately helped her make her mark in a man's profession and a man's world, and win.

Annie's birthname was Phoebe Ann Moses, although records sometimes note her family name was Mosey. There are some reports that her brother confirmed the former name to be correct; however, the official documentation is inconclusive. What is known is that Annie was born into a poverty-stricken family on August 13th, 1860 in Darke County, Ohio. Her mother was widowed in 1865, when Annie was only five. It is reported that her father, Jacob Oakley, had been caught in a blizzard that winter and eventually succumbed to pneumonia.

His widow, Susan, was left with the sole responsibility of raising six children and the family became increasingly destitute. The matriarch did her best to pull the family out of poverty by downsizing their home, remarrying, and working as a domestic nurse for $1.25 per week. Her second husband also died very suddenly, leaving behind a newborn baby. In 1868, Susan conceded to offers to loan out her children to other families, where they would work in exchange for a place in a "good home." This was known as "farming out" one's children and was not uncommon for poor families in a time when social services were not what they are today.

Annie Oakley, 1885.

Accordingly, the superintendent of a local poor farm and his wife offered to foster young Annie and teach her housekeeping skills. In exchange, she was expected to be the family seamstress and take care of the youngest children housed at the facility.

Less than a month after she moved to the poor farm, Annie was relocated to the home of a cruel couple that she always referred to as "He-Wolf" and "She-Wolf" in retrospect. Historians suggest that this couple may have been Abram and Elizabeth Boose, whom she resided with in 1870. Though assurances were made that Annie's only job would be to care for their infant, she had effectively entered a life of servitude.

As noted by Jan Collins for *Grunge*, "Oakley's workday began at 4 a.m. and consisted not only of caring for the baby, but also preparing meals, caring for livestock, maintaining the garden and hunting for food. She was beaten, starved, and perhaps, according to writer Carolyn Gage, sexually abused. When Susan Mosey sent for her daughter, she was told Oakley was attending school and was quite happy."

Beyond her abusive circumstances, she had the added burden of worrying about the family she had left behind. At age eight, Annie took to hunting and selling the game to nearby restaurants to help supplement the family income. By her mid-teens, she was developing a reputation as a remarkable shot. At age 15 she went to Cincinnati to take on prominent marksman Frank E. Butler, who traveled the country engaging in shooting competitions. Annie won the competition and the admiration of her competitor. She and Butler began dating and married a year later, in 1876.

Butler resumed his occupation, and the couple began touring the country together. Initially, Annie served as his assistant, and only occasionally did her own shooting. However, her popularity as a "marksman" was on the rise, and it was during this time that she adopted her stage name. When her husband fell ill in 1882, she filled in for him, and would forever after have a central role in their act. She received her popular nickname just two years later, when Sitting Bull, the famous Lakota Sioux leader and war hero, named her "little sure shot" after witnessing her prowess firsthand.

The couple toured with the Sells Brothers Circus for a time, then Annie joined Buffalo Bill's Wild West Show, where she became a bona fide star. Though the couple initially performed together, Butler recognized her popularity and opted to become her assistant and manager. As a show headliner, she achieved remarkable feats: Shooting flying glass balls, playing cards, and even cigarettes placed in her husband's mouth. She chose to let her talent do the talking and avoided ostentatious costumes that may have distracted the audience from her skills. In their 16-year tenure with Buffalo Bill's Wild West Show, the couple enjoyed adventures locally and abroad. In the United Kingdom, they toured Italy, France, Spain, and England, where they performed at Queen Victoria's Golden Jubilee.

In later decades, Annie achieved legendary status in popular culture as the woman who excelled in a male-dominated sport. She also championed female empowerment and encouraged women to learn how to operate pistols for self-defense. After the couple returned from Europe, they took on a less demanding touring schedule. In 1901 Annie suffered a back injury in a train accident and the couple stopped touring altogether.

Shortly thereafter, she faced a national scandal when a false rumor proclaimed that she was arrested for stealing a man's pants to help fund a cocaine addiction. Multiple national newspapers ran this baseless story, though Annie was nowhere near the incident of the crime when it occurred. The entire incident was revealed to be a callous mistake, and the true arrestee was a woman named Maude Fontanella, who adopted the fake name of "Any Oakley." Over the next seven years, Annie sued every paper involved for reputational harm, ultimately winning all but one of the fifty-five cases.

She did not manage to break every barrier she sought to break during her lifetime, however. Upon hearing that World War I was imminent, she wrote to the Secretary of War, Henry L. Stimson, offering to establish, fund, and train a regiment of female combat volunteers. She also offered to give shooting lessons to soldiers. Both offers were declined. Then a 1922 car crash delayed her plans to return to touring life with her husband.

Just three years later, Annie fell ill and the couple returned to her home state to be near her relatives. She died on November 3, 1926, and her husband followed just three weeks later. By all accounts, the couple were happily married for half a century. Annie Oakley's legacy is one of talent, perseverance, and breaking the mold. During a time when autonomy was beyond the reach of most women, she managed to shape her life on her own terms. As a married woman, she defied conventional expectations of husband–wife partnership. As a working woman, she demonstrated that it was possible to make a living doing what you love.

EDITH WILSON: AMERICA'S FIRST (UNACKNOWLEDGED) WOMAN PRESIDENT

In 1872, Edith Bolling Galt was born in western Virginia, to what was once a slave-holding family considered chief among the "plantation elite." By the year of her birth, those days of plenty had passed. During the Civil War and Reconstruction, her father lost his fortune, and Edith's early years were a far cry from the privilege she would later enjoy as First Lady. Though not intellectually gifted, she had ambition and a certain singlemindedness that seemed to work in her benefit.

As a teenager, her education was initially stalled by her own disinterest, which led her to leave her finishing school after just one semester. Her second attempt at an education was cut short by a combination of administrative mishaps, which led her father to conclude that it simply was not worth it to educate a girl. Though a setback at the time, this freed Edith to follow her sister to Washington D.C., a decision that would ultimately avail her with both status and wealth.

She met and married Norman Galt, a jeweler, who died nine years later and left her a sizeable inheritance. A society woman by that time, she was soon introduced to acting president Woodrow Wilson, who himself had been recently widowed. They married in 1915, just three months later, making Edith First Lady of the United States.

Even before assuming her husband's duties, she was heavily involved in matters of the state. Historian Carl Anthony, describes the magnitude of her role in the White House:

> Edith became a trusted advisor to Wilson. [He] won another term and, in April 1917, led the U.S. into World War I. By then, Edith never left his presence, working together from a private, upstairs office. He gave her access to the classified document drawer and secret wartime code and let her screen his mail. At the president's insistence, the first lady sat in on his meetings, after which she gave him withering assessments of political figures and foreign representatives. She denied his advisors access to him if she determined the president couldn't be disturbed.

The extent of her influence even before her husband's debilitating stroke is one reason historians believe she quietly served as acting president in its aftermath. The president's cognitive function was compromised, and the First Lady stepped in, consulting with his doctors, and to concede to suggestions of presidential resignation. Her stewardship of the nation's leader was reportedly marked by mass deception – neither the general population nor the country's political leaders knew the severity of Wilson's condition. Under these conditions of secrecy, Edith began to make executive decisions earmarked for the president.

In her 1939 biography, and in her later years as well, she maintained that this was untrue, stating that she assumed smaller, day-to-day presidential tasks, but stopped short of major decision-making related to programs, legislation, or policy. This denial may have been due to the political backlash she received once the truth of the president's condition was leaked to the public.

This scorn was, at least partially, motivated by the gender biases of the era, which simply did not have room for a woman running the nation's highest office – whether openly or otherwise. As noted by ThoughtCo, one Republican Senator "bitterly called her 'the Presidentress' who had fulfilled the dream of the suffragettes by changing her title from First Lady to Acting First Man."

In light of the speculation and scandal they endured, it is unsurprising that Edith became fiercely protective of her husband's legacy. This, too, may have encouraged her to downplay her role, the extent of which went unappreciated for many years. Decades later, however, many historians now firmly believe that First Lady Wilson was running the U.S. government from the time of her husband's stroke in late 1919, to the end of his term in March 1921.

CHAPTER FOUR

In Need of New Deals, 1930–1939

CHAPTER CONTENTS

Section 4.1 • OVERVIEW

"Overview: Women in the Workplace in America, 1930–1939," • © 2021 Omnigraphics.

The 1930s saw a spike in policy and legislation that showed bias against married female workers. In some cases, it was illegal for women to work once wed. It is telling, however, that nine states already had such laws in place prior to the Great Depression, suggesting that these actions had more to do with preserving patriarchy than rescuing the economy.

Discriminatory legislation such as this was also a reflection of the anxieties many faced over a changing status quo. Indeed, history has shown that when legitimized relations of power begin to shift, there is always some reluctance or even retaliation from those who benefitted from the way things used to be. Beyond economics, the very fabric of society was changing, and this had implications for social institutions such as marriage, family, and conventional gender roles.

Early rumblings of later movements had begun, and the activism that emerged in the following decades – during which a myriad of Black organizations emerged to tackle discriminatory policies that actively stifled both human rights and economic advancements – began during these challenging days. The 1930s would ultimately become the decade that laid the foundation for the U.S. civil-rights movement.

Other social changes, such as a 22-percent decline in marriage rates, also represent the tectonic shifts that lay ahead when the nation saw an increase in female breadwinners.

Section 4.2 • THE GREAT DEPRESSION

"The Great Depression at a Glance," "The Great Depression and Women's Work," • © 2021 Omnigraphics.

THE GREAT DEPRESSION AT A GLANCE

As the U.S. entered a new decade, it was battling an unprecedented economic decline. The Great Depression, which started in 1929, continued through the 1930s (though the national economy saw significant improvement in the second half of the decade). The following facts offer some insight into the challenges that permeated everyday life in an era marked by socioeconomic instability.

- The Stock Market Crash of 1929 undermined consumer confidence, which led to decreased spending and investment. Consequently, industrial production dropped by half, and factories began to retrench workers. Those who managed to retain their jobs typically took pay cuts. At the same time, the buying power of the dollar decreased. Thus, people were not only making less money, but the little they did make did not go as far as it once did.
- By 1930, approximately 4 million Americans were actively seeking – but were unable to secure – employment. This number rose to 6 million in 1931.
- Bread lines and soup kitchens were on the rise in urban areas and the homeless population was expanding throughout the country.

- Relying on credit to make ends meet, more Americans fell into debt while foreclosure and repossession rates steadily increased.
- Global adherence to the gold standard for the purposes of currency exchange meant that the economic blow spread to the rest of the world, and especially to Europe.
- As investors lost faith in banking institutions, they increasingly demanded cash deposits. This forced banks to liquidate loans to supplement their depleted cash reserves. The 1930 bank panic was just the first of many sweeping the nation, and thousands of banks were out of business by 1934.
- Even those in highly skilled, professional positions were not exempt from financial woes. Upper-middle-class professionals, like lawyers and physicians, saw their incomes decline by as much as 40 percent. In some cases, formerly wealthy families succumbed to financial ruin.
- By 1933, 15 million Americans were jobless. This year is remembered as the Depression at its most severe.
- It is estimated that more than two million men and women became homeless in the 1930s. Many of these were young people who left home to look for work, fearing that they had become a burden to their households. Some of them ended up in shantytowns (informal settlements/slums) that sprang up across the country, which were known collectively as "Hoovervilles," a reference to sitting President Herbert Hoover.
- Divorce rates dropped, though this was mainly because people could not afford to undergo the legal process. Instead, spousal abandonment peaked, particularly among men and often due to the burden or shame of job loss. This was sometimes called the "poor man's divorce."
- Suicide and violent crime increased during the Great Depression's early years, and the former reached an unprecedented national high in 1933. However, both began to decrease from 1934 onward, as the economy began to bounce back.

THE GREAT DEPRESSION AND WOMEN'S WORK

The economic prosperity seen at the start of the decade came to a crashing halt before the end of it. On October 29, 1929, forever known as Black Tuesday, the stock market crashed. Stocks fell by 13.5 percent that day, and nearly 12 percent the next. Ultimately, the period from 1929 and 1933 was marked by a 55-percent stock decline – the largest in U.S. history. In the years before the Great Depression, economic growth had inspired increasingly risky trading practices. The stock market expanded rapidly toward the end of the decade, and people from all social classes invested their savings.

These practices did not reflect the changing economic reality toward the end of the decade, when wages remained low for the average person and consumer spending had slowed. This left a surplus of manufactured goods in the summer of 1929, which prompted manufacturers to slow production. Thus, stocks were priced far higher than they were truly worth and continued to rise in spite of this. By fall, they reached levels that simply could not be satisfied by future earnings. Moreover, unemployment had begun to rise, and the agricultural recession already underway had impacted prices. Banks were also in trouble, due to major loans that they could not liquidate. All these factors set the stage for the ensuing economic crisis, the likes of which had never been seen before. This downturn would continue throughout the 1930s, permeating all aspects of society and subjecting men and women to extreme hardship.

Prostitution reportedly increased, as women desperately sought to keep themselves afloat. Ironically, there were some cases in which the pervasive gender biases of the time actually benefitted some working women. The U.S. economy rested heavily on "sex-typed" work, meaning various jobs were gender-exclusive. Manufacturing jobs such as steel production, and others seen as "men's work," had the most layoffs. Conversely, positions such as service-industry jobs, and others marked as "women's work," were more likely to endure. Other traditionally feminine labor, such as teaching, domestic work, nursing, phone operations, and clerical work, also continued. Yet, even in these industries, working women felt the pinch. Some employers lowered their salaries, while others did not pay on time. Moreover, as men lost their jobs, many women become the sole providers of their families, making their wages crucial to the survival of both husbands and children.

These were some of the sociopolitical issues present as the United States entered the next decade and the next presidential administration would need to address them. Yet, some policies intended to help the nation through the depression had a disproportionately negative impact on working women – restricting their freedoms and, in some cases, forcing them back into the domestic sphere.

Of course, workers of color were feeling the pinch long before the economic downtown. The Great Migration (1916–1930) had seen over a million African Americans relocate to the North in search of upward mobility. Nearly half of these migrants specifically sought to take advantage of the increased labor demand during the war. Accordingly, Black people enjoyed increased opportunity to secure industrial employment, seeing notable inclusion in steel and automobile production, as well as the shipbuilding and meatpacking industries. By 1920, there were 901,000 Black industrial employees compared to just 500,000 in 1910.

Still, Black people were primarily concentrated in low-paid, unskilled work across the country and, in the South, their unemployment rate was double that of White people. Amidst the employment scarcity of the Depression, these low-level positions disappeared – or became earmarked for White Americans in need of jobs. These racially discriminatory employment practices exacerbated already stark economic disparities and resulted in a phenomenon in which Blacks were typically the "last hired and first fired."

Seeing the disproportionately harsh impact they were being subjected to, African Americans began to create grassroots organizations to champion their socioeconomic interests. As noted by Christopher Klein for *History.com*,

> From the Great Depression's earliest days, African Americans mobilized to protest for greater economic, social and political rights. In 1929, *Chicago Whip* editor Joseph Bibb organized boycotts of city department stores that refused to hire African Americans. The grassroots protests against racially discriminatory hiring practices worked, resulting in the employment of 2,000 African Americans. The "Don't Buy Where You Can't Work" boycotts and pickets soon spread to other cities across the North.

Section 4.3 • **SECTION 213 OF THE FEDERAL ECONOMY ACT: PRESIDENT HOOVER'S LOUSY NEW DEAL FOR WOMEN**

In June of 1932, President Hoover signed the Economy Act of 1932 into law. The federal budget was beyond strained and the Act sought to balance it through spending reductions. This included cutting government salaries. Though economic and political leaders believed this action was crucial to recovery from the economic depression, modern experts conclude it was not the best choice. While the pay cuts saved money, they also prevented those potential earnings from being spent and circulated in communities that desperately needed them.

This was not the only New Deal development that increased hardship. A stipulation in Section 213 of the Economy Act required federal departments to fire one person in each married couple under their employ. In practice, those that were dismissed were primarily women, because their husbands were invariably paid more. What was ultimately a discriminatory policy was, of course, informed by the sociopolitical context of the time. Spencer Howard from the *National Archives* elaborates:

> Why did Congress think this was a good idea? It was widely accepted at that time that women could work outside the home before marriage and that women who didn't marry could have a career, but it was assumed that the wife in a two-income family was either working for frivolous "pin money" or negligent of her family. As unemployment soared during the Depression, working married women were accused of selfishly holding jobs that could help a breadwinner (assumed to be a man) support his family.

To the modern reader, this rhetoric is problematic and sexist in its presumptions about the needs, motivations, and "rightful place" of married women. Considering the advancements women had made in the workplace and the dominant gender-role expectations of the age, it also reflects the social backlash that these women were facing. Indeed, a dominant narrative during this era was that working women were infringing upon the employment opportunities for men. This was somewhat nonsensical, considering that the sex-typed labor economy simply did not leave room for this to be the case.

Indeed, women were largely still doing the same "gender-appropriate" labor they were engaged in before economic downtown. Still, they faced backlash despite this lapse in logic. Writers have characterized this criticism as an instance of scapegoating and suggest that people were simply suffering and needed somebody to blame. While this may seem like an oversimplification, it makes sense when one factors in the anxieties many faced over a changing status quo. Indeed, history has shown that when legitimized relations of power begin to shift, there is always some reluctance or even retaliation from those who benefitted from the way things used to be. Even beyond economics, the very fabric of society was changing, and this had implications for social institutions such as marriage, family, and conventional gender roles.

If married women were now family breadwinners, did that make them the head of the household? Since they earned the household income, did they now get to dictate how it was spent? While gender-role expectations certainly shape our lived experiences today, one cannot overstate how much more blatant and unrelenting they were a century ago. Those who favored the status quo or ascribed to traditional beliefs about gender roles most certainly would have preferred for women to return to the home. Even some women's colleges actively discouraged their graduates from entering the workforce, which would cheat men out of opportunities.

Perhaps surprisingly, Frances Perkins spoke out strongly against working married women even before being elected to Congress. Notably, she did so from a perspective that attempted to account for class differences among women by recognizing that some were in greater need for employment opportunities than others. Accordingly, Perkins discouraged middle-class and well-to-do wives from assuming positions that working-class women needed for survival:

> The woman "pin-money worker" who competes with the necessity worker is a menace to society, a selfish, shortsighted creature, who ought to be ashamed of herself. Until we have every woman in this community earning a living wage ... I am not willing to encourage those who are under no economic necessities to compete with their charm and education, their superior advantages, against the working girl who has only her two hands.

Though this logic is more nuanced than arguments that simply decree that women should remain in the home, it still served to reinforce sociopolitical infrastructure that encouraged discrimination against working married women. Underscored by the pin-money argument, the 1930s saw a spike in policy and legislation that showed bias against married female workers. In some cases, it was illegal for women to work once wed. It is telling, however, that nine states already had such laws in place prior to the Great Depression, suggesting that it had more to do with preserving patriarchy than rescuing the economy. As journalist Erin Blakemore observes:

> The arguments against married women working were personal. In Wisconsin, for example, lawmakers passed a resolution in 1935 stating that when married women with working husbands got jobs, they became the "calling card for disintegration of family life." The committee added that "The large number of husbands and wives working for the state raises a serious moral question, as this committee feels that the practice of birth control is encouraged, and the selfishness that arises from the income of employment of husband and wife bids fair to break down civilization and a healthy atmosphere.

The term "pin money" originally referred to petty cash that women used to treat themselves to nice things. By the depression it was being used as a blanket term for women's labor. This narrative, which trivialized women's work, had the benefit of justifying unequal pay between the genders. Indeed, as far back as the late 1800s, existing marriage bans also served to ensure that the lowest paying and least desirable jobs were earmarked for women without families. In doing so, they preserved prestigious and well-paid employment for men.

By the 1930s, this impulse was embodied by the pin-money argument, which was ultimately used to justify lower pay for women in general, and not just those of means. Thus, the intersectional argument presented by Perkins did not mirror the conditions on the ground, which discriminated equally against working-class women who needed an income as badly as anybody else.

Still, the dominant belief was that women were competing with men for jobs, and that women only needed these jobs to buy trinkets and comforts while men had families to support. Accordingly, the government went to some length to make it hard for women to circumvent the marriage ban. For instance, in 1933, women with federal jobs were forbidden from using their maiden names.

Despite the protests of individual women and women's groups, Section 213 of the Federal Economy Act endured for another four years. The efforts of activists paid off in 1937, however, when Section 213 was repealed as the Depression entered its last few years.

Women's Economic Survival

Much like those in the agricultural sector before them, everyday women had to come up with inventive ways to make household goods and dollars last longer. A common saying during this time was: "Use it up, wear it out, make it do, or do without." Women's households changed as they eschewed the convenience in favor of saving costs. Many housewives began to sew more of their family's clothes, while others started canning fruits and vegetables.

Others took on wage labor they could do from home. Known as "outwork," this helped many women bolster the household income.

The lack of financial resources, of course, impacted other social institutions and structures. More couples began to delay marriage and use contraception to avoid childbearing due to financial limitations. Unable to take on the expense of establishing a new household, others opted not to marry at all. Inter-generational cohabitation became more common as families used shared housing to save money.

Impact

The first wave of the nation's feminist movement declined, in part, due to the labor backlash and increasingly popular rhetoric that championed female domesticity. Groups that had led the movement for women's rights in the previous decade, like the National Women's Party and the League of Women Voters, were less prominent during this one. Ultimately, the momentum the feminist movement enjoyed before the Great Depression would not be regained until the 1960s.

Since the concerns of this decade were overwhelmingly economic, women involved themselves in organized labor movements. In Flint, Michigan, for instance, the Women's Emergency Brigade of the United Autoworkers (UAW union) played a significant supportive role in a protracted strike that prompted General Motors Company to sign a union contract in 1937.

Despite these advancements, professional women suffered a setback during the Great Depression too, effectively losing the career gains made in previous years. Progress made toward representation and inclusion in male-dominant spheres, such as the business sector, slowed. Moreover, the need for employment made it more socially acceptable for men to accept jobs traditionally held by women, such as teaching. Women accounted for 85 percent of teachers in 1920 and 78 percent by 1940.

Sexism and racism encouraged prejudicial hiring practices that limited employment opportunities for women, and particularly women of color. Moreover, legislation intended to improve working conditions for Americans simultaneously excluded positions largely held by racial minorities. As noted by *Encyclopedia.com*:

> Employers preferred white men, and then white women, over black or Hispanic women in most instances. Relegated to domestic work and farm work through centuries of racism and misogyny in the job market, most African American women found themselves left out of new laws passed to ensure worker safety. The Fair Labor Standards Act of 1938, with its minimum wage and maximum hour provisions, did not apply to domestic or farm workers.... Many cities developed specific locations where prospective domestic workers would stand outside and wait for wealthier women to hire them for a day's work. Given that those seeking employment were most often black and given the low wages one would earn in such arrangements, the process and the area of town associated with it became known colloquially as a slave market.

The informal arrangements described also contributed to the vulnerability of the Black women involved in domestic labor. Beyond lacking steady incomes and job security, these women also had no wage protections, nor any leverage to negotiate for decent pay. The oral nature of the employer–employee agreement was inherently flimsy, and left room for women to be underpaid for their work or exploited through dishonored contracts.

Despite the disadvantages created by Section 214, the number of working married women continued to increase that decade. These gains were not as major as those seen in previous years; however, that progress was remarkable in the context of the stagnant economy and the political pushback. Notably, however, only 10 percent of the 1,600 government workers fired under the Act, most of them women, had their employment reinstated.

Moreover, negative attitudes toward women and pushback against women in the workplace persisted – even as the country began to emerge from the throes of the depression. As noted by *Encyclopedia.com:*

> In 1936, only 15 percent of respondents to a poll in *Fortune Magazine* asking, "Do you believe that women should have a full-time job outside the home?" answered yes. "Simply fire the women who shouldn't be working anyway, and hire the men," wrote journalist Norman Cousins in 1939. "Presto! No unemployment. No relief rolls. No depression." His facetious words reflected how controversial working women were even after the repeal of Section 213. The idea of White, middle-class, married women working didn't really become socially acceptable again until the 1940s, when World War II opened up a large number of essential war jobs for women. The majority of state bans and policies against married and working women were repealed around that time due to a shortage of male labor as men went off to war. Women's work threatened men who had long held economic power – until the nation's power was threatened by absent men.

Section 4.4 • **THE NEW DEAL**

This section includes text excerpted from "History of Changes to the Minimum Wage Law" (Department of Labor) • "A New President Addresses the Three Rs," "Frances Perkins: 'Architect of the New Deal,'" "The Social Security Act of 1935," "Fair Labor Standards and a Minimum Wage," • © 2021 Omnigraphics.

A NEW PRESIDENT ADDRESSES THE THREE R'S

In response to the economic crisis, sitting president Herbert Hoover was reluctant to turn to what he perceived as excessive federal spending and overreliance on federal interventions. Instead, he tried to stabilize prices by facilitating cooperation between government and business. He also established government agencies and focused on generating local aid for public works and indirect relief from individual states and the private sector. As the depression worsened, however, he faced calls for more direct involvement and government funding from an increasingly dissatisfied American public.

Critics of President Hoover perceived his response as insufficient, while Hoover himself remained reluctant to allow the federal government to take actions he feared would lead the country down a socialist path (i.e., enforcing fixed prices, controlling currency values, and controlling businesses). These efforts, he contended, were only short-term solutions that would ultimately create deficits. Moreover, while he was open to giving aid to banks, he refused to issue direct aid to Americans, "believing the dole would weaken public morale."

Increasingly unpopular, and depicted as uncaring by his opponents, he lost by no small margin to Franklin D. Roosevelt in 1932. It was from this desperate socioeconomic context that the New Deal emerged. During his first hundred days in office, President Roosevelt endorsed numerous new laws. The New Deal included direct federal aid and increased federal control over various industries and rejected Hoover's support for volunteerism over deficit spending.

Most New Deal programs were implemented between 1933 and 1938 through executive presidential orders and legislation enacted by Congress. As noted by *ThoughtCo*, "the programs addressed what historians call the '3 Rs' of dealing with the depression, *Relief*, *Recovery*, and *Reform* – relief for the poor and jobless, recovery of the economy, and reform of the nation's financial system to safeguard against future depressions."

FRANCES PERKINS: "ARCHITECT OF THE NEW DEAL," 1931

As noted in Section 3, the Great Depression did not impact working women in the same way it did men. The pre-existing division of labor along gendered lines, known as sex-typed work, created more job losses in industries whose workforces were predominantly male. Between 1930 and 1940, the number of working women rose from 10.5 to 13 million – a growth of 24 percent. Indeed, as more and more men were laid off, women had to enter the workforce to sustain their families. Other social changes, such as the 22-percent decline in marriage rates seen in that same decade, encouraged this shift. In other words, the nation was seeing a rise in the number of female breadwinners.

First Lady Eleanor Roosevelt sought to mirror this growing female representation in the nation's highest office. Accordingly, she championed women like Frances Perkins, a key figure in New York's progress toward improved workers' rights following the Triangle Shirtwaist Fire.

Perkins was the first woman to lead the Industrial Commission of the state of New York, and soon became the first woman to occupy a cabinet position.

In 1933, Roosevelt appointed Perkins as U.S. Secretary of Labor, and she ultimately became just one of two cabinet members to serve throughout his presidency. Meticulous and persistent, Perkins was the force behind major economic recovery policies. As noted by *History.com:*

> Perkins brought to the job an unwavering devotion to social reform. She demanded, and got from Roosevelt, a commitment to support federal initiatives in the areas of unemployment relief and public works, insurance to guard workers from the hazards of old age and unemployment, and efforts to regulate child labor as well as wages and hours for adults. These became the cornerstones of the New Deal's policies for depression relief and reform. Carefully conceived under Perkins's watchful eyes and shepherded by her through the intricacies of the political process, the Social Security Act and the Fair Labor Standards Act remain monuments to her ability to make progress through incremental steps and to her mastery of the art of compromise.

THE SOCIAL SECURITY ACT OF 1935

In 1934, President Roosevelt formed the Committee on Economic Security (CES) and tasked it with developing an economic security bill that would act as a safety net for Americans in their various life stages. Led by long-time Labor organizer/new U.S. Secretary of Labor Frances Perkins, the CES drafted the Social Security Act, which was signed into law the following year.

Through payroll tax deductions, the bill provided support for various vulnerable populations. This aid came in the form of financial assistance for widowed parents and people with disabilities, health insurance for low-earning citizens, employer-funded unemployment insurance, and a pension program for the elderly.

A board was soon established to plan and implement deductions for enrolees. By November 1937, program registration had begun. That same year, a government pamphlet was circulated to encourage registration, and it summarized the Act as follows:

> In general, the Social Security Act helps to assure some income to people who cannot earn and to steady the income of millions of wage earners during their working years and their old age. In one way and another taxation is spread over large groups of people to carry the cost of giving some security to those who are unfortunate or incapacitated at any one time. The act is a foundation on which we have begun to build security as states and as a people, against the risks which families cannot meet one by one.

Unfortunately, various workers were excluded. By limiting its coverage to industry and commerce, the Act made no provisions for nearly half of the national workforce, including self-employed professionals, domestic workers, and field hands. The exclusion of groups two and three had a disproportionate impact on working African Americans. It took another two decades for amendments to be made, but, by the 1950s, social security was extended to those previously left out, along with some federal employees.

FAIR LABOR STANDARDS ACT AND A MINIMUM WAGE

President Roosevelt was again at the helm of landmark legislation in 1938, when Congress passed the Fair Labor Standards Act. Fundamentally, the Act guaranteed that workers would earn a base income for their labor: A principle more commonly referred to as a "minimum wage" (although some businesses still found ways to pay women workers less). The Act also stipulated that employers who wanted workers to exceed 44 hours a week had to compensate them at double their regular rate (i.e., time and a half/overtime pay). This weekly hour cap would gradually be reduced to 40 hours. Significantly, in a century marked by exploitative child-labor practices, the Act also outlawed the employment of children below the age of 16.

During this time, the national poverty line was calculated by multiplying estimated food costs by three. In its early years, the minimum wage of 25 cents an hour brought people above the poverty line and could sustain a family of three. This was one of the few times in history that the federal minimum wage was also a living wage. In the years since, it has typically lagged far behind the actual cost of living. By the 1980s, minimum wage was not even enough to sustain a two-person household, let alone a moderately sized family.

Still, at its peak it was a welcome benefit for many workers, helping to improve employment conditions. It also lowered income disparity – which, of course, had implications for class differences. Finally, the impact of the Act was enhanced by other socioeconomic events. The following year brought a second world war, and the demand for industrial labor spiked once again. Guaranteed a living wage and facing a reinvigorated labor market, many American workers enjoyed significant gains as the 1930s ended, a welcome change from the hellish decade they had managed to survive.

History of Changes to the Federal Minimum Wage Law

Early in the administration of the Fair Labor Standards Act (FLSA), it became apparent that application of the statutory minimum wage was likely to produce undesirable effects upon the economies of Puerto Rico and the Virgin Islands if applied to all of their covered industries. Consequently, on June 26, 1940, an amendment was enacted prescribing the establishment of special industry committees to determine, and issue through wage orders, the minimum wage levels applicable in Puerto Rico and the Virgin Islands. The rates established by industry committees could be less than the statutory rates applicable elsewhere in the United States.

On May 14, 1947, the FLSA was amended by the Portal-to-Portal Act. This legislation was significant because it resolved some issues as to what constitutes compensable hours worked under FLSA. Matters involving underground travel in coal mines and make-ready practices in factories had been decided earlier in a number of U.S. Supreme Court decisions.

Subsequent amendments to the FLSA have extended the law's coverage to additional employees and raised the level of the minimum wage. In 1949, minimum wage coverage was expanded to include workers in the air transport industry. The 1949 amendments also eliminated industry committees except in Puerto Rico and the Virgin Islands. A specific section was added granting the Wage and Hour Administrator in the U.S. Department of Labor authorization to control the incidence of exploitative industrial homework.

The 1961 amendments greatly expanded the FLSA's scope in the retail trade sector. The minimum for workers newly subject to the Act was set at $1.00 an hour effective September 1961, $1.15 an hour in September 1964, and $1.25 an hour in September 1965. Retail and service establishments were allowed to employ full-time students at wages of no more than 15 percent below the minimum with proper certification from the Department of Labor. The amendments extended coverage to employees of retail trade enterprises with sales exceeding $1 million annually, although individual establishments within those covered enterprises were exempt if their annual sales fell below $250,000.

The concept of enterprise coverage was introduced by the 1961 amendments. Those amendments extended coverage in the retail trade industry from an established 250,000 workers to 2.2 million.

Congress further broadened coverage with amendments in 1966 by lowering the enterprise sales volume test to $500,000, effective February 1967, with a further cut to $250,000 effective February 1969. The 1966 amendments also extended coverage to public schools, nursing homes, laundries, and the entire construction industry. Farms were subject to coverage for the first time if their employment reached 500 or more mandatory days of labor in the previous year's peak quarter. The minimum wage went to $1.00 an hour effective February 1967 for newly covered nonfarm workers, $1.15 in February 1968, $1.30 in February 1969, $1.45 in February 1970, and $1.60 in February 1971. Increases for newly subject farm workers stopped at $1.30. The 1966 amendments extended the full-time student certification program to cover agricultural employers and to institutions of higher learning.

In 1974, Congress included under the FLSA all nonsupervisory employees of federal, state, and local governments and many domestic workers. (Subsequently, in 1976, in *National League of Cities v. Usery*, the Supreme Court held that the minimum wage and overtime provisions of the FLSA could not constitutionally apply to state and local government employees engaged in traditional government functions.) The minimum wage increased to $2.00 an hour in 1974, $2.10 in 1975, and $2.30 in 1976 for all except farm workers, whose minimum initially rose to $1.60. Parity with nonfarm workers was reached at $2.30 with the 1977 amendments.

By eliminating the separate lower minimum for large agricultural employers the 1977 amendments set a new uniform wage schedule for all covered workers, while still retaining the overtime exemption. The amendments eased the provisions for establishments permitted to employ students at the lower wage rate and allowed special waivers for children 10 to11 years old to work in agriculture. The overtime exemption for employees in hotels, motels, and restaurants was eliminated. To allow for the effects of inflation, the $250,000-dollar volume-of-sales-coverage test for retail trade and service enterprises was increased in stages to $362,500 after December 31, 1981.

As a result of the Supreme Court's 1985 decision in *Garcia v. San Antonio Metropolitan Transit Authority et.al.*, Congress passed amendments changing the application of FLSA to public-sector employees. Specifically, these amendments permit state and local governments to compensate their employees for overtime hours worked with compensatory time off in lieu of overtime pay, at a rate of 1-1/2 hours for each hour of overtime worked.

The 1989 amendments established a single annual dollar-volume test of $500,000 for enterprise coverage of both retail and no-retail businesses. At the same time, the amendments eliminated the minimum wage and overtime pay exemption for small retail firms. Thus, employees of small retail businesses became subject to minimum wage and overtime pay in any work week in which they engage in commerce or the production of goods for commerce. The amendments also established a training wage provision (at 85 percent of the minimum wage, but not less than $3.35 an hour) for employees under the age of twenty, a provision that expired in 1993. Finally, the amendments established an overtime exception for time spent by employees in remedial education and civil money penalties for willful or repeated violations of the minimum wage or overtime pay requirements of the law.

In 1990, Congress enacted legislation requiring regulations to be issued providing a special overtime exemption for certain highly skilled professionals in the computer field who receive not less than 6 and one-half times the applicable minimum wage.

The 1996 amendments established a youth sub minimum wage of $4.25 an hour for newly hired employees under the age of 20 during their first 90 consecutive calendar days after being hired by their employer; revised the tip credit provisions to allow employers to pay qualifying tipped employees no less than $2.13 per hour if they received the remainder of the statutory minimum wage in tips; set the hourly compensation test for qualifying computer-related professional employees at $27.63 an hour; and amended the Portal-to-Portal Act to allow employers and employees to agree on the use of employer-provided vehicles for commuting to and from work, at the beginning and end of the work day, without counting the commuting time as compensable working time if certain conditions are met.

A separate provision of the 2007 amendments brought about phased increases to the minimum wages in the Commonwealth of Northern Mariana Islands and in American Samoa, with the goal of bringing the minimum wages in those locations up to the general federal minimum wage over a number of years.

Questions and Answers about the Minimum Wage

What Is the Federal Minimum Wage?

Under the Fair Labor Standards Act (FLSA), the federal minimum wage for covered nonexempt employees is $7.25 per hour effective July 24, 2009. Many states also have minimum wage laws. Where an employee is subject to both the state and federal minimum wage laws, the employee is entitled to the higher minimum wage rate. Various minimum wage exceptions apply under specific circumstances to workers with disabilities, full-time students, and youth under the age of 20 in their first 90 consecutive calendar days of employment, tipped employees, and student learners.

What Is the Minimum Wage for Workers Who Receive Tips?

An employer may pay a tipped employee not less than $2.13 an hour in direct wages if that amount plus the tips received equal at least the federal minimum wage, the employee retains all tips and the employee customarily and regularly receives more than $30 a month in tips. If an employee's tips combined with the employer's direct wages of at least $2.13 an hour do not equal the federal minimum hourly wage, the employer must make up the difference. Some states have minimum wage laws specific to tipped employees. When an employee is subject to both the federal and state wage laws, the employee is entitled to the provisions of each law which provide the greater benefits.

Must Young Workers Be Paid the Minimum Wage?

A minimum wage of $4.25 per hour applies to young workers under the age of 20 during their first 90 consecutive calendar days of employment with an employer, as long as their work does not displace other workers. After 90 consecutive days of employment or the employee reaches 20 years of age, whichever comes first, the employee must receive a minimum wage of $7.25 per hour effective July 24, 2009. Other programs that allow for payment of less than the full federal minimum wage apply to workers with disabilities, full-time students, and student learners employed pursuant to sub-minimum-wage certificates. These programs are not limited to the employment of young workers.

What Minimum Wage Exceptions Apply to Full-time Students?

The Full-time Student Program is for full-time students employed in retail or service stores, agriculture, or colleges and universities. The employer that hires students can obtain a certificate from the Department of Labor which allows the student to be paid not less than 85 percent of the minimum wage. The certificate also limits the hours that the student may work to 8 hours in a day and no more than 20 hours a week when school is in session and 40 hours when school is out and requires the employer to follow all child labor laws. Once students graduate or leave school for good, they must be paid $7.25 per hour effective July 24, 2009. There are some limitations on the use of the full-time student program.

What Minimum Wage Exceptions Apply to Student Learners?

This program is for high-school students at least 16 years of age who are enrolled in vocational education (shop courses). The employer that hires the student can obtain a certificate from the Department of Labor which allows the student to be paid not less than 75 percent of the minimum wage, for as long as the student is enrolled in the vocational education program. Other programs that allow for payment of less than the full federal minimum wage apply to disabled workers and full-time students employed pursuant to sub-minimum wage certificates.

How Often Does the Federal Minimum Wage Increase?

The minimum wage does not increase automatically. Congress must pass a bill which the President signs into law in order for the minimum wage to go up.

Who Makes Sure Workers are Paid the Minimum Wage?

The Wage and Hour Division of the U.S. Department of Labor is responsible for enforcing the minimum wage. Using both enforcement and public education efforts, the Wage and Hour Division strives to ensure that workers are paid the minimum wage. The Wage and Hour Division has offices throughout the country. The numbers and addresses for these offices may be found on the Internet or in the federal government "blue pages" section of the telephone book under "Labor Department."

To Whom Does the Minimum Wage Apply?

The minimum wage law (the FLSA) applies to employees of enterprises that have annual gross volume of sales or business done of at least $500,000. It also applies to employees of smaller firms if the employees are engaged in interstate commerce or in the production of goods for commerce, such as employees who work in transportation or communications or who regularly use the mails or telephones for interstate communications. Other persons, such as guards, janitors, and maintenance employees who perform duties which are closely related and directly essential to such interstate activities are also covered by the FLSA. It also applies to employees of federal, state or local government agencies, hospitals and schools, and it generally applies to domestic workers. The FLSA contains a number of exemptions from the minimum wage that may apply to some workers, however.

What Happens If State Law Requires Payment of a Higher Minimum Wage Than Federal Law?

Where state law requires a higher minimum wage, that higher standard applies.

A History of the Federal Minimum Wage

This sidebar includes text excerpted from "Minimum Wage" (U.S. Department of Labor)

Federal minimum-wage provisions are contained in the Fair Labor Standards Act (FLSA). Many states also have minimum-wage laws. Some state laws provide greater employee protections, and employers must comply with both.

The FLSA does not provide wage payment–collection procedures for an employee's usual or promised wages or commissions in excess of those required by the FLSA. However, some states do have laws under which such claims, sometimes including fringe benefits, may be filed.

The minimum-wage percentage of the nation's poverty level has averaged around 60 percent since 1989. By comparison, in 1968, the minimum-wage percentage of the nation's poverty level was 99 percent – which translates into a full-time worker who earns the minimum wage being 1 percent below the poverty line.

In 2019, the minimum-wage laws of four states – Arizona, Georgia, Minnesota, and Wyoming– were set lower than the federal minimum wage (which means the federal minimum automatically applied). Meanwhile, 20 states had laws that lock the state's minimum wage to the federal minimum wage. In 2020, 28 states plus the District of Columbia had minimum wages set higher than the federal minimum wage. Divvy Research reports, however, that only one state had a minimum wage higher than the living wage for a single worker in 2020. Divvy Research also reports that, for a family of four with a single wage-earner, the minimum wage was a whopping 50 percent below a living wage in 2020.

The national average for minimum wage in 2020 was $9.08 per hour.

The United States has a record-breaking 11+ years without a minimum-wage increase. A new American record. Yet the cost of living has increased 20 percent and the cost of purchasing housing, healthcare, and other essentials has increased far more than that.

The National Low Income Housing Coalition reports that, in 2009, the average rent was $1,132 (adjusted for inflation) but current rent have risen 30 percent since then. This means that, in today's housing market, a worker must earn approximately $20 per hour just to afford a one-bedroom apartment.

As of March 15, 2021, Congress has twice struck down attempts to increase the minimum wage during the first three months of the Biden Administration.

Table 4.1. Federal Minimum Wage Increases

Date	Administration	Minimum Wage
October 1938	FD Roosevelt	$0.25 per hour
October 1939	FD Roosevelt	$0.30 per hour
October 1945	Truman	$0.40 per hour
January 1950	Truman	$0.75 per hour
March 1956	Eisenhower	$1.00 per hour
September 1961	Kennedy	$1.16 per hour
September 1963	Kennedy	$1.25 per hour
February 1967	Johnson	$1.40 per hour
February 1968	Johnson	$1.60 per hour
May 1974	Nixon	$2.00 per hour
January 1975	Ford	$2.10 per hour
January 1976	Ford	$2.30 per hour
January 1978	Carter	$2.65 per hour
January 1979	Carter	$2.90 per hour
January 1980	Carter	$3.10 per hour
January 1981	Carter	$3.35 per hour
April 1990	Bush	$3.80 per hour
April 1991	Bush	$4.25 per hour
October 1996	Clinton	$4.75 per hour
September 1997	Clinton	$5.15 per hour
July 2007	GW Bush	$5.85 per hour
July 2008	GW Bush	$6.55 per hour
July 2009	Obama	$7.25 per hour

(Source: US Department of Labor)

Section 4.5 • NATIVE AMERICAN HEALTH IN A TIME OF SCARCITY

This section includes text excerpted from "First (and Only) Nursing School for Native Americans Established, 1932" (National Park Service); "Native American Health in a Time of Scarcity, • © 2021 Omnigraphics.

THE FIRST (AND ONLY) NURSING SCHOOL FOR NATIVE AMERICANS IS ESTABLISHED, 1932

Following the Indian wars, widespread public sentiment favored the killing of Native Americans.

Sage Memorial Hospital School of Nursing, situated on the Ganado Mission within the Navajo Reservation in Arizona (near Gallup, New Mexico), was the first and only accredited nursing program for Native American women in the United States. The Presbyterian founders of Ganado mission saw their work as threefold: Evangelism, education, and medical care would transform the lives of the Diné (Navajo) people (and would provide quality medical care more than evangelizing).

In an effort to improve health on the Reservation, the Presbyterian Board of Home Missions approved the construction of a twelve-bed hospital at Ganado in 1911, which was the largest medical mission among the Diné people.

In 1930, Dr. Clarence Salsbury, a persuasive Presbyterian missionary and physician associated with the hospital, founded Sage Memorial Hospital School of Nursing, which became what some called an "oasis of learning." Although many White Americans believed that Diné people lacked the ability to become nurses, Salsbury believed that these students would succeed at their training and become nurses who would be valuable "service to their people" (Taylor, 1,279).

Salsbury set about convincing the parents of these young women and the Diné medicine men that providing this training was important to both the young women and to their people. Strong ties between Presbyterian missions and churches across both the United States and the world also ensured the rapid growth of the school.

Formally accredited by the State of Arizona in 1932, the school eventually attracted not only Native American women but also women from other marginalized groups. As the first and only nursing school for Native Americans, Sage Memorial Hospital School of Nursing was a landmark institution in changing White attitudes about the abilities of Native American people. Through this training in modern medicine, these young nurses were able to "build a bridge between the old ways and the new" (Kristofic, 2019).

Sage Memorial Hospital School of Nursing was designated a U.S. National Historic Landmark on January 16, 2009. The press release announcing this designation read:

> Sage Memorial Hospital School of Nursing, Ganado Mission, AZ, the first accredited nursing program for Native American women in the United States, Sage Memorial Hospital School of Nursing provided Native American women with a professional nursing education. The school was a landmark institution in changing white attitudes toward the abilities of Native American people. The school attracted both Native American women as well as women from other minority groups.

Graduates of the Sage Memorial Hospital School of Nursing, c. 1935. This accredited school eventually attracted not only Native American students but also women from other marginalized groups. As the first and only nursing school for Native Americans, Sage Memorial was a landmark institution in changing White attitudes about the abilities of Native American people.

Eventually students representing over 50 different Native American tribes, as well as women of Mexican, Spanish, Inuit, Japanese, Filipino, and Chinese descent enrolled in the training program. The school's diverse population clearly illustrates that access to an accredited nursing education was not, at that time, generally available within the United States to non-white students.

The education provided at Sage Memorial Hospital School of Nursing was of such a high quality that many white parents agitated to have their daughters admitted to the school. However, the director of Sage Memorial Hospital School of Nursing, Dr. Clarence G. Salsbury, made a calculated decision to maintain a nursing training program solely for minority students. This decision, made at a time when public education was actively segregated and minority children were refused entry to white schools, provides a unique and different insight into the doctrine of separate but equal educational opportunities.

Section 4.6 • UNCREDITED TRAILBLAZER ELIZEBETH SMITH FRIEDMAN: THE HERO THAT HISTORY FORGOT

Crypto pioneer Elizebeth Smith was born in Huntington, Indiana, in 1892 and demonstrated an aptitude and passion for language from an early age. As a young woman, she briefly attended Wooster College, in Ohio, before switching to Hillsdale College, in Michigan, where she majored in English literature. A true linguist, she also studied Latin, Greek, and German, and took on an array of minors that piqued her eclectic interests. Her passion for language and literature extended beyond the classroom and she enjoyed drafting her own creative works in her spare time.

Her love of Shakespeare, which later underscored one of her greatest codebreaking achievements, reportedly informed one of her earliest career decisions. After graduation, Elizebeth worked at the Newberry Research Library in Chicago, and historians propose that she was attracted by their possession of an original Shakespeare folio.

From Newberry, she was recruited by George Fabyan, millionaire businessman and owner of Riverbank Laboratories – among the first cryptography facilities founded by the government. Fabyan wanted Elizebeth to join a private think tank that he operated from his expansive Illinois estate, and this opportunity marked her entry into cryptology.

At Riverbank, Elizebeth encountered other gifted minds: Fellow linguists, geneticists, and engineers. Perhaps most importantly, it was there that she met her future husband and professional partner, William Friedman. At the time, there was no better place for a codebreaker to be. Indeed, Riverbank was the only cryptologic laboratory in the country for years, and the Friedmans spent the next four years there, amassing historical information on coded language.

When the U.S. joined World War I, codebreaking became an invaluable skill. Since the country did not have a dedicated codebreaking department, Fabyan offered the services of his own workforce at Riverbank, forming a unit headed by the Friedmans. Over the next few years, the couple taught Army personnel how to decipher codes and developed their own complex coding systems. In 1921 the couple accepted federal employment and relocated to Washington, D.C.

Elizebeth soon led a cryptanalytic unit for the U.S. Coast Guard. There, she surveilled illegal smuggling rings and decoded messages between criminal organizations like the mob. The first woman to lead a project of this nature, Elizebeth and her assistant uncovered data that underscored 650 criminal prosecutions. She also served as an expert witness in 33 narcotics smuggling cases and continued to run her own codebreaking unit.

During the second world war, the government again called on her for assistance. Yet, despite an impressive resume and proven ability to serve the war effort, she faced professional limitations due to gender bias. Journalist Susan Haynes elaborates:

> While Friedman ran her own code-breaking unit in the '20s and '30s, she felt frustrated by her position during World War II. She was assigned to monitor clandestine

> communications between German operatives in South America and their overseers in Berlin, yet she did not have the kind of control she was used to, as her unit was transferred to Navy control, which did not allow civilians to be in charge of a unit. She was irritated too by the sloppiness of the FBI in interfering in code-breaking work, and felt that the agency had always looked at her with disdain and in a sexist light, yet still demanded her help because of her indispensable talents. It was a continuation of how she had been treated for much of her career [said a colleague]. "She was always fixing messes men had created or solving problems they could not solve."

Still, she managed to attain spectacular victories. While American troops were fighting in the Pacific, the government was growing increasingly worried about potential Nazi-backed coups and insurrections in South America. Indeed, the continent was home to various countries whose allyship was crucial to the U.S. war strategy. Elizebeth decoded communications from Germany that unveiled a spy network spanning the continent. Not only did she uncover its existence – she deciphered the identity and codes of its leader, something various law enforcement and intelligence agencies, including the Federal Bureau of Investigation (FBI), had failed to do. This was a turning point in the war. Once the spy ring was destroyed, Chile, Bolivia, and Argentina cut ties with Axis powers and joined the Allied powers, eliminating the threat to the latter's triumph.

She was not given credit for her work. Worse still, the credit that she was due was publicly taken by someone else. Indeed, J. Edgar Hoover claimed ownership of Elizebeth's achievements for himself and the FBI. Officially noted as the leaders of the code-breaking effort, they ensured the erasure of the true leader and her team. Perhaps most unfortunately, this cheated Elizebeth out of her rightful place in history, which immortalized this false account concerning the war. Moreover, she could not publicly challenge the official account: The Navy oath she signed had a nondisclosure clause that she never broke.

Legally silenced for the remainder of her life, little was known about her pivotal role in World War II. Moreover, public perceptions often relegated her to her husband's shadow. Indeed, he was considered the leading American cryptologist during his lifetime, though some believe Elizebeth to have been the more talented codebreaker. Accordingly, a 1956 feature in *TIME* magazine profiles his illustrious career, while describing Elizebeth as an assistant cipher clerk.

The Friedmans appeared in that publication once more the following year, having recently published a book debunking an enduring theory questioning the authorship of Shakespeare's plays. Conspiracy theorists had long contended that his works contained a code that pointed to the identity of the "true" author, which the Friedmans disproved. The piece in *TIME* magazine notes that the couple has an impressive resume but emphasizes William's accomplishments. Indeed, she was largely seen as the cryptologist's wife, instead of a formidable codebreaker her own right.

In 2008, nearly 30 years after her death, declassified government records made the details of her accomplishments public. This sparked new interest in her life's work, allowing Elizebeth to finally receive her just due. In a contemporary account, the *National Security Agency* praises her for making unique contributions to cryptology despite often working as a member of a team. Moreover, she is remembered for her unique ability to solve codes written in languages she did not speak and doing groundbreaking work without the use of modern tools like computers and calculators, or even a substantial background in mathematics.

In 2019, the Senate passed a resolution in her honor, recognizing her as a pioneer and "a beacon of inspiration for women in the national security community and for women pursuing STEM-related (Science, Technology, Engineering, and Mathematics) fields."

Section 4.7 • TRAILBLAZERS

"Mary McLeod Bethune: Equalizing Education," "Charlotte Perkins Gilman (1850–1933), a Woman Trapped by Her Time," "Hedy Lamarr, Innovator Supreme," • © 2021 Omnigraphics.

MARY MCLEOD BETHUNE

Mary McLeod Bethune was born in Mayesville, South Carolina, in 1875, just eight years before slavery was abolished. Although her parents, Samuel and Patsy, were enslaved at that time, Mary – one of the youngest of their 17 children – was born free. After abolition, the family remained on the plantation of their former master, saving money to venture out on their own.

This was not an uncommon circumstance, as enslaved people had been emancipated without social systems in place to start new lives. Moreover, a loophole in the 13th Amendment made it possible for new forms of slavery to continue throughout the South. Southern states swiftly codified and implemented the Black Codes, which effectively served to prevent the loss of cheap Black labor through exploitative conditions.

Sharecropping was one such condition. This is a form of peonage that kept most workers largely indebted to former plantation owners. Historians refer to the period that followed the Civil War as the "Reconstruction" era. For many Black families, it was a time of backbreaking labor in pursuit of true freedom. Though just a child, Mary worked in the cotton fields with her family for up to 10 hours each day. Eventually, the McLeods saved enough money to attain a small piece of land where they built a log cabin. Homeowners, finally, they called this place the Homestead.

Patsy supplemented the family income by doing laundry for their former master. Young Mary often accompanied the matriarch when she returned the garments and those trips gave her access to toys her own family could not afford. During one such visit, she grabbed a book, only to have it snatched away by a White child who remarked that she was not allowed to read. In her later years, Mary reflected that this incident motivated her to become literate. Not long after, she became the first person in her family to receive a formal education.

Early Education

When Mary was seven years old, her family was visited by a Black Presbyterian missionary named Emma Wilson. Wilson offered Samuel and Patsy the chance to send their children to a school she would soon open. Unfortunately, the couple could only afford to educate one child, and Mary was chosen. This monumental opportunity would, however, require tenacity and sacrifice from the young learner.

Each day, she walked 10 miles to get to and from the tiny, one-room institution known as Trinity Mission School. When she came home, she still had chores to do, then she would share what she had learned with her family as time permitted. Four years later, she graduated, at age 11, and had no resources to continue her education beyond this point. Lacking options, Mary rejoined her family in the cotton fields.

It was a difficult time for all. Mary's educational dreams had been dashed, and she longed to go back to school. However, this dream was waning as the family entered even greater economic hardship. The McLeods' single mule had died, and they had to mortgage their home to buy another. Struggling to stay afloat, they certainly could not pay for further education.

A year after Mary McLeod's graduation, Mary Chrisman read about the school for Black children in her former hometown. Chrisman was a Quaker teacher who sponsored a church-led program that helped educate formerly enslaved youth. Upon learning of the school in Mayesville, she offered to pay for one student's tuition, thereby allowing Mary McLeod to return to the classroom.

A Different World

Just two years later, a 13-year-old Mary left South Carolina to attend the Scotia Seminary for Negro Girls. This institution in Concord, North Carolina, gave Mary her first experience of racial integration: Black and White teachers worked, sat, and ate alongside each other – an idyllic image of harmony that made a lasting impact.

By 1890, 15-year-old Mary had completed the modern equivalent of an associate's degree, and this enabled her to work as a teacher. But the ambition of her youth was unthwarted, and she wanted to pursue higher education. She continued her studies at Scotia Seminary, spending her summers doing domestic work to help support her family.

Upon graduating in 1894, her former benefactor, Mary Christman, funded further schooling at the Moody Bible Institute in Chicago, Illinois. Already a humanitarian, Mary worked in low-income neighborhoods, assisting the homeless and hungry, in addition to visiting prisons. At school, she took classes designed to help her do missionary work abroad. Specifically, she had hoped to be stationed in Africa. After graduation, she sought permission to do so from the Presbyterian Church's mission board in New York. This dream was shattered when she was informed that "coloreds" were not permitted to serve as African missionaries.

Resilient, though disappointed, the 19-year-old embarked on a journey that would see her founding a groundbreaking college and becoming a CEO, suffragist, civil-rights icon, and trusted presidential advisor.

Starting a School

While teaching 8th graders in Augusta, Georgia, Mary met Albertus Bethune, whom she married in 1898. The couple relocated to Savannah, where she continued teaching until the birth of her son in 1899. Soon, the family relocated to Florida for another teaching opportunity, and that state would act as a home base for the remainder of her life.

Upon hearing of plans for a railroad in northern Florida, Mary saw an opportunity to fulfil her long-held dream to start a school of her own. Anticipating that the construction project would bring money and migrant families to the area, she moved her family to Daytona Beach in 1904. The Bethunes lived in one of the poorest neighborhoods in a city where Black people were lynched frequently, yet Mary also recognized that these dangers were precisely why her institution was so desperately needed.

Later that year, at just 29 years of age, Mary McLeod Bethune opened the Daytona Normal and Industrial Institute with just $1.50. She started with five girls ages 8 to 12, and one boy – her son. Parents paid 50 cents per week, and students received a school uniform and classes in business, academics, religion, and industrial skills. She also lectured to generate funds for the institution and attract new students. A Black figure of increasing influence in the Jim Crow South, she could not escape the attention of the Ku Klux Klan. Refusing to be intimidated, she reportedly stood resolute in her doorway, and the incident ended without violence.

She continued to champion education as a means for Black empowerment and began teaching evening classes for adults. By 1906, the Daytona Institute had 250 registered students, and she purchased a larger building to accommodate the growth. Shortly thereafter, her husband left the family, never to return. Undeterred, Mary continued to enhance her curriculum and purchased more property to accommodate the ever-growing student population. Still, insufficient funding again gave way to overcrowding. Though initially reluctant, the educator resolved to seek donations from wealthy White donors. A donation from James Gamble funded a new brick schoolhouse: A four-story building she named Faith Hall. Remembered as a powerful and moving orator, Mary's speaking skills were said to inspire such pledges. She subsequently received funding from Thomas H. White of White Sewing Machines, who remembered both Mary and her school in his will.

Not long after, business magnate and famed philanthropist, John D. Rockefeller, created a scholarship program for Mary through his foundation. This was the start of a lifelong association with influential allies, many of whom generously facilitated her tireless pursuit for socioeconomic equity.

Disturbed by the lack of Black-serving healthcare institutions in Daytona, she undertook more fundraising to construct a 20-bed hospital on her school campus. Philanthropist and industrial tycoon Andrew Carnegie was a benefactor of the hospital project as well as of Mary's school expansion. When her initial proposal to gain college accreditation was rejected by an all-White committee, Mary mobilized the support of her allies in response. The board approved junior-college accreditation for the school in 1913.

And the school kept growing. Always industrious, Mary took a hands-on approach to fundraising as well, often selling baked goods or traveling door-to-door on her bicycle to drum up donations. Sitting on a 20-acre campus by 1923, the school still faced financial constraints, prompting a merger with the Cookman Institute for Men in Jacksonville, Florida. Student enrollment doubled to 600, and the institution became known as the Bethune-Cookman

College in 1929. Mary also became the first Black female college president and served in that role for another 13 years.

Activism, Politics, and Legacy

Despite the demands of her educational pursuits, Mary found time to support the political interests of Black women, founding organizations to support causes that served this demographic. Once the 19th Amendment was passed, her voter-registration drive subjected her, once again, to the threatening presence of the Klan. This was but one example of the many voter-suppression tactics that kept southern Black women from the polls during this time.

In 1924, Mary won the presidency of the 10,000-member National Association of Colored Women, beating out fellow civil-rights icon Ida B. Wells. A decade later, she founded the National Council of Negro Women, which specifically sought to address issues and instances of discrimination as hindrances to African American quality of life.

Her rising profile and social connections brought her into the company of then-governor, and future president, Franklin D. Roosevelt, who later appointed Mary as advisor of minority affairs. In June 1936, she became director of the Division of Negro Affairs of the National Youth Association (NYA), making her the first Black woman to lead a federal office. She provided similar consultation at the requests of President Calvin Coolidge and President Herbert Hoover, both of whom earmarked her to join various committees.

Through much of the 1930s and early 1940s, Mary advocated for Black inclusion in New Deal policies. Toward the end of her life, yet another President, this time Harry S. Truman, selected her to attend the United Nations' founding convention. She was the sole Black woman in attendance, and this experience became the highlight of a life of extraordinary achievement.

As her health faltered, Mary retired from active employment and turned her attention to writing, while maintaining a handful of organizational affiliations. In her final moments, she wrote her last will and testament, noting that what she called her "greatest dream" – equal rights for Black people – had not yet been won. Still, her own words described her legacy as that of love across difference, a thirst for education, and an enduring hope for a better world.

Perhaps most poignantly, she understood her own sacrifices as part of the centuries-long pursuit of racial equality, stating, "[t]omorrow, a new Negro, unhindered by race taboos and shackles, will benefit from more than 330 years of ceaseless striving and struggle. Theirs will be a better world. This I believe with all my heart."

Mary McLeod Bethune died of a heart attack on May 18, 1955, at 79 years of age. She was buried on the grounds of the school she had dedicated her life to. In honor of the countless people she mentored, and those she paved the way for, her tombstone simply reads "Mother." Today, Bethune-Cookman University has nearly 3,000 students and offers 45 qualifications.

CHARLOTTE PERKINS GILMAN: A WOMAN TRAPPED BY HER TIME

American economist Charlotte Perkins Gilman was a popular lecturer who traveled widely for most of her adult years. Gilman advocated for female autonomy, outlined the need for women's financial independence, and argued that women needed to work outside of their homes. She also advocated for communal living, cooperative kitchens, and professional nurseries that would free women from the confines of domesticity.

For seven years, Gilman was also the sole writer and editor of *The Forerunner*, a magazine devoted to women and social change. Her famous novel *Herland*, about a utopian society of women, was published in installments in this magazine. She published numerous nonfiction titles as well, including her popular *Women and Economics* (1898), in which she outlined the damage done to women when society consigns them solely to the domestic sphere.

Gilman grew depressed following the birth of her child and, feeling overwhelmed by her domestic and maternal duties, escaped to California to visit friends. Her depression waned during the visit, only to return as soon as she returned to her domestic duties.

Gilman consulted with Dr. S. Weir Mitchell when she returned to New England. And Mitchell diagnosed Gilman with "hysteria." He then prescribed the then-popular "rest treatment" that was also prescribed to brilliant English writer Virginia Woolf. The treatment assumed that this skilled writer and lecturer was overtaxing her lady brain by taking on male roles instead of restricting herself to domesticity and motherhood.

Mitchell's prescription:

> Live as domestic a life as possible. Have your child with you all the time. Lie down an hour after each meal. Have but two hours' intellectual life a day. And never touch pen, brush or pencil as long as you live.

Gilman later said that this prescription nearly drove her insane.

An intellectual at heart, Gilman realized that social norms did not allow her to pursue both marriage, motherhood, and the intellectual life. And she believed her choice was between staying with her husband and "going mad" or leaving him and "staying sane."

Gilman was accused of being "unnatural" for making the decision to divorce her husband and was widely condemned for her decision to give up her daughter to the care of her ex-husband and his new wife.

In 1933, Gilman was diagnosed with breast cancer and committed suicide rather than endure a slow and painful death from the disease.

Her most enduring publication is the novella "The Yellow Wall-paper," which *The New England Magazine* published in its January 1892 edition (pp. 647–56). In the novella, ambitious women are isolated and treated for the same so-called mental exhaustion as Gilman and forbidden to engage in "unwomanly" intellectual endeavors. Nor are they allowed to speak to friends. The novella ultimately depicts how men in medical and legal positions work together to isolate, institutionalize, and harm intelligent, ambitious women.

HEDY LAMARR, INNOVATOR SUPREME

Once called the most beautiful woman in the world, Hedy Lamarr would famously say that brains are far more interesting than looks. An informed opinion, certainly, for a woman who had both. Hedwig Eva Kiesler, later known as Hedy Lamarr, was born in Vienna on

UNITED STATES PATENT OFFICE

2,292,387

SECRET COMMUNICATION SYSTEM

Hedy Kiesler Markey, Los Angeles, and George Antheil, Manhattan Beach, Calif.

Application June 10, 1941, Serial No. 397,412

6 Claims. (Cl. 250—2)

This invention relates broadly to secret communication systems involving the use of carrier waves of different frequencies, and is especially useful in the remote control of dirigible craft, such as torpedoes.

An object of the invention is to provide a method of secret communication which is relatively simple and reliable in operation, but at the same time is difficult to discover or decipher.

Briefly, our system as adapted for radio control of a remote craft, employs a pair of synchronous records, one at the transmitting station and one at the receiving station, which change the tuning of the transmitting and receiving apparatus from time to time, so that without knowledge of the records an enemy would be unable to determine at what frequency a controlling impulse would be sent. Furthermore, we contemplate employing records of the type used for many years in player pianos, and which consist of long rolls of paper having perforations variously positioned in a plurality of longitudinal rows along the records. In a conventional player piano record there may be 88 rows of perforations, and in our system such a record would permit the use of 88 different carrier frequencies, from one to another of which both the transmitting and receiving station would be changed at intervals. Furthermore, records of the type described can be made of substantial length and may be driven slow or fast. This makes it possible for a pair of records, one at the transmitting station and one at the receiving station, to run for a length of time ample for the remote control of a device such as a torpedo.

The two records may be synchronized by driv-

Fig. 2 is a schematic diagram of the apparatus at a receiving station;

Fig. 3 is a schematic diagram illustrating a starting circuit for starting the motors at the transmitting and receiving stations simultaneously;

Fig. 4 is a plan view of a section of a record strip that may be employed;

Fig. 5 is a detail cross section through a record-responsive switching mechanism employed in the invention;

Fig. 6 is a sectional view at right angles to the view of Fig. 5 and taken substantially in the plane VI—VI of Fig. 5, but showing the record strip in a different longitudinal position; and

Fig. 7 is a diagram in plan illustrating how the course of a torpedo may be changed in accordance with the invention.

Referring first to Fig. 7, there is disclosed a mother ship 10 which at the beginning of operations occupies the position 10a and at the end of the operations occupies the position 10b. This mother ship discharges a torpedo 11 that travels successively along different paths 12, 13, 14, 15 and 16 to strike an enemy ship 17, which initially occupies the position 17a but which has moved into the position 17b at the time it is struck by the torpedo 11. According to its original course, the enemy ship 17 would have reached the position 17c, but it changed its course following the firing of the torpedo, in an attempt to evade the torpedo.

In accordance with the present invention, the torpedo 11 can be steered from the mother ship 10a and its course changed from time to time as necessary to cause it to strike its target. In

U.S. Patent No. 2,292,387 for a "Secret Communication System" invented by Hedy Kiesler Markey (Hedy Lamarr) and George Antheil. The pair invented the earliest known form of a telecommunications technique called "frequency hopping." The secret system used a piano roll to manipulate radio frequencies, making it impossible for classified messages and radio-guided torpedoes to be intercepted. Years later, the invention had a global impact on everyday communications.

November 9, 1914. The only child in a wealthy Jewish family, she had the encouragement and the means to entertain big dreams.

Her father, a bank director, was a hands-on parent who desired for Hedy to develop a curious mind. She joined him on long walks, during which they had technical discussions. He would explain the mechanisms of everyday equipment they saw along the way, whether printing presses or streetcars. This intellectual foundation had a profound impact on young Hedy, giving her a healthy curiosity and a thirst for technical understanding. By age five, she was taking her music box apart to investigate how it worked.

From her mother, a concert pianist, Hedy received a talent for the arts and an array of artistic opportunities. She began piano and dance lessons at a young age, and this early introduction to a performer's life would soon serve her well. At just 16 years of age she was discovered by film director Max Reinhardt. She also took acting classes in Berlin and made her first film appearance in 1930: a minor role in a German movie called *Geld auf der Straße* ("Money on the Street"). Two years later, her role in a controversial film, *Ecstasy*, and subsequent stage acting brought her greater notoriety. Hedy was, however, yet to be a household name. Just a year later, at 19, she married Austrian munitions dealer, Fritz Mandl. Though he had been a fan of her work before he met her, the marriage proved stifling to her career ambitions and personal autonomy. As noted by *The National Women's History Museum*:

> [Hedy] once said, "I knew very soon that I could never be an actress while I was his wife.... He was the absolute monarch in his marriage.... I was like a doll. I was like a thing, some object of art which had to be guarded and imprisoned having no mind, no life of its own." She was incredibly unhappy, as she was forced to play host and smile on demand amongst Mandl's friends and scandalous business partners, some of whom were associated with the Nazi party. She escaped from Mandl's grasp in 1937 by fleeing to London but took with her the knowledge gained from dinner-table conversation over wartime weaponry.

But before the inventions came fame. A fortuitous meeting with legendary MGM studio executive Louis B. Mayer introduced Hedy to a world of opportunity. Her social circle expanded to include various accomplished, intelligent names, some of whom reinforced her inventive spirit. This was the case concerning her relationship with business mogul and aviator Howard Hughes.

Though she and Hughes were romantically involved for a time, biographers note that Hedy was primarily intrigued by his innovative mindset. The mogul encouraged her to embrace that side of herself. For instance, he gifted her with a small set of tools to use whenever she had some downtime on film sets. Moreover, Hughes introduced her to some of the engineers that he worked with, and gave her tours of his own plane factories, where she learned about the mechanisms of aviation.

Of course, Hughes was simply supporting a passion that was already there. As a working actress, Hedy was already devoting her personal time and space to inventions. In some cases, she provided the mogul with potential solutions to his own technical predicaments. For instance, Hughes wanted to produce faster planes and sell them to the military. Hedy then purchased a text about the fastest fish and birds, taking design inspiration from the shapes of their bodies to sketch a new wing design. Upon seeing this potentially more aerodynamic design, he reportedly remarked, "You're a genius."

Hedy made her most notable invention as the U.S. was gearing up for World War II. This time, her Hollywood connections introduced her to George Antheil, a formidable writer and composer also known for his multiple talents. At a dinner party, she expressed to him a desire to be more helpful during the war effort. Significantly, she had some knowledge about weaponry and munitions from her previous marriage. Thus, she and Antheil began to explore ideas. They ultimately developed a remarkable communication system intended to guide torpedoes to their targets during combat.

Neither could have predicted that this innovation would have a profound, global impact on everyday communications some decades later.

Specifically, the system used a technique called "frequency hopping," a process of switching between radio waves. Notably, the transmitter and receiver changed frequencies together, which made it impossible for radio waves to intercept, thus helping a torpedo meet its intended target. The duo secured a patent (U.S. Patent No. 2,292,387) in August of 1942 and pursued military support for their invention.

The inventive accomplishment was barely covered by the media. Moreover, the Navy chose not to adopt the proposed system. With her more direct contribution rejected, Hedy was not discouraged in her desire to serve her adopted nation. She continued to support the war effort, using her celebrity status to raise funds. A decade later, she became an American citizen.

In 1959, she and Antheil's patent expired. Her film career had ended just the year before, and she was certainly a Hollywood success story. Yet her inventive skill was largely unknown or unacknowledged by the public. Modern scholars reflect that many actors of the time were reduced to a single narrative in the eye of the public and trapped by their one-dimensional depictions onscreen. As a female actor in that overwhelmingly male-dominated industry, she was, of course, subject to the male gaze and vulnerable to sexual objectification. Ironically, this reductive process directly mirrors the dynamics Lamarr fled in her marriage: The sense of being seen as a symbol, or an item, and not a person. Widely seen as little more than the onscreen seductress, it took nearly 40 years for Lamarr to be recognized as an innovative genius.

Impact

Finally, in 1997, the Electronic Frontier Foundation gave its Pioneer Award to both Hedy and Antheil. That same year she became the first female recipient of the Invention Convention's Bulbie Gnass Spirit of Achievement Award. Though she never made a cent from her decades old patent, Lamarr was the co-inventor of frequency-hopping technology, which would later serve as a framework for today's WiFi, Bluetooth, and GPS.

As the mother of modern communication systems, Lamarr was inducted into the National Inventors Hall of Fame in 2014. Unfortunately, she did not live long enough to witness her massive impact on modern technology, having passed away at the start of the new millennium. Unfortunately, her estate has not received any compensation for the invention that is now worth billions.

Still, her descendants look upon her legacy with great pride. In an interview with *Forbes* magazine, her daughter notes that Lamarr and Betty Davis were two of the first women to own film production companies, which they used to give a platform to women's narratives and perspectives when they were few and far between.

PART TWO

Cultural Shifts and Sonic Booms, 1940–1969

Introduction: Adaptability and Innovation

Women dismantled all kinds of social, economic, and employment barriers during World War II.

Initially, a shortage of male workers forced the United States government and American businesses to actively recruit for war-industry jobs. White middle-class women were recruited first, followed by minority men, and then minority women. Integration of the workforce initially met with resistance; however, new opportunities led to profound opportunities as both civil-rights and women's movements developed in the following decades.

During World War II, six million women served in nontraditional jobs in the defense industries.

The complex challenges, hardships, and opportunities that women faced during the war years – including gender discrimination, hazardous working conditions, food rationing, and shortages of housing and childcare – occurred just after women had been scapegoated and forced back into the domestic sphere. The women who played such large roles during the war years were empowered and confident. And Eleanor Roosevelt recognized that their war-years work could be leveraged to increase workplace rights for women and marginalized populations.

CHAPTER FIVE

Calling All Women, 1940–1949

CHAPTER CONTENTS

Section 5.1 • **WOMEN IN A CHANGING WORKFORCE**

This section includes text excerpted from "The World War II Home Front" and "Rosie the Riveter Memorial" (National Park Service) • "Women in a Changing Workforce," • © 2021 Omnigraphics.

On the morning of December 7th, 1941, military forces of the Empire of Japan attacked the United States Naval Fleet and ground bases at Pearl Harbor in Hawaii. On December 8th, 1941, one day after that Day of Infamy, the United States declared war against the Empire of Japan. On December 11th, 1941, Japan's ally, Germany, declared war on the United States. Sixteen million Americans, mostly young working-age men, would serve in the military during World War II, out of an overall U.S. population of 113 million. While an unprecedented number of young men were serving in the war, the country drastically increased its war production on the home front. These production increases served not only the needs of the armed forces of the United States but of the country's allies as well, whom President Franklin D. Roosevelt referred to collectively as "The Arsenal of Democracy." The combination of so many serving in the military during a period of necessary and drastic increases in production led to unprecedented social changes on the American home front.

Top image: A munitions worker tightens nose plugs on 500-pound aerial bombs, c. 1943. • Lower image: Two Daytona Beach, Florida, housewives weld in an aircraft-construction class during World War II. Both have sons in the military, April 1942.

The nation's factories increasingly employed women whose pre-war roles kept them at home. These women helped build the aircraft, ships, and tanks vital to the war effort. Nicknamed the composite "Rosie the Riveter," these women substantially increased the production of war material to unheard of levels.

A SHORTAGE OF WORKERS

A shortage of White male workers led the United States Government and American businesses to actively recruit for war-industry jobs. Initially,

On the home front and waiting in line for rationed sugar.

White middle-class women were recruited, followed by minority men, and finally minority women. Integration of women and minorities into the workforce was initially met with resistance; however, the new opportunities for women and people of color "cracked open" the door to equal rights and would have profound impacts on the Civil Rights and Women's Movements in the following decades. During World War II, six million women served in nontraditional jobs in the defense industries. These women later came to be known as "Rosies," based on the 1943 popular song "Rosie the Riveter," about a woman building planes during the war.

BOOM TOWNS

The World War II period is when the largest number of people migrated within the United States. Individuals and families relocated to industrial centers for good-paying war jobs and out of a sense of patriotic duty. Many industrial centers became "boom towns," growing at phenomenal rates. One example, the City of Richmond, California, grew from a population of under 24,000 to over 100,000 during the war. Workers from around the nation had to intermingle with each other and overcome differences in order to meet war demands. Following World War II, many migrants decided to stay in their new homes, forever changing the cultural landscape of the United States.

Working Conditions and Challenges

Home-front workers faced many challenges and many of them led to change. Working conditions on the home front were difficult and dangerous. Between the bombing of Pearl Harbor

Poster promoting rationing on the home front during World War II

in December of 1941 and the D-Day Invasion of Europe in June of 1944, there were more home-front industrial casualties than military casualties. This high number of industrial casualties would lead to improved workplace safety and regulations. Another challenge faced by working women on the home front was childcare, as mothers comprised a significant portion of the workforce. In some progressive communities and businesses, this led to the establishment of child-development centers, although nationwide, only 10 percent of women had access to professional childcare.

Rationing on the Home Front

In addition to home front workers, everyone was expected to be an active participant in the war effort. Rationing was a way of life as twenty commodities were rationed and people were asked to "Use it up – Wear it out – Make it do – or Do without." Materials vital to the war effort were collected, often by youth groups, and recycled. Many Americans supported the war effort by purchasing war bonds. Women replaced men in sports leagues, orchestras, and community institutions. Americans grew 60 percent of the produce they consumed in "Victory Gardens." The war effort on the United States home front was a total effort.

Section 5.2 • **WOMAN WARRIORS**

This section includes text excerpted from "Women's Army Corps at Chickamauga," "Women Go to War," "Free a Marine to Fight: Women Marines in World War II," (National Park Service); "Introduction: Women Warriors,1940–1949," "Army Nurses Corps," "Cadet Nurse Corps," "Coast Guard SPARS," "Navy Nurse Corps," "Women Accepted for Volunteer Emergency Service (WAVES)," Women Airforce Service Pilots (WASP)," "Women's Auxiliary Corps (WAC)," • © 2021 Omnigraphics.

After the attack on Pearl Harbor, the United States unquestionably was in the second World War. As months passed and the American casualty rate continued to rise, the United States government recognized an urgent need for more military personnel. With much of the able-bodied male population already tapped, the government looked to the female population.

Prior to the war, women could only serve in the military in nursing and clerical positions. After the attack on Pearl Harbor, however, legislation allowed for the establishment of new military units. Women served as pilots and mechanics and in other non-combatant roles. Newly established units included the Women Accepted for Voluntary Emergency Service (WAVES), the Women's Air Force Service Pilots (WASP), the Women's Army Auxiliary Corps (WAAC initially, then WAC), and several reserve units.

1942 was a significant year for normalizing the presence of women in the armed services, but also significant because so many women had been forced or pressured out of the workplace so recently. To keep the American war effort moving forward, Congress passed a bill on May 12th,1942, that created the Women's Army Auxiliary Corps (WAAC). This bill was controversial and many opposed it. Despite the government's new propaganda campaigns that depicted women as competent and patriotic, some people in the country did not believe that women were fit for military service and others opposed the idea on a moral basis. At any rate, creating WAAC as an auxiliary force before fully integrating the unit into the army was a politically expedient decision.

Between World War I and World War II, people like Army Chief of Staff General George C. Marshall and Congresswoman Edith Nourse Rogers (who served as a Red Cross volunteer in France in 1917) periodically prodded military and elected leaders about forming an official women's corps. Marshall knew that General John J. Pershing already had specifically asked for, but not received, uniformed female troops. It is also important to note that Congresswoman Rogers was angered by the fact that so many woman warriors had been wounded and disabled during the first world war, only to be informed that they were not entitled to healthcare or veteran benefits. This is one of the reasons the Congresswoman put the armed forces on notice that "women would not again serve ... without the protection the men got."

Studies outlining how women could serve in the armed forces were readily available but, until 1941, few legislators or members of the armed forces took these studies seriously and even advocates of women serving could not agree on whether women should be enlisted directly into the military or be kept separate and consigned to an auxiliary, where they would serve – these people envisioned – as canteen workers, chauffeurs, cooks, hostesses, librarians, messengers, strolling minstrels, and waitresses.

Congresswoman Rogers eventually compromised and settled for a small women's auxiliary. In May 1941, she introduced H.R. 4906, a bill that established the WWAC, which would make available "... to the national defense the knowledge, skills, and special training of the women of the nation." Legislators argued and stalled, and even the brazen Japanese attack on Pearl Harbor was not enough to move them to pass this bill until May 15th, 1942.

The notion of an auxiliary of women who were neither military nor civilian was impractical from the start. The status failed to adequately recognize or provide benefits to women warriors whose vital leadership, sacrifices, training, and work were integral to the country's war efforts. For these reasons and more, WAAC was ultimately reclassified as the Women's Army Corps (WAC) with full military status.

Recruiting efforts for the earlier WAAC encouraged women to serve their country by working in non-combatant jobs that "freed a man" to fight on the front lines. Driven by intense patriotism, thousands of women answered the call to duty and joined the WAAC. The recruits were required to

- be between 20 and 49 years of age
- be in good health
- successfully pass an Army aptitude test, and
- have no children under 14 years of age.

Being a woman "of outstanding character" was also emphasized by WAAC, which encouraged women to "be ladies as well as soldiers."

The WAAC was a closely watched experiment that measured women's ability to participate in the armed forces and the Army wanted the best women the nation had to offer. The Army got them, and WAAC was so successful and performed so well during its first year that these women impressed both generals and government officials alike, including the president. Meanwhile, Congresswoman Rogers continued to remind people in positions of power of the brave woman warriors who served in the first world war only to be refused veteran status or benefits to cover their medical expenses when they were wounded in action.

The WAAC dropped its auxiliary status and became the Women's Army Corps (WAC), an official unit of the United States Army, on September 1st,1943. Over 150,000 women served in the U.S. Army during the war and until 1950 both on the home front and across the globe in locations such as England, France, New Guinea, North Africa, and the Philippines. By 1945, the women of the WAC drafted Army maps of war zones, drove trucks, served as Army medics and military police, and performed admirably in more than 150 other Army trades.

Woman warriors served in other branches of the military as well. The Marine Corps and Navy initially recruited women either as reservists or as Women Accepted for Volunteer Emergency Service (WAVES). The Coast Guard created a women's unit dubbed "the SPARS" (which stood for the Coast Guard motto: "Semper Paratus, Always Ready) in November. And, in 1943, two female pilot organizations merged to form the Women Airforce Service Pilots (WASP). All told, around 350,000 women served in more than 200 different capacities, gained valuable work experience, and helped the country win the war.

By the war's end, 432 women warriors had been killed and 88 had been taken prisoner, primarily in the Philippines, where they worked as nurses and cared for other American prisoners of war. Another 15 were wounded in action and awarded Purple Hearts. The Bronze Star also was awarded to 565 women, and military nurses received over 1,000 citations, commendations, and medals. These trailblazing women paved the way for later generations of American women who joined the military.

ARMY NURSE CORPS

The Army Nurse Corps was one of only two women's military units that existed before the bombing of Pearl Harbor. More than 59,000 nurses served in the Army Nurse Corps during World War II. Many of these women performed their duties under fire. These nurses evacuated, transported, and provided medical care to wounded soldiers on battlefields, in hospitals, and aboard medical transport planes, ships, and trains. With these nurses working alongside Army medics and Naval corpsmen, the military's post-injury mortality rate

Mary Lasker with President Harry S. Truman and Lucile Petry. When the U.S. Public Health Service established the Division of Nurse Education, Surgeon General Thomas Parran appointed Lucile Petry, RN, as the head of the Cadet Nurse Corps, making her the first woman to head a major division of the U.S. Public Health Service.

dropped to just 4 percent. The women in the Army Nurse Corps received commissions and full benefits.

CADET NURSE CORPS

Military Nursing Services continued to pull active graduate nurses from hospitals, health agencies, schools, and institutions, causing a drastic shortage of nurses and the shortage of trained nurses continued unabated. With no centralized recruiting effort in place and higher-paying jobs for women in the defense industry and factories further draining the pool of prospective nursing candidates, Congresswoman Frances P. Bolton introduced a bill in March of 1943 to address the crisis. The bill called for the establishment of a government program to provide grants to schools of nursing to facilitate the training of nurses to serve in the armed forces, government and civilian hospitals, health agencies, and in war-related industries.

The Bolton Act passed both houses of Congress and became law on July 1st with an initial appropriation of $65 million for the first year. Responsibility for the Cadet Nurse Corps was placed under the federal Public Health Service (PHS). The Division of Nurse

Top image: Recruiting poster for the Cadet Nurse Corps. • Lower image: The Cadet Nurse Corps was open to all, regardless of race, ethnicity or marital status. Though women of color were still underrepresented among Cadet Nurses, the common curriculum ensured that all underrepresented populations received the same training. Also, schools of nursing that discriminated against African American or other marginalized populations were at risk of losing federal funding if they continued this practice. Pictured left to right are Cadet Nurses Elizabeth Carroll, Hortense Ashe, Merdine Thompson, and Elizabeth Martin. All sat for the Ohio State Board Examinations in December of 1944.

Education was established, and Surgeon General Thomas Parran appointed Lucile Petry, RN, as the head of the corps, making her the first woman to head a major division of PHS.

On March 29th, 1943, Director Petry introduced H.R. 2326, a bill to create and fund a training program for nurses. At the insistence of powerful and influential First Lady Eleanor Roosevelt, who championed human rights and pointed out that many marginalized populations across the country lacked access to quality medical care, an amendment to the original Bolton Act resulted in the Cadet Nurse Corps being an early nondiscriminatory program. Any interested young woman could receive training. As a result of this amendment, 3,000 African Americans, 200 Asian-Pacific Island Americans, and 40 Native Americans representing twenty-five tribes were able to enroll in the program.

The only requirements a potential student had to meet were that she be between the ages of 17 and 35 years of age, be in good health, and have graduated from an accredited high school with good grades. Once these women were accepted into an accredited nursing school, qualified applicants received scholarships that covered their tuition and fees, as well as a small monthly stipend. In return, Cadets were expected to complete their training in 30 months and to provide essential nursing services for the duration of the war, either in the military or on the home front.

COAST GUARD WOMEN'S RESERVE (SPARS)

Lenah H. Sutcliffe Higbee, c. 1916, was the first chief of the Navy Nurse Corps and for her wartime efforts was awarded the Navy Cross, an award second only to the Medal of Honor. A U.S. Navy destroyer was also named in her honor. Three other nurses from the Navy Corps received the Navy Cross posthumously.

The Coast Guard Women's Reserve (SPARS) was authorized in 1941 with passage of the U.S. Coast Guard Women's Reserve Act, with the goal of placing women in roles that allowed more men to go to sea. This law was similar to the one created by the Women's Naval Reserve, or WAVES. Lieutenant Commander (later Captain) Dorothy C. Stratton was the director of the program.

Eleven thousand women eventually joined the SPARS as enlisted personnel or commissioned officers, with most serving for the duration of the war plus an additional six months. Seventy percent of these enlisted women received both recruit and specialized training, and a few worked with top-secret Long Range Aid To Navigation (LORAN) at select monitoring stations. SPARS recruits, like the women of WAVES, were restricted to service in the continental United States and were assigned to every U.S. Coast Guard district except those in Alaska, Hawaii, and Puerto Rico. Coast Guard Commodore J. A. Hirschfield noted that the SPARS women "volunteered for duty when their country needed them, and they did their jobs with enthusiasm, efficiency, and with a minimum of fanfare."

NAVY NURSE CORPS

When the war began, some 1,700 active-duty and reserve nurses formed the Navy Nurse Corps, but the corps swelled to 11,000 during World War II. When Pearl Harbor was attacked by the Empire of Japan, nurses from both the Army and Navy Nurse Corps – the only women corps in existence then – treated the casualties and cared for the wounded. In World War II, flight nurses helped evacuate wounded soldiers from combat zones. They also trained thousands of Hospital Corpsmen stationed on combat ships in how to perform nursing duties.

WOMEN ACCEPTED FOR VOLUNTEER EMERGENCY SERVICE (WAVES)

The Navy watched the unraveling of the WAAC closely as it struggled with its own version of a plan for introducing much-needed women into service. Some say there were naval officers who preferred to enlist ducks, dogs, or monkeys to solve their personnel shortage, but the decision to use women was made at the highest level. These women would be "in" the Navy.

WAVES apprentice Seaman Frances Bates inspects a Grumman Wildcat engine as part of her training at the U.S. Naval Training School (WR) Bronx, New York.

With the help of influential First Lady Eleanor Roosevelt, the Navy bill Public Law 689 was signed on July 30th, 1942. The law established the Navy Women's Reserve (WAVES) and authorized a Marine Corps Women's Reserve (MCWR), but the Marines weren't ready to concede just yet. The WAVES program was created in August 1942 as an official part of the Navy. The program, directed by Lieutenant Colonel Mildred McAfee, was initially limited to onshore tasks.

Twenty-seven thousand women joined WAVES the first year. Approximately 900 of the 27,000 performed their duties at onshore installations. They also shared the same rank as the

From left: WAFS pilots Nancy Batson, Cornelia Fort, Evelyn Sharp, Barbara J. Erickson, and Gertrude Meserve, a flight instructor who taught hundreds of students at Harvard and MIT, March 7th, 1943. When the War Department floated the idea of recruiting female pilots to meet domestic aviation needs, General Hap Arnold, Chief of the U.S. Army Air Corps, declared the idea "utterly unfeasible" and asserted that women are just too "high strung" to fly airplanes. First Lady Eleanor Roosevelt intervened and the Women's Auxiliary Ferrying Squadron (WAFS) unit was created. The WAFS team consisted of 28 commercially licensed pilots who operated under the leadership of Nancy Harkness Love. WAFS pilots initially transported military trainers and flew light aircraft from factories to domestic bases. Female pilot joined force in the Women Airforce Service Pilots (WASP) unit and their duties expanded significantly.

male sailors and were subject to comparable military discipline. The Navy's Yeomen (F) positions in World War I were primarily clerical, but women in WAVEs operated control towers, performed metalsmithing, rigged parachutes, and worked as aviation mechanics.

WOMEN AIRFORCE SERVICE PILOTS (WASP)

In 1942, pioneering racing pilot Jacqueline Cochran contacted First Lady Eleanor Roosevelt to suggest the creation of a noncombat civilian unit of female pilots. This unit would handle domestic ferrying duties, she explained, so that male pilots could serve as combat pilots. General Henry Arnold approved the program in 1942 and created the U.S. Army Air Forces Women's Flying Training Detachment (WFTD). Cochran then launched a recruiting campaign. To be accepted into the WFTD training program, recruits had to be between the ages of 21 and 35 (later 18–35), had to complete 30 weeks of flight training, and had to fly at least 35 hours before beginning her ferrying duties.

Around the same time, test pilot and fellow air racer Nancy Harkness Love, who earned her pilot's license at 16 years of age, reached out to Lieutenant General William H. Tunner of the

A WASP pilot, sometimes referred to as a "Fly Girl," circa 1943. The Women Airforce Service Pilots (WASP) pilots ferried military personnel trainers and flew light aircraft from factories to domestic bases, but also delivered bombers, fighter planes, and transport planes as well. All told, 1,070 women pilots completed WASP training and served as pilots during the war. These pioneering women paved the way for modern U.S. Air Force women pilots.

U.S. Army Air Forces about creating a Women's Auxiliary Ferrying Squadron (WAFS). This squadron would ferry planes from factories to airbases. Tunner appointed Major Love to his staff. The WFTD eventually approved this second unit.

Love commanded the WAFS and later all women's ferrying operations and was appointed to the rank of lieutenant colonel in the US Air Force reserve after the war. It is important to point out that these units were not official military units and the pilots did not have veteran status. This means the families of pilots who were killed while serving their country would receive no compensation and could not hang a gold star in their window to indicate that someone in the home had made the ultimate sacrifice in service to the country. It also meant that the army would not escort the body to the grave or drape a U.S. flag over the pilot's coffin.

In August of 1943, these two units merged to become the Women Airforce Service Pilots (WASP). Jacqueline Cochran directed the training of WASP pilots from 1943 to 1944 at Avenger Field in Sweetwater, Texas, while Nancy Harkness Love directed ferrying operations. Under her leadership, the pilots flew a full range of military aircraft, including fighter planes. They also tested aircraft, towed aerial targets for gunnery practice, ferried aircraft from factories to airbases, and ferried trainers to assigned military bases.

After the war, both of these pilots received a Distinguished Service Medal and Cochran went on to become the first woman to break the sound barrier.

WASP pilots served honorably but were among the warrior women who were told they did not qualify for veteran status when the war ended. After years of campaigning, WASP pilots did gain veteran status in the late 1970s, but Lieutenant Colonel Love was recently deceased. Jacqueline Cochran did gain veteran status, however.

WOMEN'S ARMY CORPS (WAC)

As detailed above, the Women's Army Auxiliary Corps (WAAC) was an auxiliary unit rather than an official unit of the U.S. Army. Reclassifying the auxiliary unit into a permanent unit (the Women's Army Corps), however, made WAC an official unit of the U.S. Army. WAC women received rank, benefits, and the same wage as their male counterparts, along with benefits in the event they were wounded or killed in service to their country. This reclassification also allowed African American women to serve in WAC. "The 6888," which trained at the Chickamauga Battleground, was the first all-Black female unit to serve overseas during the war. WAC women were cartographers, medics, members of the military police, and tradespeople. The women served in domestic locations as well as many theaters of war.

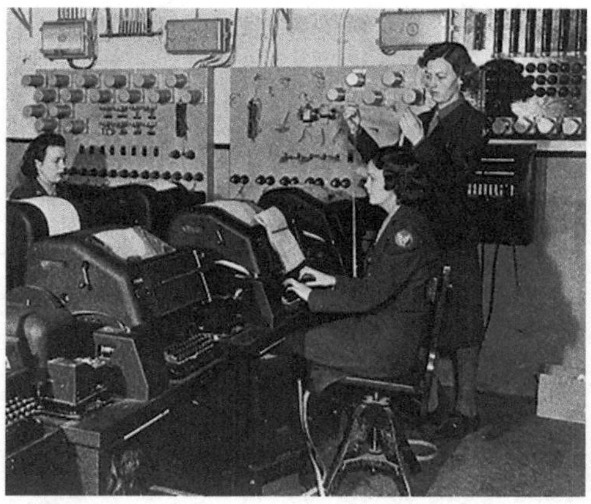

Women's Army Corps soldiers assigned to the Eighth Air Force in England operate teletype machines during World War II.

Women's Army Corps Training at Chickamauga Civil War Battleground

In July 1942, the U.S. Army converted unused school facilities at the Chickamauga Battlefield into a sprawling training complex for the Women's Army Auxiliary Corps (WAAC), established in May 1942. The next year, the WAAC received a new name, the Women's Army Corps (WAC), and the training facility at Fort Oglethorpe became the Third WAC Training Center, one of the largest training sites for women soldiers during World War II, capable of housing more than 9,000 personnel.

At Chickamauga, WACs underwent basic training before moving on to more advanced training in their individual specialties. The War Department filmed a WAC recruitment video at Fort Oglethorpe, and by the end of the war, around 50,000 women had trained at the post, including some members of the segregated 6888th Postal Battalion – the only all-Black WAC unit to deploy overseas. Women who served at Chickamauga during World War II served our country with distinction – among the women who passed through the gates of the Third WAC Training Center were Purple Heart recipients and thousands who served at or near the front lines. Some of Chickamauga's WACs gave the last full measure of devotion and are today buried in American cemeteries in France.

At the close of World War II, the Third WAC Training Center was disbanded and Fort Oglethorpe closed as a military post and became an incorporated city in the state of Georgia. Today, the legacy of Chickamauga's women soldiers can be seen not only in the lives and legacies of those who are still alive into the twenty-first century, but in the very ground at Chickamauga Battlefield. Scattered throughout the woods between Snodgrass Hill and the park visitor center are the ruins, foundations, and road traces of a once-sprawling army camp where America's young women answered the call of the duty.

WOMEN MARINES

Some stories sound too contrived to be true yet are repeated too often to be dismissed as mere folklore. One such tale was rescued and restored to its rightful place in history when Mary Eddy Furman confirmed that, yes, the portrait of Archibald Henderson, 5th Commandant of the Marine Corps, crashed from the wall to the buffet the evening that Major General Commandant Thomas Holcomb announced his decision to recruit women into the Marine Corps. Furman, then a child, was attending a military dinner party on October 12th, 1942, when the Commandant was asked, "General Holcomb, what do you think about having women in the Marine Corps?" Before he could reply, the painting of Archibald Henderson fell.

We can only surmise how Archibald Henderson would have reacted to the notion of using women to relieve male Marines "for essential combat duty." But General Holcomb's opposition was well-known. He, as many other Marines, was not happy about the prospect. But, in the fall of 1942, he was facing losses suffered during the campaign for Guadalcanal and predicted potentially significant future losses in upcoming operations. What he needed was personnel, so the Commandant did what he had to do and recommended that as many women as possible be used in noncombat billets of the Marines.

While unpopular, this idea was hardly unprecedented. Women were already serving in the Army and in Navy and Coast Guard Reserves. And, during World War I, 300 "Marinettes" had served in clerical positions, which freed male Marines working at Headquarters, Marine Corps, to go to France.

Bowing to increasing pressure from all sides, the Marine Corps proposed a women's reserve to be placed in the Adjutant-Inspector's Department. The Commandant, in the absence of reasonable alternatives, sent the recommendation to Secretary of the Navy Frank Knox, and, in the end, the matter was finally settled for the Corps on November 7th, 1942, when President Franklin D. Roosevelt gave his assent.

EARLY PLANNING

On November 5th, the Commandant wrote to the commanding officers of all Marine posts and procurement districts to prepare them for the forthcoming Marine Corps Women Reserves (MCWR) and to ask for their best estimates of the number of Women Reservists (WRs) needed to replace officers and men as office clerks, radio[wo]men, drivers, mechanics, mess[wo]men, commissary clerks, and so on. He also made clear that, within the next year, the personnel shortage would be such that it would be incumbent on all concerned with the national welfare to replace men with women in all possible positions.

Armed with the responses, planners tried to project how many women possessing the required skills would be enlisted and put to work immediately and how many would need special training in such fields as paymaster, quartermaster, and communicator. Based on their calculations, quotas were established for recruiting and training classes were scheduled.

Early estimates called for an initial target of 500 college-educated officers and 6,000 enlisted women within four months, and a total of 1,000 officers and 18,000 enlisted women by June 1944. The plan for rank and grade distribution followed the same pattern as the men's with only minor differences. For officers, there would be one major and 35 captains, with the balance of the remaining commissioned officers being first and second lieutenants. The highest rank, fixed by Public Law 689, permitted one lieutenant commander in the Women's

Private First Class Priscilla Goodrich (left) and Private Elaine Munsinger (right) of the Wrench and Hammer Brigade break down an airplane engine in the Assembly and Repair department at Marine Corps Air Station Cherry Point, North Carolina, c. 1943.

Reserve of the U.S. Naval Reserve, whose counterpart in the Marine Corps would be a major. Eventually, the law was amended so that the senior woman in the Navy and Coast Guard was promoted to captain and in the Marine Corps to colonel.

The public, anticipating a catchy nickname for women Marines, much like the WACS, WAVES, and SPARS, bombarded Headquarters with suggestions: MARS, Femarines, WAMS, Dainty Devil-Dogs, Glamarines, Women's Leather-neck Aides, and even Sub-Marines. Surprisingly, considering his open opposition to using women at all, General Holcomb adamantly ruled out all cute names and acronyms. After answering yet another reporter on the subject, the General stated his views very forcefully in an article in the March 27, 1944, issue of *Life* magazine: "They are Marines. They don't have a nickname and they don't need one. They get their basic training in a Marine atmosphere at a Marine post. They inherit the traditions of Marines. They are Marines."

Marine women of World War II were enormously proud to belong to the only military service that shared its name with them and insisted upon it. It happened that, in practice, they were most often called Women Reservists though, which was informally shortened to WRs. When referred to as women Marines, or Marine women, the "w" was not capitalized as it was later, after passage of the Armed Forces Integration Act of 1948 granted women regular status in the military. Then, Women Marines were best known as WMs. In fact, women would have to wait 30 years before the gender designator would be dropped and they at last would be simply Marines.

In 1943 the country desperately needed womanpower. By custom, working women were mainly employed in beauty shops, classrooms, hospitals, libraries, offices, retail stores, or in homes as domestics. Not many women drove trucks or buses, and they certainly didn't fix them. Women did not work in trade roles in areas such as plumbing, electrical, or carpentry (although some did in the first world war). And they rarely supervised men. Widely accepted social norms at the time deemed certain jobs too dirty, too dangerous, too strenuous, or for unspecified reasons, just not suitable for women.

In this socioeconomic climate, the Marine Corps set out to select, train, classify, and assign 18,000 newly recruited civilian women at the rate of more than 1,000 per month, and to have them on the job and making a contribution in the shortest time possible. That it was done as magnificently as it was is a tribute both to the women who made it happen and to the men who allowed it to happen.

The 1943 Marine recruiting brochures promised women openings in 34 job assignments. Final statistics indicate that women served in more than 200. Such miscalculations led to bothersome reassignments when newly identified, high-priority jobs had to be assigned but qualified women were no longer available. For example, the first calls for IBM tabulating-machine operators, teletypewriter operators, sewing-machine operators, drafts[wo]men, utility repair[wo]men, and even telephone operators came only after many women with this kind of civilian training and experience had been assigned to other duties.

Expensive errors in judgment were made because no one knew exactly how many women were needed and Marines underestimated the skills and efficiency of their female recruits. As a result, they requested far too many women, especially for office work at Headquarters, because they thought that fifty percent more women would be needed to replace the work of the men. For clerical work, the reverse was generally true.

Adding to the confusion, many men did not understand the duties involved in specific job titles and this led to Marines who could not dictate requesting stenographers, and Marines who needing filing clerks asking for clerk typists. In the end, large numbers of WMs felt let down and were bored by monotonous assignments that took only a fraction of their time and made scant demands on their skills. Colonel Ruth Cheney Streeter, the Director of the Marine Corps Women's Reserve, understood their frustration and made it a habit to visit WMs in the field often to give regular pep talks on the vital importance of every job to the overall war effort.

Contradicting the adage that there is never too much of a good thing, these women of exceptionally high caliber who were recruited in the early phases of the war were also responsible for so many underemployed WRs. In Colonel Streeter's opinion:

> In test scores, educational level, civilian experience, and special skills, these women, as a group, were well above "average." Only a few of the jobs open to them in the Marine Corps were "above average" in responsibility and demands for skill, a great majority of the jobs were quite ordinary, and many more were actually extremely simple. Yet, somebody

> had to do these simple jobs. There were not enough women sufficiently lacking in intelligence, clerical ability, education and skill to be happy in these simple jobs. So, Women Reservists capable of more skilled work had to be misassigned – especially at first and especially at Headquarters, Marine Corps.

More than half of all Women Reservists were engaged in clerical work, about the same percentage as in civilian life. But new ground was broken as women went to work as radio operators, parachute riggers, motor transport drivers, aerial gunnery instructors, cooks, bakers, Link trainer instructors, control-tower operators, motion-picture technicians, automotive mechanics, teletype operators, cryptographers, laundry managers, post exchange salespersons and managers, auditors, audiovisual librarians, assembly and repair mechanics, weather observers, artists, aerial photographers, photograph analysts, chemists, postal clerks, musicians, statisticians, stewardesses, and writers.

MATCH SKILLS TO NEEDS

World War II changed for all time the notion of proper women's work. In the armed forces as in civilian life, necessity caused the rules to be rewritten and while an effort was made to fit the women into jobs related to their former occupations, there was, by necessity, an openness to new ideas.

Fewer Marine women than civilians were used as stenographers and general clerks, but more were assigned as typists; fewer were used as office machine operators, but far more were assigned to supply and supervisory work. Fewer women Marines were considered professionals in the Corps, but this was due to the large number of schoolteachers who enlisted but were not used as instructors. Fewer women were used in skilled trades than came from these jobs in civilian life as well, but more women proportionately were used in mechanical jobs than came from these jobs as civilians – especially in aviation.

Section 5.3 • UNITED NATIONS CHARTER

"The United Nations Charter," • © 2021 Omnigraphics.

The late 19th nineteenth century saw a rise in organizations designed to facilitate international relations. The Red Cross was among the best known and earliest manifestations of this intention. By World War I, however, there were over 400 cross-border organizations of its kind. From the 1920s emerged the most prominent international governing body seen thus far: The League of Nations. Though the league endured for a quarter-century, it was largely ineffective, and its failure to prevent another global war highlighted the need for a more impactful organization.

This is the gap that the United Nations (UN) charter sought to address in 1941. Though the charter was drafted that year, it underwent a series of debates, evaluations, and alterations for another four. The end of the war revealed an even greater need for an organization of its type, and the 51 nations steering the process finalized the document on June 26th, 1945.

At the UN Conference on International Organization in San Francisco, 50 of the 51 founding nations signed the charter. The last remaining country (Poland) endorsed it two months later, and the charter came into force in October 1945. Notably, only 4 of the 850 international delegates who signed the document were women. Still, gender equality was acknowledged as instrumental to the organization's mandate to uphold human rights.

The following year, the UN made a notable step to honor this claim by establishing the Commission on the Status of Women (CSW). This was the first intergovernmental organization exclusively dedicated to facilitating gender equality and female empowerment. To that end, the CSW continues to support the advancement of women's rights, documents issues pertaining to women's lived experiences across the globe and contributes to global standards concerning gender equality.

Eleanor Roosevelt

Trailblazing human-rights advocate and First Lady Eleanor Roosevelt led the UN Commission on Human Rights. The commission obtained passage of the UN's Declaration of Human Rights, which provides that everyone is entitled to the Declaration's rights and freedoms without "distinction of any kind, such as race [and] ... sex...."

The Declaration also explicitly provides for the equality of women and men in marriage: "Men and women of full age ... are entitled to equal rights as to marriage, during marriage, and at its dissolution."

Section 5.4 • **UNCREDITED TRAILBLAZERS**

Portions of this section are excerpted from "Alice Austen" (National Park Service); "Chien-Shiung Wu," "Invisible Women Create Modern Computing: The ENIAC Women," • 2021 Omnigraphics.

ALICE AUSTEN

Elizabeth Alice Austen was born in 1866 in Staten Island, New York. She was one of the nation's earliest and most prolific female photographers.

Austen lived most of her life in "Clear Comfort," which was her maternal grandparents' home.

Oswald Muller, Alice's uncle, brought home a camera when she was ten years old. This camera was believed to be a dry plate camera. As Oswald experimented with the camera Alice watched and helped by holding the camera steady on its tripod. Oswald was a sea captain, and when it was time for him to sail away again, he gave Alice permission to use the camera. Alice's uncle Peter, a chemistry professor, taught her how to develop the glass plates she exposed and how to make prints from them.

By the time Alice was 18, she was an experienced photographer with professional standards. Her family members and the Austen house and gardens served as her first subjects. She also made early self-portraits.

Alice was active and social. And she took her equipment, which weighed as much as fifty pounds and filled a steamer trunk, everywhere she went. She photographed Midland and South Beaches in Staten Island and winter skating parties on Staten Island's frozen ponds and creeks. Alice enjoyed many sports, including the new sport of lawn tennis. In 1885 the first tennis club in the nation was established in Livingston, Staten Island. Alice spent many afternoons there, both as a player and taking photos of the other players and spectators.

During the 1890s, Alice began to travel outside of Staten Island to upstate New York, Vermont, Illinois, and Massachusetts. She also began traveling to Europe around this time. In addition to photographing her travels to these areas, Alice would take pictures of everyday people in New York City.

Alice lived a privileged life and was a prominent member of Staten Island society until the Stock Market Crash of 1929. From that point on, she struggled to survive. Alice and Gertrude Tate, her life-long companion, tried to open a Tea Room on the lawn of the family house, but were never able to achieve a profit. She began to sell off her possessions and mortgaged her house several times until she lost it in 1945. She sold off all of the remaining items in the house to a dealer in New Jersey, except for her glass-plate negatives.

Alice declared herself a pauper in 1950 and was admitted to the local poor house. At the same time Alice's negatives were discovered by a group planning to write a book on the history of American women. Alice was able to make enough money from the publishing of these photos to move into a private nursing home.

Alice died in 1952 and was buried in the Moravian Cemetery in Staten Island. Although she and Gertrude wished to be buried together, their families denied their wish.

CHIEN-SHIUNG WU

Chien-Shiung was born in China on May 31st, 1912 and grew up in a small fishing town near Shanghai. To her great fortune, her father not only believed in the importance of education but felt that girls were entitled to formal education – an uncommon belief at that time. The progressive patriarch was also the founder of the elementary school that young Chien-Shiung attended.

In 1934, at the age of 22, Chien-Shiung received a degree in physics from Nanjing University (known as the National Central University at the time) and graduated at the top of her class. Upon graduation, she obtained a position doing lab work in China. At the encouragement of her mentor, a female physicist, Chien-Shiung opted to further her education in the United States.

Financial support from extended family helped make this dream a reality, and Chien-Shiung enrolled at the University of California, Berkeley in 1936. She soon began rubbing shoulders with some academic greats in her field. In 1939, her academic advisor, Ernest Lawrence, received the Nobel Prize in Physics for inventing the cyclotron particle accelerator. By 1940, she graduated with a doctorate in physics and was well on her way to becoming a leading scientist herself.

Just two years later, she became the first female faculty member in the physics department at Princeton University. Two years after that, in 1944, she arrived in New York City to join yet another Ivy League institution: Columbia University. It is through this prestigious

The experiments of Columbia University physicists (left to right) Chien-Shiung Wu, Y. K. Lee, and L. W. Mo confirmed the theory of conservation of vector current. In the experiments, which took several months to complete, proton beams from Columbia's Van de Graaff accelerator were transmitted through pipes to strike a 2 mm. Boron target at the entrance to a spectrometer chamber.

appointment that she joined the Manhattan Project team, conducting research that helped create the world's first atomic bomb. Even in the absence of this milestone, she was already breaking barriers for minorities, being one of very few female senior researchers in the War Department, and the only person of her race.

Chien-Shiung supported the project by helping solve significant problems concerning uranium enrichment and radiation detection. In 1945, these efforts culminated in the bomb's creation, though Chien-Shiung would later express dismay concerning its devastating deployment over Hiroshima and Nagasaki. Historians note that her work ultimately helped bring the war to a much speedier end than could otherwise have been expected.

The Manhattan Project was a top-secret initiative during its time, and credit was later given to her former professor, Robert Oppenheimer, and her mentor, Enrico Fermi, but not to her. To this day, Oppenheimer and Fermi remain more prominent names and are widely acknowledged as the scientific minds behind the atomic bomb. This was not the last time that Chien-Shiung would be overlooked in this fashion.

A Second Credit Controversy

At Columbia University nearly a decade later, Chien-Shiung once again made a monumental contribution to the field of physics. She developed an experiment that tested the law of parity conservation by "observing beta decay at ultracold temperatures." Through this work, she ultimately disproved what was once believed to be an indisputable law of physics. Her results validated the theories of two male colleagues who initially made the hypothesis and subsequently received the Nobel Prize.

In an interview for *CBS*, contemporary professor of physics and mathematics at Columbia, Brian Green, states that Chien-Shiung's work "radically changed our view of the universe." Indeed, scientists had a longstanding assumption that the universe was symmetrical. Thus, it was not thought necessary to differentiate between left and right. By demonstrating that this law was false, she availed new frameworks from which to consider the nature of the atom and of the universe itself. Some propose that her discovery may be as monumental as Einstein's realization of the theory of relativity. Though the experiment she developed is now named in her honor, many believed and continue to believe that she was unfairly overlooked by the Nobel committee in 1957.

The American Association of University Women explains the controversy in greater detail:

> Her colleagues Tsung-Dao Lee and Chen Ning Yang proposed a theory that would disprove a widely accepted law of physics at the time called the Parity Law. Parity Law stated that objects that are mirror images of each other behave in the same way. Wu's experiment spun radioactive cobalt-60 nuclei at low temperatures. If the law held, the electrons would shoot off in paired directions. Wu's experiment demonstrated that they did not.
>
> Wu's work was termed the most important development in the field of atomic and nuclear physics to date; a 1959 AAUW press release called her experiment the "solution to the number-one riddle of atomic and nuclear physics." Her male coworkers Lee and Yang received the Nobel Prize for disproving the Parity Law … the prize committee overlooked Wu.

Some of the leading physicists of her time shared the view that she was unjustly overlooked. Indeed, Nobel laureates Willis Lamb, Polykarp Kusch, and Emilio Segrè advocated on her behalf. Though many believe that sexism played a part in her exclusion, others propose that there is more to the story. Contemporary chemist and historian Magdolna Hargittai proposes that Chien-Shiung's exclusion was, at least in part, due to a technicality:

> Wu and colleagues saw the first hints of parity violation on 27 December 1956. Shortly after news of this preliminary result got out, an independent group working at the Columbia cyclotron did a quick measurement in early January and observed parity violation in muons – at about the same time as Wu and colleagues were making their definitive measurements. What is more, a third group at the University of Chicago had been looking for parity violation since the summer of 1956 and had also found preliminary evidence by December.
>
> The Wu-NBS and Columbia cyclotron teams published their results in the February 1957 issue of the *Physical Review* and the Chicago paper was published in the March issue of the same journal. Therein lies a major barrier to Wu sharing the 1957 prize. According to the Nobel rules, the 1957 prize cannot be awarded for work published in 1957. Indeed,

the Nobel Prize nomination archive shows that neither Wu, nor anyone else who had measured parity violation in 1956–57, had been nominated for the 1957 prize.

Others note that the Nobel Committee also had a limit of three nominees, meaning that Chien-Shiung was excluded, among others. Finally, another school of thought is that she was left out because she was not the author of the original hypothesis: Her experiment was ultimately reliant upon the ideas of Lee and Yang, which it tested. Still, the laureates themselves acknowledged her contribution as significant when they received the award.

There are no doubts concerning the impact of Chien-Shiung's work, which was recognized as singular even during her era. Though she did not win a Nobel Prize for her discovery, she became the first person to receive a Wolf Prize, now considered the second most prestigious scientific award. Perhaps most importantly, she went on to enjoy an illustrious, highly commended career as a scientist, researcher, and professor. A testament to her enduring professional reputation, she is nicknamed "The First Lady of Physics" and "Queen of Nuclear Research."

In early 2021, Chien-Shiung was honored and immortalized by a U.S. postal stamp bearing her likeness. In an interview with the *Washington Post*, her granddaughter described the pioneer as "someone who just had no doubt in her abilities, and no doubt in the idea that women and girls had the same abilities as men ... but were simply not given the same opportunities."

She retired from Columbia University in 1981 and died in New York City, in 1997. Her ashes are buried in the courtyard of the elementary school she had the privilege to attend as a little girl. Chien-Shiung is remembered for changing the way that scientists view the world, and for the humility that led her to declare that scientific discovery itself is the "the reward of a lifetime."

INVISIBLE WOMEN CREATE MODERN COMPUTING: THE ENIAC WOMEN

During World War II, the U.S. Army partnered with physicist John Mauchly, engineer J. Presper Eckert, and their team of mathematicians and engineers at the University of Pennsylvania Moore School of Electrical Engineering to develop, design, and construct the first large-scale, programmable, "general-purpose" digital computer as part of its classified Project PX, a secret war initiative.

The government funded this $400,000 project and the team built the Electronic Numerical Integrator and Computer (ENIAC). Female mathematicians employed as "human computers" were the ones who programmed the computer and rendered it functional, though.

The ENIAC was huge. It had 1,500 mechanical relays, and programmers used plugboards to communicate with this powerful calculating device. Each new calculation also required days to program before the ENIAC could compute values accurately and at optimal speed.

Six of the army's best human computers, who had calculated ballistic trajectories before this assignment, programmed the computer to perform the rapid-fire calculations that the government needed to construct a hydrogen bomb.

Programmers Betty Jennings (left) and Frances Bilas (right) operating the ENIAC's main control panel, c.1945–1947.

Kathy Kleiman, a computer programmer, was an undergraduate student at Harvard University in 1985 when she went in search of female "role models and inspiration." She soon discovered a 1946 photo of the ENIAC and was surprised to see that the photo included women and men – and that these women appeared to be programming the computer. She also discovered what anyone who digs through archives long enough will tell you: That it is exceedingly difficult to determine who the women in a photograph are when it never occurs to the photographer or employer or engineer or coworkers or men in the same lab with the women – or perhaps an entire army – that those women might be consequential enough to at least identify along with the men. Kleiman recognized that she was looking at pioneers in her field and asked the cofounder of the nearby Computer History Museum to help her identify the women; the cofounder, however, told her that these women were just models, so there was no reason to identify them.

It took years, but Kleiman was finally able to track down and identify these six "pioneers in early programming and software": Kathleen "Kay" McNulty Mauchly Antonelli, Jean Jennings Bartik, Frances Elizabeth "Betty" Snyder Holberton, Marlyn Wescoff Meltzer, Frances Bilas Spence, and Ruth Lichterman Teitelbaum – all rendered invisible, and never before mentioned or recognized for their achievements.

Kleiman and film producer David Roland arranged to record 20 hours of the oral histories of these women, and when she learned that they had not been invited to the ENIAC fiftieth-anniversary celebration, she started amplifying their stories and nominating them for awards. By 1997, each of these pioneers had received awards at the highest levels of computing and each had been inducted into the Women in Technology International Hall of Fame.

Kleiman went on to produce the inspirational film *The Computers: The Remarkable Untold Story of the ENIAC Programmers*. She also shared the women's story in her TEDx talk "The Secret History of the ENIAC Women," during which she reminded the audience that it is not easy to change enduring American narratives that elevate the accomplishments of the people who hold the power, but it is necessary.

Section 5.5 • TRAILBLAZERS

"Trailblazing Human-Rights Advocate Eleanor Roosevelt," • © 2021 Omnigraphics.

TRAILBLAZING HUMAN-RIGHTS ADVOCATE ELEANOR ROOSEVELT

Even now, nearly sixty years after her death, Anna Eleanor Roosevelt is remembered as one of the most admired and beloved women of the twentieth century. Born in October 1884, her early life was a juxtaposition of social privilege and personal turmoil.

She was the eldest child in a family that was among the wealthiest in New York. Of course, financial security could not make her immune to the gendered expectations typical of the age. Eleanor was not a conventional beauty, a "failure" that incurred her mother's disappointment. Though her father showed her great affection, his battle with substance addiction ultimately wreaked havoc on the family.

By the time she was six, he had gone to Europe to receive treatment for his addictions, leaving his wife to raise the three Roosevelt children alone. Just two years later, Eleanor's mother came down with diphtheria (an infection of the nose and throat) and, following a surgery, died. Tragedy soon struck again when both her brothers contracted scarlet fever, and only the younger one survived. Then her father, his addictions worsened by grief, died in 1894. By age ten, Eleanor had lost all but one member of her immediate family.

She and her young brother were sent to live with their maternal grandmother, Mary Hall, and Eleanor soon left for finishing school in London. She then returned to New York to make her social debut as expected of girls of her class. There, a chance encounter with a future president changed her life forever.

The Road to the White House

In 1902, she unexpectedly ran into Franklin Delano Roosevelt on a train. Franklin was her fifth cousin, once removed and Eleanor regularly saw him during social events. This encounter, however, sparked a courtship that soon led to an engagement when she 19 and he 21. Though she was certainly young, Eleanor already had a strong sense of empathy, as evidenced by her active engagement in social-welfare initiatives. She was a prominent member of the Junior League, an organization for privileged young ladies involved in charitable work. Eleanor also visited tenement houses, where she availed her tutoring skills to impoverished families.

She married Franklin in 1905 and had six children in the next decade, though one died as an infant. Following this, a protracted extramarital affair changed the couple's marriage forever. Biographers state that Eleanor never quite trusted Franklin again, and their relationship

First Lady Eleanor Roosevelt addressing the Democratic National Convention on July 18, 1940, in Chicago.

morphed into a platonic partnership. This private agreement may explain the unconventional independence and freedom that marked Eleanor's tenure as first lady.

In 1920, Franklin joined the ticket of Democratic party presidential candidate James Cox. The pair did not win the election, but the campaign sparked Franklin's ambition for the nation's highest office. The following year, he suffered a devastating setback when he contracted polio, which left him unable to walk.

Members of his circle, including his mother, believed this to be the end of his career, but Eleanor strongly opposed this rhetoric. This show of strength put an end to family dynamics that had long been stifling and disempowering. She supported her husband during his physical recovery and began to give him political counsel, too. He returned to the political arena, and to the public eye, in 1928, winning the New York City governorship. In 1933, he won the presidential race against an increasingly unpopular Herbert Hoover, whose handling of the Great Depression was a source of national scorn.

Service and Sacrifice

Now first lady, Eleanor was hardly pleased. She had successfully crafted a life of independence in New York and was reluctant to leave it behind. Most of all, she did not want to part ways with the Todhunter School, where she was both teacher and co-owner. She recognized that the resources availed by the presidency could bring her philanthropic ambitions to life, however.

This desire to impact meaningful social change helped her distinguish herself from the first ladies before her. Traditionally, these women were relegated to supporting roles and expected to do little more than stand beside their husbands or act as dutiful hosts. Eleanor was just the opposite. The president did not want the public to know that he was immobile, so she often assumed presidential duties that required travel. She would inform him of concerns and developments through memos, often sending word about the needs she saw on the ground during the worsening economic crisis.

She also took on additional labor to advocate for equity by attending speaking engagements and championing the needs of vulnerable groups. She began to establish herself as an ally for women, racial minorities, and the socioeconomically disadvantaged, including individuals without housing security. Moreover, she proved herself a woman of the people. Her famous Sunday egg scrambles (breakfast events she hosted for civilians) were an opportunity to learn the needs and struggles of everyday Americans – in their own words, and from their own perspectives.

As many human- and civil-rights leaders before her, she did not negate the power of the written word. In 1936, Eleanor debuted a newspaper column that often engaged with contentious issues of the time, such as the rights of women and minorities. "My Day" ran six days a week for 26 years. Such was her commitment to its authorship that she missed just four publications when her husband died in 1945.

In 1940, Franklin won his second reelection, making him the first (and last) president to serve more than two terms in American history. That same year, Eleanor had a landmark moment of her own when she gave a speech to the Democratic National Convention, becoming the first woman to address a national presidential convention.

In the aftermath of World War II, she recognized that increased demand for women's labor could be leveraged into progress for women's workplace rights. She had long been a champion of diversity in the workforce, even at the highest levels of government. Indeed, a decade before, she had advocated for the hiring of Frances Perkins, whom her husband ultimately appointed as the first woman to join the presidential cabinet. The first lady believed that all people had the right to join the American labor force. She wanted to eliminate racial discrimination in the workforce, and argued for equal pay, equal employment opportunities, and rights for all.

In many instances, she also took a stance against comparatively smaller demonstrations of institutional racism. One famous example involved the Daughters of the American Revolution. The organization denied songstress Marian Anderson the chance to perform at its concert hall because she was Black. In response, the first lady issued a personal invite for Anderson to perform in front of a national audience in Washington, D.C., then promptly cancelled her membership with the offending organization. She also spoke out against the proliferation of anti-Japanese racism following Pearl Harbor and opposed the government's decision to send Japanese Americans to internment camps.

She traveled internationally to visit soldiers during the war, earning the code name "Rover" from Secret Service and "Everywhere Eleanor" from the public (because one never knew where she would be next). Because her dedication to human rights sometimes stood in stark contrast to the dominant beliefs of the time, some gave her a less light-hearted descriptor: "Public Energy Number One."

Shortly before the end of the war, Franklin was elected for his fourth presidential term, but he died the following year. Eleanor initially announced that she, too, would retreat from public life. Subsequently, President Harry S. Truman helped change her mind by asking that she serve the nation as its first delegate during the founding of the United Nations (UN). She accepted and became emersed in the role, constantly attending meetings and studiously researching political issues.

Poignantly, biographers note that she was partly motivated by a fear that failing to do well would "reflect badly on all women." Conversely, the general consensus was that she did a brilliant job, particularly in relation to the Universal Declaration of Human Rights, which she helped draft in 1948. Shortly thereafter, the declaration was ratified by 48 nations. In the years after, Eleanor held various appointments with the UN, including that of goodwill ambassador. Each was an opportunity to fashion a more equitable world and deepen her understanding of the human condition.

In 1959, Eleanor joined the faculty at Brandeis University as a lecturer on politics and human rights. In 1962, aged 78, she discovered that she had aplastic anemia and tuberculosis, and did not live to see another year. She is remembered as former President Truman once described her: "The First Lady of the World."

CHAPTER SIX

Suspicion, Purges, and Oppression, 1950–1959

CHAPTER CONTENTS

Section 6.1 • **OVERVIEW**

"Overview: Women in the Workplace in America, 1950–1959," • © 2021 Omnigraphics.

The 1950s were a hypervigilant decade during the Cold War era when social norms sometimes seemed like cloaks people donned to keep themselves under the radar.

The image of women that the mass media pushed during those years was the ideal of a modern, White, middle-class suburban housewife who blissfully moved through her days of "natural" domestic tranquility while using shiny new consumer products. But trailblazing women were working behind the scenes to usher in new technologies, new understandings, and a broader range of opportunities for women in the workplace and beyond.

Section 6.2 • **THE MYTH OF FEMALE INFERIORITY**

"The Myth of Female Inferiority," • © 2021 Omnigraphics.

Physical anthropologist Ashley Montagu questioned the myth of female inferiority in his provocative article "The Natural Superiority of Women," published in the *Saturday Evening Post* to widespread media attention. Montagu also challenged Dr. Sigmund Freud's assertion that women are incomplete men and demonstrated that, chromosomally, men are incomplete women who have unconscious "womb and breast envy."

Montagu cited research showing that women are not vulnerable and delicate at all, as had been claimed for years, but instead resist physical and emotional stress far better than their

Biologist working in a lab

male counterparts. He also explained that "the mother–child relationship has the advantage of having to be more considerate, more self-sacrificing, more cooperative, and more altruistic than usually falls to the lot of the male."

Section 6.3 • TRAILBLAZERS

"Grace Hopper," "Clare Booth Luce," "Rosa Parks," and "Margaret Chase Smith," • © 2021 Omnigraphics.

MATHEMATICAL AND PROGRAMMING PIONEER COMMANDER GRACE HOPPER HELPS CREATE COBOL

Grace Brewster (Murray) Hopper was born to Walter Fletcher and Mary Campbell in New York City in 1906. As an undergraduate at Vassar College, her academic prowess won her a place in the Phi Beta Kappa National Honor Society. In 1828, at the age of 22, she graduated with degrees in both physics and mathematics. She then pursued a M.S. degree in mathematics at Yale University, where her father had studied before her. Then the budding mathematician opted to remain at the University for her doctorate degree, which she earned in 1934.

After the bombing of Pearl Harbor, Grace felt a strong desire to join the war effort. She was in her late thirties by then and stood only 4 feet and 8 inches tall. Her age and stature prompted the Navy to deny her initial petition to join Women's Reserve. However, in 1943, she was granted permission to undergo intensive military conditioning, so she promptly took a sabbatical from Vassar, where she was an assistant professor. Hopper then completed a two-month training program through the Midshipmen's School for Women at Smith College and became a Navy lieutenant junior grade. Assigned to the Bureau of Ships Computation Project at Harvard University, she joined a team working on the first electromechanical computer in the country, known as MARK I. A pioneering programmer, she was also responsible for authoring the machine's nearly 600-page manual. Beyond this, she was working on classified mathematical assignments (e.g., calculating rocket trajectories) deemed crucial to the U.S. war effort.

When the war ended, Grace was offered a full professorship at Vassar, which she ultimately turned down to continue her work with computers. In 1946, the Navy refused her request for a regular commission because of her age, and she ended her active service (though she remained a naval reservist). A three-year research fellowship at Harvard followed. When this opportunity ended, she found the institution had no permanent positions for women, which left her little choice but to move on. As fate would have it, she took a senior mathematician position at the Eckert-Mauchly Computer Corporation in Philadelphia. Under army contracts, the company had successfully built the first electronic computer. By the time Grace joined the team, it had another major development underway: The first commercial electronic computer, known as UNIVAC. While working on the UNIVAC I and II, Grace took an interest in developing new coding methods and suggested the novel concept of automatic programming. In 1952 she created the first compiler to translate mathematical codes into data that machines could read, thereby laying the foundation for modern programming languages.

The following year, Grace had another innovative idea and suggested that programs be written in words instead of symbols. This proposition was met with skepticism and resistance, but she began developing an English-language compiler anyway. Her determination paid off with the 1956 debut of FLOW-MATIC: The first programming language to operate through word commands. Notably, Grace also accounted for the need to write programs in languages other than English, providing foundational guidance on how this could be done.

The prospect of using word-based languages made computers much more user-friendly for the average person who did not have specialized training in engineering or mathematics. Since computer manufacturers were looking to enter the private sector, this development vastly extended their potential reach. Grace also recognized that computer technology could simplify and streamline common business processes such as payroll and wanted to make computers better suited for the regular working world.

As she expected, the use of personal computers soon skyrocketed and, with their popularity, several computer languages emerged. This development necessitated a standardized business language, and Grace sought to fill this gap. The COmmon Business-Oriented Language (COBOL) emerged from the 1959 Conference on Data Systems Languages. While its development was a collaborative effort, Grace's contribution stood out. She is credited with designing COBOL, developing its compilers and fostering its massive reach.

Just a decade later, COBOL was a leading global computer language. However, as technology advanced, COBOL's popularity began to decline. Moreover, many programmers skilled in the language had reached retirement age and left the labor market. Still, the language retains popularity among institutions. Despite being over 60 years old, companies and businesses still favor this program for business, finance, and administrative systems. As recently as 2017, COBOL boasted over 200 million global lines of usage and many of our regular financial transactions are made possible by this system. Indeed, a report from Reuters found that COBOL supports:

- 43 percent of all banking systems
- The generation of approximately $3 trillion in daily commerce
- 95 percent of all card swipes at ATMs
- 80 percent of all in-person credit-card transactions.

Legacy

In addition to her obvious intellect, Grace was also a testament to what women workers could do in a more equitable world. Biographers note that her entry into young adulthood coincided with a period of unusual opportunity for American women. In the 1920s and 1930s, the number of women earning doctorates was at a relative high, a phenomenon that would not be seen again for some decades. Not long after Grace received her doctorate, labor demands associated with the war helped to expand women's opportunities to join the workforce.

This is, of course, not to dismiss the obstacles she certainly faced. Ageism, in particular, repeatedly prevented her from providing the level of military service that she aspired to, both in her thirties and in her later years, when she resumed her naval career.

In 1991, Grace was awarded the National Medal of Technology, becoming the first woman to receive it independently. In her remarks, she noted that teaching and mentorship were her greatest source of professional pride, stating, "all the young people I've trained over the years; that's more important than writing the first compiler." Today, the Grace Hopper Celebration of Women in Computing Conference honors its namesake's love of mentorship by encouraging women to venture into computing. Similarly, the Association for Computing Machinery offers an award named after the pioneer, who passed away in 1992.

In 2013, she was commemorated with a "Google Doodle" on what would have been her 107th birthday. In 2016, she posthumously received the Presidential Medal of Freedom. Known as "Amazing Grace" to her military subordinates, she is remembered as a retired navy commander, a formidable teacher, and a mathematician of monumental aptitude.

CLARE BOOTH LUCE BECOMES FIRST WOMAN AMBASSADOR TO A MAJOR POSTING

Clare Boothe Luce made a name for herself early on. By age 32, she was a well-known author, journalist, and a managing editor affiliated with publications like *Vogue* and *Vanity Fair*. She also had penned a classic Broadway play led by an all-female cast: The 1936 comedy, *The Women*. Though she would ultimately write eight plays, three books, and numerous movie scripts, she is also remembered as a politician and a diplomat.

In 1942, Clare won a Republican seat in the House of Representatives, ultimately representing the state of Connecticut for two terms. Along with her husband, a renowned media magnate, she became an early supporter of Dwight D. Eisenhower's presidential candidacy. Upon winning the election, the president sought to reward the couple for their patronage and offered Clare the position of Secretary of Labor.

Ultimately, it was decided that she would serve as U.S. ambassador to Italy, an opportunity deemed a better fit for various reasons. Not only did she speak Italian, she was one of the most prominent Catholic converts in the U.S. – a fact expected to garner some warmth in the majority-Catholic European country. Clare's conversion to the faith was noteworthy because anti-Catholicism was still rampant in the United States during this time. Beyond her beliefs, the opportunity complemented her politics as a staunch anti-communist who wanted to serve American interests during the Cold War. In 1953, she became the first woman to command a major U.S. embassy, a position she held for three years.

ROSA PARKS

Seamstress and civil-rights activist Rosa Parks invigorated the movement for racial equality when she refused to give up her bus seat to a White man in Montgomery, Alabama. Parks' arrest on December 1st, 1955, launched the Montgomery Bus Boycott, which took place from December 5th, 1955, to December 20th, 1956. Notably, on December 5th, the first day of the boycott, 40,000 of Montgomery's Black bus drivers – a majority the city's drivers – boycotted the system.

Before the boycott began, African Americans represented 75 percent of Montgomery's bus riders. During the boycott, over 17,000 Black citizens walked or carpooled or used a taxi to travel to and from work each day rather than use the segregated bus system.

The Montgomery Bus Boycott is considered to be the first mass demonstration against racial segregation in the country. When a Supreme Court ruling, along with declining revenues, forced the city to desegregate its buses thirteen months after the boycott began, Parks became an instant icon, but her resistance was a natural extension of a lifelong commitment to social activism. Over the years, Rosa had repeatedly disobeyed bus-segregation regulations. Once, she even had been put off a bus for her defiance.

Born Rosa Louise McCauley, she spent the first years of her life on a small farm with her mother, grandparents, and brother. She witnessed night rides by the Ku Klux Klan and listened in fear as lynchings occurred near her home. The family moved to Montgomery, where Rosa went to school and became a seamstress employed by a local department store. She married barber Raymond Parks in 1932, and the couple joined the Montgomery National Association for the Advancement of Colored People (NAACP). When she inspired the bus boycott, Parks had been the secretary of the local NAACP for twelve years. Parks founded the Montgomery NAACP Youth Council in the early 1940s, and later, as secretary of the Alabama State Conference of the NAACP, she traveled throughout the state interviewing victims of discrimination and witnesses to lynchings.

In the wake of the Montgomery Bus Boycott, Parks lost her tailoring job and began received death threats. Montgomery also found a workaround to the mandate that it integrates its bus service by maintaining segregated bus stops. Snipers also shot at buses with Black passengers, and one bullet shattered the legs of a pregnant Black passenger.

In January of 1957, the homes of prominent local civil-rights leaders were bombed, as were four Black churches. Seven Ku Klux Klan bombers were ultimately charged, but Rosa and her family relocated to Detroit, Michigan, which is the nation's largest Black-majority city. Rosa remained an active member of the NAACP and worked for Congressman John Conyers (1965–1988), helping the homeless find housing. The Rosa and Raymond Parks Institute of Self-Development was established in 1987 to offer job training for Black youth. In 1999, Parks received the Congressional Gold Medal of Honor, the highest honor a civilian can receive in the United States. The Southern Christian Leadership Conference (SCLC), cofounded by Martin Luther King Jr., also sponsors an annual Rosa Parks Freedom Award.

Section 6.4 • BROWNIE WISE AND THE TUPPERWARE® PARTY

In 1946, Tupperware® was introduced to the American homemaker by chemist Earl Tupper. Tupperware is a product line of lightweight, unbreakable plastic containers and were a new, innovative solution for food storage. Their patented locking lids make burping sounds as they expelled air from the containers, so food stayed fresh. It has become an iconic American brand and is commonly used as a generic name for its category.

Designing, obtaining the patent, and manufacturing Tupperware was only part of building the brand and commercial success of the product. The company needed to figure out the best way to sell it to homemakers who were not sure how to use Tupperware. After attempting to

Tupperware® party, 1950s

sell it through the traditional channel in stores, they saw negligent sales results. It became clear that there was a disconnect between the product offering and customer engagement. Something was not working.

In the 1940s, a new selling model called the "hostess party" was quickly gaining momentum. A successful Fuller Brush Company door-to-door salesman saw great success by tapping local housewives to run home parties. The hostess party direct-selling model was now established and on its way. The hostess party presented the ideal opportunity for women to enter or re-enter the working world. It is important to note that the timing of this product is immediately after WWII when the majority of jobs held by women had been terminated after soldiers returned home and reclaimed them. Hostess parties were seen as the perfect opportunity for the happy homemaker to make some extra "pin" money. Women volunteered their homes and invited their friends to attend a fun, social gathering called a Tupperware party. Of course, these parties were sales pitches where multiple purchase orders could be placed at one time. It was the beginning of a very efficient and lucrative business model that is still in practice today. Hostess parties provided women with a new income opportunity, independence, and autonomy to control their own work schedules. It was seen as the perfect job for a busy mom.

Brownie Wise was a divorced, single mother from Detroit who needed to make a living to support her family. There were far fewer income opportunities for women in the 1940s than there are today. Fortunately, she was an intuitive salesperson who understood the value of the personalized demonstration in the welcoming and safe home environment. Wise began selling Stanley Home products and within a year, became one of the most successful unit managers in Detroit. She knew that she was good at selling and she also understood the value of tapping into the homemaker target audience. She was sure the new Tupperware product would be a hit with homemakers and began to showcase Tupperware at her Stanley Home products hostess parties. She was right. Sales were strong, and she was soon hired as the Vice President, General Manager of Tupperware Home Parties.

Wise insisted on the nontraditional strategy of selling Tupperware products exclusively through hostess parties. Her strategy was not only commercially successful for Tupperware, but also provided a career path and income opportunity for hundreds of thousands of women who eagerly sponsored Tupperware® parties. In the 1950s, the social norm was for women to be tied to the home and the family rather than to a traditional workplace. This nontraditional job allowed women to work and be home at the same time. Tupperware revenue continued to grow, and Wise became the face of the brand. In 1954 she became the first woman to appear on the cover of *Business Week*. Brownie Wise is remembered as being the pioneer of the multi-level marketing industry (MLM) which inspired several successful business launches that are still around today, including Mary Kay, Avon, the Pampered Chef, and LuLaRoe. According to the Direct Selling Association, the MLM industry grossed over $35 billion in 2019.

CHAPTER SEVEN

Breaking Ground, Gaining Ground, 1960–1969

CHAPTER CONTENTS

Section 7.1 • PRESIDENTIAL COMMISSIONS AND TASK FORCES ON WOMEN

This section includes text excerpted from "Presidential Commission on the Status of Women," "White House Task Force on Women's Rights and Responsibilities," (Wikipedia); "A Few Good Women: Advancing the Cause of Women in Government, 1969–84," (Richard M. Nixon Presidential Library and Museum).

PRESIDENT KENNEDY'S 1961 PRESIDENTIAL COMMISSION ON THE STATUS OF WOMEN

On December 14, 1961, President John F. Kennedy established, through Executive Order 10980, a Presidential Commission on the Status of Women (PCSW) and placed former First Lady and human-rights advocate Eleanor Roosevelt at the helm. Roosevelt chaired the commission until her death in 1962.

The Equal Rights Amendment (ERA) was a hot-potato issue with passionate opinions on all sides. Kennedy supported the ERA but could not afford to alienate the labor base that helped him win the election, which made pro-labor Roosevelt a particularly wise choice to lead the commission.

Women typically fell into two camps where the ERA was concerned and support for the amendment, or lack thereof, was typically tied to one's socioeconomic status. Like the 19th Amendment, the ERA was written by middle-class White women who lacked direct experiences of women who worked in sweatshops and factories. Until the ERA was proposed, legislation related to women in the workplace had always been protective legislation.

Working-class women and unions supported such protective legislation, which they believed protected women in dangerous occupations from injury and exploitation. The flip side of this argument, however, is that the existence of special rights made it more likely that employers would hire men instead or pay women less because of the hassle of meeting special accommodations.

When the PCSW began in 1961, Congress was considering 412 pieces of legislation related to the status of women.

By 1962, the national commission was encouraging states, cities, and universities to study the status of women in their domains. By 1967, all fifty states had operational commissions, which eventually formed the Interstate Association of Commissions on the Status of Women (IACSW).

On October 11, 1963 – on what would have been Eleanor Roosevelt's 79th birthday – the PCSW issued a final report on "American Women." The report outlined its finding, criticized the inequalities that women face, and made recommendations for further action. The report also stated that constitutional equality between the sexes is essential but should be achieved through judicial means. Let the Supreme Court decree that women are protected under the equal protection clause of the 14th Amendment, it recommended, instead of amending the Constitution.

The PCSW made plain that discrimination against women was a significant problem in the United States and state commissions began meeting annually with the Department of Labor to discuss best practices for eliminating discrimination.

During the 1966 meeting, several attendees began discussions about how the Equal Employment Opportunity Commission (EEOC) had failed to enforce the provision banning sex-based discrimination in the workplace.

The Virginia chapter of the National Women's Party convinced Representative Howard W. Smith to add the word "sex" in the employment section (Title VII) of the 1964 Civil Rights Act. When the Act passed, a law banning sex discrimination in private employment was on the books for the first time.

Meanwhile, when the women discussing EEOC failures were unable to get a resolution passed, they decided to create an "NAACP for women" to advocate for enforcement of this law and to move forward on other initiatives to address inequities based on sex. These women formed the National Organization for Women (NOW) in October 1966 as the first new feminist organization of the second-wave feminist movement. They also placed former EEOC Commissioner Richard Graham on its board as vice president.

PRESIDENT NIXON'S 1969 WHITE HOUSE TASK FORCE ON WOMEN'S RIGHTS AND RESPONSIBILITIES

On February 6th, 1969, President Nixon held his second news conference, which was broadcast on television and radio, in the East Room of the White House. Among the journalists who had questions for the President was a woman reporter who wanted to know more about women's role in the new administration. Vera R. Glaser of the North American Newspaper Alliance asked: "Mr. President, in staffing your administration, you have so far made about 200 high-level Cabinet and other policy position appointments, and of these, only three have gone to women. Could you tell us, sir, whether we can expect a more equitable recognition of women's abilities or are we going to remain a lost sex?" The President replied amid laughter, "Would you be interested in coming into the Government?" He continued, "Very seriously, I had not known that only three had gone to women, and I shall see that we correct that imbalance very promptly."

President Nixon and his staff forged an action plan that would bring more women into the government. After a period of research, the Presidential Task Force on Women's Rights and Responsibilities sent a memorandum dated December 15th, 1969, to the President about the administration's role in providing leadership to promote the advancement of women in government.

Barbara Hackman Franklin, a business-school graduate from Harvard University, was recruited by Fred Malek, a staff assistant from 1971 to 1973, to lead the successful recruitment of qualified women into upper-level government jobs. Malek, then Deputy Undersecretary for the Department of Health, Education, and Welfare, had been a classmate of Franklin at Harvard University.

Franklin was appointed U.S. Secretary of Commerce during President George H. W. Bush's administration and served in this role from February 1992 to January 1993. Her acute interest in the advancement of women in government positions led to her exceeding the goals established by the Nixon administration.

Section 7.2 • **LEGISLATION**

This section includes text excerpted from "Equal Pay for Equal Work" (U.S. Department of Labor); "The Civil Rights Act of 1964 and the Equal Employment Opportunity Commission," U.S. National Archives and Records Administration, August 25, 2018; "Facts About Age Discrimination," (U.S. Equal Employment Opportunity Commission (EEOC)); "Overview, 1960–1969."

EQUAL PAY ACT OF 1963

The Equal Pay Act of 1963 amended the Fair Labor Standards Act (FLSA) and protected against wage discrimination based on sex.

All forms of compensation were covered, including salary, overtime pay, bonuses, life insurance, vacation and holiday pay, cleaning or gasoline allowances, hotel accommodations, reimbursement for travel expenses, and benefits. If there was an inequality in wages between women and men who perform substantially equal jobs, the Act required employers to raise the female workers wages to equalize pay, but they were not allowed to reduce the wages of other individuals.

What Is Required to Substantiate an Equal Pay Act Claim

Several elements must be met in compensation discrimination complaints under the Equal Pay Act. The jobs being compared must require substantially equal skill, effort, and responsibility and be performed under similar working conditions within the same establishment.

Skill: Measured by factors such as the experience, ability, education, and training required to perform the job. The issue is what skills are required for the job, not what skills the individual employees may have.

Effort: The amount of physical or mental exertion needed to perform a job.

Responsibility: The degree of accountability required to perform the job.

Working Conditions: This encompasses two factors: (1) physical surroundings like temperature, fumes, and ventilation; and (2) hazards.

Establishment: The prohibition against compensation discrimination under the EPA applies only to jobs within an establishment. An establishment is a distinct physical place of business rather than an entire business or enterprise consisting of several places of business. In some circumstances, physically separate places of business may be treated as one establishment. For example, if a central administrative unit hires employees, sets their compensation, and assigns them to separate work locations, the separate work sites can be considered part of one establishment.

"Equal" work does not mean identical jobs; rather, they must be "substantially equal" in overall job content, even if the position titles differ. In order to be considered substantially equal, the job duties must be "closely related" or "very much alike." Thus, minor differences in the job duties or the skill, effort, or responsibility required for the jobs will not render the work unequal. An agency may have a defense if compensation is based on a seniority system, merit system, systems which measure earnings by quantity or quality of production, or any factor other than sex.

CIVIL RIGHTS ACT OF 1964

In 1964, Congress passed Public Law 88-352 (78 Stat. 241), popularly known as the Civil Rights Act of 1964. The provisions of this Act prohibited discrimination on the basis of sex as well as race in the hiring, promoting, and firing of women in the workplace.

The word "sex" was added at the last minute. According to the *West Encyclopedia of American Law*, Representative Howard W. Smith (D-VA) added the word. His critics argued that Smith, a conservative southern opponent of federal civil rights, did so to kill the entire bill (a so-called poison-pill amendment). Smith, however, argued that he had amended the bill in keeping with his support of Alice Paul and the National Women's Party, with whom he had been working. Martha W. Griffiths (D-MI) led the effort to keep the word "sex" in the bill.

In the final legislation, Section 703 (a) made it unlawful for an employer to "fail or refuse to hire or to discharge any individual, or otherwise to discriminate against any individual with respect to [her or] his compensation, terms, conditions or privileges of employment, because of an individual's race, color, religion, sex, or national origin." The final bill also allowed sex to be a consideration when sex is a *bona fide* occupational qualification for the job.

Title VII of the Act created the Equal Employment Opportunity Commission (EEOC) to implement the law. Further laws expanded the role of the EEOC. Today, the Commission enforces federal laws that make it illegal to discriminate against a job applicant or an employee because of the person's race, color, religion, sex (which includes, under some administrations, pregnancy, gender identity, and sexual orientation), national origin, age (40 or older), disability, or genetic information. This discrimination protection applies to all types of work situations, including hiring, firing, promotions, harassment, training, wages, and benefits.

The regulatory authority of the EEOC includes enforcing a range of federal statutes prohibiting employment discrimination. According to the EEOC website, these include:

- Title VII of the Civil Rights Act of 1964, that prohibits employment discrimination on the basis of race, color, religion, sex, or national origin
- The Pregnancy Discrimination Act that amended Title VII to make it illegal to discriminate against a woman because of pregnancy, childbirth, or a medical condition related to pregnancy or childbirth
- The Age Discrimination in Employment Act of 1967, and its amendments, that prohibit employment discrimination against individuals 40 years of age or older
- The Equal Pay Act of 1963 that prohibits discrimination on the basis of gender in compensation for substantially similar work under similar conditions
- Title I of the Americans with Disabilities Act of 1990 that prohibits employment discrimination on the basis of disability in both the public and private sector, excluding the federal government
- The Civil Rights Act of 1991 that provides for monetary damages in cases of intentional discrimination
- Sections 501 and 505 of the Rehabilitation Act of 1973, as amended, that prohibit employment discrimination against federal employees with disabilities
- Title IX of the Education Amendments Act of 1972 that forbade gender discrimination in education programs, including athletics, that received federal dollars

Presidents have weighed in on how best to offer equal opportunities to women in the workplace. In 1965, President Lyndon B. Johnson's Executive Order 11246 established nondiscriminatory practices that government contractors must follow. President Richard Nixon's Executive Order 11478 executive order required that every level of federal service offer equal opportunities for women and established a program to implement that action. The Department of Labor then adopted a plan that required federal contractors to assess their employees to identify gender and race and to set goals to end any under-representation of women and other underrepresented populations. By the 1990s, Democratic and Republican administrations had taken a variety of actions that resulted in 160 different federal affirmative action programs. State and local governments followed suit.

In addition to addressing race, color, creed, and age, from the 1970s forward, the courts dealt with gender questions. It voided arbitrary weight and height requirements (*Dothard v. Rawlinson*), erased mandatory pregnancy leave (*Cleveland Board of Education v. LaFleur*), allowed public employers to use carefully constructed affirmative-action plans to remedy certain past discriminatory practices that resulted in women and minorities being underrepresented in the workplace (*Johnson v. Transportation Agency, Santa Clara County*), and upheld state and local laws prohibiting gender discrimination.

By the late 1970s, all branches of the federal government and most state governments had taken at least some action to enhance and fulfill the promise of equal protection under the law. The EEOC continues to design policies that help the historically disadvantaged, including women and other underrepresented populations.

AGE DISCRIMINATION IN EMPLOYMENT ACT OF 1967

The Age Discrimination in Employment Act of 1967 (ADEA) protects employees 40 years of age or older from workplace discrimination based on their age. The ADEA's protections apply to both employees and job applicants. Under the ADEA, it is unlawful to discriminate against a person because of their age with respect to any term, condition, or privilege of employment, including hiring, firing, promotion, layoff, compensation, benefits, job assignments, and training.

The ADEA applies to employers with 20 or more employees, including state and local governments. It also applies to employment agencies and labor organizations, as well as to the federal government. ADEA protections include:

Apprenticeship Programs

It is generally unlawful for apprenticeship programs, including joint labor–management apprenticeship programs, to discriminate on the basis of an individual's age. Age limitations in apprenticeship programs are valid only if they fall within certain specific exceptions under the ADEA or if the EEOC grants a specific exemption.

Job Notices and Advertisements

The ADEA generally makes it unlawful to include age preferences, limitations, or specifications in job notices or advertisements. A job notice or advertisement may specify an age limit only in the rare circumstances where age is shown to be a "bona fide occupational qualification" (BFOQ) reasonably necessary to the normal operation of the business.

Pre-Employment Inquiries

The ADEA does not specifically prohibit an employer from asking an applicant's age or date of birth. However, because such inquiries may deter older workers from applying for employment or may otherwise indicate possible intent to discriminate based on age, requests for age information will be closely scrutinized to make sure that the inquiry was made for a lawful purpose, rather than for purposes prohibited by the ADEA. If the information is needed for a lawful purpose, it can be obtained after the employee is hired.

Benefits

The Older Workers Benefit Protection Act of 1990 (OWBPA) amended the ADEA to specifically prohibit employers from denying benefits to older employees. Congress recognized that the cost of providing certain benefits to older workers is greater than the cost of providing those same benefits to younger workers and that those greater costs might create a disincentive to hire older workers. Therefore, in limited circumstances, an employer may be permitted to reduce benefits based on age, as long as the cost of providing the reduced benefits to older workers is no less than the cost of providing benefits to younger workers.

Although both of these laws cover older female and male workers, research indicates that working women are less protected by age-discrimination laws than their male counterparts.

"These women are falling through the cracks," said researcher Joanne Song McLaughlin, PhD.

Kristen Dalli of Consumer Affairs summarizes McLaughlin's findings this way: "ADEA is focused on age-related discrimination while Title VII focuses on gender discrimination. This becomes problematic because the two laws are consistently being forced apart; consumers can fight against either age or gender, but when it comes to both, the laws can't be combined."

McLaughlin says her evidence indicates "that both state age discrimination laws and the ADEA improved the labor market outcomes for older men but had a far less favorable effect on older women. In some cases, she found that "age discrimination laws did not improve the labor market outcomes for older women at all."

For these reasons, McLaughlin believes it is necessary to update these laws in an effort to address the specific kinds of discrimination that older women encounter in the workplace.

Section 7.3 • ADDRESSING DISCRIMINATION IN THE WORKPLACE WITH AFFIRMATIVE ACTION

"Affirmative Action" in the United States refers to a set of laws and administrative practices within organizations to increase the representation of particular groups that have been historically discriminated against in education and/or employment based on their gender, race, or nationality. Affirmative action includes government-mandated, government-approved, and private voluntary programs to end and correct the effects of specific forms of discrimination. The main focus of affirmative programs is to grant special consideration and provide better access to education and employment to women and racial minorities who were historically denied equal opportunity in these fields.

Affirmative-action programs currently tend to favor "targeted goals," rather than exact quotas, to redress past discrimination in a particular organization or larger society through specific initiatives used to identify, select, and empower women and other historically underrepresented workers. Examples of affirmative action in employment include outreach initiatives, targeted hiring, women and other so-called minority executive development, and various employee-support policies.

In recent years, several campaigns have aimed to make institutions and organizations more inclusive in terms of gender diversity and to provide access to educational and employment opportunities for people with disabilities, members of the LGBTQ+ community, and covered veterans.

Affirmative Action Can Level The Playing Field

Affirmative-action policies conceptualize these policies as going beyond equal opportunity toward a more proactive anti-discrimination position. Affirmative action aims to level the playing field by proactively supporting disadvantaged groups from a holistic perspective rather than remedying injuries tied to specific individuals.

In 1981, the U.S. Commission on Civil Rights clarified the intention of affirmative action, defining it as "seeking to remedy past and present discrimination and its effects." In sum, affirmative action aims to:

1. Directly address and overcome historical discrimination and its legacy
2. Increase diversity and representation in education, the labor force, and housing
3. Reduce economic disparities and poverty caused by discrimination.

Affirmative Action in Employment

In employment, "affirmative action" refers to any positive anti-discrimination action or initiative that is designed to secure access to preferred occupational positions for individuals that are currently underrepresented in such positions. Affirmative action may be used in hiring decisions and also in decisions and initiatives about career advancement, and it may be applied either explicitly through preferential policies or implicitly through facilitative policies. For instance, an organization might set a target of 10 percent of all interviewees for a senior

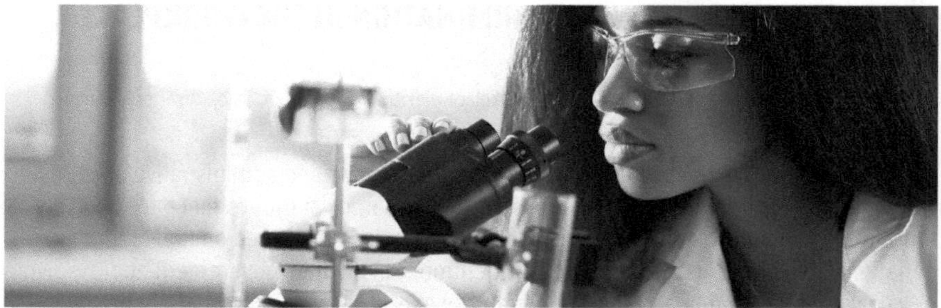

A student chemist conducting research in the lab

position to be female, Black, or a member of another marginalized group. Alternatively, the organization might develop advancement or talent-management programs specifically for women.

There are, however, drawbacks to the use of affirmative action in employment. In particular, the conflation of affirmative action with "reverse discrimination" has negative connotations that can cause a backlash against women workers and others who may be perceived as benefiting from it. For example, new hires who are thought to be privileged as a consequence of affirmative action may receive negative attention from colleagues. Other policies may be more appropriate to help enact change, such as conducting internal reviews and audits of pay and positions to ensure that there are no injustices on the basis of gender, race, ethnicity, or any other marginalizing characteristic. Another strategy is to adopt an equality and diversity policy, which corporations are currently requiring at an increasing rate.

Section 7.4 • **TRAILBLAZERS**

ENVIRONMENTAL SCIENTIST RACHEL CARSON'S *SILENT SPRING*

In 1962, marine biologist Rachel Carson published a book that ushered the United States into a new age of environmental consciousness. Nearly ten years prior, she found herself concerned by emerging reports that human-made insecticides created adverse impacts for other wildlife. Not long after, the Audubon Society (a conservation organization) commissioned her to write a book on the subject. *Silent Spring* was the product of years of research on the effects of the now-infamous chemical dichlorodiphenyltrichloroethane (commonly known as DDT) and other pesticides like it. Carson argued that these pesticides were harmful to both humans and animals and posed a significant danger to ecosystems. She also pointed out major flaws in the government's approach to pesticides, including the clear conflict of interest that existed when the Department of Agriculture (USDA) regulated pesticides and promoted the agriculture industry.

The publication was delayed due to Rachel's battle with cancer, but the project finally reached the public in the form of a serial in the *New Yorker*. Carson faced a slew of criticism, particularly from the chemical industry, which stood to lose its profits in the wake of the revelation. Her detractors called her "a fanatic defender of the cult of the balance of nature" and a "probabl[e] communist," yet the merit of the work was evident. Meticulously researched, substantial, and scientifically sound, it was difficult to dismiss on the grounds of credibility.

Despite being unwell, the scientist powered through a series of media appearances to support the monumental text. Testifying before President Kennedy's Science Advisory Committee, her stance made a strong case for new, protective environmental policy and was influential in the creation of the U.S. Environmental Protection Agency (EPA), which was created just after her death. Beyond alerting everyday Americans to the dangers of pesticide use, her work highlighted the reality that humans have a symbiotic relationship with nature. Indeed, as one thrives or perishes, so does the other.

This awareness of our ability to do irreparable harm to the planet underpins most contemporary efforts to live more sustainably, be it through recycling, using solar panels, or reducing our carbon footprint.

Carson was posthumously awarded the prestigious Presidential Medal of Freedom by President Jimmy Carter in 1980.

DOLORES HUERTA

American labor leader and civil-rights activist Delores Clara Fernández Huerta (b. 1930) cofounded the Stockton chapter of the Community Service Organization to advocate for economic improvements for Latino, Mexican, and Chicano migrant farmworkers and later cofounded the Agricultural Workers Association. In 1965, she joined forces with labor organizer Cesar Chavez to cofound the National Farmworkers Association, now United Farm Workers (UFW).

Huerta organized the 1965 Delano grape strike, which amplified the plight of migrant farmworkers and resulted in a nationwide boycott of California grapes. Huerta then negotiated an end to the boycott with California's table grape industry, which resulted in a three-year collective-bargaining agreement with the UFW.

In 1969, Huerta stood beside former U.S. Attorney General and current senator Robert F. Kennedy on the speaker's platform as he delivered a statement after winning the California Democratic presidential primary election just moments before he and five other people were shot at the Ambassador Hotel in Los Angeles. Kennedy died the following day.

Huerta and women's movement leader Gloria Steinem also championed intersectionality in activism before it even had a name.

Huerta, a role model for in the Hispanic/Latino community and beyond, coined the phrase "Si, se puede" (if you can), and is widely recognized for her advocacy for workers, immigrants,

Luci Baines Johnson, Mary Wilson, and Dolores Huerta at the Summit on Race in America at the LBJ Presidential Library on April 8, 2019. Huerta, a Presidential Medal of Freedom recipient, cofounded the United Farm Workers of America with Cesar Chavez in the 1960s and has spent decades advocating for laborers, women and children.

and women's rights. She is the recipient of the U.S. Presidential Eleanor Roosevelt Award for Human Rights and the Presidential Medal of Freedom and served as honorary cochair of the Women's March on Washington on January 21st, 2017.

Section 7.5 • BETTY FRIEDAN'S GROUNDBREAKING BOOK *THE FEMININE MYSTIQUE* LAUNCHES SECOND-WAVE WOMEN'S MOVEMENT

"Betty Freidan's Groundbreaking Book *The Feminist Mystique* Launches Second-Wave Women's Movement," •

In the 1960s, new legislation granted working women more rights and protections in the workplace. Still, middle- and upper-class working women faced growing pressure to consign themselves solely to the domestic sphere. By the 1960s, women had been pressured for decades to marry early, stay home, have babies, and restrict themselves to their family's care and feeding. And, as so many American women before them, these women who worked outside the home or refused to adhere to the dominant narrative regarding a woman's "place," were both scorned and labeled as "unfeminine."

Betty Friedan's book *The Feminine Mystique* was an instant best-seller in 1963 and is widely credited with launching the second-wave feminist movement.

After graduating from Smith College (a prominent East Coast women's college), Friedan studied psychology at University of California, Berkeley. In 1957, Freidan sent a questionnaire to Smith College classmates. The answers they returned became the basis for her book.

Friedan found that numerous suburban housewives suffered in silence from a "problem that has no name." In the process of trying to identify the source of their discontent, Freidan not only coined a famous term but published an enduring work with a global impact. *The Feminine Mystique* would ultimately sell millions of copies in a slew of languages. It would change feminist discourse forever.

The Feminine Mystique, or women's so-called natural domesticity, refers to an intriguing and pervasive issue women in mid-century, post-war society faced. Dominant beliefs at the time held that "real women" were entirely fulfilled by domestic roles. This message was, of course, reinforced by the mainstream media, which relentlessly framed marriage, motherhood, and homemaking as the greatest possible (and most noble) achievements for White middle- and upper-class women.

From this perspective, the very desire for more – be it education, employment, or political activity – was unfeminine. Wanting more was considered shameful because, according to the dominant narrative, dissatisfaction with traditional domestic life indicated an internal flaw. In this way, women who were not satisfied with domestic, suburban life were effectively blamed for their own unhappiness. Indeed, the underlying logic was that this unhappiness was a consequence of their own inappropriate and "masculine" ambitions.

This theory did not readily apply to the realities of women from lower social classes, and specifically to marginalized women of color. These women typically had no choice but to work to sustain themselves, a lived experience essentially not accounted for in Friedan's work. *The Feminine Mystique* instead spoke to a challenge facing women of relative means, who had been relegated to rigid domestic roles they believed to be their only option.

The so-called mystique was fundamentally a problem of lack and entrapment. Women were being told what sort of life they should be content with, and many tried to be. When they failed, they blamed themselves, not realizing they had bought into a one-size-fits-all construct of womanhood that simply could not hold them.

Freidan's book questions the mythical existence of a woman's feminine mystique and argues that women's maladjustment to so-called natural domesticity indicates a need for a change in the social order rather than a change in women.

American women of means, Freidan points out, were taught in

> the millions of words written about women, for women, in all the columns, books and articles by experts telling women their role was to seek fulfillment as wives and mothers ... that truly feminine women do not want careers, higher education, political rights – the independence and the opportunities that the old-fashioned feminists fought for. Some women, in their forties and fifties, still remembered painfully giving up those dreams, but most of the younger women no longer even thought about them. A thousand expert voices applauded their femininity, their adjustment, their new maturity. All they had to do was devote their lives from earliest girlhood to finding a husband and bearing children.

Freidan again: "By 1962 the plight of the trapped suburban housewife had become a national parlor game. Whole issues of magazines, newspaper columns, books ... educational conferences and television panels were devoted to the problem (yet) no other road to fulfillment was offered to [these] women."

"This is not what being a woman means, no matter what the experts say," Friedan observed. "For human suffering there is a reason; perhaps the reason has not been found because the right questions have not been asked, or pressed far enough."

"If I am right," continued Friedan, then

> the problem that has no name stirring in the minds of so many American women today is not a matter of loss of femininity or too much education, or the demands of domesticity. It is far more important than anyone recognizes. It is the key to these other new and old problems which have been torturing women and their husbands and children, and puzzling their doctors and educators for years. It may well be the key to our future as a nation and a culture. We can no longer ignore that voice within women that says "I want something more than my husband and my children and my home."

Friedan's book is credited with changing the national conversation about traditional gender roles and inspiring a generation of women to prioritize themselves while working for full autonomy and equality. Now considered a classic, Friedan's work is credited with sparking renewed support for gender equality in the workplace, reproductive rights, and women's autonomy and education.

Section 7.6 • **NATIONAL ORGANIZATION FOR WOMEN (NOW) FOUNDED, 1967**

A group of women attending the Third National Conference of Commissions on the Status of Women in 1966 were frustrated by the lack of action they saw on display at the convention. This inaction was even more disturbing because the theme of the conference was "Targets for Action," which had raised their expectations. The women decided to create an "NAACP for women" that would allow them to advocate for enforcement of laws that ensure the equal treatment of both sexes.

Betty Friedan wrote "N.O.W." on a napkin and invited these fifteen women, including trail-blazer Pauli Murray, to her hotel room, where Catherine Conroy placed a five-dollar bill on the table and said, "Put your money down and sign your name." And the women did.

They discussed an action plan for enforcing Title VII of the Civil Rights Act of 1964, which prohibits employers from discriminating against employees based on sex, race, color, nationality, and religion.

A few months later, at the National Organization of Women (NOW) founding conference, attendees finalized their Statement of Purpose:

> We, men and women who hereby constitute ourselves as the National Organization for Women, believe the time has come for a new movement toward true equality for all women in America, and toward a fully equal partnership of the sexes, as part of the world-wide revolution of human rights now taking place within and beyond our national borders.

NOW set up seven task forces: Equal Opportunity of Employment; Legal and Political Rights; Education; Women in Poverty; The Family; Images of Women; and Women and Religion, and author Betty Friedan was recognized as the founding president. NOW also strategically placed former Equal Employment Opportunity Commission (EEOC) Commissioner Richard Graham on the board as vice president.

NOW began petitioning the EEOC to enforce its prohibition against sex discrimination and filed a formal petition with the EEOC for hearings to amend regulations on sex-segregated "help wanted" ads.

At its second national conference, NOW created a "Bill of Rights for Women" and prioritized passage of the Equal Rights Amendment, the repeal of all abortion laws, and funding for publicly funded childcare. The board also adopted bylaws that allowed for the creation of NOW chapters.

In 1977, NOW created a political action committee (PAC) that supports politicians who share the organization's goals.

NOW continues to advocate for equal rights for women and enforcement of comparable-worth legislation (equal pay for work of comparable value).

This organization remains a cornerstone of the women's rights and liberation movement and is the largest feminist group in the United States, with over 500,000 current members.

PART THREE

Revolution and Equality for All, 1970–1999

Introduction: "Living the Revolution"

"Introduction to Part Three, Revolution and Equality for All, 1970–1999: Living the Revolution,"

Some scholars say that the second-wave women's liberation movement first entered main-stream public consciousness when footage of the 1968 Miss America protest aired. That may be so, but it was feminist leader Gloria Steinem who said, in her commencement speech "Living the Revolution" at Vassar in 1970:

> This is the year of Women's Liberation. Or at least it is the year the press has discovered a movement that has been strong for several years now, and reported it as a small, privileged, rather lunatic event instead of the major revolution in consciousness – in everyone's consciousness – male or female, that I believe it truly is.

Steinem went on to describe the importance of women and men having "the scales fall from our eyes, not just learn, but unlearn." She added: "Some call the movement feminist, but it should more accurately be called humanist; a movement that is an integral part of rescuing this country from its old, expensive patterns of elitism, racism, and violence:"

> We are filled with the Popular Wisdom of several centuries just past, and we are terrified to give it up. Patriotism means obedience, age means wisdom, woman means submission, black means inferior – these are preconceptions imbedded so deeply in our thinking that we honestly may not know that they are there.

White people took notice of the women's movement as well. "Female equality will be a major cultural/political force of the 1970s," President Nixon's Urban Affairs Advisor Daniel Patrick Moynihan told the president. "The essential fact is that we have educated women for equality but have not really given it to them." The task force's report recommended passage of the ERA (which Nixon endorsed), promoting equal rights and opportunities and advancing more women to executive positions in the federal government.

In 1972 President Nixon signed the Equal Employment Opportunity Act, which mandated that personnel decisions in all federal agencies be free of inequality. Title IX of the Civil Rights Act also prohibited discrimination by any educational institution that received federal dollars. President Nixon also initiated the White House Women Recruiting Program and by May 1973:

- The number of women in high-level jobs paying more than $28,000 annually increased from 36 to 130

- More than 1,000 women were hired or promoted to mid-level government positions.
- A PR function on women's issues was created within the White House to provide "substantive input to the Domestic Council on a number of issues of concern to women."

Gloria Steinem asserts that "Nixon's Commission on Women concluded that the Supreme Court was sanctioning discrimination against women – discrimination that it had long ago ruled unconstitutional in the case of blacks – but the Commission report remains mysteriously unreleased by the White House" (Steinem, "Living the Revolution" Commencement speech). And it's true that the Equal Pay Act had been around for seven years by 1970, yet women made up only 5 percent of all the people in the country earning $410,00 per year or more. In fact, many laws were on the books calling for equal pay for equal work, but American women in the workplace have yet to receive it.

CHAPTER EIGHT

"Unbought and Unbossed," 1970–1979

CHAPTER CONTENTS

Section 8.1 • **OVERVIEW**

"Overview: Women in the Workplace in America, 1970–1979," • © 2021 Omnigraphics.

By the 1970s, women were demanding equality and speaking out about gender-based discrimination. Yet, in the 1970s, creditors still required the signed permission of a woman's husband (or that of another man) before they would extend credit to her. Banks also required married women to change the name on their accounts to reflect their marital status. For example, if Jane Doe had an account in her own name before getting married, she was required to change the name on that account to Mrs. James Buck (or whatever), regardless of whether she took her husband's name when they married. Such practices were especially infuriating to women who earned more than their husbands. Bank policies such as these also continued the once-legal practice of defining American women as the property of their husbands.

In the 1970s, U.S. Representative Shirley Chisholm, a National Organization for Women (NOW) member who declared herself "unbought and unbossed," was blazing new trails and sharing truths about just how many women and children live in poverty in this nation of plenty. One of her favorite pieces of advice was to bring a folding chair if you aren't offered a seat at the proverbial table. Similarly, Ruth Bader Ginsburg, a longtime legal advocate for gender equality and pay equity for working women, was blazing trails of her own. Ginsburg won five of the six cases she argued before the U.S. Supreme Court in this decade. Ginsburg also continued to advocate for women's autonomy and right to privacy, both of which were central in the landmark *Roe v. Wade* Supreme Court decision. This decision removed control of a woman's body from the state and provided working women who were focused on their careers another option to consider should they become pregnant.

Working women also benefitted from the collective power of the women's liberation movement. Workplace culture shifted significantly during these years as women made inroads into areas of work that had once been defined solely as "men's work." These new opportunities also highlighted a need for legislation that ensured the equal application of the law for both sexes. Meanwhile, it was time for the movement to launch its own magazine that was owned, produced, written, edited, and managed by and for women.

Section 8.2 • **LEGISLATION AND JUDICIAL DECISIONS**

This section includes text excerpted from "Equal Credit Opportunity Act of 1974" (U.S. Department of Justice), "The Pregnancy Discrimination Act of 1978," "The Rehabilitation Act of 1973," (U.S Equal Employment Opportunity Commission). "*Roe v. Wade* and Women's Reproductive Rights," • © 2021 Omnigraphics.

EQUAL CREDIT OPPORTUNITY ACT OF 1974

This important civil-rights law made it possible for working (and nonworking) women to qualify for credit based on their own creditworthiness and without having to provide a man's signature granting her the right to submit the credit application. Before passage of this Act, bank routinely required a man's signature, even when the working woman was the primary breadwinner. Banks also required women to reference their husband's name on their bank accounts (i.e., Mrs. John Doe), even if the woman did not take her husband's name when they married.

What Is the ECOA?

The Equal Credit Opportunity Act (ECOA) protects women from being discriminated against by lenders, based on any of the following reasons:

- Age (as long as the applicant is old enough to enter into a contract)
- Color
- Exercising your rights under certain consumer protection laws
- Marital status
- National origin (the country you or your ancestors were born in)
- Race
- Receiving money from any public assistance program, such as Social Security Disability Insurance (SSDI) or the Supplemental Nutrition Assistance Program (SNAP)
- Religion
- Sex (including gender)

For example, a lender generally cannot deny loan applications or charge higher costs, such as a higher interest rate or higher fees, for any of the reasons listed above. ECOA applies to various types of loans, including car loans, credit cards, home loans, small-business loans, and student loans.

Why ECOA Became the Law

ECOA was passed at a time when discrimination against women applying for credit was common. For example, mortgage lenders often discounted a married woman's income, especially if she was of childbearing age. Things weren't much better for single women, either. Organizations that lobbied for the passage of ECOA also claimed that mortgage lenders were more likely to deny credit to single women relative to other applicants.

Congress originally passed ECOA in October of 1974. When it was enacted, ECOA prohibited lending discrimination based on sex or marital status. Not long after the original law was passed, in March of 1976, Congress amended the law to further prohibit lending discrimination based on age, color, exercising one's rights under certain consumer-protection laws, national origin, race, the receipt of public-assistance income, or religion.

PREGNANCY DISCRIMINATION ACT OF 1978

This Act amended Title VII of the Civil Rights Act of 1964 to prohibit sex discrimination on the basis of pregnancy (which is another form of discrimination on the basis of sex). The Act ensured that pregnant women who are capable of working had the right to do so, identical to employees with other, but similar, medical conditions. The Act also mandated that employers provide the same benefits to women at any stage of pregnancy, delivery, or recovery from delivery when they are medically unable to work as to all other employees with temporarily disabling conditions. It also disallowed workplace discrimination against women based on the mere possibility of pregnancy.

The Pregnancy Discrimination Act

Be it enacted by the Senate and House of Representatives of the United States of America in Congress assembled, that section 701 of the Civil Rights Act of 1964 is amended by adding at the end thereof the following new subsection:

(k) The terms because of sex or on the basis of sex include, but are not limited to, because of or on the basis of pregnancy, childbirth, or related medical conditions; and women affected by pregnancy, childbirth, or related medical conditions shall be treated the same for all employment-related purposes, including receipt of benefits under fringe benefit programs, as other persons not so affected but similar in their ability or inability to work, and nothing in section 703(h) of this title shall be interpreted to permit otherwise. This subsection shall not require an employer to pay for health insurance benefits for abortion, except where the life of the mother would be endangered if the fetus were carried to term, or except where medical complications have arisen from an abortion: Provided, That nothing herein shall preclude an employer from providing abortion benefits or otherwise affect bargaining agreements in regard to abortion.

Sec. 2. (a) Except as provided in subsection (b), the amendment made by this Act shall be effective on the date of enactment.

(b) The provisions of the amendment made by the first section of this Act shall not apply to any fringe benefit program or fund, or insurance program which is in effect on the date of enactment of this Act until 180 days after enactment of this Act.

Sec. 3. Until the expiration of a period of one year from the date of enactment of this Act or, if there is an applicable collective-bargaining agreement in effect on the date of enactment of this Act, until the termination of that agreement, no person who, on the date of enactment of this Act is providing either by direct payment or by making contributions to a fringe benefit fund or insurance program, benefits in violation with this Act shall, in order to come into compliance with this Act, reduce the benefits or the compensation provided any employee on the date of enactment of this Act, either directly or by failing to provide sufficient contributions to a fringe benefit fund or insurance program: Provided, That where the costs of such benefits on the date of enactment of this Act are apportioned between employers and employees, the payments or contributions required to comply with this Act may be made by employers and employees in the same proportion: And provided further, That nothing in this section shall prevent the readjustment of benefits or compensation for reasons unrelated to compliance with this Act.

Approved October 31, 1978.

THE LANDMARK *ROE V. WADE* DECISION AND EXPANSION OF WOMEN'S REPRODUCTIVE RIGHTS

In a landmark decision on January 22nd, 1973, the U.S. Supreme Court ruled (7–2) in favor of a woman's right to abortion. The court's decision established that privacy rights protected a woman's right to choose an abortion under the 14th Amendment. *Roe v. Wade* struck down many state laws that criminalized abortion and divided U.S. citizens into two groups – those who supported abortion and those who were against it.

The case took place in 1970 when Norma McCorvey, or "Jane Roe," an unmarried woman, wanted to legally and safely terminate her pregnancy. Residing in Dallas, Texas, at the time, she filed a federal action against District Attorney Henry Wade. At the time of this case, many states had made abortion illegal, except for preserving a woman's life or health, cases of incest or rape, or viability of the fetus out of the womb. However, the court did not agree with Roe's assertion of an absolute right to abortion.

The court then attempted to balance out a woman's right to privacy while preserving the state's interest in regulating abortion. *Roe v. Wade* came to be known as the case that legalized abortion nationwide. This ruling legalized women's autonomy over their own bodies and enabled working women to manage their careers and decide whether they would (or if they would) have children.

In September 2020, the death of Justice Ruth Bader Ginsburg, a fierce advocate of women's rights, led to a vacancy in the Supreme Court with less than six weeks before the presidential election. Ginsburg's death brought to the forefront the possibility of *Roe v. Wade* being overturned. In light of the vacancy, President Donald Trump nominated Judge Amy Coney Barrett for the position of Associate Justice of the Supreme Court. In one of his interviews on *Fox and Friends Weekend*, Trump affirmed Barrett's conservative views, adding that he had not discussed abortion rights with her before nominating her for the court. On October 26th, 2020, the Senate confirmed Barrett's nomination and she took the judicial oath the very next day. Barrett's confirmation gives the Supreme Court a 6–3 conservative majority, and the risk of *Roe v. Wade* being overturned is still an imminent possibility.

REHABILITATION ACT OF 1973

The Rehabilitation Act of 1973 replaced the Vocational Rehabilitation Act,

- to extend and revise the authorization of grants to states for vocational rehabilitation services, with special emphasis on services to individuals with the most severe disabilities
- to expand special federal responsibilities and research and training programs with respect to individuals with disabilities
- to create linkage between state vocational rehabilitation programs and workforce investment activities carried out under Title I of the Workforce Investment Act of 1998
- to establish special responsibilities for the Secretary of Education for coordination of all activities with respect to individuals with disabilities within and across programs administered by the federal government
- and for other purposes.

This is a precursor to the Americans with Disabilities Act.

HYDE AMENDMENT OF 1976

The Hyde Amendment is a legislative provision that bans federal funds from being used to pay for an abortion "except where the life of the mother would be endangered if the fetus were carried to term." Before the amendment went into effect in 2010, U.S. taxpayers paid for some 300,000 abortion procedures annually. The amendment is named after sponsor U.S. Representative Henry Hyde of Illinois. Passage of this amendment represents what Justice Ruth Bader Ginsburg referred to as the "chipping away at a woman's reproductive rights" and represents one of the first successful efforts to undermine the ability of women to obtain an abortion after the *Roe v. Wade* decision legalized the procedure. In 1993, President Bill Clinton signed a 1994 appropriations act that expanded the category of abortions that federal funds would pay for to include cases of rape or incest. Pro-choice advocates sometimes describe the amendment as "government so small it fits in your uterus," a commentary on the small-government sponsors who argue for small government, then pass legislation focused on the bodies of women.

Section 8.3 • TRAILBLAZERS

NOW MEMBER SHIRLEY CHISHOLM IS FIRST BLACK WOMAN ELECTED TO THE HOUSE, 1968

Shirley Chisholm was a first-generation American. In 1924, she was born to Guyanese and Bajan parents who had settled in New York. The first of their four daughters, she was born, raised, and educated in the city. She attended a girls' school in Brooklyn and later enrolled at Brooklyn College. Always a talented speaker, she won awards for school debates, and her professors suggested she pursue a political career. Shirley was initially hesitant to entertain this option, citing what she called the "double handicap." Today, this is more commonly known as the status of being a double minority. Black and female in the pre-civil rights era, she knew political success was an uphill battle. She graduated with academic honors in 1946 and accepted employment as a nursery-school teacher.

Not long after, Shirley went back to school and graduated from Columbia University with a master's in early childhood education. Though she continued to work in this field, she got involved with a long list of sociopolitical organizations, including the National Association for the Advancement of Colored People (NAACP), the League of Women Voters, the Urban League, the National Organization for Women (NOW), and the Democratic Party Club of Bedford-Stuyvesant, Brooklyn.

By the 1960s, part-time activism was no longer enough for Shirley, who wanted to formally represent the political interests of her community. The opportunity soon came through court-mandated redistricting. Under those orders, her neighborhood now had a new, majority-democratic district that she could potentially win. In 1968, she successfully campaigned for a seat in Congress.

There, she introduced over 50 pieces of legislation to support gender and racial equality, end the Vietnam War, and provide resources for the impoverished. A staunch ally of vulnerable populations, she soon earned the nickname "Fighting Shirley." Beyond supporting legislative change, she cofounded the National Women's Political Caucus, all while climbing the Congressional ranks. She continued her upward trajectory by becoming the first Black woman (and just the second woman) to join the highly influential House Rules Committee.

Many perceive the professional advancement of women of color as proof that the complex interaction of racial and gender bias is overstated – or that such discriminations are the exception. Yet, a closer look often reveals that they are, in fact, the status quo. In many cases, what we do not see and what the history books leave out are the many times successful women were told no. Typically, we see the breakthroughs and mistake them as outnumbering the barriers.

Despite her professional status, Shirley Chisolm faced these discrete barriers behind the scenes. In 1972, she decided to pursue the nation's highest office and began campaigning for her party's presidential nomination. Yet, she was barred from engaging in televised primary debates. Moreover, she had to turn to legal action to rectify this discrimination.

Shirley Chisholm (D-NY), the first Black woman elected to the U.S. House of Representatives, announcing her candidacy for president in 1972.

Despite appealing to the law, she was only allowed to support her campaign with a single speech.

Despite these manufactured limitations, she had the organic support of students, racial minorities, and women – many of whom proudly joined the so-called Chisholm Trail. A true underdog, her campaign performed well despite being underfunded and unsupported by the predominantly male Congressional Black Caucus (of which she was, ironically, a founding member). The congresswoman entered 12 primaries and won 152 delegate votes, which accounted for 10 percent of the total voting population.

Though this was a fight she did not win, Shirley became the first woman – and the first Black American – to pursue a presidential nomination from one of the two major political parties in the United States. Moreover, her legacy stood firm even without the presidency, as she is the first African American congresswoman and a seven-term member of the House of Representatives.

In 1983, Shirley retired from Congress and took a faculty position at Mount Holyoke College. She then co-founded the National Political Congress of Black Women and subsequently retired to Florida in 1991. Toward the end of her life, Chisholm was offered an ambassadorship, which she turned down due to declining health. She died in 2005, at the age of 80. Fittingly, the titles of her two biographies are apt descriptors of her persona and her purpose: She was *Unbossed and Unbought* (1970) as she fought *The Good Fight* (1973).

ELLEN T. GRASSO

In 1974, Ella T. Grasso became the 83rd governor of Connecticut. Moreover, she was the first woman to win a governorship without being married to a man who had previously held that position. In this way, her achievement was integral to the national realization that women were inherently and independently capable of civic leadership.

Born Ella Rosa Tambussi in Windsor Locks, Connecticut, the future governor received both her bachelor's and master's in economics from Mount Holyoke College. Not long after, she served as an assistant director of research for the War Manpower Commission of Connecticut during World War II. In 1952, Ella was elected to the Connecticut General Assembly and re-elected two years later. This trend would continue for the rest of her career.

Between 1959 and 1970, Ella completed three successful terms as Connecticut Secretary of State. An ardent advocate for human rights, she was elected to U.S. Congress in 1970 (and again in 1972), during which time she established a decisively liberal voting record. Just two years later, she won the Democratic nomination for governor and narrowly defeated her Republican competitor, Richard Kilborn.

In 1975, Ella became the first female governor in the history of her home state. Of course, the greater victory was knowing she had done so on the strength of her own merit. Having proven herself in the role, she was re-elected by a sizeable majority in September 1978. Unfortunately, her crowning achievement came near the end of her life. She resigned from public service in 1980, due to illness, and died the following year at 61 years of age. In 1993, she was inducted into the National Women's Hall of Fame.

HELEN THOMAS

After covering the Washington beat for 30 years – that's ten presidents – pioneering journalist Helen Thomas (1920–2013) was finally formally named a White House reporter and received well-earned recognition as another female American trailblazer who broke down barriers and led numerous battles to gain equal access to jobs, news, and newsmakers for female journalists.

In the 1950s and 1960s, Thomas, reporter Fran Lewine, and writer Elsie Carper took on the National Press Club for barring women from membership or access to its news-making luncheons – and, when the Press Club finally did grant them access, they consigned the women to the balcony and censored them from asking questions. The journalists were finally "allowed" access to join the Press Club as full members in 1971.

But those aren't the only barriers Thomas broke through. She went on to become the National Press Club's first female officer, the first woman admitted to the Gridiron Club, and the first woman to serve as president of the White House Correspondents' Association. And she received a slew of lifetime achievement awards. She also was the only female print reporter to accompany President Richard M. Nixon on his trip to China.

Thomas was adept at scooping information that federal officials tried to keep from the public and famously asked Nixon what his "secret plan" was for the Vietnam War. She also stopped President George Bush (the former) in his tracks after he announced that his defense budget would remain the same despite the recent collapse of the Soviet Union, fall of the Berlin Wall, and virtual elimination of communism across Europe by asking, in her simple but razor-sharp way, simply "Who's the enemy?"

"I respect the office of the presidency, but I never worship at the shrines of our public servants," Helen Thomas said. "They owe us the truth."

Section 8.4 • TENNIS GREAT BILLIE JEAN KING WINS THE BATTLE OF THE SEXES

The year before the Battle of the Sexes, Title IX was passed, decreeing that "no person in the United States shall, on the basis of sex, be excluded from participation in, be denied the benefits of, or be subjected to discrimination under any education program or activity receiving Federal financial assistance." Though it brought hope for the advancement of female student athletes, sportswomen remained something of an afterthought in the nation at large. Despite this, Billie Jean King had managed to establish herself as a leading tennis player. By 1973, she had won 10 major singles titles and ranked among the top female players in the country. Moreover, at 29 years of age, she was an athlete in her prime.

Conversely, the heyday of her future competitor Bobby Riggs seemed far behind him. He was considered one of the tennis greats of the World War II era, though he lost some playing years to the all-consuming conflict. By the 1970s he maintained a regular office job, while

American tennis great Billie Jean King, 1978

"hustling" players on the golf course in his spare time. It was a far cry from the sports stardom of the past, and Riggs craved a return to the spotlight.

He began to challenge King to a competition, requests she repeatedly denied over a three-year period. He had no current ranking, and there was nothing to be gained from the endeavor. Moreover, she likely recognized that the offer was part of an ongoing publicity stunt. For the first time in a while, Riggs had garnered notable media coverage by disparaging women's tennis and challenging many of its stars, most of whom ignored him.

Ignored by King, he began to pursue top-ranking player Margaret Court. Though the challenge itself was simply par for the course, her acceptance was surprising. In May 1973, she suffered a major defeat to the veteran player in what became known as the "Mother's Day Massacre." She later remarked that his style of playing was foreign to anything she had experienced. Court had made a name for herself by achieving more Grand Slam titles than any player in history – of either gender. Indeed, she had a lot to lose. But she did not anticipate Riggs' drops shots, lobs, and various other tricks; the resultant loss was a major blow.

This was precisely the publicity that Riggs sought. Moreover, he was spurred on by the crushing victory. He returned his focus to King, whom he described as a "women's libber leader." A self-described "chauvinist," he essentially taunted King in the media in the hopes of "keep[ing] this sex thing going." In July of that year, she conceded to a winner-takes-all match for a $100,000.

Throughout the summer, Riggs continued to drum up publicity through sexist taunts. Among his choice quotes was the declaration that he would beat King because "[s]he's a woman and they don't have the emotional stability." In response, she called him a "creep." After months of public anticipation, the athletes were greeted by 30,000 fans and various celebrities at the Houston Astrodome on September 20th, 1973. While this was remarkable in itself (such indoor venues were relatively new to U.S. sports), a whopping 50 million viewers tuned in to watch the highly publicized event.

Having resigned herself to the spectacle, King was ready for primetime. She "entered the playing court in the style of Cleopatra on a gold litter carried by four shirtless members of the Rice University track team, while Riggs arrived via rickshaw, flocked by his bevy of "Bobby's bosom buddies." They then exchanged pregame gifts: A baby pig for the chauvinist Riggs, a giant Sugar Daddy lollipop for King."

The pre-game shenanigans over, she won a sweeping 6–4, 6–3, 6–3 victory, undeterred by Riggs' so-called usual bag of tricks. To the surprise of many, her opponent was somewhat gracious, noting that he had underestimated her prowess on the court. Still, he demanded a rematch several times in the ensuing decades, always to no avail.

King's performance brought much-needed respect to women's tennis and to women in sports. She became the first superstar female athlete in the nation's history, landing an array of endorsements for major brands from Adidas to Colgate. Moreover, this recognition had tangible outcomes, among them addressing the long-existing pay gap between male and female players. That same year, the U.S. Open became the first Grand Slam to dole out equal

Title IX

Title IX of the Education Amendments of 1972 protects people from discrimination based on sex in education programs or activities that receive federal financial assistance. Title IX states that

> [n]o person in the United States shall, on the basis of sex, be excluded from participation in, be denied the benefits of, or be subjected to discrimination under any education program or activity receiving Federal financial assistance.

Scope of Title IX

Title IX applies to institutions that receive federal financial assistance from the U.S. Department of Education (ED), including state and local educational agencies. These agencies include approximately 16,500 local school districts, 7,000 postsecondary institutions, as well as charter schools, for-profit schools, libraries, and museums. Also included are vocational rehabilitation agencies and education agencies of 50 states, the District of Columbia, and territories and possessions of the United States.

Educational programs and activities that receive ED funds must operate in a nondiscriminatory manner. Some key issue areas in which recipients have Title IX obligations are recruitment, admissions, and counseling; financial assistance; athletics; sex-based harassment; treatment of pregnant and parenting students; discipline; single-sex education; and employment. Passage of this legislation translates into more budding young Billie Jean Kings having more of an opportunity to compete in school athletic programs.

prize money to champions of either gender. Though two more Grand Slams followed suit, the road to pay equity was a long one. It took over three decades for the fourth and final holdout, Wimbledon, to finally pay women equal prize money.

By the time she retired in 1983, King had amassed 12 major titles, including 6 Wimbledon titles and 4 U.S. Opens. In furtherance of gender equity in sport, she also cofounded a nonprofit that advocated for female athletes, a women players' union, and even a publication dedicated to women's sports. Yet biographers note the irony of the fact that she was still remembered for a single match.

Indeed, the true indication of sexism at work may not be the barrage of snark and gendered commentary surrounding the infamous Battle of the Sexes. It may be the very fact that a tennis great could routinely see her legacy reduced to a single association with a man. This essentialization did not escape King herself, who once said, "I know that when I die, nobody at my funeral will be talking about me. They'll all just be standing around telling each other where they were the night I beat Bobby Riggs."

Still, she remained gracious and even developed a fondness for Riggs in the years that followed, noting that his antics ultimately did some good by promoting the game of tennis. Decades after they faced off on the court, she called him, knowing that he was dying of cancer. Unlike the jabs they traded before the match of the ages, their final conversation ended with "I love you."

Section 8.5 • GLORIA STEINEM AND THE FIRST NATIONAL MAGAZINE PRODUCED, WRITTEN, EDITED, AND MANAGED BY AND FOR WOMEN

"Gloria Steinem and the First National Magazine Owned, Produced, Written, Edited, and Managed by Women for Women," • © 2021 Omnigraphics.

In 1963, social activist, journalist, writer, editor, lecturer, and pioneering feminist leader Gloria Steinem's two-part series chronicling the eleven days she spent undercover as a Bunny in Hugh Hefner's New York Playboy Club made her famous.

Steinem graduated from Smith College, spent two years in India working for Independent Research Service (as a CIA operative), and then moved to New York City, already sure that marriage and motherhood were not for her. "In the 1950s, once you married you became what your husband was, so it seemed like the last choice you'd ever have.... I'd already been the very small parent of a very big child – my mother. I didn't want to end up taking care of someone else," she told *People* magazine years later.

Steinem helped launch *New York* magazine and was writing a regular column for it when she became more involved with the second-wave women's liberation movement after covering the Redstockings' abortion hearing.

In 1971, Steinem, Betty Friedan (author of the groundbreaking book *The Feminine Mystique* and cofounder of the National Organization for Women (NOW)), and Congresswoman Bella Abzug created the National Women's Political Caucus (NWPC) as a way to influence policy and participate in the political process. Steinem and Dorothy Pitman Hughes cofounded and launched *Ms.* Magazine – the nation's first woman-owned, woman-produced, woman-written, woman-edited, woman-focused, and woman-targeted magazine that brought feminism and women's-rights issues into the mainstream.

off our backs, an important but less slick feminist periodical of the time, compared purchasing *Ms.* Magazine at newsstands and stores as something akin to slipping feminist ideas "into American homes concealed in bags of groceries like tarantulas on banana boats" (Foussianes). And, when *Ms.* Magazine officially launched in 1972, newscaster Harry Reasoner quipped, "I'll give it six months before they run out of things to say" (ibid.).

Ms. Magazine refused to run advertisements it deemed to be sexist and rejected any ad that required the magazine to include content that promoted or adhered to a company's products. The magazine aspired to present diverse content and employ a diverse staff too, but the staff remained largely White women of privilege, and the magazine's content reflected this viewpoint. *Ms.* Magazine covered topics and viewpoints of vital importance to women, including articles about domestic violence and, later, female genital mutilation and global human rights, all of which were less likely to appear in mainstream publications.

The magazine took hits from all sides. Old-school feminists were upset because the magazine hadn't hired the people they deemed to be "the established voices" of the movement. Writer Alice Walker was upset because she and only one other person of color appeared on the cover over the course of a year. Some public librarians were upset that a feminist magazine existed at all and banned it. And some newsstands and stores selectively boycotted issues,

Gloria Steinem at a news conference, Women's Action Alliance, January 12, 1972.

but the magazine had a large readership (3 million during its heyday) and was and remains influential.

Ms. Magazine amplified and explained feminist arguments and ideals at a time when few other mainstream publications were doing so and few conversations outside of feminist circles were familiar to a wide swathe of America. The magazine also provided news of special interest and importance to women that went far beyond the newest brownie recipe that other mainstream self-identified women's magazines always seemed to publish. It is also important to note that the mainstream magazines of the time that targeted women were typically produced by men and reflected their version of what they determined to be of interest to American women.

Steinem's 1983 collection of essays, *Outrageous Acts and Everyday Rebellions*, covered a full range of topics, including her experiences during those years, and was influential. After coming out on the other side of breast-cancer treatment, she also wrote *Revolution from Within: A Book of Self-Esteem* and was surprised when a subset of feminists accused her of retreating from the women's liberation movement.

"I was saying that many institutions are designed to undermine our self-authority in order to get us to obey their authority," Steinem told *Interview* magazine, but some of her readers missed that point.

Steinem, who continues to write, lecture, travel, and champion women, offered this insight to the *New York Daily News*:

> We've demonstrated that women can do what men do, but not yet that men can do what women do. That's why most women have two jobs – one inside the home and one outside it – which is impossible. The truth is that women can't be equal outside the home until men are equal in it.

The current pandemic has revealed the reality that this unequal balance remains, but it remains to be seen how the chasm will be addressed.

CHAPTER NINE

A Decade of Firsts, 1980–1989

CHAPTER CONTENTS

Section 9.1 • OVERVIEW

"Overview: Women in the Workplace in America, 1980–1989," • © 2021 Omnigraphics.

In the 1980s, women continued to pursue economic and social equality, but navigating family and work responsibilities remained a challenge. Women still faced a significant wage gap and still worked a second shift at home. Finding and affording quality childcare continued to be an issue for working mothers as well.

George Guilder of *The Atlantic* reported that "from 1890 to 1985, the participation in the workforce of women between the ages of twenty-five and forty-four soared from 15 to 71 percent, with the pace of change tripling after 1950" (1). Women in management positions increased from 44 percent in 1972 to 49 percent in 1985. From 1960 to 1983, women working in banking and financial management rose from 9 to 39 percent, and women practicing law rose from 2 to 15 percent. By 1985, a solid half of college graduates were women and a good many of these women pursued advanced degrees in male-dominant fields such as accounting, business, computers, and information sciences.

A continuing pattern of women moving into fields traditionally dominated by men was apparent. While the overall percentage of married women participating in the workplace increased significantly – from 26 percent in 1950 to 67 percent by the mid-eighties – it is important to note that many of these women worked on a part-time basis, with only 29 percent of married women working full-time, year-round jobs in 1984.

Yet, despite the passage of the Equal Pay Act in 1963, married women with a graduate-level education earned 11 percent less than married men with high-school educations in 1983 (ibid.).

Section 9.2 • JUDICIAL DECISIONS

"Rostker v. Goldberg," "Meritor Savings Bank v. Vinson," • © 2021 Omnigraphics.

ROSTKER V. GOLDBERG

The Military Selective Service Act of 1967 authorized single-sex registration for the military draft, but that registration was discontinued in 1975. Growing unrest in Southwest Asia in 1980 convinced President Carter that it was time to reactivate the draft, and he recommended that Congress authorize the registration and conscription of qualified men and women. Congress responded by allocating the funds necessary to register only men, however, so the president ordered reactivation based on Congress's decision.

A group of men promptly filed a lawsuit challenging the constitutionality of the male-only draft. When a lower court declared that the Act violated the due process clause of the 5th Amendment and was, therefore, gender-based discrimination, the case moved to the U.S. Supreme Court. *Rostker v. Goldberg* was argued in March of 1981, and the Supreme Court decision was issued in June. In a 6–3 decision, the Supreme Court held that the single-sex registration was constitutional and did not violate the due process clause. The Court also noted that Congress had considered evaluative evidence before reaching its decision.

In his dissent, Justice Thurgood Marshall notes that the decision "categorically excludes women from a fundamental civil obligation" and relies upon "ancient canards about the proper role of women."

MERITOR SAVINGS BANK V. VINSON

A former bank employee filed a lawsuit against the bank and her former supervisor there, claiming that the supervisor had sexually harassed her and acted in violation of Title VII of the Civil Rights Act of 1965. One party claimed that the two had instead had a consensual sexual relationship, but the other party denied this claim. Nevertheless, the District Court denied relief.

The Court of Appeals disagreed, said a remand was necessary, and noted that a person's clothing and personal fantasies "had no place in litigation." The U.S. Supreme Court then held that incidents of sexual harassment created a hostile or abusive work environment for the former employee, and that, even though the case did not involve economic loss for the person who was being harassed, it was still in violation of Title VII of the Civil Rights Act of 1965.

Section 9.3 • MAY CHEN CO-ORGANIZES THE 1982 NEW YORK CITY CHINATOWN STRIKE

New York City's 1982 Chinatown strike was one of the largest-ever Asian American worker strikes, and May Chen of the International Ladies' Garment Workers' Union co-organized it. Twenty thousand garment-factory workers spilled into the streets of Lower Manhattan to demand that their Chinese employers practice the Confucian principles of fairness and respect, improve their working conditions, and increase their wages. Factory owners responded by withdrawing their demand that workers forego holidays and accept reduced benefits. They also decided against the wage cuts they were proposing. This well-organized strike led to these same factory owners establishing English-language classes and offering transportation services and on-site bilingual interpreters to benefit workers.

The International Ladies' Garment Workers' Union (ILGWU) was once one of the largest labor unions in the United States and one of the first U.S. unions to have a primarily female membership. This union was a key player in labor history of the 1920s and 1930s. The ILGWU union in the United States and Canada represented workers in the women's clothing industry. When ILGWU formed in 1900, most of its members were Jewish immigrants employed in sweatshops – i.e., small manufacturing establishments that employed workers under unfair, unsafe, and unsanitary conditions. Successful strikes in 1909 and 1910 in New York City by the ILGWU resulted in a "protocol of peace" between the women's clothing industry and the union. The protocol greatly improved conditions for the garment makers. Wages were increased, working hours were reduced, the union was recognized by the clothing manufacturers, and a board of arbitration was established to handle labor-management disputes. David Dubinsky, who later served as the union's president from 1932 to 1966, led a successful battle against a Communist attempt to gain control of the ILGWU in the 1920s. When resolutions that would have allowed craft unions to organize the workers in mass-production industries were defeated at the convention of the American Federation of Labor (AFL) in 1935, the ILGWU and seven other AFL unions formed the Committee for Industrial Organization (CIO). All eight were expelled from the AFL in 1937. When the CIO became the Congress of Industrial Organizations in 1938, the ILGWU withdrew and two years later returned to the AFL.

Section 9.4 • TRAILBLAZERS

"Supreme Court Justice Sandra Day O'Connor," "Congresswoman Geraldine Ferraro Chosen as Walter Mondale's Running Mate," "Trailblazing Talk Show Host and Media Mogul Oprah Winfrey," "Bombshell Badass Jane Fonda," •

TRAILBLAZING SUPREME COURT JUSTICE SANDRA DAY O'CONNOR

On September 21st, 1981, Sandra Day O'Connor's seat on the highest court in the land was confirmed by the U.S. Senate with a vote of 99 to 0. Though this unanimous approval was certainly impressive, so was the fact that history had been made: A woman had finally been appointed to the U.S. Supreme Court. O'Connor would ultimately serve as an Associate Justice for 24 years before retiring from her position in 2006.

An alumna of Stanford University (class of 1950), she graduated with a B.A. in economics. She then attended the university's law school, taking an active role in the *Stanford Law Review*. Always an intellectual, O'Connor maintained the high academic standards she was already known for even in her high-school days. She was admitted to the prestigious Order of the Coif (a society for high-achieving law students) and graduated in the top 10 percent of her class in 1952.

Though highly qualified, and more than competent, she was braced to enter a field notoriously resistant to women. Accordingly, her applications to join various legal teams were unsuccessful. Typical of the overt gender biases of the time, one firm even offered her a position as a secretary instead. Offers for paid positions were scarce, but she was eager to kickstart her career. With few alternatives, she accepted an unpaid position at the office of an attorney in San Mateo, California.

Slowly and steadily, she worked her way up, building a reputation as a talented lawyer. She spent some time working in Germany, then took a few years off to raise her children before re-entering the workforce. By 1965, O'Connor had become assistant Attorney General of Arizona, a position she held until the close of the decade. She then transitioned to state politics after then-Governor Jack Williams appointed her to the fill a vacancy in the Senate. Notably, O'Connor won re-election two times before her successful pursuit of a judgeship in the Maricopa County Superior Court.

A moderate conservative, O'Connor was reputed to be firm but fair in the courtroom. In 1979, five years after securing a judgeship, she was chosen to serve on the state's court of appeals. Just two years later, President Reagan nominated her as an Associate Justice of the U.S. Supreme Court.

The unjust reality of the first women to fill any prominent position is that they are often looked upon to prove both their individual abilities along with those of women in general. Added to this expectation is the burden many members of marginalized populations feel to forge a smoother, easier path for those to follow, while knowing that any personal failures will likely have the opposite effect. Meticulous, conscientious, and equity-minded, O'Connor's legacy in the Supreme Court certainly laid a strong foundation for the women who followed.

Though O'Connor "tended to vote in line with her politically conservative nature," she is remembered for her concerted effort to remain unswayed by political agendas. Despite her own conservative beliefs regarding abortion, she voted to uphold the ruling in *Roe v. Wade*, a landmark case concerning reproductive rights. Often, she was the deciding vote in Supreme Court decisions that had implications for voting rights, civil rights, individual privacy, and environmental conservation.

Sandra Day O'Connor, first female Associate Justice of the Supreme Court of the United States

As noted by *Encyclopedia Britannica*:

> O'Connor quickly became known for her pragmatism and was considered, with Justice Anthony Kennedy, a decisive swing vote in the Supreme Court's decisions. In such disparate fields as election law and abortion rights, she attempted to fashion workable solutions to major constitutional questions, often over the course of several cases. In her decisions in election law, she emphasized the importance of equal-protection claims (*Shaw v. Reno* [1993]), declared unconstitutional district boundaries that are "unexplainable on grounds other than race" (*Bush v. Vera* [1996]), and sided with the Court's more liberal members in upholding the configuration of a congressional district in North Carolina created on the basis of variables including but not limited to race.

O'Connor is also remembered for a strong sense of duty. Diagnosed with breast cancer in 1988, she underwent a successful surgery and never missed a court day. Some media accounts describe her appearance as noticeably frail during this time, indicating the physical toll of her ordeal. Still, she did her job with stoicism and discretion, traits she was reportedly known for. By the mid-2000s, however, her husband's protracted battle with Alzheimer's disease called her beyond the courtroom. She cited this as a major factor in her decision to retire in 2006. Three years later, she received the Presidential Medal of Freedom, and a decade after that, she announced that she had been diagnosed with early-stage dementia and would be retiring from public life.

CONGRESSWOMAN GERALDINE FERRARO CHOSEN AS WALTER MONDALE'S RUNNING MATE

Born to an Italian immigrant father and a first-generation Italian American mother, Geraldine Anne Ferraro was raised in New York. The early death of her father prompted a move to the South Bronx, where her mother worked in the garment industry, a popular vocation for women in the 1940s. Her family supplemented its income with a rental property, which allowed her to transfer to an elite boarding school in a suburb north of the city.

A stellar student, Geraldine skipped the seventh grade, and had a virtually permanent position on the honor roll. An academic scholarship took her to Marymount Manhattan College; however, it did not cover all her expenses. To fund her tuition and living costs, she had to maintain two jobs while studying full time. Finally, in 1956, she graduated and received a public-school teaching certification.

Dissatisfied with the teacher's life, she decided to go to law school, again taking classes while working full time. The sacrifice paid off in 1961, when she passed the bar exam. Through her legal work, Geraldine established contacts with Democratic Party members in New York. In 1974, she became the assistant district attorney of Queens County, stationed in the Special Victims Bureau. There, she prosecuted cases involving child abuse, domestic violence, and sexual assault. Within a few years she became head of that unit, and soon gained admission to the United States Supreme Court Bar.

Despite this success, the nature of the work was difficult and exacted an emotional toll. After years of handling tough cases, Geraldine needed a professional change. She had built a solid reputation as a prosecutor, and an associate encouraged her to use this as a springboard to join the U.S. House of Representatives.

Pledging to remain tough on crime and prioritize neighborhood development, she won a House seat in 1978. She was popular among her Queens constituents, who appreciated the fact that she honored her campaign promises. She also made inroads in the party, becoming well-liked and notably influential in a short space of time. Accordingly, she was re-elected in 1980 and again in 1982.

Two years later, the Democratic party was gearing up for the imminent presidential election. Senator Walter Mondale was preparing to vie for the presidency and was inclined to pick a female running mate. Of the five candidates he considered, two were women: Ferraro and San Francisco Mayor at the time, Dianne Feinstein. In the summer of 1984, Ferraro was announced as Mondale's running mate, making her the first woman as well as the first Italian American, to run for national office with the backing of a major party.

Some were critical of the appointment, believing that Mondale was "pander[ing] to pressure groups" to secure their support. For many, however, no alleged agendas could undercut the impact of the momentous event. Indeed, feminist icon Gloria Steinem, dismissed the critiques – remarking that "[h]alf the human race is not a special interest." For her part, Ferraro was well aware that she was poised to break an enduring barrier.

In the early days of her run, it appeared that the self-described "Queens housewife" had mass appeal. A woman from a no-frills background, and familiarity with hardship and hard work, she appeared to be a candidate that everyone could relate to – including those on the margins. A *New York Times* article cited this accessibility as the core of her appeal, describing her as: "A down-to-earth, streaked-blond, peanut-butter-sandwich-making mother whose personal story resonated powerfully."

When the novelty of a woman candidate wore off, however, the candidate faced the same gendered obstacles encountered by any working woman of her time. Unlike other women however, she had to negotiate these stumbling blocks while under a microscope. Perhaps more newsworthy than a female presidential candidate, was a female candidate caught in controversy. Tellingly, reporters often presented her with complex and controversial topics while failing to do the same for her running mate. Throughout the campaign, she fielded questions that he simply was not asked, despite the reality that he was the primary candidate.

In a perhaps more discrete manifestation of sexism, the press also ran content that questioned her womanhood, an example of coded language that perpetuated the notion that femininity and leadership were mutually exclusive. Then, her family's finances were questioned. Calls were made for her husband, a business owner, to release his tax returns to congressional committees. He eventually did, and the documents showed no financial indiscretions, however the speculation itself had injured the candidate's public image.

On November 6th, 1984, Mondale and Ferraro lost the presidential run to Ronald Reagan and George H.W. Bush, amassing just 41 percent of the popular vote. Moreover, the latter won the electoral votes in every state but two: The District of Columbia and Mondale's home state of Minnesota. Ferraro did not give up on her political ambitions, and ran for the Senate a few times, though unsuccessfully. She did, however, find professional success as a business consultant and political commentator on CNN. In the late 1990s, she became an ambassador to the United Nations Human Rights Commission.

Unfortunately, her legacy was tainted by questionable remarks made during the 2008 presidential race. A supporter and associate of Hillary Clinton, Ferraro publicly attributed the success of the Obama campaign to the fact that he was Black: Describing his identity markers as a stroke of "luck" that he would not have fared as well without. She then characterized the public criticism she faced in the aftermath as a form of reverse racism.

Ultimately, there is some valuable nuance in the story of Geraldine Ferraro. Indeed, a fundamental reality of all historical figures is that they lack perfection. As history itself has shown us, many pioneers have demonstrated insight in certain areas, while lacking it in others. Though Ferraro never won another bid for public service, she is remembered for her willingness to try. By entering the race for the nation's highest office, she inspired a sea of female politicians-to-be.

In 2011, she passed away after a long battle with cancer.

TRAILBLAZING TALK-SHOW HOST AND MEDIA MOGUL OPRAH WINFREY

Around the world, Oprah is known on a first-name basis. Ironically, this is not the name she was born with, nor even a stage name she chose, but a common mispronunciation that eventually grew on her. Born Orpah Gail Winfrey, her name was taken from a woman in the biblical book of Ruth. However, people often got it wrong, calling her Oprah so much that she eventually embraced it.

Like many self-made successes, she came from the humblest roots and established herself over time. Born in 1954, her mother was an unwed teenage girl from an impoverished,

President Barack Obama awards the 2013 Presidential Medal of Freedom to Oprah Winfrey during a ceremony in the East Room of the White House, November 20, 2013.

rural part of segregated Mississippi. Oprah's early years were spent with her grandmother, Hattie Mae, who looked after her so that her mother could find work. For her part, Hattie Mae earned an income as a maid for a White family, and the home she shared with her grandchild had no electricity or running water. In a poignant quote, Oprah notes the limited sense of possibility that disadvantage often creates:

> I grew up in rural Mississippi, obviously a Black girl. At the time, we were called "colored" people [or] negroes. My grandmother was a maid; that's all she ever knew. The only real expectation she had for me was that I'd become a maid and – in her words – have some "good White folks." Meaning, people who would not speak negatively about me, who would allow me to take food home, be good to me, and treat me with some level of dignity and respect. That was my grandmother's dream for me.... I remember watching her hang up clothes on the line one day, and saying "you have to watch me Oprah Gail, cause one day you'll have to do this for yourself," and knowing inside myself that this would not be my life.... I believed there was something bigger, greater, more for me.

This early ambition was complemented by remarkable aptitude. By three years old, Oprah learned to read and recite Bible verses. In the absence of other luxuries, church on Sundays gave her an opportunity to hear stories that inspired her to envision a grand, exciting future for herself. It worked, and by the time she was in high school, she already had a job reading the news on the air. At 19, she became the youngest news anchor and the first African American woman to join Nashville's WTVF-TV. This was followed by some time in Baltimore, where she co-anchored the six o'clock news for WJZ-TV.

Then came her first major setback. Station heads felt she became too emotionally invested in the stories she covered – a tendency they deemed "unfit for TV." Just 22 years old, and far from home, she was fired from her evening news gig, an experience she remembers as devastating. Yet, it was also entirely necessary. Oprah herself recognized that she did not have a passion for the news. While she may have gotten too attached to certain stories, she was detached from others, often zoning out while reading more perfunctory accounts. In one instance, she recalled being so distracted that she accidentally mispronounced the word "Canada." In retrospect, she cites this moment as an epiphany: If she were doing something she genuinely loved, she would not be working on autopilot.

What appeared to be a setback was a push in the right direction. The station offered her a hosting position on the network's failing daytime talk show. They had nothing to lose, and neither did she. On August 14th, 1978, she made her debut on *People Are Talking* and found her calling. On this new platform, the traits once deemed professional hindrances turned out to be assets. Personable, emotional, and sometimes theatrical, she gained a following among viewers and the show became a hit.

In 1984, she moved to Chicago, taking over yet another rating failure for WLS TV. Again, station heads had low expectations. She recalls being pointedly told that she would never surpass the ratings of talk show king Phil Donahue. In fact, she did so in a matter of weeks, transforming *AM Chicago* into a local hit. After a year, it was given a new, hourlong format, and renamed *The Oprah Winfrey Show*. By 1986 the program received national syndication and was well on its way to becoming the global phenomenon that nobody anticipated. Perhaps most remarkably, it remained a cultural fixture for a quarter of a century. With an estimated viewership of 40 million each week, Oprah cornered the daytime television market for 25 seasons and 25 years.

Unsurprisingly, her reach had major implications for industries beyond the media. A feature in her book club segments could turn obscure writers into bestsellers, while the segment itself was credited with inspiring a renewed love of reading in the U.S. Similarly, business owners whose products she praised saw exponential sales increases. Her tougher, more gritty episodes provided a national platform for difficult conversations, from racism to homophobia to personal trauma; critics often praised her for handling these issues with empathy and due sensitivity.

A daily presence in the living rooms of millions of people, she expanded her brand. In the early days, she established a production company, naming it Harpo (after the character she famously played in the film adaption of *The Color Purple*). She then developed the Harpo Production studio, where her show and others were taped from the 90s onward. This made her the third woman in the American entertainment industry to own her own studio, preceded only by Hollywood legends Mary Pickford and Lucille Ball. Harpo Productions eventually became the force behind other successful syndicated shows, including *The Dr. Oz Show* (2009–present) and *Dr. Phil* (2002–present).

In 2000 she debuted a self-titled, long-running publication. At its height, *The Oprah Winfrey Magazine* – also known as "*O*"– had local versions published in the U.S. and in South Africa. It averaged millions of monthly sales in the former, and hundreds of thousands in the latter. To adapt to changing times, the publication eventually discontinued its print edition and went fully digital, maintaining a healthy readership even in a difficult era for magazines. By 2003, she was the first Black female billionaire.

In 2011 Oprah shocked the world by announcing that the end was nigh. Despite its continued popularity, she would not extend the show for a 26th season. Undeterred by professional risk or uncertainty, she felt herself called to higher pursuits, notably stating: "In every job I've taken and every city in which I've lived, I have known that it's time to move on when I've grown as much as I can. Sometimes moving on terrified me. But always it taught me that the true meaning of courage is to be afraid, and then, with your knees knocking, to step out anyway."

The endeavor that she stepped into made her the first Black woman to start a television network. The Oprah Winfrey Network, commonly known as OWN, was certainly a challenge, being an entirely new start. Without the faithful daily viewership of the talk show, the network saw underwhelming success in its early years. Still, she built it up over time, in the same way she did her brand many years before. By 2021, the network found its feet, and Discovery Communications purchased a majority stake in the company. Oprah remains chief executive of the network, as well as producer and host of some of its signature shows.

Legacy

Oprah show segments involving car giveaways and fancy gifts garnered the greatest media coverage during the program's later years. Today, they remain some of the most talked about aspects of the show. Though exciting and certainly entertaining, they sometimes distract its arguably more meaningful and enduring legacy – which is not giving in general but giving equitably. While one is a momentary joy or convenience, the other often changes the very trajectory of a person's life.

A strong believer in empowerment through education, Oprah has championed equitable giving: Supported countless scholarships, both directly and through institutions. In the most famous example of the latter, she pledged 25 million dollars to Morehouse College, an endowment that will change the futures of Black men and their families for decades to come.

Perhaps most notably, she started a private boarding school for girls in Johannesburg, South Africa. The Oprah Winfrey Academy educates high-achieving students from impoverished or otherwise disadvantaged backgrounds. They pay no tuition or fees, receive uniforms, and have most of their everyday needs taken care of. For many, it is a welcome opportunity to learn in the absence of socioeconomic burden. The institution has the capacity for approximately three hundred students from grades 8 through 12, many of whom continue to prestigious colleges in their home country or abroad.

Her philanthropy is certainly the crux of her impact, Oprah is also a pioneer several times over. Her mainstream status has perhaps obscured the fact that she effectively broke racial barriers, not only in her "crossover'" appeal, but through the power of representation. For many, she stood in welcome defiance of the often stereotypical and limited depictions of African Americans in the mainstream media. An advocate for education and social service, a self-made media mogul, and a true rags-to-riches story: Oprah is the embodiment of triumph over circumstance.

BOMBSHELL BADASS JANE FONDA

There are so many trailblazing women in the entertainment industry that have had a significant impact on the empowerment of women in America – women like Hattie McDaniel, Bette Davis, Katharine Hepburn, Mary Tyler Moore, Dolly Parton, and Jane Fonda, just to name a few. All of these women were or continue to be forces to be reckoned with, achieving huge accomplishments against all odds. Jane Fonda, however, is in a class of her own. She brings her unique, cultivated, and fine-tuned talents to the forefront of American culture and has been a "go to" inspiration for generations of women.

Fonda has broken barriers, risked public acceptance, and has led the way for women of all ages, demonstrating that women can be strong, opinionated, firm in their convictions, and multilayered. Over her long career – spanning over 60 years and still going strong – she has been a bombshell sex kitten, an outspoken revolutionary, an Academy Award-winning actress, a film producer, a workout queen, and a billionaire's wife.

Fonda was born into a complicated and privileged family. Her father Henry Fonda was considered to be Hollywood royalty and was known to be emotionally distant from his children. Her mother Frances Ford Seymour battled mental illness and committed suicide when Jane was just 12 years old. Jane struggled with the eating disorder bulimia, along with health issues related to the disorder, for decades. "I was raised in the '50s. I was taught by my father that how I looked was all that mattered, frankly," she told *Harper's Bazaar*. "He was a good man, and I was mad for him, but he sent messages to me that fathers should not send: Unless you look perfect, you're not going to be loved" (Brown). A very tough message for any young woman to hear, and without a doubt, particularly profound when received within the context of the 1950s Hollywood scene.

As Jane moved into her 40s, the effects of bulimia were becoming increasingly more difficult to manage. She was at a decision point in her life. She could either continue down an unhealthy and potentially fatal path, or she could fight hard to get her health under control and continue to move forward with her successful, award-winning professional career and family life. Fortunately, she chose the path of recovery over 40 years ago, around the same time that she founded her fitness empire in the early 1980s.

In 1982, with the guidance of fitness professionals, Jane had the confidence and entrepreneurial foresight to create an exercise video targeted at women, combining the use of then state-of-the-art VHS videotape technology, and the draw of exercising at home with a celebrity. The video "*Workout Starring Jane Fonda*" was part of a series of exercise products and not surprisingly, the VHS videotape became a bestseller. The original 1982 tape was the first non-theatrical home video release to top the sales charts. It was the top-selling VHS tape for six years. In total, Fonda sold 17 million videos in the 1982–1995 series, which was a huge success in a previously unproven market (Garcia 2018). This success served as a great inspiration, encouraging other women to create original exercise content packaged up in an easy-to-use format.

Hollywood starlet Jane Fonda in 1963

Jane Fonda opened up the formerly male-dominated fitness industry to women and established the celebrity-as-fitness-instructor model (Stillwell 2019). The success of Fonda's exercise business is what enabled her to fund her political activism, which was her original goal (Ferrise 2018).

Jane had tremendous early success in her acting career, beginning with stage performances in the late 1950s and moving into her film career in the 1960s. She was hard at work averaging nearly two movies a year throughout the 1960s. *Tall Story*, released in 1960, was her first film where she played a college cheerleader pursuing a basketball star played by Anthony Perkins. This performance won her a Golden Globe for Most Promising Newcomer. The 1965 film *Cat Ballou* was a major

Jane Fonda at a political rally in 1975

breakthrough and solidified Fonda's career. This Western Comedy received five Oscar nominations with Fonda's co-star Lee Marvin winning an Oscar for best actor. It attracted considerable attention from the media and ranked as one of the year's top-ten films at the box office. After the success of *Cat Ballou*, Fonda was seen not only as being talented and hard-working, but perhaps even more importantly, she was now being recognized as a bankable actress.

In 1968, she played the lead role in the science-fiction film *Barbarella*, directed by her then husband Roger Vadim. The film opens with Barbella (Jane Fonda) undressing while floating in zero gravity. The viewer is able to see her breasts and full body for a short time. While by today's standards this may seem tame and mainstream, in 1968 this pushed the accepted boundaries of the time, was viewed as being racy, and in turn created a buzz around the film that drove ticket sales. As strategically crafted by her husband, this film established her sex-symbol status.

Fonda won her first Academy Award for Best Actress in 1971, playing the prostitute Bree Daniels in Alan J. Pakula's murder mystery *Klute*. A non-exhaustive list of Jane Fonda's awards spanning her 60-year career includes two Academy Awards (*Klute* in 1971 and *Coming Home* in 1978), seven Golden Globe Awards, four People's choice awards, one Emmy, two American Movie Awards, and in 2019 the Women Film Critic's Circle Award for Acting and Activism. She has had and continues to have a remarkable career and has granted many interviews over the years reflecting on the industry, the personalities, the publicity demands, the challenges, the opportunities, along with the reality for women in Hollywood in America. In a 2018 *Harvard Business Review* interview by Gabriel Joseph-Dezaize, Jane was asked if she had faced sexism in her career. Jane's response to this direct question: "Well, I wasn't paid as much as my male costars. I felt very judged by how I looked, and it made me extremely uncomfortable for a long time. We're talking about the late 1950s and early 1960s, and at that time objectification and sexism were all around you in the movie business. There wasn't a sense that you could do anything about it. It was just life. There were directors who tried to have sex with me before they would give me a job, but I would just laugh. It wasn't until later, with the rise of the women's movement in America, that this began to change" (Joseph-Dezaiza 2018).

In 1972 she changed her focus from being an award-winning Hollywood bombshell to political activism when she became involved in the anti-Vietnam War movement. In an article published by Fox News Entertainment on August 8, 2018, Jane said: "Prior to me becoming an anti-war activist, I had lived a meaningless life, so when I decided to throw in my head in with the anti-war movement everything changed" (Fox News 2018).

As is well-documented, there was historic civil and political unrest in the United States during the late 1960s and early 1970s during the Vietnamese War. This unrest, sometimes peaceful and at other times violent, included protests against the establishment, the civil-rights movement, the feminist movement, and anti-war demonstrations. Fonda was deeply opposed to the war. She began to research and network and then traveled to witness the war firsthand. In July of 1972, she visited Hanoi in North Vietnam. She stated that the United States was intentionally targeting a dike system along the Red River, which was seen as being an anti-American perspective and considered to be North Vietnamese propaganda. Once a photo of Fonda seated on a North Vietnamese anti-aircraft gun was released, there was widespread

The Bechdel Test

Award-winning cartoonist Alison Bechdel created the informal Bechdel test as a way to evaluate bias against women in films, fiction, and other media. To pass the Bechdel test, a work must feature at least two women, these women must talk to each other, and their conversation must concern something other than a man.

Although Bechdel created the test as a bit of fun, it has launched important discussions about both the lack of female characters in movies and the racial disparities prevalent in films. Too often, the female characters in films are insubstantial in comparison to the male characters in the work.

New York Times writer Manohla Dargis coined the phrase the "DuVernay Test" as a way of measuring whether a film portrays "fully realized" African Americans and other characters from marginalized populations as opposed to characters of color who are merely informed by White characters. Do these characters have their own plot lines, motivations, desires, and actions? This test was created in response to growing criticism of the film industry's treatment of and inclusion of people of color, which too often means a filmmaker merely creates a gratuitous character of color in order to check off the diversity box.

outrage from Americans. Jane Fonda's name and reputation were both tarnished. From this point onward she has been known as "Hanoi Jane." In her 2005 autobiography *My Life So Far*, she wrote that she was manipulated into sitting on the battery and had been horrified at the implications of the pictures.

During an episode of *Oprah's Master Class*, Fonda described the scenario in which she was seen laughing and smiling while sitting on an enemy anti-aircraft battery: "These soldiers sang a song; I sang a song in feeble Vietnamese. Everyone was laughing. I was led to a gun site and I sat down. And I was laughing and clapping, and there were pictures taken.... I understand the anger about that" (Robinson 2015). Jane was accused of treason by many. She has acknowledged how that photo sent a terrible message to the American soldiers and their families who were risking their lives on behalf of the country and has apologized for her thoughtlessness at the time (Fox News).

This visit to Vietnam changed Jane's priorities and from this point on, she was only interested in acting roles with substance and typically focused on important issues. She was no longer interested in winning over her viewers and increasing her popularity. In order to deliver a message, she was now willing to alienate viewers, if necessary. When asked if her outspoken political views damaged her acting career, Jane states: "The suggestion is that because of my actions against the war my career had been destroyed.... But the truth is that my career, far from being destroyed after the war, flourished with a vigor it had not previously enjoyed" (Fonda 2005).

At age 83, Jane Fonda is as sharp as a tack and continues to stay true to herself, using her voice in both her acting career and political activism. She is the co-lead in the Netflix series *Grace and Frankie*, in which she and her real-life close friend Lily Tomlin play two unlikely friends who are brought together after their husbands announce they are in love with each other and plan to get married. She is on the frontlines of social justice with her unrelenting activism. After 60 years of delivering her message, it has become very clear that her mission is to help others by providing a platform for marginalized groups and to educate the public on important issues on climate change, sexism, and racism. And this is what makes Jane Fonda an 83-year-old bombshell badass.

GUERRILLA GIRLS EXPOSE GENDER AND ETHNIC BIAS IN THE ART WORLD

The artist–activists who comprise the Guerrilla Girls came together in 1984 to "expose sexual and racial discrimination in the art world." These women use creative means to "undermine the idea of a mainstream narrative by revealing the understory, the subtext, the overlooked, and the downright unfair." Their 1984 founding coincided with the Museum of Modern Art (MOMA) *International Survey of Painting and Sculpture*, which featured 169 artists – less than 10 percent of whom were women despite the prevalence of prominent women artists who could have been featured. The group calls itself "the conscience of the art world" (and the gorilla masks they wear in public serve to remind museums and galleries that they could be anyone, anywhere).

The Guerrilla Girls' first action was a poster campaign that combined statistics with eye-catching graphic design to highlight the longstanding discriminatory practice of excluding women and non-White artists from publications, exhibits, and galleries. This campaign targeted specific artists, critics, curators, dealers, and New York City museums that the women determined to be complicit in this exclusion.

The collective is best known for its interventions, however. Sometimes the women project images and messages onto the walls of an offending institution to call attention to its discriminatory practices, as the Guerrilla Girls did before the 2015 Whitney exhibit.

One poster the Guerrilla Girls produce annually asks, "How many women had one-person exhibitions at NYC museums last year?" (The answer is consistently either zero or one.) Another popular poster features the rear view of a nude woman posing on a chaise lounge and wearing a gorilla mask. The poster asks, "Do women have to be naked to get into the Met?" Of course, another question is, "How are women and non-White artists supposed to earn recognition and a living in this kind of closed system?"

CHAPTER TEN

Stepping Up and Pushing Back, 1990–1999

CHAPTER CONTENTS

Section 10.1 • OVERVIEW

"Overview: Women in the Workplace in America, 1980–1989," • © 2021 Omnigraphics.

Economists describe the 1990s as the golden age for working women. This is true in various respects. From the perspective of social and psychological safety, various legal proceedings helped set a precedent for women to seek legal recourse for discrimination – particularly in the form of sexual harassment. In *Harris vs. Forklift Systems*, for instance, the U.S. Supreme Court ruled that workplace discrimination was grounds for a lawsuit regardless of whether it resulted in outcomes deemed injurious or severe. This was but one of many cases which collectively addressed the policy gaps which allowed sexual harassment to continued unchecked for generations.

In 1993, the Family and Medical Leave Act of 1993 provided legal protections for many women who faced the possibility of termination for taking necessary time away from work. Although parental leave remains unpaid, the Act stipulates that if an employee is away for qualified family and/or medical reasons, employers must preserve their position for up to three months. The qualifying circumstances include adoption, foster-care placement, and pregnancy.

The Women's Legal Defense Fund (now the National Partnership) drafted the legislation that became the Family and Medical Leave Act, which was introduced in Congress in 1984. The Act was then reintroduced every year until it finally became law in 1993. (Congress passed this legislation in 1991 and 1992, but then-President George H. W. Bush vetoed it both times.) President Bill Clinton signed FMLA into law not long after his inauguration in January of 1993.

The National Partnership reports that the FMLA has been used more than 200 million times since its passage, despite it not covering every worker and despite the fact that many working women and men cannot afford to take three months of unpaid leave even if the law provides for it.

Women also made strides in terms of representation and compensation. Admittedly, the nation began the decade on a commendable note: Boasting the sixth-highest women worker participation rate in the world. By the end of the 1990s, women's participation rate reached an all-time high of 60 percent. Simultaneously, women's wages were climbing, and the gender wage gap shrank. By 1999, women were making 76.5 cents for every dollar earned by men. Still, women of color did not enjoy the same progress. Indeed, Black and Hispanic women still earned far lower, at 64 and 54 cents to every male dollar, respectively.

The working woman was also becoming a pop-culture staple. Thanks to increased representation in film and TV, the educated, professional woman entered the mainstream. This was accompanied by an emergence of strong, assertive female characters in youth-directed shows, including animated programs. These expanded media depictions of womanhood, along with national initiatives like "Take Our Daughters to Work Day," helped to inform and inspire the professional expectations of young girls.

Perhaps the decade's crowning achievement for women in the labor force, four women were elected to the Senate in 1992: Carol Moseley Braun of Illinois (the first Black woman elected to the Senate), Dianne Feinstein and Barbara Boxer of California, and Patty Murray of Washington state. Moreover, 24 women joined the House of Representatives. One year later, Janet Reno became the first woman to serve as the U.S. Attorney General – and we finally had a female lawyer in the White House. Welcome, First Lady Hillary Rodham Clinton.

Section 10.2 • AMERICANS WITH DISABILITIES ACT OF 1990

This section contains text excerpted from "Facts about the Americans with Disabilities Act," "Americans with Disabilities Act," (U.S. Department of Justice (DOJ).

The Americans with Disabilities Act (ADA) is a federal law that provides enhanced protections in the workplace for workers with disabilities. For women workers, this translates into an equal opportunity to benefit from the full range of employment-related opportunities that are available to others. For example, discrimination against people with disabilities is now prohibited in recruitment, hiring, promotions, training, pay, social activities, and other privileges of employment. The law restricts questions that can be asked about an applicant's disability before a job offer is made and it requires that employers make reasonable accommodations to known physical or mental limitations of otherwise qualified individuals with disabilities, unless this would result in an undue hardship.

Transportation provisions in Title II of the Act cover public transportation services, such as city buses and public rail transit (e.g., subways, commuter rails, Amtrak) and states that public transportation authorities may not discriminate against people with disabilities in the provision of their services. This means they must comply with requirements for accessibility in newly purchased vehicles, make significant efforts to purchase or lease accessible-use buses, remanufacture buses in an accessible manner, and unless it would result in an undue burden, provide paratransit where they operate fixed-route bus or rail systems. (Paratransit is a service that picks and drops off individuals who are unable to use the regular transit system independently because of physical or mental impairment). Title III provisions also require that buildings make reasonable modifications, such as the addition of ramps, so that people with mobility disabilities are provided access. Other important improvements are that courses and examinations related to professional, educational, or trade-related applications, licensing, certifications, or credentialing must now be provided in a place and manner accessible to people with disabilities, or alternative accessible arrangements must be offered.

Examples of reasonable accommodations include

- Providing or modifying equipment or devices
- Job restructuring
- Part-time or modified work schedules
- Reassignment to a vacant position
- Adjusting or modifying examinations, training materials, or policies
- Providing readers and interpreters
- Making the workplace readily accessible to and usable by people with disabilities

The ADA makes it unlawful to discriminate in all employment practices, such as:

- Recruitment
- Firing

- Hiring
- Training
- Job assignments
- Promotions
- Pay
- Benefits
- Lay off
- Leave
- All other employment-related activities

Section 10.3 • LEGISLATION AND JUDICIAL DECISIONS

This section includes text excerpted from "Family and Medical Leave Act," (U.S. Department of Labor), "*U.S. v. Virginia*: A Judicial Decision That Opened New Doors and Career Paths for Women," • © 2021 Omnigraphics.

U.S. V. VIRGINIA: A JUDICIAL DECISION THAT OPENED NEW DOORS AND CAREER PATHS FOR WOMEN

In *U.S. v. Virginia,* the Supreme Court held that the Virginia Military Academy, a state-supported military academy previously limited to men, must admit women in order to cease violating the equal protection clause of the 14th Amendment, or must cease operating with the use of taxpayer funds. The Court notes that separate would not be equal if Virginia were to create a military program solely for women at another school, and that categorization by sex "may not be used ... to create or perpetuate the legal, social, and economic inferiority of women." The Court also explicitly held that no government unit may "den[y] to women, simply because they are women, full citizenship stature – equal opportunity to aspire, achieve, participate in and contribute to society based on their individual talents and capacities."

FAMILY AND MEDICAL LEAVE ACT OF 1993

The Family and Medical Leave Act (FMLA) entitles eligible employees of covered employers to take unpaid, job-protected leave for specified family and medical reasons with continuation of group health insurance coverage under the same terms and conditions as if the employee had not taken leave. Eligible employees are entitled to:

- Twelve workweeks of leave in a 12-month period for
  - the birth of a child and to care for the newborn child within one year of birth
  - the placement with the employee of a child for adoption or foster care and to care for the newly placed child within one year of placement
  - to care for the employee's spouse, child, or parent who has a serious health condition
  - a serious health condition that makes the employee unable to perform the essential functions of his or her job
  - any qualifying exigency arising out of the fact that the employee's spouse, son, daughter, or parent is a covered military member on "covered active duty," or
- Twenty-six work weeks of leave during a single 12-month period to care for a covered servicemember with a serious injury or illness if the eligible employee is the servicemember's spouse, son, daughter, parent, or next of kin (military caregiver leave).

Section 10.4 • SUPREME COURT JUSTICE RUTH BADER GINSBURG

Ruth Bader Ginsburg was notorious for her brilliant legal mind and the trails she blazed; her tireless work fighting for gender, LGBTQ+, and racial equality, and for the rights of women in the workplace; and for her consistent rulings that protected workers from discriminatory practices.

Ginsburg grew up in a low-income neighborhood in Brooklyn in an observant Jewish family, devoted herself to her studies, and earned a full scholarship to Cornell University, where she met her soon-to-be-husband "Marty," who encouraged her intellectual pursuits. And like Justice Sandra Day O'Connor before her, Ginsburg discovered the full force of gender bias and bias against working mothers when she graduated from law school and no one would hire her.

A law professor intervened on her behalf and convinced a judge to offer Ginsburg a two-year clerkship. She published a book based on the research she did over those two years and was soon offered an assistant-professor position at Rutgers School of Law (which asked her to accept a low salary because her husband had a well-paying job).

When Ginsburg discovered she was pregnant with her son James, she feared that her contract might not be renewed and so wore baggy clothes to hide her pregnancy, and earned tenure there in 1969.

Ginsburg was a moderator on a panel that was exploring issues of gender equality and subsequently published law review articles on the subject. She offered an early seminar on the topic of gender discrimination in 1970 and was quickly recognized as a highly successful litigator in gender-discrimination cases. In 1972, she cofounded the ACLU Women's Rights Project. Her successful litigation of *Struck v. Secretary of Defense* led to protections for pregnant women in the workplace. Before this ruling, women were routinely fired for being pregnant. And in 1973, she coauthored *Sex-Based Discrimination*, the first law-school casebook to address the topic. Ginsburg then accepted a tenured position at Columbia Law School, where she continued her legal work on gender discrimination.

During the 1970s, she argued six gender-discrimination cases before the Supreme Court and won five of them. She also was instrumental in expanding the concept of gender discrimination, and helped others understand that these principles apply broadly and cover gender identity and sexual orientation as well.

In 1980, President Jimmy Carter appointed Ginsburg to the U.S. Court of Appeals in Washington, D.C. In 1993, President Bill Clinton nominated Ginsburg to the U.S. Supreme Court, where she served on the bench as the second woman justice from 1993 until her death in 2020.

Justice Ginsburg wrote the majority opinion for *United States v. Virginia* (1996), a high-profile gender-discrimination case which held that Virginia Military Academy's male-only admission policy violated the equal protection clause of the 14th Amendment. Addressing VMA's argument that its program was unsuitable for women, Justice Ginsburg wrote:

President Jimmy Carter with Ruth Bader Ginsburg at a reception for women federal judges, October 3, 1980

> Generalizations about "the way women are," estimates of what is appropriate *for most women*, no longer justify denying opportunity to women whose talent and capacity place them outside the average description.

That decision resulted in state-funded schools opening their doors to women.

Ginsburg also joined the majority in the *Babb v. Wilkie* (2020) age-discrimination case, a decision that makes it easier for people older than 40 years of age to sue the federal government for age discrimination. And she famously dissented the 2007 *Ledbetter v. Goodyear Tire and Rubber Co.* decision on gender-based pay discrimination and read her dissent aloud, as she sometimes did when she found a majority decision to be especially prolematic.

"When [Justice Ginsburg] was in the minority, she was a powerful voice in dissent in ways that changed the game," said Emily Martin, general counsel at the National Women's Law Center in Washington, D.C. "For example, when five justices ruled against Lilly Ledbetter in her pay discrimination case, Justice Ginsburg's call to action inspired the public and Congress to change the law and strengthen equal pay protections."

Even in death, Justice Ginsburg was a trailblazer, becoming the first woman in history to lie in state at the Capitol.

Justice Ginsburg showed women and girls what a confident woman exercising both her intelligence and her power looks like and showed aspiring lawyers how game-changing federal policy decisions protect not only women but all American workers.

Section 10.5 • ADA DEER

Ada Deer was born in 1935 in Kenosha, Wisconsin. Her mother was a nurse whose passion for Native American culture led her to work on the Menominee Indian Reservation. It was there that Ada was born and raised. Her father, Joe Deer, a tribal lumber mill worker, was a heavy drinker with a dark disposition. Biographers note that the patriarch was perpetually angry, while his daughter describes him as a "hard" man.

In retrospect, Ada traces these issues to socioeconomic challenges unique to his time. He lost his own mother to the 1918 flu epidemic. He then endured the cultural erasure that many Indigenous people faced when forcefully removed from their families and made to attend anglicized boarding schools. There, many had their names changed without consent and were punished for speaking their mother tongues. This is not an uncommon experience of trauma among Native American families, and these forms of cultural suppression often unfolded in contexts compounded by stark poverty.

Ada was exempt from neither of these social ills, making her well-equipped to voice and champion the socioeconomic interests of Indigenous Americans facing similar obstacles.

As early as age four, Ada would accompany her mother to Menominee general council meetings. This was the matriarch's way of broadening Ada's concept of the world: Encouraging her to think beyond the reservation. She would later note that these gatherings had a profound impact, though she did not recognize it at the time. Indeed, they encouraged her to develop a sense of perspective that many of her peers did not have. These early traits of ambition and curiosity were enhanced through her love of reading and learning.

As a teenager, Ada attended public schools in Milwaukee and Shawano, since there were no high schools on the reservation. Through a federal leadership program for students, she was able to visit the University of Wisconsin's Madison campus, her first exposure to college life. Not long after, she returned and enrolled there on a tribal scholarship.

It was not uncommon for women at the time to attend college as a precursor to marriage and motherhood, but Ada had no interest in earning a so-called Mrs. Degree. Deciding she did not want to marry or procreate, she turned her focus to education and embarked on what biographers refer to as her lifetime of firsts.

In 1957, Ada became the first Menominee member to graduate from UW Madison – completing a bachelor's degree in social work. Four years later, she became the first Native American to attain a master's degree in social work from Columbia University. Then Ada promptly began a service-oriented career, working as a social worker in both New York and Minneapolis, then completing a stint with the Peace Corps in Puerto Rico. She later returned to her alma mater, intending to pursue a law degree. However, she felt called to serve and support her tribe instead and promptly discontinued her studies after one semester.

POLITICAL ACTIVISM

In the 1950s, the U.S. government began a process known as "termination" which caused tribes to lose their federal recognition (along with the accompanying protections and benefits). The Menominee reservation was terminated in 1961 and became a county in Wisconsin. Moreover, a corporation, Menominee Enterprises, Inc., was established to manage tribal assets.

In response, Ada helped lead a grassroots movement to protect Indigenous people from the loss of social services and self-determination that the change would bring. The loss of subsidized healthcare was of particular concern, as her community would be left with neither a hospital nor a residential doctor. Moreover, the commercial sale of former reservation land would change the nature of the community. These were some of the issues that residents resisted as they petitioned that Menominee's federal status be reinstated. In service of this cause, Ada helped establish the Determination of Right and Unity for Menominee Shareholders organization, known as DRUMS.

These efforts proved successful when President Nixon approved the Menominee Restoration Act of 1972. The following year, Ada reflected on that protracted journey in *The Washington Post*, saying, "You don't have to collapse just because there's federal law in your way. Change it!" The victory won, she moved on to another landmark achievement as the first chairwoman to lead her Wisconsin tribe, maintaining this position from 1974–1976.

LEADERSHIP

In 1977, Ada returned to UW Madison's School of Social Work as a lecturer in the American Indian Studies program. There, she debuted classes on issues facing Native American communities and others which centered on multicultural perspectives. Perhaps most notably, she developed the first social-work program that prepared students to work on reservations. She remained an instructor there until 1993, when she became the first woman to head the Bureau of Indian Affairs (BIA) following an endorsement from President Clinton.

Cognizant of her own impact and acutely aware of her social responsibilities, Ada said the following during her confirmation hearing:

> At Menominee, we collectively discovered the kind of determination that human beings only find in times of impending destruction.... Against all odds, we invented a new policy – restoration. This legislation is a vivid reminder of how great a government can be when it is large enough to admit and rectify its mistakes. It is also indicative of my tribe's spirit, tenacity, and ability to hold other sovereign entities accountable.

She brought this trailblazing spirit to her role as BIA leader, informing policy decisions for over 500 federally recognized tribes. In 2000, she returned to her old university once more, this time as director of the American Indian Studies Program and a fellow of the Harvard Institute of Politics. In 2010, Ada received a pioneer award from the National Association of Social Workers in recognition of her advocacy for Native Americans. Beyond this, she is also recognized for paving the way for women – and particularly women of color – in civic and federal leadership.

Section 10.6 • **THE RISE AND FALL AND RISE AGAIN OF ELLEN DEGENERES**

America's television viewers first encountered the rising-star, stand-up comic Ellen DeGeneres on the popular ABC sitcom *These Friends of Mine* (1994). Ellen was the clear standout, and when the show returned for a new season it also had a new name: *Ellen* (as in bookstore manager Ellen Morgan, the character Ellen DeGeneres played on TV).

A (carefully cultivated) rumor soon spread that *Ellen* might become the first prime-time sitcom to feature a gay lead character, and Ellen the comic kept the rumor in the news. When interviewers asked her about her own sexuality, she threw out titillating lines such as "I'm a … I'm a… Leeeee … banese."

TIME magazine hit the shelves just before her one-hour special aired, and she was on the cover, along with the headline "Yep. I'm gay."

ABC estimates that 42 million viewers watched Ellen's special, which featured cameos by big-name entertainers, including out lesbian singer k.d. lang and popular media mogul Oprah Winfrey (in the role of therapist for Ellen, the bookstore manager).

Then interest in Ellen waned. Was it her coming out? The writing? Mercury in retrograde? Whatever it was, the show ended the following year and newly out Ellen was out of a job, and deemed too big a risk for some in the entertainment industry to take on.

DeGeneres moved to CBS and tried again with *The Ellen Show*, but her audience just wasn't there. And so she shifted to voice gigs on animated films for a while.

Meanwhile, the world was evolving and inclusion was too, so she tried again with the 2003 *Ellen DeGeneres Show*.

And this Emmy Award–winning syndicated talk show was an instant hit.

Ellen taught us to be who we are.

Section 10.7 • **ANITA HILL**

Foreshadowing a decade of heightened awareness around professional propriety, Americans were captivated by the infamous case of Anita Hill and Clarence Thomas. The former – a female law professor – had accused the latter – a male Supreme Court nominee – of sexual harassment. Moreover, the Senate Committee hearing was televised, creating a spectacle that brought gender and racial politics to the fore. It was the first time a woman had discussed the experience of sexual harassment on such a major platform. For many viewers at home, Hill's public testimony mirrored the workplace challenges that they had endured in silence.

Long before they ever met, Hill and Thomas had a lot in common. Both were educated, self-made Black professionals with roots in impoverished families and the segregated South. Both eventually graduated from Yale Law School and moved to Washington, D.C., though they met for the first time as potential co-workers in 1981. Within the U.S. Department of Education, Thomas had become Assistant Secretary of Education for the Office for Civil Rights. Needing a special assistant, he hired Hill, and the saga that would later capture the nation ensued. It continued as the two joined the Equal Employment Opportunity Commission (EEOC), where Thomas became chair while Hill remained his assistant – a fact that would later be used to question her credibility.

In the decades since Hill's testimony, the general public has gained a greater appreciation of the complexities of harassment and discrimination at work. This includes the knowledge that many survivors do not come forward for fear of retaliation, nor do they resign for fear of career setbacks, economic loss, and various other reasons. Hill did not have the benefit of modern developments (like the #MeToo movement) and contemporary discourses to ensure her testimony was handled with sensitivity.

Instead, she was mocked, subjected to sarcasm, and forced to recount the same details over and over. Significantly, these events unfolded at the hands of an all-White, all-male committee that seemed simultaneously dismissive and invasive. Hill was made to describe the alleged harassment with humiliating detail, while the responses of her audience revealed the extent to which the sexual harassment of women had been legitimized in the American workforce.

In response to Hill's claim that Thomas had inappropriately brought up pornographic materials and discussed them in sexually graphic detail, Senator Arlen Specter remarked that it was normal for people to discuss breasts at work. Other commentary was similarly questionable and often lacking in delicacy or tact. Beyond the stated allegations, Hill's complaint alleged that Thomas repeatedly requested that she go on dates with him, ignored her refusals, and made disturbing sexual jokes and comments.

One aspect of Hill's legacy is the enduring belief that she would not have been subjected to an interrogation so severe if she were a White woman. Ultimately, the reason that historians emphasize the races of the accuser, accused, and those who questioned them, is because these proceedings were unavoidably framed by the biases and stereotypes of the time. More specifically, Hill was almost certainly made vulnerable by age-old beliefs that undermine Black femininity: Placing it beyond the parameters of fragility and deeming it impervious to experiences of trauma or harm. Decades later, many still perceive Hill as essentially unprotected, even by those tasked with safeguarding the proceedings. In the years since, then-Democratic chair (and current President of the United States) Joe Biden faced particular backlash for his failure to adequately mediate.

As noted in a 1993 article by the *Stanford University News*:

> As chairman of the Senate Judiciary Committee at the time, it fell on Biden to preside over the hearings. Critics of his performance tend to hone in on three things. First, he did little to stop members of the committee from attacking Hill. The Republicans were the most relentless. Arlen Specter asked her why she didn't report the behavior to HR and

> said that discussing "large breasts" at work was common. Howell Heflin asked if she was a "scorned woman" and if she had "militant attitude relative to the area of civil rights" or a "martyr complex." Charles Grassley accused her of lifting the pubic hair story from *The Exorcist.*
>
> Second, Biden failed to call additional witnesses who could have corroborated Hill's testimony. One of those women, Angela Wright Shannon, told *Roll Call* in 2016 that it was probably a good thing that she didn't testify. "I don't think I could have maintained the grace and dignity of Anita Hill," she said. Hill, in 2014, said Biden declining to put the other witnesses in front of the committee was "a disservice to me" and "a disservice more importantly, to the public," as allowing those women to testify would have "helped the public to understand sexual harassment. He failed to do that."
>
> Lastly, Biden's critics say that his own questioning of Hill was unfair, blaming him for "setting an accusing, sceptical tone and losing control..." Charles Ogletree, a Harvard law professor and Hill's attorney at the time, told *Politico* that he still blames Biden for mishandling the hearing ... Ogletree said he's brought up the hearings with Biden in the years since, but hasn't been satisfied with the response.

President Biden would later publicly apologize for failing to protect Hill during the interrogation, noting that she did not get a fair trial, and "the system did not work." Thomas, for his part, maintained that the allegations were false and part of a racially and politically motivated effort to discredit him and undermine his professional ascent. After a three-day investigation, the Federal Bureau of Investigation compiled a report stating it believed Hill's accusations to be unfounded, and Clarence Thomas soon became Associate Justice of the Supreme Court, which he remains.

Impact

In 2018, Anita Hill was met with a standing ovation from a sea of female executives at *Fortune* Magazine's twentieth annual "Most Powerful Women" Summit in California. Contemporary social-justice movements have changed the national conversation about sexual harassment. Moreover, they have done so to an extent that Hill likely never imagined possible during her time. Two decades later, many credit her for paving the way for women to take a stand against sexual harassment and voice their related experiences.

Though she is heralded as a trailblazer now, some saw her as such even back then, though her impact was perhaps more discrete. In the aftermath of her widely publicized testimony, the EEOC was flooded with complaints of sexual harassment, and the National Women's Law Center faced a deluge of legal inquiries. Working women were empowered and emboldened to speak up and to take legal recourse. That same year, Congress passed the Civil Rights Act of 1991, guaranteeing the same for women across the country.

There were also legislative changes at the state level, and anti-harassment programs became a staple in various offices and organizations, which they remain today. These developments primed the decade for more gender-inclusive social spaces. Of course, this had a positive impact on women's participation in the labor market. Accordingly, the year that followed, 1992, was decreed the "Year of the Woman," and it certainly was.

Twenty-four women were elected to the House of Representatives, thereby doubling the total number at the time. Four women were also elected to the Senate – tripling the total number at the time. Discussions of sexual harassment in the workplace would feature prominently in the public sphere through the remainder of the decade and then resurge time and time again as the decades rolled by. Through it all, many remember Anita Hill as the woman whose testimony opened the gates for others to tell their stories.

PART FOUR

Diversity: The New Normal, 2000–2021

Introduction, 2000–2021

"Introduction to Part Four, Diversity: The New Normal, 2000–2021," • © 2021 Omnigraphics.

A December 1999 U.S. Department of Labor report indicates that women made up a majority of the workforce (50.04%) at the turn of the century, but few women held executive-level positions. The Equilar Gender Diversity Index (GDI) reports that only 6 percent of Fortune 500 companies had a female CEO at the dawning of the new century and only 2 percent of *Russell 3000* companies had a board comprised of at least 50 percent women. While these numbers remain low, a glance back at the previous decade confirms a steady increase in representation, and a McKinsey and Company report also confirms an increase in female C-level executives. Meanwhile, three out of every five (59.8%) working-age women in the United States worked in the labor force by 1998.

We open Part 4 with a detailed report from the U.S. Department of Labor on women in the workforce in America. This report indicates that the last time women made up a majority of the workforce was during the Great Recession, which officially ended in June 2009, although many of the statistics that describe the U.S. economy had yet to return to their pre-recession values before the 2020 Covid-19 pandemic upended the nation's economy and workforce. We also explore the Great Recession as well as the "Female Recession" that the pandemic created, the role millennial women play in the workforce now and moving forward, and the unequal burdens working women continue to face. We also offer what evidence suggests will lie ahead for America's working women.

CHAPTER ELEVEN

Unequal Pay, Unequal Work, 2000–2009

CHAPTER CONTENTS

Section 11.1 • "STANDING UP FOR FAIR PAY": THE LILLY LEDBETTER FAIR PAY ACT OF 2009

"'Standing Up for Equal Pay': The Lilly Ledbetter Fair Pay Act of 2009," •

Lilly Ledbetter was employed as a supervisor at the Gadsden, Alabama, Goodyear Tire and Rubber Company plant from 1979 to 1998. The salary Ledbetter earned in her final year at the plant was $3,727 but she learned that the lowest paid male in the same position earned $4,286 and the highest earned $5,236.

Ledbetter filed a complaint with the Equal Employment Opportunity Commission (EEOC) and then sued the company under Title VII of the Civil Rights Act of 1964, arguing that her poor performance evaluations were based on her sex rather than her job performance and that they resulted in her earning a lower wage than any of her male coworkers. A jury found for Ledbetter and awarded her over $3.5 million in back pay and damages, but a district judge later reduced that amount to $360,000.

The Court of Appeals, Eleventh Circuit, reversed that ruling on the basis that Ledbetter's claim was time barred. (Title VII requires that a charge be filed with the EEOC within 180 or 300 days of the violation, depending on the state.) The Court of Appeals also concluded that there was insufficient evidence to prove that the company acted with discriminatory intent during the two pay decisions that met the filing deadline.

Ledbetter's case was then brought before the U.S. Supreme Court, which was charged with determining the circumstances under which a plaintiff can bring an action under Title VII alleging illegal pay discrimination, specifically when the disparate pay is received during a statutory-limitation period and is the result of intentionally discriminatory pay decisions that occurred beyond the limitation period.

Justice Samuel Alito authored the 5–4 decision, which held that discriminatory intent must occur during the 180-day statutory period and that Ledbetter's claim was filed outside of the statutory period. Justices Breyer, Ginsburg, Souter, and Stevens disagreed and Justice Ruth Bader Ginsburg – a lifelong advocate for gender equality and worker rights – famously donned her "dissent jabot" and read her *Ledbetter v. Goodyear Tire and Rubber Co.* dissent aloud in the chambers, as she sometimes did when she found a decision to be especially egregious. Ginsburg argued that pay disparities are significantly different from other types of discrimination (such as termination), which are "easy to identify" and which allow workers to seek immediate redress. Pay discrimination, on the other hand, is typically "hidden from sight," occurs in increments, and only becomes evident over time.

Justice Ginsburg then said that the correct approach to deciding this case is one consistent with Title VII's purpose and with the Court's precedent: "Treat each payment of a wage or salary infected by sex-based discrimination" as an unlawful employer act and therefore "outside the 180-day charge-filling period." She also found that the majority's interpretation of Title VII was "incompatible with the statute's broad remedial purpose."

"When [Justice Ginsburg] was in the minority, she was a powerful voice in dissent in ways that changed the game," noted Emily Martin, general counsel at the National Women's Law Center in Washington, D.C. "For example, when five justices ruled against Lilly Ledbetter in her pay discrimination case, Justice Ginsburg's call to action inspired the public and Congress to change the law and strengthen equal pay protections." And, indeed, it did. The Lilly Ledbetter Fair Pay Act of 2009 reversed the Supreme Court's decision and outlined plainly that each discriminatory paycheck resets the 180-day limit to file a claim. The Act also addressed wage discrimination on the basis of age, religion, national original, race, sex, and disability. This was the first bill that President Barack Obama signed into law.

Section 11.2 • **THE GREAT RECESSION AND ITS IMPACT ON WOMEN**

A major factor that contributed to the growth of the U.S. labor force in the second half of the twentieth century was the remarkable increase of participation by women. During this time, the U.S. economy experienced economic growth that increased the demand for labor. Baby boomers (those born between 1946 and 1964) began entering the workforce in large numbers in the early 1960s as they reached working age. Coupled with the rapidly increasing participation of women workers, this resulted in a large influx of women into the labor market. After peaking in 1999, the participation rate of women has continuously declined. During this time, the baby-boom generation aged and the economy experienced the impacts of the severe 2007–2009 recession. The Bureau of Labor Statistics (BLS) projects women's participation in the workforce will continue its decline in the 2014–2024 decade.

The participation rate of women in the workforce increased throughout the 1960s, 1970s, and 1980s, and peaked at 60.0 percent in 1999. Over these four decades, the participation rate increased even during several economic downturns. Historically, increases in the number of working women offset the decline in the rate of male workers. Decreases after the 1999 peak are now contributing to a decline in the overall rate of American workers, however. Since the midpoint of the Great Recession in 2008, women's rate of participation has declined by 2.8 percentage points to 56.7 percent in 2015. The BLS projects that this rate will continue its decline and fall by 0.9 percent to 55.8 percent in 2024.

From the 1960s to the 1990s, large numbers of women in the baby-boom generation entered the labor market. In 1950, 18.4 million women accounted for about one-third of the total workers. In 2000, there were 66.3 million (46.5%) women workers. By 2015, that number had increased to 73.5 million (46.8%). According to BLS projections, the number of women workers will increase to 77.2 million (47.2%) in 2024.

The gender gap has significantly narrowed in the past several decades. Men made up more than two-thirds of the labor force in 1950. By 2000, that gap had narrowed to just 7.0 percent. By 2024, the gender gap is projected to be 5.6 percent.

The share of women in the labor force continued to grow at a higher rate than that of men and has done so for the past six decades. The first wave of baby boomers began working in the early 1960s. From 1964 to 1974, women's participation grew by 43 percent, but growth for men was around 17 percent. Women's participation continued to grow until the early 1980s; then the gap between growth rates of women and men narrowed through the following

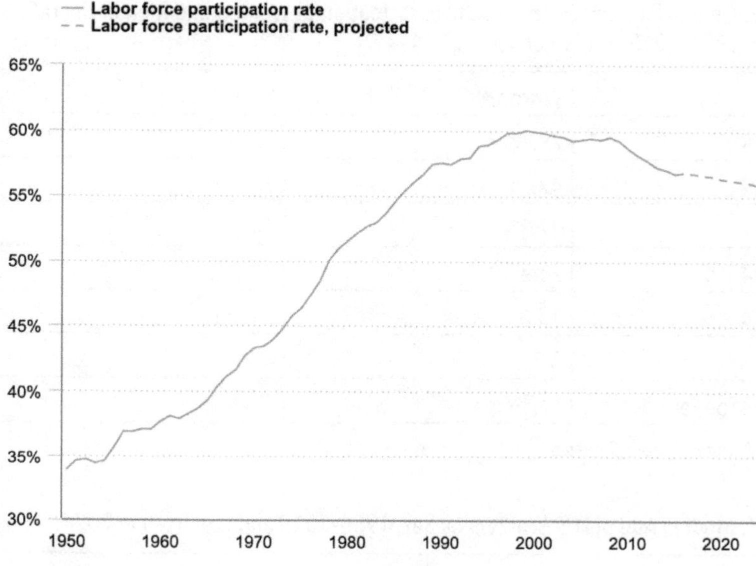

Source: U.S. Bureau of Labor Statistics.

Chart 11.1. Participation of Women in the Labor Force, 1950–2015 and Projected to 2024

Table 11.1. Participation of Women and Men in the U.S. Labor Force, 1950–2015 and Projected to 2024

Year	Percent women in overall labor force	Percent men in overall labor force
1950	29.6%	70.4%
1960	33.4%	66.6%
1970	38.1%	61.9%
1980	42.5%	57.5%
1990	45.2%	54.8%
2000	46.5%	53.5%
2010	46.7%	53.3%
2015	46.8%	53.2%
2020 (projected)	47.0%	53.0%
2024 (projected)	47.2%	52.8%

Source: U.S. Bureau of Labor Statistics

Table 11.2. Growth Rate Per Decade of the Participation of Women and Men in the U.S. Labor Force, 1954–2015 and Projected to 2024

Decade	**Women**	**Men**
1954–1964	29.1%	8.4%
1964–1974	42.5%	16.9%
1974–1984	37.3%	14.5%
1984–1994	21.2%	10.9%
1994–2004	13.6%	11.5%
2004–2014	6.7%	4.9%
2014–2024 (projected)	5.8%	4.4%

Source: U.S. Bureau of Labor Statistics

Table 11.3. Median Age of U.S. Workers by Sex, 1950–2015 and Projected to 2024

Year	**Total Labor Force**	**Women**	**Men**
1950	38.6%	36.7%	39.3%
1960	40.5%	40.4%	40.5%
1970	39.0%	38.3%	39.4%
1980	34.6%	34.0%	35.1%
1990	36.4%	36.2%	36.5%
2010	41.7%	42.0%	41.5%
2015	41.9%	42.0%	41.8%
2024 (projected)	42.4%	42.8%	42.0%

Source: U.S. Bureau of Labor Statistics

decades. From 2014 to 2024, the growth in participation of women in the workplace is projected to be a bit larger than that for men (5.8 percent compared with 4.4 percent).

The median age indicates the age distribution of the working population; it is the age at which half the labor force is above the age and half below. Changes in the median age indicate rapid aging of the U.S. labor force, which has had a measurable impact on labor-market behavior, such as worker participation rates. As the baby-boom generation entered the workforce, the median age of the workers decreased steadily until 1980. Since then, as the baby boomers have aged, so has the labor force. For the decades before 2000, the median age of male workers has been older than that of women. However, since 2000, the median age of women in the labor force has surpassed that of men. This trend is expected to continue, reflecting a higher level of participation by older women than in previous decades.

Table 11.4. Share of Women in the U.S. Labor Force by Age Group, 1950–2015 and Projected to 2024

Year	16-24	25-54	55+
1950	23.8%	63.0%	13.2%
1960	19.9%	63.3%	16.8%
1970	25.8%	57.7%	16.5%
1980	25.7%	61.3%	13.0%
1990	18.5%	70.2%	11.3%
2000	16.2%	71.2%	12.6%
2010	14.0%	66.2%	19.8%
2020 (projected)	12.2%	63.1%	24.7%
2024 (projected)	11.6%	61.3%	25.3%

Table 11.5. Participation Rates of Young Women in the U.S. Labor Force by Age, 1950–2015 and Projected to 2024

Year	16-19	20-24
1950	43.9%	36.8%
1951	44.8%	38.1%
1952	43.6%	38.5%
1953	42.8%	38.3%
1954	42.6%	38.7%
1955	43.1%	39.7%
1956	44.4%	41.0%
1957	43.7%	41.5%
1958	43.0%	42.0%
1959	41.8%	42.3%
1960	42.8%	42.9%
1961	43.4%	43.3%
1962	43.3%	43.4%
1963	42.9%	44.2%

Table 11.5, continued

Year	16-19	20-24
1964	43.3%	44.5%
1965	44.0%	45.2%
1966	46.5%	46.2%
1967	47.6%	47.3%
1968	48.5%	47.9%
1969	50.4%	49.1%
1970	51.3%	50.1%
1971	51.1%	50.3%
1972	53.0%	51.0%
1973	54.9%	52.3%
1974	56.6%	53.9%
1975	57.2%	55.1%
1976	58.0%	56.8%
1977	59.6%	58.5%
1978	61.7%	60.6%
1979	62.5%	62.3%
1980	61.9%	64.0%
1981	61.9%	65.3%
1982	62.0%	66.3%
1983	61.9%	67.1%
1984	62.8%	68.2%
1985	63.7%	69.6%
1986	64.3%	70.8%
1987	64.6%	71.9%
1988	64.5%	72.7%
1989	64.4%	73.6%
1990	62.9%	74.0%
1991	61.7%	74.1%

Table 11.5, continued

Year	16-19	20-24
1992	61.8%	74.6%
1993	62.0%	74.6%
1994	62.5%	75.3%
1995	62.3%	75.6%
1996	62.2%	76.1%
1997	62.6%	76.7%
1998	63.3%	76.5%
1999	62.9%	76.8%
2000	51.2%	73.1%
2001	49.0%	72.7%
2002	47.3%	72.1%
2003	44.8%	70.8%
2004	43.8%	70.5%
2005	44.2%	70.1%
2006	43.7%	69.5%
2007	41.5%	70.1%
2008	40.2%	70.0%
2009	37.7%	69.6%
2010	35.0%	69.3%
2011	34.6%	67.8%
2012	34.6%	67.4%
2013	34.7%	67.5%
2014	34.5%	67.7%
2015	34.4%	68.3%
2016 (projected)	32.1%	67.1%
2017 (projected)	31.2%	67.0%
2018 (projected)	30.6%	66.9%
2019 (projected)	29.8%	66.8%

Table 11.5, continued

Year	16-19	20-24
2020 (projected)	28.9%	66.7%
2021 (projected)	28.0%	66.6%
2022 (projected)	27.3%	66.6%
2023 (projected)	26.6%	66.6%
2024 (projected)	25.9%	66.5%

Source: U.S. Bureau of Labor Statistics

Over time, women born during the baby boom have affected the shares of each age group in the overall labor force. The highest participation rate of young (16–24) women was 27.4 percent in 1975 but has declined since then and is expected to decline further by 2024. The participation rate of women workers in the 25–54 age category increased from the 1980s until 2000 but their share has declined since then. The BLS expects their share to decline even more by 2024, but women in this age range will remain the largest share of women in the workforce. Since 2000, the share of women 55+ years of age has increased from 12.6 percent in 2000 to 22.2 percent in 2015. Their share is projected to grow even more by 2024.

The rate of participation of young (16–24) women in the labor force reached its high point of 64.6 percent in 1987 and has declined considerably since 2000. This decline is expected to continue, and the rate is projected to be 48.6 percent in 2024. Increased school enrollment is a major reason for the declining participation rate of young women. Also, their participation rate is affected by economic downturns, expansions, and competition from older and foreign-born workers for jobs.

Women's participation rates are at their highest when working women are 25–54 years old. Since 1999, the participation rate of these women has declined. The participation rate of women in this age group is least sensitive to economic downturns because these women typically have gained the necessary skills and experience needed to perform their work and they have strong ties to the labor market. By 2024, their participation is projected to trend up to 75.2 percent. This increase is mainly due to a higher projected participation rate for 45–54 years old women workers.

The participation rate of women who are 55 years old or older increased to 26.1 percent in 2000, reached its peak in 2010 (at 35.1%), and remained there until 2013. This rate edged down to 34.7 percent by 2015 and, by 2024, is projected to edge up to 35.4 percent. The historical, sharp increase in participation for older women can be attributed to several factors. Older women are living longer and healthier lives than in the past. Today's older women are more educated and more skilled than ever before. Higher education levels result in higher participation in the labor market. Other factors include an increase in the Social Security retirement age and the elimination of the Social Security earnings test. Also, more employers are offering defined contribution retirement plans instead of defined benefit plans, which

Table 11.6. Participation Rates of Women in the U.S. Labor Force by Age, 1950–2015 and Projected to 2024

Year	16-24	25-54	55+
1950	43.9%	36.8%	18.9%
1951	44.8%	38.1%	18.8%
1952	43.6%	38.5%	19.3%
1953	42.8%	38.3%	19.6%
1954	42.6%	38.7%	19.7%
1955	43.1%	39.7%	21.6%
1956	44.4%	41.0%	22.8%
1957	43.7%	41.5%	22.4%
1958	43.0%	42.0%	22.6%
1959	41.8%	42.3%	23.1%
1960	42.8%	42.9%	23.6%
1961	43.4%	43.3%	23.9%
1962	43.3%	43.4%	23.9%
1963	42.9%	44.2%	23.8%
1964	43.3%	44.5%	24.3%
1965	44.0%	45.2%	24.6%
1966	46.5%	46.2%	24.8%
1967	47.6%	47.3%	25.0%
1968	48.5%	47.9%	25.0%
1969	50.4%	49.1%	25.5%
1970	51.3%	50.1%	25.3%
1971	51.1%	50.3%	25.3%
1972	53.0%	51.0%	24.5%
1973	54.9%	52.3%	23.8%
1974	56.6%	53.9%	23.0%
1975	57.2%	55.1%	23.1%
1976	58.0%	56.8%	23.0%

Table 11.6, continued

Year	16-24	25-54	55+
1977	59.6%	58.5%	22.9%
1978	61.7%	60.6%	23.1%
1979	62.5%	62.3%	23.2%
1980	61.9%	64.0%	22.8%
1981	61.9%	65.3%	22.7%
1982	62.0%	66.3%	22.7%
1983	61.9%	67.1%	22.4%
1984	62.8%	68.2%	22.2%
1985	63.7%	69.6%	22.0%
1986	64.3%	70.8%	22.1%
1987	64.6%	71.9%	22.0%
1988	64.5%	72.7%	22.3%
1989	64.4%	73.6%	23.0%
1990	62.9%	74.0%	22.9%
1991	61.7%	74.1%	22.6%
1992	61.8%	74.6%	22.8%
1993	62.0%	74.6%	22.8%
1994	62.5%	75.3%	24.0%
1995	62.3%	75.6%	23.9%
1996	62.2%	76.1%	23.9%
1997	62.6%	76.7%	24.6%
1998	63.3%	76.5%	25.0%
1999	62.9%	76.8%	25.6%
2000	63.0%	76.7%	26.1%
2001	62.0%	76.4%	27.0%
2002	61.1%	75.9%	28.5%
2003	59.2%	75.6%	30.0%
2004	58.7%	75.3%	30.5%

Table 11.6, continued

Year	16-24	25-54	55+
2005	58.6%	75.3%	31.4%
2006	57.9%	75.5%	32.3%
2007	57.2%	75.4%	33.2%
2008	56.5%	75.8%	33.9%
2009	55.2%	75.6%	34.7%
2010	53.6%	75.2%	35.1%
2011	53.3%	74.7%	35.1%
2012	53.2%	74.5%	35.1%
2013	53.5%	73.9%	35.1%
2014	53.6%	73.9%	35.1%
2015	53.8%	73.7%	34.7%
2016 (projected)	51.9%	74.3%	35.5%
2017 (projected)	51.4%	74.4%	35.7%
2018 (projected)	51.0%	74.5%	35.8%
2019 (projected)	50.6%	74.6%	35.9%
2020 (projected)	50.2%	74.8%	35.9%
2021 (projected)	49.8%	74.9%	35.9%
2022 (projected)	49.4%	75.0%	35.7%
2023 (projected)	49.0%	75.1%	35.5%
2024 (projected)	48.6%	75.2%	35.4%

Source: U.S. Bureau of Labor Statistics

results in more uncertainty about retirement savings. In addition, women may continue working to keep their employer-provided health insurance.

A significant decline in the participation rate of young (16–24) women has pushed down the overall participation rate of women. The participation rate of teen women (16–19) reached its peak in 1989, at 53.9 percent, and a declining trend followed. This rate has declined by nearly 17 percentage points since 2000. The high point of the labor-force participation rate of 20–24-year-old women was in 1999, at 73.2 percent. Since 2000, this rate also has declined for a drop of nearly 5.0 percentage points by 2015. Increased school enrollment, economic downturns, and competition for jobs have contributed to lower participation rates for young women. The projected participation rate of teen women, at 25.9 percent in 2024, reflects a decline of 7.0 percentage points since the latest recession. The projected decline for women ages 20 to 24 for that same time period is smaller, at 2.6 percentage points (66.5 percent).

All groups of women in the 25–54 years old category show decreases in labor participation rates since 2000. Along with this decline their relative share has also decreased from 72.4 percent in 1996 to 63.8 percent in 2015. An important factor in this declining share can be attributed to women born from 1965 to 1975. In 2015, these women were between 40 and 50 years of age. Both the declining size of the age group and their declining participation rates have put downward pressure on the overall participation rate of women.

There has also been a long-term shift in the age composition of 25–54 years old women. The higher participation shares from these women and women who are 35–44 years old have fallen, while the share of women who are 45–54 years of age has risen. This has pushed down the overall labor-force participation rate of women in the 25–54 and 45–54 age range, and older women are projected to participate at higher rates than younger women.

Rates for women in the 25–34 and 45–54 age range tracked closely together in recent years and were the same in 2015, at 73.4 percent. By 2024, participation by older women in these groups is projected to be 77.0 percent. The projected rate of women who are 35– 44 years of age, at 73.9 percent, changes very little.

Participation rates of older women workers have increased significantly since the end of the 1990s and are projected to continue to do so in the next 10 years. The rate of 55–64 years old women increased by 6.6 percentage points, from 51.9 percent in 2000 to 58.5 percent in 2015. Their rate is projected to be even higher in 2024, at 62.9 percent. Even women 65+ years of age saw rising participation rates in 2000, from 9.4 percent to 15.3 percent in 2015. The BLS projects their rate to increase to 18.4 percent in 2024.

With the aging of the baby-boom generation, people 55+ years of age are expected to make up a much larger share of both the population and the labor force than in the past. Because age is a major determinant of the labor supply, the aging of the U.S. population will lower the participation rates of women, men, and the overall rate, which in turn will affect the growth of the labor force.

The overall participation rate of 25–54 years old women increased from 65.7 percent in 1950 to 84.1 percent in 1999, as more of these women began working. Their participation growth not only caused the overall rate for the age group to increase but offset declines in men's participation rate. Between 1950 and 1999, the participation rate of these working women increased from 36.8 percent to 76.8 percent. The participation rate of men in this age group declined from 96.5 percent to 91.7 percent over the same period. Since then, the rates for this age group have declined for women, men, and overall. The BLS projects the workforce participation rate of these women to rise slightly to 75.2 percent in 2024, while the men's rate will continue its decline to 87.2 percent in 2024. The overall

Table 11.7. Workforce Participation Rates of Women Ages 55+ Years of Age, 1950–2015 and Projected to 2024

Year	55-64	65+
1950	27.0%	9.7%
1951	27.6%	8.9%
1952	28.7%	9.1%
1953	29.1%	10.0%
1954	30.0%	9.3%
1955	32.5%	10.6%
1956	34.9%	10.8%
1957	34.5%	10.9%
1958	35.2%	10.3%
1959	36.6%	10.2%
1960	37.2%	10.8%
1961	37.9%	10.7%
1962	38.7%	10.0%
1963	39.7%	9.6%
1964	40.2%	10.1%
1965	41.1%	10.0%
1966	41.8%	9.6%
1967	42.4%	9.6%
1968	42.4%	9.6%
1969	43.1%	9.9%
1970	43.0%	9.7%
1971	42.9%	9.5%
1972	42.1%	9.3%
1973	41.1%	8.9%
1974	40.7%	8.1%
1975	40.9%	8.2%
1976	41.0%	8.2%

Table 11.7, continued

Year	55-64	65+
1977	40.9%	8.1%
1978	41.3%	8.3%
1979	41.7%	8.3%
1980	41.3%	8.1%
1981	41.4%	8.0%
1982	41.8%	7.9%
1983	41.5%	7.8%
1984	41.7%	7.5%
1985	42.0%	7.3%
1986	42.3%	7.4%
1987	42.7%	7.4%
1988	43.5%	7.9%
1989	45.0%	8.4%
1990	45.2%	8.6%
1991	45.2%	8.5%
1992	46.5%	8.3%
1993	47.2%	8.1%
1994	48.9%	9.2%
1995	49.2%	8.8%
1996	49.6%	8.6%
1997	50.9%	8.6%
1998	51.3%	8.6%
1999	51.5%	8.9%
2000	51.9%	8.9%
2001	53.2%	9.8%
2002	55.2%	9.8%
2003	56.6%	10.6%
2004	56.3%	11.1%

Table 11.7, continued

Year	55-64	65+
2005	57.0%	11.5%
2006	58.2%	11.7%
2007	58.3%	12.6%
2008	59.1%	13.3%
2009	60.0%	13.6%
2010	60.2%	13.8%
2011	59.5%	14.0%
2012	59.4%	14.4%
2013	59.2%	14.9%
2014	58.8%	15.1%
2015	58.5%	15.3%
2016 (projected)	59.8%	16.0%
2017 (projected)	60.2%	16.3%
2018 (projected)	60.6%	16.6%
2019 (projected)	61.0%	17.0%
2020 (projected)	61.4%	17.3%
2021 (projected)	61.8%	17.7%
2022 (projected)	62.1%	17.9%
2023 (projected)	62.5%	18.1%
2024 (projected)	62.9%	18.4%

Source: U.S. Bureau of Labor Statistics

Table 11.8. Workforce Participation Rates of Women and Men, 25–54 Years of Age, 1950–2015 and Projected to 2024

Year	Women	Men	Overall
1950	36.8%	96.5%	65.7%
1951	38.1%	96.8%	66.2%
1952	38.5%	97.2%	66.6%

Table 11.8, continued

Year	Women	Men	Overall
1953	38.3%	97.4%	66.9%
1954	38.7%	97.3%	67.0%
1955	39.8%	97.4%	67.6%
1956	41.0%	97.3%	68.2%
1957	41.5%	97.1%	68.3%
1958	42.0%	97.1%	68.6%
1959	42.3%	97.1%	68.7%
1960	42.9%	97.0%	68.9%
1961	43.3%	96.9%	69.1%
1962	43.4%	96.8%	69.0%
1963	44.2%	96.8%	69.4%
1964	44.5%	96.8%	69.6%
1965	46.2%	96.7%	69.9%
1966	46.2%	96.6%	70.3%
1967	47.3%	96.6%	70.9%
1968	47.9%	96.3%	71.1%
1969	49.1%	96.1%	71.6%
1970	50.1%	95.8%	72.0%
1971	50.3%	95.5%	72.0%
1972	51.0%	95.1%	72.2%
1973	52.3%	95.0%	72.9%
1974	53.9%	94.7%	73.6%
1975	55.1%	94.4%	74.1%
1976	56.8%	94.2%	74.9%
1977	58.5%	94.2%	75.8%
1978	60.6%	94.3%	76.9%
1979	62.3%	94.4%	77.9%
1980	64.0%	94.2%	78.6%

Table 11.8, continued

Year	Women	Men	Overall
1981	65.3%	94.1%	79.3%
1982	66.3%	94.0%	79.8%
1983	67.1%	93.8%	80.1%
1984	68.2%	93.9%	80.7%
1985	69.6%	93.9%	81.5%
1986	70.8%	93.8%	82.0%
1987	71.9%	93.7%	82.5%
1988	72.7%	93.6%	82.9%
1989	73.6%	93.7%	83.4%
1990	74.0%	93.4%	83.5%
1991	74.1%	93.1%	83.4%
1992	74.6%	93.0%	83.6%
1993	74.6%	92.6%	83.4%
1994	75.3%	91.7%	83.4%
1995	75.6%	91.6%	83.5%
1996	76.1%	91.8%	83.8%
1997	76.7%	91.8%	84.1%
1998	76.5%	91.8%	84.1%
1999	76.8%	91.7%	84.1%
2000	76.7%	91.6%	84.0%
2001	76.4%	91.3%	83.7%
2002	75.9%	91.0%	83.3%
2003	75.6%	90.6%	83.0%
2004	75.3%	90.5%	82.8%
2005	75.3%	90.5%	82.8%
2006	75.5%	90.6%	82.9%
2007	75.4%	90.9%	83.0%
2008	75.8%	90.5%	83.1%

Table 11.8, continued

Year	Women	Men	Overall
2009	75.6%	89.7%	82.2%
2010	75.2%	89.3%	82.2%
2011	74.7%	88.7%	81.6%
2012	74.5%	88.7%	81.4%
2013	73.9%	88.4%	81.3%
2014	73.9%	73.9%	80.9%
2015	73.7%	88.3%	80.9%
2016 (projected)	74.3%	88.0%	81.0%
2017 (projected)	74.4%	89.9%	81.1%
2018 (projected)	74.5%	87.8%	81.1%
2019 (projected)	74.6%	87.7%	81.1%
2020 (projected)	74.8%	87.6%	81.1%
2021 (projected)	74.9%	87.5%	81.1%
2022 (projected)	75.0%	87.4%	81.2%
2023 (projected)	75.1%	87.3%	81.2%
2024 (projected)	75.2%	87.2%	81.2%

Source: U.S. Bureau of Labor Statistics

Table 11.9. Share of Women in the Workforce by Race and Ethnicity, 1950–2015 and Projected to 2024

Year	White	Black	Asian	All Other Groups
1980	86.00%	11.50%	2.40%	0.00%
1990	84.10%	12.20%	3.70%	0.00%
2000	81.60%	13.10%	4.40%	0.90%
2010	79.80%	13.10%	4.70%	2.40%
2015	77.00%	13.90%	5.80%	3.30%
2020 (projected)	76.40%	14.10%	6.20%	3.20%
2024 (projected)	75.50%	14.40%	6.60%	3.60%

Source: U.S. Bureau of Labor Statistics

Table 11.10. Share of Women's Labor Force by Hispanic Ethnicity, 1980–2015 and Projected to 2024

Year	Hispanic Women	Non-Hispanic Women
1980	5.10%	94.90%
1990	7.30%	92.70%
2000	10.20%	89.80%
2010	12.80%	87.20%
2015	15.10%	84.90%
2020 (projected)	16.70%	83.30%
2024 (projected)	18.10%	81.90%

NOTE: The U.S. Department of Labor uses the term "Hispanic" as an umbrella term to identify women of Hispanic and Latina origin.
Source: U.S. Bureau of Labor Statistics

participation rate of all workers in this age group is projected to rise slightly, to 81.2 percent in 2024. Women in the U.S. labor force are projected to become more diverse. Reflecting the greater racial and ethnic diversity of today's population, diversity has also increased in the past several decades for both women and men. Over the next 10 years, working women will become even more racially and ethnically diverse. Immigration is the main engine of population and labor-force growth. White women are projected to retain the largest share of working women in 2024, but their share is projected to decline to 75.5 percent. The shares held by Asian, Black, and "all other groups" of working women are projected to increase in the next decade.

Hispanic/Latina workers make up a growing share of the female labor market. The nation's female workforce has become more diverse in recent decades, as the share held by Hispanic people has grown. (NOTE: The U.S. Department of Labor uses the term "Hispanic" as an umbrella term to identify women of Hispanic and Latina origin.) In 1980, Hispanic women comprised just 5.1 percent of women workers. By 2024, they are projected to account for 18.1 percent. At the same time, the share held by non-Hispanic workers has been declining and is projected to fall further by 2024.

Women workers have become more diverse in the past several decades, with increasing shares of Asian, Black, and Hispanic workers. Black women have the highest participation rate and Hispanic women the lowest. White non-Hispanic women have the second highest participation rate. The participation rates of women in each race and ethnic group increased from the 1960s to the 1990s. However, rates peaked at the end of the 1990s and started declining around 2000. The BLS projects that Asian women's participation rate will trend up in the next 10 years and converge with the rate for White non-Hispanic women in 2024. The rate for White non-Hispanic women is projected to move down in

Table 11.11. Labor-force Participation Rates of Women by Race and Ethnicity, 1980–2015 and Projected to 2024

Year	Black	Asian	Hispanic	White Non-Hispanic
1980	53.20%	55.40%	47.40%	51.30%
1990	53.50%	54.40%	48.30%	52.10%
2000	53.70%	54.80%	48.10%	52.70%
2010	54.20%	55.20%	47.70%	53.00%
2015	55.20%	55.60%	49.60%	53.50%
2020 (projected)	56.50%	56.80%	49.30%	54.50%
2024 (projected)	56.90%	57.00%	50.10%	55.40%

NOTE: The U.S. Department of Labor uses the term "Hispanic" as an umbrella term to identify women of Hispanic and Latina origin.
Source: U.S. Bureau of Labor Statistics

2024. The participation rate for Black women is projected to decline slightly. And the participation rate of Hispanic women is projected to increase in 2024.

Section 11.3 • **AGE DISCRIMINATION IS A WOMAN'S ISSUE**

This section includes text excerpted from "The State of Age Discrimination and Older Workers in the U.S. 50 Years after the Age Discrimination in Employment Act {ADEA}," (U.S. Equal Employment Opportunity Commission) and other cited sources.

Research confirms that older workers who lose a job face more barriers in their search for new employment than younger workers. Research also makes clear that, while both male and female workers who are 40+ years of age report widespread age discrimination in the workplace, older women are significantly more vulnerable than are older men. This is explained, in part, by the fact that older working women are members of at least two historically underrepresented populations of workers – they are both older and female – which leaves them more likely to encounter bias in their later years.

A 54-year-old worker who lost her job in early 2008 at the beginning of the Great Recession is now 68 years old. The average unemployment duration for a 54-year-old was almost a year, and it may have taken her many more years than that to find a new job. Further, this new job may not have been on a par with the one she had before the recession. To make up for that financial loss, she will likely need to work longer than originally planned and may still be in the workforce.

Intersectional Claims

The EEOC reports that the commission has "long recognized the theory of 'intersectional discrimination' under both Title VII and the ADEA" when an individual is treated differently because she or he belongs to more than one protected category and is subjected to a set of stereotyping unique to her or his status. The commission also reports that the availability of an intersectional claim has become increasingly important for older women in the workplace as more older women experience both age and sex discrimination. Yet, as outlined in section 7.3, recent research indicates that, until these laws are rewritten, older women will remain less protected by them than their male counterparts.

Today's Baby Boomers range in age from 57 to 75. Because of that nearly 20-year span in age, these workers have widely different considerations about work and retirement. While about 10,000 Baby Boomers retire every day, many have inadequate savings for retirement. Work life has changed dramatically since Boomers entered the workforce. Instead of a career spanning one industry and a few positions, as was expected at the beginning of their careers, most workers today are expected to have 11 different jobs in our modern, dynamic economy. Behind the Boomers, the leading edge of Generation X workers are now in their early fifties. And, in 2016, Millennials surpassed Baby Boomers as the largest segment of the workforce in the United States.

Today's older female workers face more unfounded and outdated assumptions about their abilities than older men (Whitehill).

Despite decades of research finding that age does not predict ability or performance, employers often fall back on precisely the ageist stereotypes that the Age Discrimination in Employment Act (ADEA) of 1967 was enacted to prohibit. The purpose of this federal law was to promote the employment of older workers based on ability.

Writing for Anchor Business Brokers, Steven Whitehill notes that evidence indicates that older female workers are far more likely to be discriminated against than older male workers. "When taken together," Whitehill explains, "age discrimination and gender discrimination against women in the workplace means that women are constantly fighting an uphill battle for equality in the workplace."

Whitehill also cites a National Bureau of Economic Research study that researchers say provides evidence that "age discrimination laws do not deal effectively with the situation of older women who face both age and gender bias" at the workplace and, as a result, "older women are discriminated against … more so than their old[er] male counterparts" (Neumark et al.). This study further notes that:

> Based on evidence from over 40,000 job applications, we find robust evidence of age discrimination in hiring against older women, especially those near retirement age. But we find that there is considerably less evidence of age discrimination against men after correcting for the potential biases this study addresses.

Writing for the *Harvard Business Review*, Lauren Stiller Rikleen offers a firsthand account of how one older woman in the American workforce was forced out of her workplace:

> Susan [not her real name] is a woman in her 60s who has spent decades working in the insurance business. After years of performance reviews describing her outstanding work ethic, her fortunes turned once she started reporting to a woman 20 years her junior. Under her new manager, Susan felt set up to fail – she was assigned more cases and held to much higher standards than her younger colleagues. Susan's manager issued a formal performance evaluation that characterized her as failing in her duties. Although Susan was supposed to have 90 days to improve, her manager fired her after a few days. Susan has since sued her employer for age discrimination.

Unfounded assumptions about age and ability continue to drive age discrimination in the workplace. Research on ageist stereotypes demonstrates that most people have specific negative beliefs about aging and that most of those beliefs are inaccurate. These stereotypes are most often directed at older women workers, which can lead to negative evaluations and firing, rather than coaching or retraining.

Today's experienced workers are healthier, more educated, and work and live longer than previous generations. And experienced workers have talent that our economy cannot afford to waste. Age-diverse teams and workforces can improve employee engagement, performance, and productivity by actively promoting a multigenerational workforce.

Research indicates that company profits and share performance can be close to 50 percent higher when women are well represented at the top (Dixon-Fyle, et al.). This means that discriminatory practices that weed out older women may also be harmful to the employer. Younger women also lose a vital opportunity to be mentored by older women in positions of responsibility, as a McKinsey & Company study notes.

It is important to acknowledge the significant harm and costs to older workers, their families, and employers that age discrimination causes. The financial and emotional harm of age discrimination on older workers and their families is significant. Once an older woman worker loses a job, she will likely endure the longest period of unemployment compared to other age groups and will likely take a significant pay cut should she become re-employed. The loss of a job has serious long-term financial consequences as older workers often must draw down their retirement savings while unemployed and are likely to suffer substantial losses in income if they become re-employed.

The emotional harm of any discrimination is traumatic. For older workers, they typically feel betrayed when they have given many years of their working lives to one employer. Research shows that perceived age discrimination also results in serious negative health effects, in part, because with advancing age, older individuals are exposed to more negative ageist stereotypes that make them feel older than their chronological age. Forced retirement correlates with significant declines in mental and physical health that can lead to shortened life spans.

Changing employment practices can help change attitudes and increase appreciation for a multigenerational workforce. Simply put, our economy cannot afford to waste the knowledge, talent, and experience of older workers.

Section 11.4 • THE WHISTLEBLOWERS

"The Whistleblowers," • © 2021 Omnigraphics.

In 2002, three courageous female whistleblowers revealed widespread corruption and ethical and leadership failures.

In 2001, **Sherron Watkins**, then the Vice President of Corporate Development for the multi-billion-dollar energy company Enron Corporation, alerted CEO Kenneth Lay to what appeared to be internal accounting irregularities that she had discovered. She also contacted a friend at the Arthur Andersen accounting firm, which audited the company, and this friend alerted the firm's partners to the burgeoning scandal.

What Watkins found were special-purpose entities, accounting loopholes, and shoddy and deliberately misfiled financial reports that the company's executive team used to hide from shareholders and the company's board of directors billions of dollars in company debt and other failings. The group also pressured accountants from the top-five Arthur Andersen firm to keep quiet about these irregularities during their audits. When the inevitable Enron scandal erupted, it was considered to be the largest audit failure in the nation's history and, all told, 16+ executives or associates either pleaded guilty or were found to be guilty of various crimes.

Enron's stock price plummeted following word of the scandal, which led to shareholders filing suit against the company and the U.S. Securities and Exchange Commission (SEC) and Congress launching investigations. When Enron filed for Chapter 11 bankruptcy, this filing of $63.4 billion in assets represented the largest corporate bankruptcy in the nation's history – at least until the 2002 Worldcom scandal, which is summarized below.

Enron whistleblower Sherron Watkins, an accountant, was employed by three large multi-billion-dollar global companies during her career – the aforementioned accounting firm Arthur Anderson, the German metal mega-corporation Metallgessellschaft, and the infamous Enron, and all three imploded because of scandals.

Today, this courageous whistleblower lectures widely on ethics and leadership in business and shares what these corporations taught her firsthand about the high cost of eroded values. Watkins is coauthor of the book *Power Failure, the Inside Story of the Collapse of Enron* (Doubleday, 2003).

Whistleblower **Cynthia Cooper** was the Vice President of Internal Audit at the telecom giant WorldCom when she discovered evidence of what was later deemed to be the largest accounting fraud in history.

Cooper was urged to back off and delay audits soon after she began her investigation, which led her and her team to work behind closed doors to continue their investigation. What she ultimately discovered was that CFO Scott Sullivan was running a multi-billion-dollar fraud.

Sullivan is the employee who convinced WorldCom's then-CEO Bernie Ebbers to buy MCI.

Cooper believes that the CEO's "propensity for taking risks contributed to both the rise and fall of the company." Those high-risk decisions ultimately resulted in his net worth

CEO in a meeting with her staff

plummeting to rock bottom and his missteps racking up a debt of $400 million in loans owed to WorldCom.

Cooper wrote about her experiences challenging WorldCom executives in her best-selling book *Extraordinary Circumstances*. And Cooper, like Sherrod, is now a motivational speaker. She is also credited with changing Corporate America through her actions.

CFO magazine writers Julia Homer and David Katz note that internal audits improved considerably in the wake of this scandal, but some aspects of the Sarbanes-Oxley Act of 2002 actually decreased the amount of time an auditor can devote to performing risk-based audits:

> Section 404 wasn't initially a part of the Sarbanes Oxley Bill that passed the House. It was added in the Senate only after the WorldCom fraud. These two paragraphs … have proven to be an albatross to Corporate America. What WorldCom and a lot of the recent corporate scandals have in common is collusion at the very highest levels of the company, which means most of the basic controls can be bypassed.

But one positive effect, they continue, "is that executive management and the board now recognize the importance of a strong internal-control framework, which means support for internal-audit departments that have often struggled for resources and stature."

Following the 9/11 terrorist attacks in 2001, whistleblower **Coleen Rowley**, a Chief Division Counsel for a Minnesota branch of the Federal Bureau of Investigation (FBI), exposed the Bureau's failure to respond to warnings from her field office about conspirator and suspected terrorist Zacarias Moussaoui, and a looming potential attack on the United States. Rowley testified before the Senate Judiciary Committee about the problems she saw in this oversight and suggested needed improvements in FBI and intelligence-community responses.

The Whistleblower Protection Enhancement Act of 2012 clarifies the disclosures of information protected from prohibited personnel practices. It also requires a statement in nondisclosure policies, forms, and agreements so that they conform with disclosure protections.

She also wrote a memo to then-FBI Director Robert Mueller criticizing the FBI for ignoring and mishandling information about this potential attack on the country. This led to a two-year Department of Justice Inspector General Investigation.

The FBI reorganized in response to Rowley's memo and the subsequent Department of Justice investigation.

These three whistle-blowers were named *TIME* magazine's Persons of the Year in 2002.

Section 11.5 • **TRAILBLAZERS**

"First Lady Michelle Obama," "Trailblazing Senator Tammy Duckworth," •

FIRST LADY MICHELLE OBAMA

First Lady Michelle Obama is a lawyer, community organizer, writer, and wife of former U.S. President Barack Obama. Before serving as First Lady from 2009 to 2017, she was a lawyer, Chicago city administrator, and a community-outreach worker.

Michelle Obama graduated *cum laude* from Princeton University with a B.A. in sociology before studying law at Harvard University, where she was awarded a J.D. in 1988. As a law student there, she took part in demonstrations calling for the hiring of more minority professors.

After three years of working with a corporate firm, she decided to pursue a career in public service. In 1993, she became executive director of the Chicago branch of Public Allies, a leadership-training program that prepares young adults for careers in the public sector. In 1996, she developed a community-service program for the University of Chicago. As First Lady, she amplified social issues such as education, poverty, and health, and encouraged children (and adults) to eat healthy meals and to be physically active.

The first lady's "Let's Move!" campaign was a comprehensive initiative that sought to solve the public-health crisis of childhood obesity. The goal was to raise a healthier generation of physically active kids. The campaign included a Let's Move! blog in which parents and kids could learn facts about the importance of a healthy diet and physical activity. The blog also featured the annual White House Kitchen Garden Planting, described the benefits of various vegetables, and encouraged families to grow their own food.

"In the end," First Lady Michelle Obama said, "this isn't just a policy issue for me. This is a passion. This is my mission. I am determined to work with folks across this country to change the way a generation of kids thinks about food and nutrition."

First Lady Michelle Obama, Official Portrait

In 2018, Michelle Obama published her best-selling memoir *Becoming*, which discusses the life experiences that shaped who she is today.

More recently, former first lady Michelle Obama and Dr. Jill Biden, the current first lady, launched the national initiative "Joining Forces." This comprehensive initiative focuses on mobilizing various sectors of people across the nation in a manner that provides more

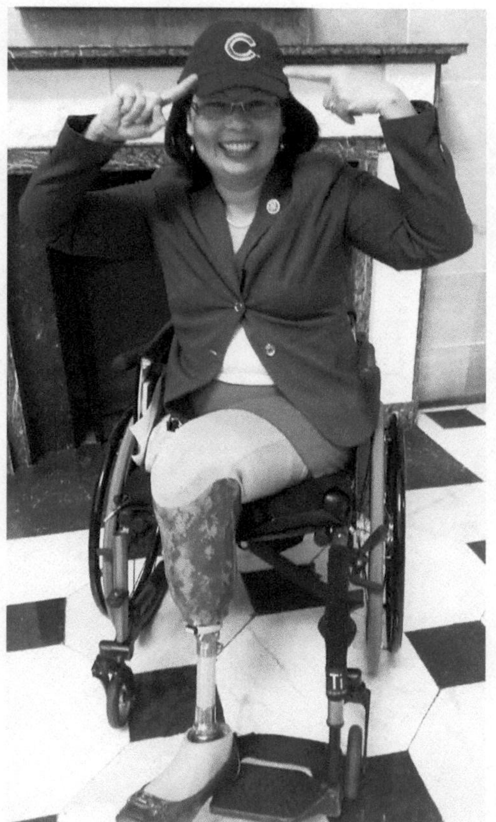
U.S. Senator Tammy Duckworth of Illinois wearing a Chicago Cubs cap on Capitol Hill, October 7, 2015

support and opportunities to service members and their families.

TRAILBLAZING SENATOR TAMMY DUCKWORTH

U.S. Senator Tammy Duckworth is a trailblazer on multiple fronts. She is an Iraq War veteran, a Purple Heart recipient, the former Assistant Secretary of the U.S. Department of Veterans Affairs, one of the first female pilots to fly combat missions during Operation Iraqi Freedom, the first American female double amputee wounded in battle, the first disabled woman elected to Congress, the first Thai American woman elected to Congress, one of the first Asian Americans elected to Congress, and the first sitting senator to give birth during her term in office (and, as such, was instrumental in helping to establish maternity-leave policies for the Senate).

Senator Duckworth has had a variety of careers in the American workplace. She served in the Army Reserve Forces for 23 years before retiring at the rank of Lieutenant Colonel. She was deployed to Iraq as a Blackhawk helicopter pilot for the Illinois Army National Guard in 2004. On November 12th of that same year, her helicopter was hit by a rocket-propelled grenade, and she lost her legs and partial use of her right arm. After spending a year recovering at Walter Reed Army Medical Center, she became Director of the Illinois Department of Veterans Affairs. Five years later, President Obama appointed Duckworth as the U.S. Assistant Secretary of Veterans Affairs. In this role, she addressed many of the unique challenges that female and Native American active soldiers and veterans face. Duckworth was elected to the U.S. Senate in 2016 after representing Illinois's Eighth Congressional District in the U.S. House of Representatives for two terms. As of this writing, She remains a sitting Senator.

"I understand that not everyone thinks about [accessibility] because for most of my adult life, I didn't either," she tweeted. "But the truth is that everyone is one bad day away from needing accessible options the #ADA requires to help them get around." The Americans with Disabilities Act (ADA) protects roughly 40 million American citizens with disabilities, including trailblazing Senator Tammy Duckworth.

CHAPTER TWELVE

Don't Ask, Do Tell, 2010–2019

CHAPTER CONTENTS

Section 12.1 • **OVERVIEW**

"Overview: Women in the Workplace in America, 2010–2019," • © 2021 Omnigraphics.

The United States experienced its lowest unemployment rate in 18 years during this decade, but as the economy gained jobs, wage disparities persisted.

In 2016, women earned $0.82 for every dollar all man earned; Black women earned $0.79 for every dollar a White man earned; and Latina women earned $0.60 for every dollar a White man earned.

The Bureau of Labor Statistics reported:

> In 2018, 57.1 percent of all women participated in the labor force. This was about the same as the 57.0 percent who participated in 2017, and still about 3 percentage points below the peak of 60.0 percent in 1999. By comparison, the labor force participation rate for men was 69.1 percent in 2018, unchanged from the previous year and 17.5 percentage points below its peak of 86.6 percent in 1948.
>
> The rapid rise in women's labor force participation was a major development in the labor market during the second half of the 20th century. Overall, women's labor-force participation increased dramatically from the 1960s through the 1980s, before slowing in the 1990s. With the dawn of the 21st century, labor force participation among women began a gradual decline, until the participation rate hit a recent low in 2015 at 56.7 percent.
>
> Women's involvement in the labor market has changed in several notable ways over the past several decades. For example, women became much more likely to pursue higher levels of education: from 1970 to 2018, the proportion of women ages 25 to 64 in the labor force who held a college degree quadrupled, whereas the proportion of men with a college degree about doubled over that time. Women also have become more likely to work full time and year round. In addition, women's earnings as a proportion of men's earnings have grown over time: women working full time earned 62 percent of what men earned in 1979 and 81 percent in 2018. More recently, women in the baby-boom generation (defined as people born between 1946 and 1964) have begun to retire in large numbers, which has put downward pressure on their labor force participation rate over the past decade or so.

During this decade, the Don't Ask, Don't Tell Act – the discriminatory policy that caused numerous women who served in the military to be dismissed – was repealed, the Defense of Marriage Act was nullified, and a landmark ruling resulted in working women in same-sex relationships gaining over 1,000 rights that had previously been granted only to opposite-sex marriages, including the right to marry and include members of their families on their employer health insurance plans.

Passage of the Patient Protection and Affordable Care Act of 2010 (Obamacare) made health insurance affordable for people with pre-existing conditions and for gig workers – and at a time when most bankruptcies in the nation were tied to medical bills.

The military ban on women in combat was lifted and trailblazer Hillary Rodham Clinton – lawyer, First Lady, Senator, U.S. Secretary of State, and then Democratic candidate for president – ran a historic race in 2016.

Section 12.2 • **SENATE MAJORITY BLOCKS EQUAL PAY FOR WOMEN WORKERS**

"Senate Majority Blocks Equal Pay for Women Workers," • © 2021 Omnigraphics.

In 2014, a majority of Senators blocked the Paycheck Fairness Act, an Act that the bill's sponsors said would bring transparency to worker salaries by making it illegal for employers to penalize workers who discuss their earnings. The Act also required the Equal Employment Opportunity Commission (EEOC) to collect wage information from employers in an effort to ensure equity and compliance.

In a floor speech, Senate Majority Leader Harry Reid of Nevada noted that the majority of senators who blocked passage of this bill "don't seem to be interested in closing wage gaps for working women." Senate Minority Leader Mitch McConnell also noted that a growing number of working women had experienced declining wages during the Great Recession. "When it comes to American women overall, what we've seen in the past five and a half years is less income and more poverty."

The Great Recession, which is officially described as occurring globally between 2007 and 2009, was determined by the International Monetary Fund (IMF) to be the most severe economic and financial meltdown since the Great Depression. The crisis left millions of American workers unemployed and some areas of the U.S. economy did not reach pre-recession levels until 2016.

After the Paycheck Fairness Act failed to pass, President Barack Obama signed executive orders that imposed similar requirements on government contractors.

Section 12.3 • **MILITARY BAN ON WOMEN IN COMBAT LIFTED**

"Military Ban on Women in Combat Lifted," • © 2021 Omnigraphics.

In 1994, U.S. Defense Secretary Les Aspin of the Clinton Administration rescinded the Risk Rule that restricted where women in the military could serve, but military women were still "excluded from assignment to units below the brigade level whose primary mission is to engage in direct combat on the ground." In 2013, U.S. Secretary of Defense Leon E. Panetta lifted the Department of Defense Combat Exclusion Policy in the Women's Armed Services Integration Act of 1948 with the unanimous approval of the Joint Chiefs of Staff. This policy change allowed both women and men to participate in front-line combat and comprehensive combat operations.

At a Pentagon press conference announcing this policy change, Secretary Panetta explained that women serving in the military are integral to the Defense Department's ability to fulfill its mission. He also reminded the nation that "[o]ver more than a decade of war, [women warriors have] demonstrated courage, skill and patriotism," and that "152 women in uniform ... died serving this nation in Iraq and Afghanistan." If members of our military "can meet the qualifications for a job," he added, "then they should have the right to serve, regardless of creed, color, gender, or sexual orientation."

President Obama released a subsequent statement noting that this milestone reflected "the courageous and patriotic service of women through more than two centuries of American history and the indispensable role of women in today's military." The Armed Forces Press Service later noted that this policy change opened up 237,000 new positions to women employed by the U.S. armed forces.

BACKGROUND

The Women's Armed Services Integration Act of 1948 was originally proposed by U.S. Congresswoman Margaret Chase Smith. This Act expanded women's employment opportunities by allowing women to serve as permanent members of the armed forces. Prior to passage of the Act, only military nurses were able to serve on a permanent basis, while other women who wished to serve were restricted to reserve positions.

The Navy swore in its first women enlistees less than a month after President Truman signed the bill into law, but Section 402 of the Act excluded women from aircraft and Navy vessels that might engage in combat. When the Risk Rule was lifted in May of 1994, the Navy assigned 59 Navy women to the combatant nuclear-powered vessel the *Dwight D. Eisenhower* (CVN-60). The crew of this vessel participated in operations Uphold Democracy in the Caribbean, Southern Watch in the Arabian Gulf, and Deny Flight, Provide Promise, and Sharp Guard in the Mediterranean in 1994. The first female chaplain was also aboard the *Eisenhower*.

Historians have documented the fact that thousands of U.S. military nurses in the late-nineteenth and early-twentieth centuries came under fire, particularly in the Spanish-American War, World War I, World War II, the Korean War, and the Vietnam War. Some of these were killed in the line of duty and others were held as prisoners of war.

A Final Note

Despite passage of the 1948 Act, the army established a regulation that barred mothers of dependent children from service and enforced this regulation well into the 1970s.

Section 12.4 • TRAILBLAZERS

This section includes text excerpted from "Biographies of the Secretaries of State: Hillary Rodham Clinton (1947–)," (U.S. State Department); "Stacy Cunningham Named Head of the New York Stock Exchange," "U.S. Women's Soccer Team," • © 2021 Omnigraphics.

HILLARY RODHAM CLINTON'S HISTORIC RUN

Hillary Rodham Clinton seems to have done it all. Or nearly all. A successful Yale-educated lawyer, law professor, diplomat, first lady of Arkansas and then of the United States, U.S. Senator (2001–2009), U.S. Secretary of State (2009–2013), and the first woman nominated by a major U.S. political party to be on its presidential ticket.

Clinton has championed women and children throughout her career. She founded Arkansas Advocates for Children and Families in the 1970s, served as the first female chair of the

Secretary of State Hillary Rodham Clinton, September 28, 2010

Legal Services Corporation, and was the first female partner of the Rose Law Firm in the late 1970s. In her famous speech in Beijing in 1995, she declared that "human rights are women's rights, and women's rights are human rights." This declaration inspired women worldwide and helped galvanize a movement for women's rights in the workplace and across the globe.

As first lady, she championed healthcare reform and advocated for child and family protection legislation at the national level. With Secretary of State Madeleine K. Albright, Secretary Clinton worked to launch the government's Vital Voices Democracy Initiative. Today, Vital Voices is a nongovernmental organization that continues to train and organize women leaders across the globe. And at the 1995 United Nations Conference on Women, she championed gender equality.

In 2000, Clinton made history as the first first lady elected to the U.S. Senate, and the first woman elected statewide in New York to the Senate. She served on the Armed Services Committee; the Health, Education, Labor and Pensions Committee; the Environment and Public Works Committee; the Budget Committee; and the Select Committee on Aging. She was also a Commissioner on the Commission on Security and Cooperation in Europe.

Senator Clinton worked across party lines to build support for causes important to her constituents and the country, including the expansion of economic opportunity and access to quality, affordable health care. After the terrorist attacks on September 11, 2001, she was a strong advocate for funding the rebuilding of New York City and addressing the health concerns of the first responders who risked their lives working at Ground Zero. She also championed the cause of our nation's military and fought for better healthcare and benefits for wounded service members, veterans, and members of the National Guard and Reserves. She was also the only Senate member of the Transformation Advisory Group to the Department of Defense's Joint Forces Command.

In 2006, Senator Clinton won reelection to the Senate, and in 2007 she began her historic campaign for President. In 2008, she campaigned for the election of Barack Obama and Joe Biden, and in November, she was nominated by President-elect Obama to be Secretary of State.

The *National Law Journal* has twice listed Clinton as one of the 100 most influential lawyers in the United States.

Clinton became the first woman nominated by a major U.S. political party to be on its presidential ticket. She won the popular vote, but not the Electoral College vote. She wrote *What Happened* following her loss, and then launched her new political action organization Onward Together. Clinton currently serves as the chancellor of Queens University in Belfast, Northern Ireland.

STACEY CUNNINGHAM NAMED HEAD OF THE NEW YORK STOCK EXCHANGE

The New York Stock Exchange (NYSE) has been operational in the U.S for 226 years. This male-dominated field did not have its first woman chair holder until 1967, when Muriel Siebert bought her seat on the exchange. Stacey Cunningham began working at the NYSE as a summer intern in 1994. At the time, the women's restroom was inside an old phone booth on the seventh floor. She worked her way up from her first opportunity as an intern to working as a floor clerk, then becoming a market marker for less than a year. Cunningham was then promoted to head of sales and, in 2015, to her last position as Chief Operating Officer before stepping into the president's chair.

In 2018, Stacey Cunningham became the first female president of the NYSE. Cunningham's appointment came as many firms began seeing pushback for their treatment of women in the workplace and from the #MeToo movement. The NYSE wanted to show they had moved beyond the culture of the past. In 2020, as the COVID pandemic loomed, Cunningham decided to shut down in-person trading at the NYSE in March. While the exchange board reopened in May 2020, Cunningham has stated that she does not expect in-person trading until everyone can be vaccinated.

U.S. WOMEN'S SOCCER TEAM

In a month-long tournament, the U.S Women's Soccer team won their final match against the Netherlands in a 2–0 victory. But their fight to victory was just the beginning for this team. In March 2019, just months before the US. Women's National (WNT) team's World Cup victory and the U.S Men's National (MNT) team's loss, failing to qualify for the World Cup, the women filed suit against the U.S. Soccer Federation stating violation of the Civil Rights Act of 1964 and the Equal Pay Act of 1963.

"For each win, loss, and tie that women players secure, they are paid less than men who play the same sport and who do the same work; that is gender discrimination," the players' spokeswoman Molly Levinson said in a statement. "A pervasive atmosphere of sexism drove this pay discrimination."

When comparing the WNT and MNT salaries, one can see that women make 38 percent of what men earn. For each match the women play, they earn approximately $4,950 per match compared to men at $13,166 per match.

"Each of us is extremely proud to wear the United States jersey, and we also take seriously the responsibility that comes with that," forward Alex Morgan said in a statement reported by the Associated Press. "We believe that fighting for gender equality in sports is a part of that responsibility. As players, we deserved to be paid equally for our work, regardless of our gender."

All 28 players are named in the lawsuit against the U.S. Soccer Federation. They stand together as a team, hoping to receive compensation equal to their male counterparts who play the same game.

Section 12.5 • SEXUAL VIOLENCE IN THE WORKPLACE AND THE #METOO MOVEMENT

The Me Too (#MeToo) movement is a social movement that amplifies how widespread sexual abuse and sexual harassment are, particularly in the American workplace, where men often hold disproportionate power over women. At the height of this movement, people publicized or posted online allegations of sex crimes mostly committed by prominent, powerful men, and often prominent men in the entertainment industry and political arena.

In 2006, Tarana Burke, an American activist, started the Me Too movement in an effort to help impoverished Black women and girls of color who had survived sexual violence stand up for themselves and feel empowered. The movement encouraged survivors to share their personal experiences in an effort to shed light on the prevalence of sexual crimes committed, primarily, against women. The hashtag "#MeToo" gained popularity on social media in 2017 when it was utilized by Hollywood actress Alyssa Milano, who sparked this worldwide movement. The movement helped spread awareness of the impacts of sexual violence not only toward women, but toward other groups as well, including differently abled communities. The movement provided people with the opportunity to stand in solidarity against sexual violence and to speak out about their experiences. In 2017, *TIME* magazine recognized Tarana Burke as one of "the Silence Breakers."

Several high-profile actresses associated with Harvey Weinstein's Miramax company shared their experiences of being sexually harassed or assaulted by the producer while working (or seeking to work) on Miramax films. After years of rumors, in October 2017, several women openly accused Weinstein of sexual harassment and violence. In March 2020, he was sentenced to 23 years in prison for sex crimes. Another well-known man in the entertainment industry who was imprisoned for sex crimes is Bill Cosby, a famous actor and U.S. comedian. Cosby was accused by multiple women of drugging and raping them. Larry Nassar, former USA Gymnastics national team doctor, also was sentenced to prison for sexual violence after victims came forward in light of the #MeToo movement.

The American #MeToo Movement

SEXUAL HARASSMENT AND SEXUAL ASSAULT

"Sexual harassment" and "sexual assault" generally refer to any form of inappropriate or unwanted sexual behaviors, especially in a school or workplace, although they can occur under a variety of circumstances. It is important to note the following:

- The victim, as well as the harasser, may be a woman or a man.

- The harasser can be the victim's coworker, supervisor, or a family member.
- The victim does not have to be the person harassed but could be anyone affected by the offensive conduct.

The #MeToo movement called attention to the prevalence of sexual assaults in the United State and empowered victims of these crimes.

SEXUAL VIOLENCE IN THE WORKPLACE

Jenifer Kuadli reports on the Legal Jobs blog that 90 percent of adult rape victims in the United States are female, that 40 percent are adult women, and that 41.8 percent of all women have been victimized by sexual violence other than rape. Women employed by the U.S. armed services reported nearly 20,000 sexual assaults in 2020 and research indicates that women with disabilities are twice as likely to be sexually assaulted. Current evidence indicates that approximately 70 American women commit suicide daily as a result of sexual violence. This number is growing, but fewer than 20 percent of rapes are reported. Statistically speaking, for every 1,000 rapes committed in this country, 995 perpetrators are never punished for their crimes.

Multiple sources indicate that 652,676 American women were rape victims in 2019, but that figure excludes non-rape sexual assaults. Adding non-rape sexual assaults increases this number to close to one million American women. Meanwhile, 1 in 6 women in the United States are predicted to be raped annually, which translates into a woman being sexually assaulted every 73 seconds.

Sexual Violence and Workplace Research Findings

The connections between sexual violence and the American workplace remain understudied but research is available. American employees experienced approximately 36,500 rapes and sexual assaults from 1993 to 1999, and women were the victims in 80 percent of the assaults that occurred in the workplace (Duhart, 2001). A 2011 study found that, between 2005 and 2009, rape/sexual assault accounted for 2.3 percent of all nonfatal violence in the workplace (Harrell, 2011). Another study found that 38 percent of working women had experienced sexual harassment in the workplace (Potter and Banyard 2011).

Sexual harassment also is a serious concern for working women, and a 2007 study found that women who both work and receive public assistance – in other words, low-paid workers – are frequently the victims of sexual harassment in the workplace. This harassment is more likely to occur when these workers transition from public assistance into unsubsidized employment, but 8–13 percent of workers who returned to public assistance also reported experiencing sexual harassment in the workplace (Siegel and Abbott, 2007).

Women working in traditionally male-dominated professions, such as in the military, also experience more sexual harassment and sexual violence. In fiscal year 2010, for example, 3,158 military sexual assaults were reported to the Department of Defense (U.S. Department of Defense, Sexual Assault Prevention and Response), but the Defense Department estimates that only 13.5 percent of survivors of sexual assault reported their assaults (SAPRO, 2011).

The Impact of Sexual Violence on Working Women

Interrupted Work Can Be Traced to Sexual Violence

Research indicates that sexual violence in the workplace causes interruptions in work for a significant number of working women. In one study, researchers found that 50–95 percent of women who were raped at their workplace experienced posttraumatic stress disorder (PTSD) (Heise, Ellsberg, and Gottemoeller, 1999). Another study found that rape survivors' reactions to the assault were so debilitating and severe that they were initially unable to return work (Ellis, Atkeson, and Calhoun, 1981). In fact, researchers who assessed a survey of outcomes of sexual violence perpetrated against working women found that over 20 percent of workplace rape survivors reported that the sexual assault caused them to take time away from work (Tjaden and Thoennes, 2006). And a similar study found that 21 percent of working women who were raped by an intimate partner likewise resulted in these women averaging 8 days of leave taken from work because of the assault (U.S. Department of Health and Human Services, Centers for Disease Control and Prevention [CDC], 2003). Research indicates that adults who survived childhood sexual violence continue to be impacted by the assault, too. A 2004 study found that early sexual violence often translates into difficulties in the workplace for adult survivors, leading to poor job performance and high work absentee rates (Anda et al., 2004).

Financial Losses Associated with Sexual Violence in the Workplace

Victimization costs associated with each rape that occurred in 2008 were estimated to be $151,423 (DeLisi et al., 2010). Another study found that lifetime income loss resulting from sexual violence is estimated to be $241,600 (MacMillan, 2000). And an Iowa study found that the cost of lost work associated with sexual violence is actually more than $130 million (Yang, Zhang, Miller, et al., 2012). The lower productivity rates of sexual-assault victims result in lower wages too and those victims are estimated to lose approximately $2,200 in the aftermath of sexual violence (MacMillan, 2000). Meanwhile, a 1994 study determined costs associated with sexual harassment in the federal government to be $327 million. These researchers reported a loss of $24.7 million as a result of job losses; $14.9 million associated with the cost of sick leave and job turnover tied to the harassment; and productivity losses of $287.5 million (U.S. Meritor, 1995).

CHAPTER THIRTEEN

The Audacity of Work, 2020–2021

CHAPTER CONTENTS

Section 13.1 • **OVERVIEW**

Multiple sources report that 2020 was the worst year for economic growth since the days following World War II. The economy shrank 3.5 percent and women suffered disproportionate job losses in the early days of the pandemic, with over 12.1 million women's jobs lost between February and April of 2020 alone. The Bureau of Labor Statistics (BLS) reports that, by August, more than 1.1 million workers had dropped out of the labor market altogether and were no longer looking for work, and 865,000 (80%) of those workers were women (including 324,000 Latina workers and 58,000 Black women).

By September 2020, approximately 1 in 9 Black women (11.1%) 20 years of age or older were unemployed. This was more than double their pre-pandemic unemployment rate of 4.9 percent in February. That same month, the unemployment rates for Black women and Latinas were more than one-and- a-half times higher than the rate for White men 20 years of age and older (6.5%):

- Men's overall unemployment 7.45%
- Women's overall unemployment 7.7%
- Black women's overall unemployment 11.1%
- Latinas overall unemployment 11.0%
- Women ages 20–24 12.2%
- Women with disabilities 15.1%

No wonder people are referring to our economic woes as the "She-cession."

During the pandemic, working women with children have either left their jobs or are trying to work from home while parenting, handling the bulk of the housework, and ensuring that their children are keeping up with their online classes.

Uneven Burdens, Uneven Pay, and Now You're a Teacher, Too

One possible reason for the gender disparity in the number of people who left the workforce is that women earn less and still bear the brunt of caretaking responsibilities at home (and often care for elderly family members as well as their children). With so many childcare centers and schools closed, parents had to supervise their children during the workday, and that responsibility largely fell on women who had been part of the workforce before the pandemic.

Section 13.2 • **WOMEN WITH DISABILITIES HIT HARDEST BY PANDEMIC JOB LOSSES**

In March 2020, 17.9 percent of people with a disability were employed, down from 19.3 percent in 2019.

Prior to the first U.S. pandemic shutdowns in March 2019, the U.S. Bureau of Labor Statistics (BLS) reported that the unemployment rate for people with disabilities was 7.3 percent but that number climbed to 12.6 percent in 2020. The nonpartisan advocacy group RespectAbility reported that 34.6 percent of working-age women (18–64) with at least one disability were unemployed nationwide, despite polls indicating that many wanted to work. Around 22.5 percent of these unemployed women with disabilities lived in poverty, compared to 14.7 percent of U.S. women without a disability. RespectAbility also reported that, during the first month of pandemic shutdowns, 3,736 American women with disabilities lost their jobs.

RespectAbility examined employment rates for people with disabilities at the state level in 2017 and found that the number of American women with a disability who were employed in the workplace varied widely from state to state. The state with the highest female disability employment rate in 2017 was South Dakota, where 53 percent of these women were employed, but many states reported women with disabilities leaving the workforce that same year. North Carolina reported the biggest job losses of any state, with 12,142 women with disabilities leaving the workforce.

In June 2020, Allison Norlian of *Forbes* magazine reported that, since the pandemic began in the United States, 1 in 5 workers with disabilities had lost their jobs, which translates into nearly 1 million jobs lost in the disabled community alone.

Section 13.3 • **TRAILBLAZERS**

KAMALA HARRIS

Vice President Kamala Devi Harris is the nation's first female, Black, and South Asian American vice president and the first vice president to have graduated from a historically Black university (HBCU). This trailblazer of heroic proportions was sworn into office by America's first trailblazing Latina Supreme Court Justice Sonia Sotomayor.

Kamala Harris, May 12, 2017

Harris has been shattering barriers throughout her career. In 2010, she became California's first female and first Black attorney general. Then she was the second Black woman and the first South Asian American to serve in the U.S Senate. Harris then became the first Black and first Asian-American woman to win a major political party's nomination – and to do so in a country where few Black women have made it to the top of their field.

After she was sworn in as Vice President, Harris then swore in three other barrier-breaking senators in her role as the nation's newest president of the upper chamber: Alex Padilla, the first Latino senator from California; Rev. Raphael Warnock, the first Black senator from Georgia; and Jon Ossoff, the first Jewish senator from Georgia.

Harris said that, when she was on the campaign trail, she frequently reminded herself of something her mother Shyamala Gopalan told her: "You may be the first to do many things, but make sure you are not the last."

Vice President Harris also swore in the nation's first Native American cabinet member, U.S. Secretary of the Interior Deb Haaland.

DEB HAALAND

As a member of Congress, Deb Haaland (D-New Mexico), a citizen of the Laguna Pueblo and self-described 35th generation New Mexican, broke barriers as one of the first Native Americans elected to Congress. She is also one of the few members of Congress who put herself through college and law school using food stamps and student loans.

In her opening remarks at the Department of the Interior, Secretary Haaland said:

> I'm not a stranger to the struggles many families across America face today. I've lived most of my adult life paycheck to paycheck. It's because of these struggles that I fully understand the role Interior must play in the president's plan to build back better; to responsibly manage our natural resources to protect them for future generations – so that we can continue to work, live, hunt, fish, and pray among them.

As Secretary of the Interior, Haaland oversees 500 million acres of public lands, the federal oil-and-gas program, and the U.S. Bureau of Indian Affairs. This makes her responsible for the well-being of the nation's 1.9 million Indigenous people, who are citizens of one or more of the nation's 574 federally recognized tribes.

The U.S. Department of the Interior has a long, well-documented, and consistent history of mistreating Native Americans, so Secretary Haaland's role in the Biden cabinet is expected to be transformational, as she not only ensures the well-being of Native Americans but also works with the administration to ban fracking on all public lands. (Secretary Haaland also opposes oil and gas exploration on public lands.)

Indigenous belief systems commonly consider the earth to be holy, a gift to be cared for rather than mined for short-term gains with long-term negative consequences. In keeping with this belief, Secretary Haaland cosponsored the Green New Deal, a resolution written by Rep. Alexandria Ocasio-Cortez and Sen. Edward Markey. This resolution calls for the U.S. to eradicate fossil-fuel pollution in no more than a single decade.

A letter signed by environmental groups supporting Secretary Haaland's nomination noted that "Representative Haaland is a proven leader and the right person to lead the charge against the existential threats of our time – tackling the climate, extinction and COVID-19 crises, and racial justice inequities on our Federal public lands."

RACHEL LEVINE

American pediatrician Rachel Levine is the country's newest Assistant Secretary for Health. Levine served as Secretary of the Pennsylvania Department of Health from 2017 to 2021 and served as the Pennsylvania Physician General from 2015 to 2017. During that time, she made the anti-overdose medication naloxone available to law-enforcement officers, which is credited with saving the lives of almost a thousand opioid users who had overdosed.

Levine is also a professor of pediatrics and psychiatry at the Penn State College of Medicine and created the adolescent medicine division and eating-disorders clinic at the Penn State Hershey Medical Center. She is known at the medical center for her expertise in helping young teens who routinely cut or otherwise harm themselves as well. Levine was in charge of the unit she created until she accepted the nomination for Pennsylvania Physician General.

Levine is also a trailblazer: One of only a few openly transgender government officials in the country and the first openly transgender federal official in a Senate-confirmed post.

Section 13.4 • MILLENNIAL WOMEN IN THE WORKPLACE

WHO ARE MILLENNIAL WOMEN?

Millennials, defined as the group of people born between the years of 1980 and 1996, are the largest generational cohort to date and the largest generation in the American workforce as of 2017. Research shows that Millennial women are generally confident, empowered, and optimistic when taking on projects. Socially groomed for teamwork and collaboration, native to technology, and yearning to make a positive impact on communities and the world at large, Millennials can provide a lot of value in the workplace. However, plenty of negative stereotypes continue to haunt them (including, but not limited to being high maintenance, lazy, unfocused, and entitled) and many organizations fail to recognize the value they can bring.

Millennial women in particular face a myriad of challenges in addition to these stereotypes. Gender bias, wage gaps, and "the glass ceiling" – to name a few – are still prevalent, though not unique to this generation of women. It is important to note the added difficulty of COVID-19 and its significant impact on this group by way of remote-schooling for their children and shouldering the majority of household responsibilities. Although Millennial women face many challenges that are similar to those faced by previous generations, there is at least one stark difference – their attitude. Many women of this generation declare that their mothers explicitly told them to "act as individuals, stand on their own two feet, and to not rely on anyone else but themselves."

Moreover, studies show that girls with working mothers are more likely to embrace traditionally masculine traits such as ambition and independence. Twice as many Millennials' mothers worked than mothers in the late 1970s (67 percent and 31 percent, respectively) and the impact is clear. In 2012, only one out of 1,000 incoming female college students selected "full-time homemaker" as their expected career.

This change in attitude, along with shifts in personality, help define the Millennial woman. One study that utilized data from more than 11 million college students measured stereotypical masculine and feminine traits and found that there has been an increase in so-called masculine traits among Millennial women. For example, in 2012, 77 percent of college women said they had an above average drive to achieve compared to 75 percent of college men. In 1989, these numbers were 69 percent and 72 percent, respectively. These changes signify the reversal of gender roles where young women are in line with, if not surpassing, young men in prioritizing their education, career, independence, and autonomy. In fact, according to another study conducted in 2015, two-thirds of young women between the ages of 18 to 34 ranked having a high-paying career as their first priority in life, compared to 59 percent of young men of the same age group. These trends are deeply rooted in women's movement toward individualism and self-actualization.

On a similar note, 83 percent of Millennial women recently surveyed said they wanted to start their own business. When businesses are led by female Millennial entrepreneurs, revenues rise between 9 and 22 percent. These numbers reflect that, if women had the same access to capital as men, the gross domestic product (GDP) of emerging markets would have a higher chance of increasing. Unsurprisingly, Millennial women face gender bias within the Venture Capital (VC) industry, resulting in greater challenges when raising funds and less money secured overall than their male counterparts. In 2018, women overall held a meager 2.2 percent share of the $130 billion given out in venture capital. The percentage won by Millennial women was even smaller. Additionally, recent studies show that almost half of American female entrepreneurs reported experiencing gender bias. Many are asked different questions than men when pitching to VCs – more invasive questions about their personal lives rather than about their business idea. Indeed, women report needing to "do more, be more, grow faster, show more proof points, and do it all with so much less to get a seat at the table." During the COVID-19 pandemic, it's evident that raising capital has become even harder for Millennial women.

When not seeking entrepreneurship, Millennial women are most interested in working for companies with a strong record of diversity. Eighty-five percent of those surveyed said an employer's policy on diversity, equity, and workforce inclusion was important when deciding whether or not to work for them. An inclusive, international approach is a plus, with opportunities to take on diverse global assignments. Millennial women also look for employers who uphold a culture of flexibility, open communication (including clear and regular feedback), and purpose. Millennial women want to contribute to the world and to be proud to work for their employer.

Gender Bias and Related Obstacles

Generally, organizations understand that attracting and retaining female talent is imperative to their success. Yet traditional business practices and rigid company cultures persist in upholding gender biases and socially constructed gender norms, both of which have a negative impact on women. For instance, research shows that having children can be one of the worst career moves a woman can make, and although companies are increasingly offering flex programs, employees remain hesitant to use them. By recognizing the unique needs of Millennial women and working to meet those needs, women workers feel empowered, and therefore, they thrive. In turn, so does the bottom line.

Inherent gender biases still persist despite the increase of highly educated Millennial women entering the workforce. For example, as of 2015, women were still paid 22 percent less than their male counterparts for doing the same job. Even with the significant shifts in attitude and personality traits noted previously, there is still a large conflict for women in the workplace and in leadership in comparison to men. In her book *Lean In: For Graduates*, Sheryl Sandberg states, "As a culture, we still carry an incredible amount of ambivalence toward working mothers that working fathers are still able to neatly sidestep. These attitudes have persisted into the 2010s" (28).

In addition to the controversy around parenthood, according to research cited by Pepperdine University, there has also been a recent increase in the percentage of women who feel that employers are too male biased in the following areas: Attracting, promoting, developing, and retaining employees. In 2011, 29 percent of Millennial women felt their employers were male biased in promotions. This percentage jumped to 43 percent in 2015. In these same years, 19 percent felt employers were too male biased in developing their employees, compared to 30 percent four years later. Additionally, 18 percent of women felt that their employers were male biased in their retaining efforts, and by 2015 this number jumped up to 31 percent.

There is a need for reform and more targeted approaches to resolving gender inequality. As of 2015, at the start of their careers, less than half of women felt they would be able to rise to the most senior levels of their companies, compared to 71 percent of their male counterparts. Furthermore, many studies show that women consistently underestimate their own abilities while men overestimate theirs, despite equal performance levels. These obstacles are further enforced by the microaggressions experienced by Millennials, which are subtle in nature and can show up in the form of someone telling a Millennial employee they are old enough to be their parent, or citing a pop culture reference that was "way before your time." In addition to age-related microaggressions, Millennial women often receive unsolicited advice about altering their communication styles to conform to more traditional business styles. Women in the workplace are also often told to alter how they present themselves in order to be taken more seriously, like by speaking in a lower tone of voice or sitting up straighter in a meeting, or boosting their chair in order to be as tall as the men at the table. While usually well intended, these types of advice and comments can undermine credibility and uphold age and gender barriers. Furthermore, these strategies often backfire since they create a feeling of disingenuousness and incongruency for women.

In addition to microaggressions and unsolicited advice, many double standards exist for Millennial women in the workplace. For example, competitiveness – a trait that many Millennial women display – is perceived as a positive attribute for men but a negative attribute for women. Ambition creates a double standard as well. Ambitious men are viewed as driven, focused, and as someone with leadership potential, but ambitious women are dismissed as difficult to manage and not team players. On a similar note, recent research shows that men win more promotions, receive more challenging assignments, and have more access to top leaders than women do. Women, meanwhile, have a much more challenging journey to the top and do not see themselves reflected in leadership or organizational cultures to the degree that men do. Many women report gender as a key factor in missed raises and promotions and believe that their gender makes it harder for them to advance than their male counterparts. Many also feel invisible at work compared with male colleagues. These sentiments are not lost on Millennial women.

Other intangible, gender-related obstacles women face include the glass ceiling, the glass cliff, and the glass elevator. The most commonly known of the three, the glass ceiling, refers to the organizational hierarchy that prevents women and other marginalized individuals from achieving leadership positions. For Millennial women, this can look like being assigned dead-end projects or low-visibility projects, a lack of mentoring, assumptions about family life and child-rearing, and exclusion from informal networks. The glass cliff is a more recent phenomenon, referring to women being promoted into leadership positions when the chances of failure are highest, such as during an economic crisis. Research shows that times of crisis, economic or otherwise, tend to trigger the appointment of female leaders, who then get blamed for any negative outcomes that were set in motion long before they assumed their position of leadership. Finally, the glass escalator refers to the phenomenon of men moving up the corporate ladder at a much quicker pace than their female counterparts. While some progress has been made over the past few decades, Millennial women still experience these phenomena across all industries, but particularly in nontraditional male occupations, like teaching.

One exceptionally significant example of gender bias happened in 2020 at the Pentagon, where its most senior leaders at the time, Mark T. Esper and General Mark A. Milley, agreed that the two top generals should be promoted to elite, four-star commands. However, their nominations were put on hold because the nominees are women. Under the administration of President Donald Trump, Esper and Milley feared that because the generals were not White men, their nomination would create unrest in the White House. Seemingly well-intentioned, the two delayed their recommendation of General Jacqueline D. Van Ovost of the Air Force and Lieutenant General Laura J. Richardson of the Army in hopes that Democratic presidential nominee Joseph R. Biden Jr. would win the election and be more supportive of the Pentagon picks than Trump, who has a history of disparaging women. Esper and Milley worried that if they did not delay their recommendation, the Trump Administration would replace the two women with its own candidates before Trump left office. The decision to postpone the promotion of Ovost and Richardson is reflective of greater, systemic issues of gender inequality and discrimination in the United States.

Workplace Performance, Evaluation, and Management

Millennial women often struggle to conform and thrive in traditional business structures because these structures were not designed for them. In order to thrive, these women want several things from an employer, including well-defined career trajectories, opportunities for advancement, transparent communication (including clear goals and feedback, visibility and power), autonomy, and true flexibility – meaning they want to be able to choose the time and place they work, not just be offered flex programs. Flexibility is especially empowering to working parents, and women are more likely than men to require flexibility in this area because they continue to shoulder the majority of childcare and household responsibilities.

Understanding the policies and practices that empower Millennial women can help businesses cultivate a corporate culture that is worth seeking out, ultimately enhancing their ability to recruit and retain talent. However, companies still have a long way to go. In one study, the vast majority (90 percent) of Millennial women indicated that their performance was evaluated differently than the performance of men. Eighty percent of men agreed. Perhaps because of this, Millennial women indicated that they were more nervous at work, worried more, and were uncertain about appropriate types of behavior, particularly around confrontation and adversity. Forty-four percent of women said that confrontation led them to question their own abilities, whereas only 26 percent of men said the same. Millennial women also experienced disparities both in salary and career-advancement opportunities, diminishing their ambitions to move into leadership positions. Experiencing these regular, systemic slights wears on the generation's confidence and self-esteem, adding to the more overt challenges of equal pay, maternity leave, and sexual harassment.

In addition, young female leaders manage conflicting perceptions about their identities. Tasked with being hardworking, tenacious, and successful employees, women workers are also expected to be compliant, pleasant, and modest. These competing expectations may leave some Millennial women feeling pressured to continuously improve their skills in order to prove themselves as valuable in the workplace. In leadership, this double bind is particularly sharp as women navigate the fine line of being a fierce and focused leader and being liked. "Double bind" refers to the prescriptions and expectations of the female gender role as being communal, helpful, and warm, to name a few, which are not attributes traditionally associated with leadership. This contradiction creates a natural resistance to female leaders, which results in female leaders being more risk-adverse than male leaders. When women are direct, authoritative, and confident – traits traditionally associated with leadership – these traits directly oppose what society has been conditioned to believe about women. When working women violate these societal norms, their actions often incite a negative reaction.

The bar is very high – sometimes unattainably so – for young women. Due to societal norms and professional pressures, women tend to feel the need to be perfect and to constantly prove themselves in order to be taken seriously in the workplace, much more so than men. As a result, female managers are more likely than male managers to micromanage. Research indicates that this style of management is disempowering, particularly to Millennials and other women. It is important to note the extent to which businesses value women's work and management styles affects how women manage. Organizations can help mitigate micromanagement by creating environments in which women feel confident and valued, therefore no longer feeling the need to excessively prove themselves. By placing higher value on women's work styles, organizations can encourage managers to allow more autonomy for their employees and to better support them.

Millennial women themselves can also leverage the following strategies to help build their confidence and diffuse perfectionist tendencies, according to the Georgetown Institute for Women, Peace, and Security:

- **Fail Fast:** Failing fast entails "trying something, getting fast feedback, and then rapidly inspecting and adapting." For women, this tactic can be instrumental for building confidence since it creates an ecosystem where there is less to lose, which in turn, alleviates the pressure of perfectionism. Failing fast requires a leap of faith and is inherently uncomfortable, although it does become less so with practice.

Focus on accomplishments and positive outcomes, instead of negative ones, and rinse and repeat until confidence has grown.

- **Manage Your Micromanagement:** Awareness is the first step toward lending employees more autonomy. Receiving confidential feedback from team members about management styles can be very helpful. Use an anonymous survey or one conducted by a third party. Once feedback has been received, it can be leveraged to prioritize the team's tasks and build slack into the process where appropriate. Clear communication is critical during this process, both around determining new processes and around reformed expectations.

Senior Positions, Leadership, and Mentorship

Equality in the workplace is of critical importance for all marginalized individuals, but it is particularly important for allowing Millennial women to move into leadership roles. Leadership plays a key role in empowering Millennial women, and although they are entering the workforce in nearly equal numbers as men, they are still highly underrepresented at leadership levels. In fact, as of 2015, only 17 percent of C-Suite positions in the United States were held by women, and representation of women on corporate boards was equally as low. Despite the low representation of women in leadership, research consistently shows that companies with higher numbers of women in leadership perform significantly better financially than companies without women at the top. These companies report a greater than 47-percent average return on equity and a greater than 55-percent average earnings (before interest and taxes).

Women are empowered when they see other women in leadership positions and when companies communicate that they value women's leadership styles, which usually tend to be more democratic and collaborative, less hierarchical, and oriented to enhancing others' self-worth. In general, women tend to use communication to foster connections and form relationships, while men tend to use communication to achieve tangible outcomes and exercise dominance. Women workers also tend to use more polite language and speak more tentatively than men and also tend to interrupt others less than men. These tendencies result in women being interpreted as less confident and less capable than male counterparts. Furthermore, research shows that women in leadership who communicate openly and collaboratively are often viewed as weak despite the proven benefits of this type of communication style. Men, on the other hand, are viewed as being more competent when communicating unilaterally.

Women face a multitude of barriers that preclude them from advancing in their careers at the same rate as men, despite equal levels of ambition around advancing to senior leadership roles. Thus, stereotypically masculine communication and leadership styles persist as men continue to hold the majority of leadership positions. Despite being less effective than stereotypically feminine styles of leadership, masculine styles are still viewed by the majority as superior, both unconsciously and consciously. Research finds that these prevailing communication and leadership styles do not help women move into leadership positions.

Of note, Millennial employees feel most empowered when leaders are transparent about the "why" behind their strategic decisions. Millennials view this type of high-level transparency as critical to the quality of their work, allowing them to connect the dots between the broader landscape and the impact they can make within the organization. Understanding what is required of them for collaboration, cooperation, and collective decision-making allows them to feel more competent, work toward clear goals, and find greater meaning in their work. Millennial women, in particular, are empowered even more by strong mentoring relationships. Mentors – male and female alike – have the experience and resources to guide women toward leadership positions. A recent study showed that 72 percent of women interviewed had a preference for female mentors, yet only 33 percent of the women interviewed had a female mentor. The remainder of women interviewed expressed frustration in their search to find one.

Despite women's preference for female-to-female mentorship, several of the women interviewed stated that they had positive relationships with male mentors, who are essential for allyship. The balance is tricky though, as male executives can often be reluctant to mentor female employees for fear that basic forms of mentorship, like one-on-one meetings or working lunch sessions, could be misinterpreted as romantic advances. While mentorship from both genders is important, without experienced women available to serve as mentors, many women are left without the empowering support they desire. There is a clear gap between the number of entry- and mid-level women seeking mentorship and the number of senior-level women who can mentor them. Another challenge Millennial women face is a lack of access to informal networks, which can be instrumental in accelerating promotion. Informal networks can help shape and accelerate careers in the following ways:

- Create opportunities for communication
- Help with the flow of information
- Assist with access to referrals and jobs
- Strengthen influence and reputation
- Provide emotional support and professional advice.

Household Dynamics, Childcare, and Maternity Leave

Studies show that Millennial men and women aspire to be more equal than previous generations in parenting and household chores. Many Millennial men are willing to take on more responsibilities at home than men of past generations and, in turn, many Millennial women have higher expectations for their male partners' involvement in household chores and childcare. Yet in reality, both parties tend to mirror the parenting styles of their own parents. Additionally, the combination of social expectations and pressure at work often derail this aspiration and continue to force parents into making tough decisions around work and life. Millennials, in particular, find it challenging to envision a balance that fulfills both parenting and career expectations. Notably, many Millennial men aspire to be involved fathers, and many Millennial women are committed to continuing their careers after having children.

However, the tough decisions made at home frequently result in women stepping back at work so that men don't have to, even if both parties have equal expectations regarding roles at work and at home. One reason working mothers may be more willing to cut back at work is because of the level of guilt they experience – guilt that is greatly influenced by the expectations projected onto working mothers. While working mothers are consistently judged and challenged when prioritizing childcare, fathers are admired and praised. This double standard is not new, but it persists in the experience of Millennial women and significantly affects their self-perceptions. Research shows that 31 percent of full-time working women who have families report having more to do than they can possibly handle. Only 13 percent of men with full-time positions and families said the same.

Research also indicates that only 35 percent of employed Millennial men without children believe that men should be primary breadwinners and that women should be primary caregivers, but after becoming fathers, 53 percent of Millennial men said it was better for parental dynamics to take on more traditional roles. The gap becomes even wider among highly educated Millennial men, with two-thirds of Harvard Business School MBA graduates expecting their partners to manage the majority of childcare and household responsibilities. This percentage is down from previous generations, indicating a shift in social attitudes and expectations toward more egalitarian dynamics; however, workplace policies are still deeply rooted in the old-fashioned ideals of the past. Indeed, the absence of male-specific work–life balance policies amplifies the tendency to revert to traditional, heteronormative dynamics.

Despite the generational rise of working women and mothers, expectations of women as caregivers and homemakers is deeply engrained in American culture.

A recent study indicated that 39 percent of working mothers have experienced family-related career interruptions compared to only 24 percent of working fathers. More than half of these women stated that being a working parent has made it more challenging to achieve career advancement compared to only 16 percent of working fathers. Additionally, women take more time off for maternity leave than men do for paternity leave, resulting in an increased risk of feeling disempowered throughout their parental-leave experience. These expectations and societal norms influence how working women are viewed by others and by themselves. Recent data reveals that mothers are "less likely to be hired for jobs, to be perceived as competent at work, or to be paid as much as their male colleagues with the same qualifications." Unsurprisingly, fathers do not experience any of these effects. In fact, it is quite the opposite. Fathers are viewed by employers as more stable and even more committed to their work since they have a family to provide for.

Despite the praise received by men for being involved fathers, taking paternity leave continues to carry a stigma for many men. While Millennial men tend to value and use paternity leave to a greater extent than men of previous generations, they are not exempt from experiencing this stigma. Designing, implementing, and supporting equal parental-leave policies can empower Millennial men and women alike. Specifically, companies can help level the playing field by offering gender-neutral parental leave. Gender-neutral leave alleviates the pressure on new moms and lessens the social stigma for new dads. Ninety-seven percent of Millennials (male and female) feel that work–life balance is important to them but believe that taking advantage of work–life balance and flexibility programs will negatively impact their careers. Granting all employees greater flexibility, such as gender-neutral parental leave, can help support Millennial parents in achieving a better balance between family and work, and empower working fathers to take on more responsibilities at home. That said, it is imperative that employers encourage employees to actually utilize these programs and support them when they do so.

Work–Life Integration, Mental Health, and COVID-19

In a time when we are more digitally connected than ever, the age-old adage of work–life balance seems to evade all employees regardless of age or gender. Now, the emphasis is on work–life integration, especially for Millennials who view work as an integral part of life, not something separate that needs to be "balanced." Work–life integration is defined by the Georgetown Institute for Women, Peace, and Security as "when what you do at work and what you do outside of it with family, friends, and community are driven by the same fundamental values and passions." Ideally, under the guise of work–life integration, employees can bring their personalities to work along with their skills and strengths, which will contribute to a feeling of congruency and authenticity in both work and life.

Work–life integration empowers Millennial women yet much like work–life integration balance, the idea is also elusive and takes on different meanings to different people. For many Millennials, work–life integration means aligning their work with their passions, personal interests, values, and principles. For Millennial women specifically, work–life integration also means finding work that accepts and values their natural talents, strengths, and styles. This is imperative since women often feel the need to show up differently at work in order to fit in and make valuable contributions, which threatens their ability to show up seamlessly and wholly in work and life alike. When Millennial women achieve true work–life integration, they are more willing to make sacrifices and work harder to ensure company success.

According to the Georgetown Institute for Women, Peace and Security, companies can work to value women's contributions by recognizing differences and touting the benefits of diversity. While it is difficult to shift corporate cultures, leaders can encourage a supportive environment that fosters an appreciation of employees' differences. Educational events such as workshops and seminars can help create greater awareness and easier discussions around differences in communication styles, work styles, schedules, and so on. Furthermore, when leaders consistently discuss the benefits of diversity, it can help move the needle on company culture and create a safer and more empowered environment for employees who are in lower-level positions to do the same.

When women feel undervalued and unsupported, it can contribute to feelings of dissatisfaction and have a negative impact on overall well-being. In a study conducted in 2020 by WebMD Health Services, nearly half of women reported greater dissatisfaction than their male counterparts in the areas of financial well-being and vocational well-being (i.e., participating in work that is satisfying and consistent with one's values). On a similar note, Millennial women reported experiencing stress at higher rates, particularly for those that are caregivers. Millennials, sometimes called the "burnout generation," are no strangers to stress, anxiety, and depression. A recent survey by Blue Cross Blue Shield revealed that less than half of Millennials think their mental health is good or excellent. Notably, Millennial women are far more likely than their male counterparts to experience burnout and depression.

Additionally, a recent survey revealed that more than half (56%) of all working women feel lonely and isolated sometimes or always compared with 44% of men. The survey also indicated vast differences in parental satisfaction with well-being: 73 percent of men with children reported satisfaction with their physical well-being, while only 49% of women with children reported the same. Other studies show that despite constant connection through technology and social media, Millennials are often anxious, stressed, irritable, fatigued, and feeling disconnected from other people in their lives. In the WebMD Health Services survey, more than half of this generation reported experiencing significantly more workplace symptoms of stress than their older colleagues.

Stress, anxiety, depression, and isolation have been compounded for everyone due to COVID-19, but the virus has been particularly impactful on Millennial women in the workplace. Research shows that the hiring gap between Millennial men and women has grown larger, with millennial men taking up 1.5 percent more of available jobs. In addition to, or perhaps because of the hiring gap, women are assuming even more family and household responsibilities during the pandemic, bearing the double burden of expectations to be full-time caregivers and work full-time as well. Recent research conducted by the Center for American Progress found that throughout the pandemic, Millennial mothers are almost three times more likely than Millennial fathers to report being unable to work due to a school or childcare closure. Despite working full-time outside of the home, women spend two hours more each day on caregiving and household tasks and are ten times more likely to stay home with sick children. This data highlights the unpaid caregiving work done by women in their households as one of the biggest barriers they face to equal opportunity in the workforce. Post-pandemic, the risk for falling further behind is even greater.

While the pandemic will eventually come to an end, economists worry about the long-term impact on women's careers, since past recessions have proven that women often feel the brunt of these types of events. Research shows that women's lifetime earnings are significantly affected when they leave the workforce for even a couple of years, exacerbating the gap in pay between genders. The country has been in dire need of policy reform around maternity leave and childcare for a long time, but it is becoming even more critical as COVID-19 continues to take a detrimental toll on Millennial women in the workplace.

Looking Forward

According to a recent study conducted by the Pew Research Center, 75 percent of young women think changes are needed to achieve equality in the workplace. Further research shows that if we continue at the current rate of progress, it could take 118 years for women to obtain gender parity in pay and 81 years to reach gender equality in overall economic engagement. Most employees feel their organizations aren't doing enough to affect real change, and although they believe their CEOs support diversity, less than half think their company is doing the necessary work to achieve gender parity. To help equalize disparities, companies can invest in workshops and training sessions, advocate for acceptance and flexibility within corporate cultures (and uphold these practices, encourage employees to use flex programs, and support and praise them when they do), connect promising female managers with executive leaders, and hire coaches for both men and women before, during, and after parental leave.

A recent article by Melinda Gates, cofounder of the Bill and Melinda Gates Foundation, the world's largest private charitable organization as of 2015, states that lawmakers can start by expanding access to paid sick and family leave for the duration of the pandemic. They can also include future stimulus packages that offer extended access to childcare facilities, so they can stay partially open to serve essential workers. Congress can also enact national paid family and medical leave policies that guarantee employees the ability to take time away from their jobs to care for a loved one or recover from an illness without threatening their financial stability.

In addition to law and policy reform, Gemma Wolfe, cohead of Strategy, Consumer, and Wealth Management at Goldman Sachs, emphasizes the importance of continuing the progress, albeit slow, made in the venture capital arena. Research shows that diverse founders are often more capital efficient, which has become increasingly important amidst the pandemic. Wolfe, along with others in the industry, is concerned by the year-over-year decline in funding to all women teams. Her concern is amplified by the longstanding impacts that COVID-19 will have on female entrepreneurship.

Millennial women must focus on putting themselves first, which continues to be a major existential challenge as they struggle to move beyond society's deeply engrained expectations and assumptions. Taking time to care for themselves, both personally and professionally, will be imperative as they keep fighting an uphill battle toward gender equality in the workplace and beyond.

Section 13.5 • **STORIES CELEBRATING AND SHOWCASING 100 YEARS OF WOMEN'S BUREAU SUCCESSES**

This section is excerpted from "Your Story," (Women's Bureau, U.S. Department of Labor)

To celebrate and honor 100 years of working to improve the lives of the nation's working women, the Women's Bureau of the U.S. Department of Labor asked women workers to celebrate this milestone with them by sharing stories about their training for and participation in the American workplace. A sampling of stories follows.

Jude Antonyappan (District of Columbia)
My brilliant mother couldn't even complete eighth grade, because of customs that devalued women's contributions in domains outside their homes. I dared to dream of becoming a lawyer someday. Each step was a struggle, riddled with obstacles that seemed insurmountable. My mom reminded [me] with a smile, "Live in infinity." I tried. With each setback, the next step unfolded with an uncanny sense of hope steeped in faith – with a sliver of happiness. I got my doctorate from one of the top universities in the world, raised my three amazing children with an unshakable belief in their sense of self and goodness to respectable stations in life; became a tenured professor; dedicated my work to help first-generation learners get their degrees; and finally, in my 60th year, I am going to become a LAWYER! Naysayers aside, with enormous goodwill for justice and service, I raise my voice and dare to argue, mastering the art of advocating zealously the case of another human who needs an empowering voice! Oh, Amma, how I wish you were here. I share the hope you gave me with your granddaughter and with countless other women who need hope above all else. WHB!

Laura Lindsey (Texas)
I am a retired African American woman who served active duty in the U.S. Air Force from May 29, 1984, until my retirement on February 1, 2014 (30 years). I was raised by my grandmother who did not have a high-school education but instilled a strong sense of

perseverance and endurance in spite of circumstances. I attained my associate degree, Bachelor of Science degree, and a Master of Science degree.

My grandmother raised 8 children of her own and 5 grandchildren. My grandmother encouraged me to join the U.S. Air Force, although I was hesitant of the unknown.

As a result of her encouragement, I entered the Air Force and was eventually promoted to the rank of Chief Master Sergeant – which is the highest enlisted rank in the Air Force. I was the second African American woman promoted to the rank of Chief Master Sergeant in the history of the Air Force Recruiting Service.

I am currently an Aerospace Science Instructor at Western Hills High School in Fort Worth, Texas, where I have been employed for the past 6 years, firmly believing I can help students also realize the potential that is within them that they sometimes cannot see in themselves.

Heidi Turner (Arkansas)
I started a career in welding and got my first job as a structural welder. I decided to continue my education as a certified welding inspector, which landed me a safety director position while pursuing my Certified Welding Inspector certificate. I love that there is such a vast amount of opportunity for women in the construction industry.

Evelyn Jorgenson, Ph.D. (Arkansas)
Community college higher education is my passion. I have worked in education since 1976 and specifically community college education since 1986. During those many years, I moved from part-time to full-time and from an entry-level educator to a community college president.

When I became president in Missouri in 1996, I was the only female community college president in the state. I feel so fortunate to be a part of and be witness to the changing roles of women in higher education and to see the steady progression to impactful leadership roles. During my tenure of 24 years as a community college president, I am pleased to say that I've seen the recognition and acceptance of women presidents rise considerably. It's exciting to live in an era where there are women in nearly every leadership role. Potential is being permitted to flourish!

I personally have come a long way, from little farm girl to a first-generation college student to a community college president. It's been an interesting journey and it is wonderful to see the progress that women have made, and continue to make, in all facets of our society. We need female leaders and we are creating them!

Seaira Goetz (New York)
I am a first-generation college student who grew up in Central Florida. I moved to New York in 2015 to pursue my education in conservation biology. I have volunteered on many organic farms as agriculture is very important to me. I am deeply passionate about feeding people healthy food and sustaining a better environment for the future.

After college, I took a seasonal position with the U.S. Department of Agriculture (USDA) as a Plant Protection Technician. I quickly climbed the ranks and took a term position as a Plant

Protection & Quarantine Officer. I now coordinate surveys in Western New York. I also serve as a representative for women on the PPQ EEO Committee.

I am proud to help cherry farmers and protect American agriculture. I look back and cannot believe I have come this far. I am thankful for the teachers who encouraged me to attend college and look beyond life in my little hometown.

Stephanie Bahar (Missouri)
As women who grew up during the beginning of the woman's movement, we have been sandwiched between choosing a career and choosing a family. We have had to navigate the way without much history for guidance and have faced much discrimination. Now, as a woman in a predominately male field (automotive), I find what personally drives me is keeping the memory of women who have fought for equal rights alive by mentoring and coaching other women.

My joy does not come in meeting company or departmental expectations, but in knowing I have planted seeds in other women and am helping strengthen the next generation.

Each day, I arrive to work with passion knowing I have an opportunity to tell a story, to passion knowledge, and to coach women who are on their own journey. Yes, there are days that I still experience the "ole boys club," or being talked down to or ignored. However, this only makes me more determined to continue to stand tall as a leader and encourage fellow women in the industry.

Alexandra Phillips (Illinois)
I am a woman, a partner, mother, a friend. I am a therapist, an executive coach, a business owner, a community member, and a travel enthusiast. I am a passionate advocate for women and children. I work to empower women by helping them to discover their strengths, uncover their limiting beliefs, and create a plan for success.

I believe, as women, we must know our value in order to communicate that value to others. I believe that by empowering women we effect change on a systemic level because anything that holds women back holds the entire system back.

I am a mother of two girls and I want to create a better, more equal playing field for the next generation of women. Becoming a mother was one of life's greatest gifts and losing my mother when I was 38 was one of my biggest losses. I believe that WE ARE THE SOLUTION; that we are the people we have been waiting for to solve the problems we struggle with as women, families, schools, and communities. Elevate the conversation.

Dama Brown (Texas)
Eternal gratitude to the DOL Women's Bureau and the many trailblazing women who secured for me and other generations of women the right to inherit, own, and control property; to engage in trade, commerce, and professions; to be free from physical abuse at the hands of a spouse; to vote, hold office, and serve on juries; to secure housing, employment, and pay parity; and to control my own bodily integrity.

Not all of these rights were available to women in the 100 years before I was born, and we must be vigilant in safeguarding those rights for the next 100 years.

A Final Note

So many strong, focused, bright, dedicated, and brave trailblazers are highlighted throughout this book. And their stories barely skim the surface! Editorial restraints required us to restrict the women we included in these pages, but the stories and experiences of so many other working women are equally compelling. The women we featured all, in some way, influenced the trajectory of women in the workplace today. They taught us many lessons, including the necessity of standing up for what we believe in and having the confidence and tenacity to keep pushing forward while questioning the established societal and cultural norms and how they might or might not serve us. In many cases, these women risked their lives in order to open new doors and establish new guidelines and greater opportunities for generations to come. Without the progress made by yesterday's trailblazers, the younger generation of women today would not be in today's work environments – where, in many cases, issues such as work–life balance, flexible work schedules, childcare, and training to help us recognize covert and overt bias, are all at the fore in corporate human-resources departments. Understanding the history of the workplace in which American women found themselves at various points in our past increases awareness of the struggles and challenges these women faced head-on in order to move us incrementally forward, creating more equality and opportunity along the way for women working in America.

PART FIVE

Resources

Additional Data, Resources, Help and Information

CHAPTER CONTENTS

100 Years of Women in the Workplace in America

Year	No. of Women in the Labor Force	Share of Women Employed in Top-10 Occupations	Top-10 Occupations of Employed Women	No. of Employed Women in Occupation
1920	8,179,017	52.8%	Other domestic & personal service	669,491
1920	8,179,017	52.8%	Teachers	622,877
1920	8,179,017	52.8%	Stenographers and Typists	567,784
1920	8,179,017	52.8%	Clerks (n.e.c.)	442,753
1920	8,179,017	52.8%	Farm laborers, home farm	396,625
1920	8,179,017	52.8%	Launderers and Laundresses	384,083
1920	8,179,017	52.8%	Salesmen and saleswomen, stores	350,552
1920	8,179,017	52.8%	Bookkeepers and cashiers	337,418
1920	8,179,017	52.8%	Cooks	266,801
1920	8,179,017	52.8%	Farmers, general farms	240,385
1930	10,500,803	66.2%	Operatives (n.e.c.)	1,386,515
1930	10,500,803	66.2%	Other domestic and personal service	1,056,567
1930	10,500,803	66.2%	Teachers	834,686
1930	10,500,803	66.2%	Stenographers and typists	720,533
1930	10,500,803	66.2%	Clerks	623,131
1930	10,500,803	66.2%	Salesmen or saleswomen	494,337
1930	10,500,803	66.2%	Bookkeepers and cashiers	435,255
1930	10,500,803	66.2%	Farm laborers, unpaid, family workers	363,806
1930	10,500,803	66.2%	Cooks	341,186
1930	10,500,803	66.2%	Launderers and laundresses	330,241

NOTE: Occupation estimates include women ages 16 and over in the labor force (1920) and civilian employed women ages 16 and over (1930–2018). Labor force estimates include all women ages 16 and over who are employed or unemployed. The classification of occupations changes every 10 years. Some occupations increase or decline in size as a result of being combined or split out from other occupations. Individual occupation categories are not strictly comparable over time. The occupations presented here are the top-10 occupations in the decade in which they occurred. "Operatives, n.e.c." were primarily employed in manufacturing jobs and "n.e.c." means "not elsewhere classified." *(Data: 1920–2000 Decennial Census and 2010 and 2018 American Community Survey public-use microdata files)*

100 Years of Women in the Workplace in America, continued

Year	No. of Women in the Labor Force	Share of Women Employed in Top-10 Occupations	Top-10 Occupations of Employed Women	No. of Employed Women in Occupation
1940	12,812,181	67.9%	Operatives (n.e.c.)	1,848,824
1940	12,812,181	67.9%	Private household workers (n.e.c.)	1,430,286
1940	12,812,181	67.9%	Stenographers, typists and secretaries	1,022,543
1940	12,812,181	67.9%	Teachers	783,205
1940	12,812,181	67.9%	Clerks (n.e.c.)	687,593
1940	12,812,181	67.9%	Salesmen and saleswomen	520,291
1940	12,812,181	67.9%	Bookkeepers, accountants, and cashiers	443,570
1940	12,812,181	67.9%	Waiters and waitresses	360,424
1940	12,812,181	67.9%	Proprietors, managers and officials (n.e.c.)	339,282
1940	12,812,181	67.9%	Housekeepers, private family	330,497
1950	16,663,485	69.8%	Operatives (n.e.c.)	2,461,939
1950	16,663,485	69.8%	Stenographers, typists and secretaries	1,558,546
1950	16,663,485	69.8%	Clerks	1,508,694
1950	16,663,485	69.8%	Salesmen and saleswomen	1,284,339
1950	16,663,485	69.8%	Private household work (n.e.c.)	1,140,029
1950	16,663,485	69.8%	Teachers	867,229
1950	16,663,485	69.8%	Nurses	604,329
1950	16,663,485	69.8%	Bookkeepers	584,381
1950	16,663,485	69.8%	Waiters and waitresses	568,036
1950	16,663,485	69.8%	Managers, officials and proprietors (n.e.c.)	558,545

NOTE: Occupation estimates include women ages 16 and over in the labor force (1920) and civilian employed women ages 16 and over (1930–2018). Labor force estimates include all women ages 16 and over who are employed or unemployed. The classification of occupations changes every 10 years. Some occupations increase or decline in size as a result of being combined or split out from other occupations. Individual occupation categories are not strictly comparable over time. The occupations presented here are the top-10 occupations in the decade in which they occurred. "Operatives, n.e.c." were primarily employed in manufacturing jobs and "n.e.c." means "not elsewhere classified." *(Data: 1920–2000 Decennial Census and 2010 and 2018 American Community Survey public-use microdata files)*

100 Years of Women in the Workplace in America, continued

Year	No. of Women in the Labor Force	Share of Women Employed in Top-10 Occupations	Top-10 Occupations of Employed Women	No. of Employed Women in Occupation
1960	22,226,500	56.1%	Clerks (n.e.c.)	1,725,420
1960	22,226,500	56.1%	Salesmen and saleswomen	1,423,980
1960	22,226,500	56.1%	Secretaries	1,423,660
1960	22,226,500	56.1%	Operatives (n.e.c.)	1,323,320
1960	22,226,500	56.1%	Private household workers (n.e.c.)	1,146,260
1960	22,226,500	56.1%	Teachers	1,106,800
1960	22,226,500	56.1%	Nurses	824,320
1960	22,226,500	56.1%	Bookkeepers	766,040
1960	22,226,500	56.1%	Waiters and waitresses	709,220
1960	22,226,500	56.1%	Managers, officials and proprietors (n.e.c.)	619,980
1970	30,688,800	42.1%	Secretaries	2,625,600
1970	30,688,800	42.1%	Teachers	1,823,800
1970	30,688,800	42.1%	Sales clerks, retail	1,446,900
1970	30,688,800	42.1%	Bookkeepers	1,265,400
1970	30,688,800	42.1%	Nurses	1,042,800
1970	30,688,800	42.1%	Waiters	931,000
1970	30,688,800	42.1%	Typists	915,800
1970	30,688,800	42.1%	Sewers and stitchers	811,300
1970	30,688,800	42.1%	Cashier	677,800
1970	16,663,485	42.1%	Maids, private household	660,500

NOTE: Occupation estimates include women ages 16 and over in the labor force (1920) and civilian employed women ages 16 and over (1930–2018). Labor force estimates include all women ages 16 and over who are employed or unemployed. The classification of occupations changes every 10 years. Some occupations increase or decline in size as a result of being combined or split out from other occupations. Individual occupation categories are not strictly comparable over time. The occupations presented here are the top-10 occupations in the decade in which they occurred. "Operatives, n.e.c." were primarily employed in manufacturing jobs and "n.e.c." means "not elsewhere classified." *(Data: 1920–2000 Decennial Census and 2010 and 2018 American Community Survey public-use microdata files)*

100 Years of Women in the Workplace in America, continued

Year	No. of Women in the Labor Force	Share of Women Employed in Top-10 Occupations	Top-10 Occupations of Employed Women	No. of Employed Women in Occupation
1980	44,649,804	41.1%	Secretaries	3,820,700
1980	44,649,804	41.1%	Teachers	2,398,240
1980	44,649,804	41.1%	Bookkeeping, accounting and auditing clerks	1,635,320
1980	44,649,804	41.1%	Nurses	1,628,020
1980	44,649,804	41.1%	Cashiers	1,426,940
1980	44,649,804	41.1%	Managers and administrators (n.e.c.)	1,352,680
1980	44,649,804	41.1%	General office clerks	1,194,800
1980	44,649,804	41.1%	Waiters and waitresses	1,194,800
1980	44,649,804	41.1%	Sales workers (n.e.c.)	1,150,800
1980	44,465,840	41.1%	Nursing aides, orderlies, and attendants	1,136,960
1990	56,553,832	36,3%	Secretaries	3,823,250
1990	56,553,832	36,3%	Teachers	2,987,327
1990	56,553,832	36,3%	Nurses	2,148,271
1990	56,553,832	36,3%	Cashiers	1,993,017
1990	56,553,832	36,3%	Bookkeepers, accounting and auditing clerks	1,565,513
1990	56,553,832	36,3%	Managers and administrators (n.e.c.)	1,615,184
1990	56,553,832	36,3%	Nursing aides, orderlies, and attendants	1,497,257
1990	56,553,832	36,3%	General office clerks	1,158,162
1990	56,553,832	36,3%	Supervisors and proprietors, sales occupations	1,157,845
1990	56,553,832	36,3%	Sales workers (n.e.c.)	1,148,866

NOTE: Occupation estimates include women ages 16 and over in the labor force (1920) and civilian employed women ages 16 and over (1930–2018). Labor force estimates include all women ages 16 and over who are employed or unemployed. The classification of occupations changes every 10 years. Some occupations increase or decline in size as a result of being combined or split out from other occupations. Individual occupation categories are not strictly comparable over time. The occupations presented here are the top-10 occupations in the decade in which they occurred. "Operatives, n.e.c." were primarily employed in manufacturing jobs and "n.e.c." means "not elsewhere classified." *(Data: 1920–2000 Decennial Census and 2010 and 2018 American Community Survey public-use microdata files)*

100 Years of Women in the Workplace in America, continued

Year	No. of Women in the Labor Force	Share of Women Employed in Top-10 Occupations	Top-10 Occupations of Employed Women	No. of Employed Women in Occupation
2000	64,553,954	33.6%	Secretaries and administrative assistants	3,597,416
2000	64,553,954	33.6%	Teachers	3,466,434
2000	64,553,954	33.6%	Nurses	2,602,376
2000	64,553,954	33.6%	Cashiers	2,028,267
2000	64,553,954	33.6%	Retail salespersons	1,780,975
2000	64,553,954	33.6%	Bookkeeping, accounting and auditing clerks	1,523,026
2000	64,553,954	33.6%	Nursing, psychiatric and home-health aides	1,465,386
2000	64,553,954	33.6%	Customer-service representatives	1,396,406
2000	64,553,954	33.6%	Childcare workers	1,254,786
2000	64,553,954	33.6%	Waiters and waitresses	1,235,786
2010	74,279,640	33.3%	Teachers	3,984,836
2010	74,279,640	33.3%	Secretaries and administrative assistants	3,427,510
2010	74,279,640	33.3%	Nurses	3,139,854
2010	74,279,640	33.3%	Cashiers	2,410,152
2010	74,279,640	33.3%	Nursing, psychiatric and home-health aides	1,926,489
2010	74,279,640	33.3%	Retail salespersons	1,735,213
2010	74,279,640	33.3%	Customer-service representatives	1,504,923
2010	74,279,640	33.3%	Waiters and waitresses	1,480,519
2010	74,279,640	33.3%	First-line supervisors of retail sales workers	1,309,252
2010	74,279,640	33.3%	Maids and housekeeping cleaners	1,269,181

NOTE: Occupation estimates include women ages 16 and over in the labor force (1920) and civilian employed women ages 16 and over (1930–2018). Labor force estimates include all women ages 16 and over who are employed or unemployed. The classification of occupations changes every 10 years. Some occupations increase or decline in size as a result of being combined or split out from other occupations. Individual occupation categories are not strictly comparable over time. The occupations presented here are the top-10 occupations in the decade in which they occurred. "Operatives, n.e.c." were primarily employed in manufacturing jobs and "n.e.c." means "not elsewhere classified." *(Data: 1920–2000 Decennial Census and 2010 and 2018 American Community Survey public-use microdata files)*

100 Years of Women in the Workplace in America, continued

Year	No. of Women in the Labor Force	Share of Women Employed in Top-10 Occupations	Top-10 Occupations of Employed Women	No. of Employed Women in Occupation
2018	78,607,961	32.8%	Teachers	34,239,366
2018	78,607,961	32.8%	Nurses	3,910,538
2018	78,607,961	32.8%	Nursing, psychiatric and home-health aides	2,965,314
2018	78,607,961	32.8%	Secretaries and administrative assistants	2,745,575
2018	78,607,961	32.8%	Cashiers	2,419,322
2018	78,607,961	32.8%	Customer-service representatives	2,083,533
2018	78,607,961	32.8%	Retail salespersons	1,680,330
2018	78,607,961	32.8%	Waiters and waitresses	1,571,530
2018	78,607,961	32.8%	First-line supervisors of retail sales workers	1,468,669
2018	78,607,961	32.8%	Managers (n.e.c.)	1,428,557

NOTE: Occupation estimates include women ages 16 and over in the labor force (1920) and civilian employed women ages 16 and over (1930–2018). Labor force estimates include all women ages 16 and over who are employed or unemployed. The classification of occupations changes every 10 years. Some occupations increase or decline in size as a result of being combined or split out from other occupations. Individual occupation categories are not strictly comparable over time. The occupations presented here are the top-10 occupations in the decade in which they occurred. "Operatives, n.e.c." were primarily employed in manufacturing jobs and "n.e.c." means "not elsewhere classified." *(Data: 1920–2000 Decennial Census and 2010 and 2018 American Community Survey public-use microdata files)*

Section 2 • **RESOURCES**

GENDERED CAREER PATHS AND SELF-FULFILLING PROPHECIES

Gender bias disadvantages women not by suppressing their ability to advance, but by encouraging professional detours. In the legal industry, for instance, research shows that biases about gender roles encourage superiors to push women into more "domestic" areas of practice, like family and matrimonial law. Therefore, women are often relegated to specialties that are far less prestigious and have lower earning potential than other areas of litigation. Beyond being less lucrative for women themselves, these areas of litigation tend to bring in less money than others, making them inherently less valued by firms.

Beyond occupying less visible roles, women sometimes perform less visible labor. Scholars observe that organizations tend to overlook the work that happens behind the scenes, like team building and crisis management. Incidentally, this work is more likely to be done by women. On the other hand, front-and-center "heroic" work is witnessed and rewarded, but these tasks are more likely to be assigned to men.

Gender biases lead those making high-level assignments to believe that women are less capable of completing them. Then, the fact that women are rarely seen doing these tasks reinforces the bias that they are not suited for them. This is another kind of double-bind known as the "self-fulfilling prophecy." It is a no-win situation in which women are believed to be inherently incapable of excelling at certain tasks, and those who hold this bias make decisions that create outcomes that "prove" it to be true.

The "glass cliff" is another example of gender bias as a self-fulfilling prophecy. There is some evidence that when women do receive high-reward assignments, they are at greater risk of being given dead-end tasks. The glass cliff describes a tendency to assign tasks with significant professional risk (and a high chance of failure) to women and people of color. This phenomenon appears to particularly impact women in leadership. Similarly, scholars suggest that female CEOs are far more likely to be appointed when a company is struggling than during prosperity. Of course, the likelihood that an organization in crisis will continue to decline is great, as is the probability that this almost inevitable outcome will still be considered a failure in leadership.

In the words of educator and equitable recruitment expert, Kate Slater:

> The glass cliff phenomenon presents a problem to the sustainability of an organization. When the going gets rough, a board might be more likely to make a leadership nomination that's seen as risky or radical. Translated: They're more likely to take a chance on someone who isn't a white man. But without the infrastructure to support the leadership transition through tricky times, the leader becomes "tokenized." They're simply a figurehead; and this, in essence, dooms them to fail. And it's reflected in the leadership disparities at the top of the top. In 2019, there was an increase in female CEOs in Fortune 500 companies – 33 women CEOs out of 500, up from 24 in 2018. And in June 2020, Fortune reported only five Black CEOs – a scant 1%.

UNEQUAL BURDENS

As noted in the *Harvard Business Review*, many organizational structures and work practices were designed to fit men's lives and situations at a time when women made up only a very small percentage of the workforce. Even the requirements of senior-level positions are skewed in favor of men. For instance, senior male workers are far more likely to have a spouse or partner who does not work. This provides males more flexibility to relocate for their job, travel frequently despite being a parent, or assume an international placement.

On the other hand, careers that conflate productivity with time ignore the reality of many women – which involves labor in the office and labor in the home. In the legal field, for instance, the use of measures like billable hours as determinants of success tends to disadvantage women with families. The evidence shows that heterosexual, partnered women with husbands and/or children typically have far less freedom than men to take on after-hours work or travel assignments.

This is partly due to traditional gender roles, which create expectations for women to shoulder the bulk of domestic labor – even when they work as much as their male partners. According to *The Guardian*, study after study has shown that even as women have stepped forward in the workforce, they still shoulder the bulk of household chores within married, heterosexual couples. One such study by the Boston Consulting Group included over 3,000 individuals from the U.S. and Europe and found that working women spend an average of 15 more hours on domestic work each week than men do. There is also contemporary evidence that women have been largely responsible for home-based learning amidst COVID-related school closures.

Despite the added burden of after-hours labor, research suggests that women must still put in twice as much effort to get the same level of recognition as men. According to evidence taken from studies involving over 1,200 leaders, Catalyst found that while men's leadership abilities are often assumed, women are required to repeatedly prove themselves. In addition to showing others that they are fit to lead time and time again, senior women note the need to monitor stereotypical expectations. These factors not only result in unequal burden, but they also take a personal toll on the well-being of women who work outside of the home – an outcome often referred to as an "emotional tax."

In another example of unequal burden, the careers of women are disproportionately impacted by child-rearing. Many face career setbacks due to the expectation that they will eventually put their career on hold to start a family, even if they have no intention to do so. This is commonly referred to as the "motherhood penalty" or "pregnancy penalty," and is grounded in two assumptions. First, that all working women will choose to have children at some point, and second, that women who do choose to have children will become less dedicated employees. These biases limit women's career-growth opportunities, particularly when it comes to leadership positions. Furthermore, studies show that women's careers suffer greater detriment with each additional child they have.

In studying this phenomenon, University of Massachusetts sociologist Michelle Budig found that women lose approximately 4% of their lifetime earnings with each child. The loss is not due to extenuating factors like working reduced hours or finding more flexible employment, but likely due to workplace stereotypes. Notably, the motherhood penalty is paid over time, making it an especially discrete form of bias that is difficult for women to counteract. As Budig states, "It's not like you immediately get a lower-paying job, but you miss out on the next promotion, you don't get the next raise, [and/or] your performance is evaluated lower."

EVERYDAY GENDER BIAS: WHAT DOES IT LOOK LIKE?

CODED LANGUAGE

The use of coded language in the workplace is an especially insidious form of gender bias because it often goes unnoticed. By communicating biases (and sometimes prejudices) in covert ways, coded language upholds stereotypes that limit the progress of working women. One example is the different ways that male and female behaviors are discussed. Research has frequently shown that when men show their emotions at work, particularly anger, it is perceived and discussed differently than when women show their emotions. Often, anger when demonstrated by men is described as passion, or it is attributed to an external cause (i.e., a challenging circumstance). Conversely, when women demonstrate anger, it is commonly attributed to an internal cause – meaning a personal character flaw (i.e., being an angry person overall).

Moreover, women who get angry are more likely to be described as emotional, which is taken as evidence of unprofessionalism, incompetence, and/or a lack of self-control. According to a 2008 study published in *Psychological Science*, women who expressed anger were consistently associated with lower status, given lower wages, and were seen as less competent. In another study, participants' beliefs about the salary women deserve dropped by 35 percent when they demonstrated an "aggressive" communication style. When men demonstrated an equally aggressive style, perceptions of the pay they deserved dropped by half as much as it did for women. This is an example of a phenomenon known as "assertiveness backlash." Working women tend to be seen much less favorably when they are direct or outspoken, and sometimes face severe professional consequences for it. This is because assertiveness is perceived as a masculine trait that is more "appropriate," "natural," or acceptable when exhibited by men.

As noted in the *Harvard Business Review*:

> Because of widely held societal beliefs about gender roles and leadership, when most people are asked to picture a leader, what they picture is a male leader. Even when women and men behave in "leaderly" ways among peers – speaking up with new ideas, for example – it's men who are seen as leaders by the group, not women. And as our study shows, even in this era of talent management and diversity and inclusion initiatives, our formal feedback mechanisms are still suffering from the same biases, sending subtle messages to women that they aren't "real leaders"– men are.

To understand how coded language translates to gendered disadvantages, consider the following example. Age-old cultural biases characterize women as being inherently maternal and nurturing. This, in turn, is presumed to make them more community-oriented than men. These biases then emerge in the workplace and often pigeonhole women into certain roles or frame them with unwanted labels. Research shows that performance reviews routinely discuss women's accomplishments from a communal perspective. In other words, even in instances where the achievement should be credited to an individual woman, it is more likely to be discussed as a win by the team. Men, on the other hand, are far more likely to be discussed as individuals, which makes them more likely to be acknowledged for their individual work. In this way, women's professional achievements are made less visible than those of men, who are more likely to be perceived as individual actors.

Even when women and men are assigned positive descriptors, they are often informed by gender stereotypes. For instance, a study of over 4,000 participants and 81,000 performance evaluations taken from a military dataset found that where male leaders were most likely to be praised as analytical, female leaders were likely to be described as compassionate. Although both terms are positive and beneficial in the workplace, the reality is that the candidate described as analytical is far more likely to receive a promotion or to keep their job during company downsizing.

After all, analytical is a performance-related term, so its association to company growth and revenue is clear. By comparison, the seemingly positive terms assigned to women are often personality-related (compassionate, enthusiastic, supportive), and their relationship to company performance is less obvious. Thus, these traits are deemed less valuable. Additionally, the same study found that when leaders were described in negative ways, men were typically considered "arrogant," while women were described as "inept." While men were criticized as being somewhat unpleasant, women were described as unable to do their jobs. A person making promotional or hiring decisions is far more likely to hire the former than the latter.

The study also found that despite objective measures of performance showing that both genders were equal in terms of physical fitness scores, grades, class performance, etc., even with all other factors being equal, women received more poor reviews than men. Additionally, evaluators still assigned women with far more negative descriptors. This echoes existing research, which notes that women tend to receive less favorable performance evaluations than men across the board.

Beyond this, the feedback given to women is less detailed or contradictory, making it difficult for them to determine the cause. Since reviews are a key component of workplace advancement in many sectors, gender bias in evaluation processes directly impacts women's ability to receive raises and promotions. This is just one of the many reasons for the underrepresentation of women in senior and executive positions. For instance, in 2019, just one in five C-suite executives (e.g., CEO, CFO, etc.) was a woman.

A 2017 study shows a more direct relationship between gender bias, coded language, and women's economic disadvantage. To analyze an entrepreneurial funding process, researchers observed discussions between the venture capitalists that evaluated each candidate. The language they used often reinforced stereotypes that framed women as lacking the qualities required for successful entrepreneurship. Somewhat shockingly, traits deemed negative among women were seen as positive among men. For instance, women were described as "young and inexperienced," while men were "young and promising." Similarly, while men were "cautious, sensible, and level-headed," women were "too cautious" and "undaring."

In a much more overt demonstration of both gender bias and sexism, a male candidate was described as a "very competent innovator that already has money to play with," while a woman was said to be "good-looking and careless with money." Unsurprisingly, the venture capitalists awarded men an average of 52 percent of the amount they applied for, while women were given just 25%. Similarly, over half of women's financing applications were denied, compared to 38 percent of men's. Reflecting on their findings, researchers believe they illustrate that "stereotyping through language underpins the image of a man as a true entrepreneur, while undermining the image of a woman as the same."

Often, people think that sexist language does nothing more than cause offense or ruffle a few feathers when in reality, there is far more at stake. Bias and prejudice use language to hide in plain sight. This creates company cultures where coded language pervades, and actively undercuts women's ability to thrive. On a societal level, lost wages, lost promotions, and lost opportunities come together to place women in general – but particularly women of color and women with disabilities – closer to the poverty line.

WOMEN AND POVERTY: A GENERAL OVERVIEW

- According to the U.S. Census Bureau data, there are more women than men living in poverty in the United States. In 2018, of the 38.1 million people living in poverty, 56 percent (21.4 million) were women.
- The 2019 Coronavirus (Covid-19) pandemic has also disproportionately affected women, pushing women out of the workplace at an unprecedented rate. This is predicted to undo some of the progress made for gender equity and female representation in the workplace.
- Research suggests that nearly two-thirds of women (60%) would earn more if working women were compensated equally to men of the same age, educational background, and hours worked. Under these circumstances, 65.9 percent of working single mothers would get a pay raise.
- The gender wealth gap is about more than just the fact that women largely earn less than men. Women are also more likely to have mortgages denied and to be overcharged for them. They are also at greater risk for unfair and abusive loan terms, and to have greater debt. These are just some of the challenges that undercut women's ability to establish savings and create wealth. Moreover, these factors make women less able to absorb and overcome the financial setback of unexpected life changes.
- Biases that undervalue women's work result in the overrepresentation of women in low-wage jobs. Approximately two-thirds of workers earning the federal minimum wage of $7.25 per hour are women. Conversely, women are largely underrepresented in the highest-paying careers.

WOMEN AND POVERTY: AN INTERSECTIONAL OVERVIEW

- Across nearly all races and ethnicities, women experience greater poverty rates than their male counterparts. American Indian or Alaska Native (AIAN) women experience the greatest poverty rates, followed by Black women and Latinas. Approximately 25 percent, or 1 in 4, AIAN women live in poverty – more than anyone in another racial or ethnic group, men and women included.
- While women, in general, account for the vast majority of workers earning federal minimum wage, women of color are especially likely to earn low wages.
- The poverty rate of women with disabilities is greater (22.9%) than both men with disabilities (17.9%) and women without disabilities (11.4%).
- Two-thirds of U.S. student-loan debt holders are women, and Black women, specifically, graduate with more debt than any other demographic. Simultaneously, Black women are most impacted by pay inequality, due to both gender-based and racial discrimination.

THE DOUBLE BIND: LIKEABILITY V. CAPABILITY

The double bind is a manifestation of gender bias in the workplace. The double bind refers to the widespread phenomenon in which women who work outside of the home are forced to choose between two equally unpleasant extremes. Take, for example, the issue of assertiveness backlash. For leaders, in particular, clear and direct communication is essential to the job. Yet women who take this approach also run the risk of losing the support of their teams. Thus, they must often choose between being seen as likable versus competent – with no option to be both. Perceived likeability has a direct impact on networking opportunities and the quality of professional relationships. It can make the difference between a positive or negative review, a glowing or indifferent reference letter, and even a promotion being granted or denied.

In terms of relationship quality, perceived likeability can make the difference between a pleasant versus hostile work environment, which then determines how long women may be willing or able to stay in their place of employment. Furthermore, research shows that having a friend in the workplace fosters employee well-being, resilience, and retention. Conversely, social exclusion can be extremely detrimental.

Studies have shown that informal work relationships also serve as channels for employees to access help, feedback, collaboration, advice, and important work-related information. Thus, one of the most damaging ways in which gender bias is manifested in the workplace is by excluding women from communication circles. World-renowned expert in gender equality and organizational culture Michelle King notes that this backlash entails:

> Lack of communication towards women; workplace information being withheld from women; the unwritten rules of the workplace not being shared with women; and lack of face-to-face communication with women. These types of behaviors can be considered gaslighting – intentionally altering information in order to create a disadvantage. Consider that interpersonal communication can be more important than written communication, especially in regards to gender-specific topics in the workplace. When communication is weaponized against women in the workplace, it is no wonder that women are so underrepresented in leadership roles.

Beyond this, existing biases that favor male candidates mean that women who are poorly perceived will only incur even further disadvantage. For decades, researchers have believed that access to informal (social) networks directly influences career outcomes. Yet, women consistently note limited access to mentors and colleagues of influence, which significantly hinders their advancement. Moreover, researchers find that the connections women do have tend to be less efficacious, meaning that men's networks provide more informal help than women's do, and men are more likely to have mentors who help them get promoted. Meanwhile, men in positions of power tend to direct developmental opportunities to junior men, whom they view as more likely than women to succeed.

THE IMPACT OF DISCRIMINATION ON ECONOMIC WELL-BEING: SYSTEMIC PAY DISPARITY

Various forms of discrimination are prevalent in the workplace, but the pay gap between men and women remains one of the most glaring markers of inequality. According to PayScale, women in the U.S. were still earning an average of just 81 cents to every dollar earned by men in 2020. Glassdoor, on the other hand, found that for some occupations, the pay gap was as wide as 73 cents to every male dollar earned. Moreover, progress toward pay equity has been painfully slow – the gender pay gap has narrowed by less than ten cents in the past five years.

While the difference may not seem like much at first, the impact of pay disparity becomes monumental over time. Using the numerical data, PayScale calculated women's potential lost earnings over a lifetime and found that they stood to lose between $80,000 and $900,000 over a 40-year career. Taking in additional factors like investment choices and compound interest, these numbers could be even higher. Clearly, pay disparity is not a minor issue. It creates substantial differences in the socioeconomic statuses of men and women, often being what prevents the latter from attaining upward mobility by building wealth.

It is important to note that the pay gap is not simply a case of employers actively lowballing women. Although this form of brazen discrimination exists, the U.S. has legal protections in place to support employment equity. Often, pay disparities between the genders is the result of much more discrete processes. Research shows that in the working population overall, women largely hold less prominent positions in less desirable or lucrative roles and employment settings than men. This is the case across various businesses, industries, and fields, giving a clear indication that women are being held back by systemic forces and processes that produce unequal outcomes. Accordingly, the research reveals gender bias consistently manufactures different work experiences, career trajectories, and financial rewards for men and women.

HOW TO ADVOCATE FOR THE ECONOMIC EMPOWERMENT OF UNDERREPRESENTED COMMUNITIES

Cross-gender Mentorship. This is a great way for nonminority, nonfemale employees to support diversity. Traditionally, mentorship between senior men and junior women has been held back by concerns about public opinion (i.e., that others will misinterpret them and question their propriety). However, the reality is that senior White males have the capacity to advocate for mentees in circles to which the women have little access. Beyond this, allies are a great asset to have because their voices will likely have more sway in spaces and situations where bias is at play.

Mentor by Extension. Many people recognize the value in mentorship, but struggle to find the time to be a mentor as their careers advance. High-level professionals who actively mentored people in the past can continue their streak in a hands-off way. For example, mentoring lineage involves referring people early in their careers to your own former protégés. Not only does this direct people to someone with more room to meet their needs, but it enhances your own professional network in the process. The next time someone asks you for career advice or guidance, put them in touch with someone who can provide more hands-on support.

Offer Work Shadow. This is a much easier goal than mentorship for the seriously time-strapped. When a promising candidate reaches out to you with a mentorship request, flag upcoming events or obligations that you may need help with. Give them a few options to choose from and offer an opportunity to take on an entry-level task. The support you receive can make up for any time you take to provide instruction or feedback during the project.

Remember to keep tasks simple and fair, as this cannot be an equitable initiative if there is exploitation of any kind. Ultimately, this is more about facilitating someone's access to spaces that may be, or may seem to be, beyond their reach. Maintaining an intersectional perspective can help you be broad about who you select. For instance, you can mentor a first-generation college student one quarter, a person with a disability the next, and a racial minority in the quarter after. This option is also great for a recent college graduate in need of hands-on experience. You can provide additional benefits by allowing those who complete the work-shadow to use you as a referee for other professional opportunities. The point here is to promote equity through access.

Refer Minority-Owned Businesses. This can be a major help to fledgling entrepreneurs, contractors, or consultants. If you receive quality work from a freelancer, for instance, you can mention them to your peers. Beyond the prospect of additional income, this can introduce someone to an entirely new network of people they may not have otherwise met. Connecting people from vastly different fields can also help people enhance the scope of their services or discover opportunities to branch out. Next time you visit a minority-owned business or hire a freelancer through a platform, consider who you know that may find their service useful and connect them based on mutual needs.

PREVENTING AND RESPONDING TO DISCRIMINATION IN THE WORKPLACE

This section includes text excerpted from "Prohibited Employment Policies/Practices," U.S. Equal Employment Opportunity Commission (EEOC).

PROHIBITED EMPLOYMENT POLICIES AND PRACTICES

The Equal Employment Opportunity Commission (EEOC) is the federal agency that enforces laws against employment discrimination, harassment, and retaliation. Under the laws enforced by the EEOC, it is illegal to discriminate against someone (applicant or employee) because of that person's race, color, religion, sex (including gender identity, sexual orientation, and pregnancy status), national origin, age (40 or older), disability, or genetic information. These laws forbid discrimination in every aspect of employment. It is also illegal under the EEOC to retaliate against a person because they complained about discrimination, filed a charge of discrimination, or participated in an employment discrimination investigation or lawsuit.

The laws enforced by the EEOC also prohibit an employer or other covered entity from using neutral employment policies and practices that have a disproportionately negative effect on applicants or employees of a particular race, color, religion, sex (including gender identity, sexual orientation, and pregnancy status), or national origin, or on an individual with a disability or class of individuals with disabilities, if the policies or practices in question are not job-related and not necessary to the operation of the business. Additionally, these prohibit an employer from using neutral employment policies and practices that have a disproportionately negative impact on applicants or employees age 40 or older, if the policies or practices in question are not based on a reasonable factor other than age.

Job Advertisements, Recruitment, and Referrals

It is illegal for an employer to publish a job advertisement that shows a preference for or discourages someone from applying for a job because of his or her race, color, religion, sex (including gender identity, sexual orientation, and pregnancy status), national origin, age (40 or older), disability or genetic information. For example, a help-wanted ad that seeks "females" or "recent college graduates" may discourage men and people over 40 from applying and may violate the law.

It is also illegal for an employer to recruit potential new employees in a way that discriminates against them because of race, color, religion, sex (including gender identity, sexual orientation, and pregnancy status), national origin, age (40 or older), disability or genetic information. For example, an employer's reliance on word-of-mouth recruitment by its mostly Hispanic workforce may violate the law if the result is that almost all new hires are Hispanic. The same laws apply when making decisions about job referrals.

Application and Hiring

It is illegal for an employer to discriminate against a job applicant because of his or her race, color, religion, sex (including gender identity, sexual orientation, and pregnancy status), national origin, age (40 or older), disability or genetic information. For example, an employer may not refuse to give employment applications to people of a certain race. An employer also may not base hiring decisions on stereotypes and assumptions made about a person based on the aforementioned factors.

If an employer requires job applicants to take a test, the test must be necessary and related to the job, and the employer must not exclude people of a particular race, color, religion, sex (including gender identity, sexual orientation, and pregnancy status), national origin, or individuals with disabilities. In addition, the employer may not use a test that excludes applicants who are 40 or older if the test is not based on a reasonable factor other than age.

If a job applicant with a disability needs an accommodation (such as a sign-language interpreter) to apply for a job, the employer is required to provide the accommodation, as long as the accommodation does not cause the employer significant difficulty or expense.

Job Assignments, Promotions, and Employment References

It is illegal for an employer to make decisions about job assignments and promotions based on an employee's race, color, religion, sex (including gender identity, sexual orientation, and pregnancy status), national origin, age (40 or older), disability or genetic information. For example, an employer may not give preference to employees of a certain race when making shift assignments and may not segregate employees of a particular national origin from other employees or from customers.

An employer also must not base assignment and promotion decisions on stereotypes and assumptions about a person based on the aforementioned factors.

If an employer requires employees to take a test before making decisions about assignments or promotions, the test may not exclude people of a particular race, color, religion, sex (including gender identity, sexual orientation, and pregnancy status), or national origin, or individuals with disabilities, unless the employer can show that the test is necessary and related to the job. In addition, the employer may not use a test that excludes employees who are 40 or older if the test is not based on a reasonable factor other than age.

Additionally, it is illegal for an employer to give a negative or false employment reference (or refuse to give a reference) based on the aforementioned factors.

Pay and Benefits

It is illegal for an employer to discriminate against an employee in the payment of wages or employee benefits on the basis of race, color, religion, sex (including gender identity, sexual orientation, and pregnancy status), national origin, age (40 or older), disability or genetic information. Employee benefits can include sick and vacation leave, insurance, access to overtime as well as overtime pay, and retirement programs. For example, an employer may not pay Hispanic workers less than African American workers because of their ethnicity, and men and women in the same workplace must be given equal pay for equal work.

In some situations, an employer may be allowed to reduce some employee benefits for older workers, but only if the cost of providing the reduced benefits is the same as the cost of providing benefits to younger workers.

Discipline, Dismissal, and Forced Resignation

An employer must not take into account a person's race, color, religion, sex (including gender identity, sexual orientation, and pregnancy status), national origin, age (40 or older), disability, or genetic information when making decisions about discipline or discharge. For example, if two employees commit a similar offense, an employer may not discipline them differently because of the aforementioned factors. When deciding which employees will be laid off, an employer may not choose the oldest workers because of their age. Employers also may not discriminate when deciding which workers to recall after a layoff.

Under the laws of the EEOC, it is illegal to force an employee to resign ("constructive discharge") by making the work environment so intolerable that a reasonable person would not be able to stay.

Reasonable Accommodation and Religion

The law requires that an employer provide reasonable accommodation to an employee or job applicant with a disability unless doing so would cause significant difficulty or expense for the employer.

A reasonable accommodation is any change in the workplace (or in the ways things are usually done) to help a person with a disability apply for a job, perform the duties of a job, or enjoy the benefits and privileges of employment. Reasonable accommodation might include, for example, providing a ramp for a wheelchair user or providing a reader or interpreter for a blind or deaf employee or applicant.

The law also requires an employer to reasonably accommodate an employee's religious beliefs or practices, unless doing so would cause difficulty or expense for the employer. This means an employer may have to make reasonable adjustments at work that will allow the employee to practice their religion, such as allowing an employee to voluntarily swap shifts with a co-worker so that they can attend religious services.

Training and Apprenticeship Programs

It is illegal for a training or apprenticeship program to discriminate on the basis of race, color, religion, sex (including gender identity, sexual orientation, and pregnancy status), national origin, age (40 or older), disability, or genetic information. For example, an employer may not deny training opportunities to African American employees because of their race. In some situations, an employer may be allowed to set age limits for participation in an apprenticeship program.

Harassment

It is illegal to harass an employee because of race, color, religion, sex (including gender identity, sexual orientation, and pregnancy status), national origin, age (40 or older), disability, or genetic information. It is also illegal to harass someone because they have complained about discrimination, filed a charge of discrimination, or participated in an employment discrimination investigation or lawsuit.

Harassment can take the form of slurs, graffiti, offensive or derogatory comments, or other verbal or physical conduct. Sexual harassment (including unwelcome sexual advances, requests for sexual favors, and other conduct of a sexual nature) is also unlawful. Although the law does not prohibit simple teasing, offhand comments, or minor isolated incidents, harassment is illegal if it is so frequent or severe that it creates a hostile or offensive work environment, or if it results in an adverse employment decision (such as the victim being fired or demoted).

The harasser can be the victim's supervisor, a supervisor in another area, a co-worker, or someone who is not a direct employee, such as a client or customer. Harassment outside of the workplace may also be illegal if it is connected to the workplace in some way. For example, if a supervisor harasses an employee while driving the employee to a meeting.

Terms and Conditions of Employment

It is illegal for an employer to make any employment decision because of a person's race, color, religion, sex (including gender identity, sexual orientation, and pregnancy status), national origin, age (40 or older), disability, or genetic information. That means an employer may not discriminate when it comes to things like hiring, firing, promotions, and pay. It also means an employer may not discriminate, for example, when granting breaks, approving leave, assigning workstations, or setting any other term or condition of employment, no matter how small.

Pre-employment Inquiries

General

As a general rule, the information obtained and requested through the pre-employment process should be limited to those essential for determining if a person is qualified for the job, whereas information regarding race, sex, national origin, age, and religion are irrelevant in such determinations. Employers are explicitly prohibited from making pre-offer inquiries about disability.

State and federal equal-opportunity laws do not clearly forbid employers from making pre-employment inquiries that relate to, or disproportionately screen out members based on race, color, sex, national origin, religion, or age. However, such inquiries may be used as evidence of an employer's intent to discriminate unless the questions asked can be justified by some business purpose. Therefore, inquiries, that may indicate an applicant's race, sex, national origin, disability status, age, religion, or ancestry (for example, questions about any organizations, clubs, or societies to which they might belong) should generally be avoided. Similarly, employers should not ask for a photograph of an applicant. If needed for identification purposes, a photograph may be obtained after an offer of employment is made and accepted.

Race

In general, it is assumed that pre-employment requests for information will form the basis for hiring decisions. Therefore, employers should not request information that could disclose an applicant's race unless there is a legitimate business need for this information. If an employer legitimately needs information about the race for affirmative action purposes and to track applicant flow, necessary information may be obtained and simultaneously guarded against discriminatory selection by using mechanisms like a "tear-off" sheet. These types of mechanisms allow the employer to separate the race-related information from the information used to determine if a person is qualified for the job. Asking for race-related information over the phone or by email is rarely, if ever, justifiable.

Height and Weight

Height and weight requirements tend to disproportionately limit employment opportunities for some protected groups. Unless the employer can demonstrate how the need is related to the job, it may be viewed as illegal under federal law. There are a number of state and local laws specifically prohibiting discrimination on the basis of height and weight unless based on actual job requirements. Therefore, unless job-related, inquiries about height and weight should be avoided.

Religious Affiliation or Beliefs

Questions about an applicant's religious affiliation or beliefs (unless the religion is a bona fide occupational qualification (BFOQ)) are generally viewed as non-job-related and problematic under federal law.

Religious corporations, associations, educational institutions, or societies are exempt from the federal laws that the EEOC enforces when it comes to the employment of individuals based on their particular religion. In other words, an employer whose purpose is primarily religious is permitted to lean toward hiring people of that same religion. This exception relieves religious organizations only from the ban on employment discrimination based on religion. It does not exempt such organizations from employing individuals due to their race, gender, national origin, disability, and/or age. Other employers should avoid questions about an applicant's religious affiliation, such as place of worship, days of worship, and religious holidays, and should not ask for references from religious leaders (e.g., a minister, rabbi, priest, imam, pastor, or similar leader).

Citizenship

Most employers should not ask whether or not a job applicant is a United States citizen before making an offer of employment. The Immigration and Nationality Act (INA) requires employers to verify the identity and employment eligibility of all employees hired after November 6th, 1986, by completing the Employment Eligibility Verification (I-9) Form and reviewing documents showing the employee's identity and employment authorization. Other state and federal laws require some employers to use E-Verify, which electronically matches the information provided by an employee on their I-9. Federal law prohibits employers from rejecting valid documents or insisting on additional documents beyond what is required for the I-9 Form or E-Verify process, based on an employee's citizenship status or national origin. For example, an employer cannot require only those who the employer perceives as "foreign" to produce specific documents, such as Permanent Resident ("green") cards or Employment Authorization Documents. Employees are allowed to choose which documents to show for employment eligibility verification from the Form I-9 Lists of Acceptable Documents. Employers should accept any unexpired document from the Lists of Acceptable Documents as long as the document appears to be genuine and relates to the employee.

Federal law also prohibits employers from conducting the Form I-9 and E-Verify processes before the employee has accepted an offer of employment. Applicants may be informed of these requirements in the pre-employment setting by adding the following statement to the employment application:

In compliance with federal law, all persons hired will be required to verify identity and eligibility to work in the United States and to complete the required employment eligibility verification form upon hire.

E-Verify employers must use the system consistently and without regard to the citizenship, immigration status, or national origin of employees. They must also notify every employee who receives a Tentative Nonconfirmation (TNC) and should not make assumptions about employment authorization based on the TNC issuance. If an employee contests a TNC, employers cannot fire, suspend, modify a work schedule, delay job placement or otherwise take any adverse action against the employee just because the employee received a TNC.

As stated above, the INA prohibits employment discrimination on the basis of national origin by smaller employers (with four to 14 employees). The INA prohibits retaliation against individuals for asserting their rights under the INA, or for filing a charge or assisting in an investigation or proceeding under the INA. Discrimination charges under the INA are processed by the Immigrant and Employee Rights Section (IER) within the Department of Justice's Civil Rights Division. For more information, contact the IER at the numbers below (9:00 am–5:00 pm ET, Monday–Friday) or visit their website. Calls can be anonymous and in any language.

- 1-800-255-7688 (employees/applicants)
- 1-800-255-8155 (employers)
- 1-800-237-2515 and 202-616-5525 (TTY for employees/applicants and employers)
- www.justice.gov/ier

Marital Status, Number of Children

Questions about marital status and the number and ages of children are frequently used to discriminate against women and may violate Title VII if used to deny or limit employment opportunities.

It is discriminatory to ask such questions only of women and not of men (or vice versa). Even if asked of both men and women, such questions may be seen as evidence of intent to discriminate against, for example, women with children.

Generally, employers should not use non-job-related questions involving marital status, number and ages of children or dependents, or names of spouses or children of the applicant. Such inquiries may be asked after an employment offer has been made and accepted if the information is needed for insurance or other legitimate business purposes.

The following pre-employment inquiries may be regarded as evidence of intent to discriminate when asked in the pre-employment context:

- Whether the applicant is pregnant
- Marital status of the applicant or whether the applicant plans to marry
- Number and age of children or future childbearing plans
- Childcare arrangements
- Employment status of spouse
- Name of the spouse

Gender

Questions about an applicant's sex (unless it is a bona fide occupational qualification (BFOQ) and is essential to a particular position or occupation), marital status, pregnancy status, medical history of pregnancy, future childbearing plans, number and/or ages of children or dependents, provisions for childcare, abortions, birth control, ability to reproduce, and name or address of spouse or children are generally viewed as non-job-related and problematic under Title VII.

Any pre-employment inquiry in connection with prospective employment expressing or implying limitations or special treatment because of sex (unless based upon a BFOQ) or any inquiry made of members of one sex and not the other is similarly troublesome.

Disability

Under the law, employers generally cannot ask disability-related questions or require medical examinations until after an applicant has been given a conditional job offer. This is because, in the past, this information was frequently used to exclude applicants with disabilities before they were fairly evaluated.

Before extending an offer, employers are permitted to ask limited questions about reasonable accommodation if they believe the applicant may need it because of an obvious or voluntarily disclosed disability, or where the applicant has disclosed a need for accommodation. Employers may also ask if the applicant will need accommodation to perform a specific job duty, and if the answer is yes, the employer may then ask what the accommodation would be.

The employer may not ask any questions about the nature or severity of the disability before extending an offer. However, after making a conditional job offer, an employer may ask any disability-related question or require a medical examination, as long as all individuals selected for the same job are asked the same questions or are also asked to undergo the same examination.

Dress Code

In general, an employer may establish a dress code that applies to all employees or employees within certain job categories. However, there are a few possible exceptions.

While an employer may require all workers to follow a uniform dress code even if the dress code conflicts with some workers' ethnic beliefs or practices, a dress code must not treat some employees less favorably because of their national origin. For example, a dress code that prohibits certain kinds of ethnic dress, such as traditional African or East Indian attire, but otherwise permits casual dress would treat some employees less favorably because of their national origin. Moreover, if the dress code conflicts with an employee's religious practices and the employee requests an accommodation, the employer must modify the dress code or permit an exception to the dress code, unless doing so would result in an undue hardship. Similarly, if an employee requests an accommodation to the dress code because of their disability, the employer must modify the dress code or permit an exception, unless doing so would result in an undue hardship.

Glossary of Terms Related to Women in the Workplace

This glossary contains terms excerpted from documents produced by several sources deemed reliable. Resources in this chapter were compiled from several sources deemed reliable; all contact information was verified and updated in May 2021.

Accessibility • The extent to which a facility is readily approachable and usable by individuals with disabilities, which refers especially to personnel offices, worksites, and public areas.

Advocate • Someone who speaks up for themselves and members of their identity group; e.g., a woman who lobbies for equal pay for women.

Affirmative Action • Positive steps taken to ensure equal employment or educational opportunities for members of marginalized groups that include women, people of color, and people with disabilities. In federal employment, extra effort must be made to include members of such marginalized populations at grade levels and in job categories where they are underrepresented.

Age discrimination • Unfair and discriminatory treatment of a person based on the person's age. The Age Discrimination in Employment Act (ADEA) forbids employment discrimination based on age. Members of the workforce who are 40 years of age or older are guaranteed equal protections by this law and may file a complaint and sue employers who discriminate against them in any facet of employment, including, but not limited to, hiring, firing, wages, benefits, hours worked, projects assigned, and the availability of overtime, based on age.

Ageism • Prejudicial thoughts and discriminatory actions based on a person's age, usually present when younger people discriminate against and stereotype older people.

Ally • A person of one social identity group who stands up in support of members of another identity group. Typically, a member of a dominant group stands beside member(s) of a targeted group; for example, a man advocates for equal pay for women.

Amicus brief • An amicus brief, also called "amicus curiae," literally means a "friend of the court." Non-parties in a legal case may file an amicus brief to assist the court in reaching a decision. Typically, a candidate for amicus-brief participation will present one or more important legal questions involving the interpretation or application of a statute that the Civil Rights Division enforces.

Assimilation • A process through which members of marginalized groups acquire the dominant group's culture, practices, language, and values – in short, they take on the dominant culture's way of life.

Autonomy • The capacity and freedom to act independently. The "bodily autonomy" of women typically refers to a woman's right to make decisions regarding her own body and decisions that impact her body; e.g., her decision to have or not to have children. Direct measures of a woman's autonomy include access to and control over resources, participation in economic decisionmaking, self-esteem, mobility, and freedom from domestic violence.

Bias • Prejudicial or preferential favoritism that interferes with impartial judgment.

Bropropriation • A neologism in English formed by combining the prefix "bro" (a term that refers to a boy or man) and "propriating" (from the word "appropriating," or "appropriation," meaning to take or use something, usually without permission). The term refers to situations in which a man appropriates a woman's idea and takes sole credit for it.

Carbon footprint • The total amount of greenhouse gases emitted into the atmosphere each year by a person, family, building, organization, or company. A person's carbon footprint includes greenhouse gas emissions from fuel that an individual burns directly, such as from heating a home or riding in a car. It also includes greenhouse gases that come from producing the goods or services that an individual uses, including emissions from power plants that make electricity, factories that make products, and landfills where trash is stored.

Chattel • A legal term used to define property. Under the English doctrine of coverture, a woman was legally defined as the chattel of her husband, as his possession. As such, any property that belonged to her before the marriage became her husband's on the day they were wed and, as chattel, she had no right to sue, or appear in court, or sign contracts, or conduct business. Wives existed legally only as the property of their husbands.

Coded language • Words used to convey layers of meaning identifiable only to a specific group. Using coded language allows speakers to express an opinion that others can interpret without specifically naming, say, a negative opinion or stereotype about another person.

Common law • The legal system that originated in England and is now in use in the United States. This system relies on the articulation of legal principles in a historical succession of judicial decisions. Common law principles can be changed by legislation.

Coverture • The English common-law concept that defines certain people as chattel.

Crosscultural Community • A concept or practice that identifies and honors differences – such as gender, nationality, economic status, and ethnicity – within a community and the ways in which these differences are bridged.

Cultural erasure • Actions by a dominant culture that attempt to negate, suppress, or force members of marginalized populations to adapt to their dominant practices, which results in erasing the unique cultures and practices of members of marginalized populations. The American practice of removing Native American children from their parents and communities, giving them new (European) names, and teaching them the practices and beliefs of the dominant culture in missionary schools where Native American practices and speech were forbidden is an example of cultural erasure.

Cultural Resistance • The use of meanings and symbols to contest and combat a dominant power or cultural way of being, which typically employs a different lens through which one can view the dominant world in the process.

Demographic • A particular sector of a population; e.g., race, sex, geography, ethnicity, and sexual orientation.

Disability Discrimination • Treating an applicant, employee, or former employee less favorably because the person or someone the person associates with has a disability, had a disability in the past, or is believed to have a disability.

Discrimination • Discrimination is defined in civil-rights law as unfavorable or unfair treatment of a person or class of people, or protected class of people, by members of a dominant group.

Diversity • The range of human differences, including but not limited to race, ethnicity, gender, sexual orientation, age, social class, physical ability or attributes, religious or ethical value systems, national origin, and political beliefs.

Disenfranchised • The act of taking away a person's or group's right to vote.

Direct Discrimination • A type of discrimination which occurs when individuals explicitly receive less favorable treatment based on protected attributes. An example of direct discrimination is rejecting a qualified female's application to a university based solely on her gender.

Double Bind • A situation in which the expectation of adherence to certain culturally enforced expectatons results in members of the dominant culture assuming that a person behaving in accordance with enforced expectations lacks capacity for, as an example, a leadership position. For example, if workplace expectations are that female employees behave in a manner that is helpful, communal, and warm, then managers often define only men as having leadership potential.

Double standard • A rule or set of principles with different standards for different groups of people. One example is an unwritten code of sexual behavior that permit men more freedom than women.

Economic hegemony • This is an economic concept in which a single state holds significant influence over the functions of the international monetary system.

Emotional tax • This term refers to the reality that women exert twice the effort to gain the same level of recognition as men in climates in which men's leadership abilities are taken for granted. In such scenarios, women are required to repeatedly demonstrate to others that they are fit to lead. These factors result in an unequal burden and take a personal toll on the well-being of women – an outcome that requires women to pay an "emotional tax" that is not required of men.

Enfranchisement • Having the right to vote.

Equal Employment Opportunity Commission (EEOC) • The federal commission responsible for ensuring that employers adhere to employment law as well as the agency that responds to and investigates employment discrimination complaints.

Erasure • The act of erasing, deleting, or removing something. Examples of cultural erasure are laws or regulations that mandate English-only classrooms or school-uniform policies that disallow hijabs or other pieces of clothing associated with a nondominant religion or culture.

Exoticized • A stereotype that is typically applied to women of color that results in these women being objectified, glamorized, and sexualized in a manner that defines them as objects subject to the male gaze rather than full human beings.

Explicit bias • Conscious attitudes and beliefs about a person or group. These biases and their expression typically arise as the direct result of a perceived threat. When people feel threatened, they are more likely to draw group boundaries to distinguish themselves from others. White factory workers feeling threatened by and attempting to remove the presence of people of color from their workplace is an example of explicit bias.

Fail fast • The tactic of trying something, receiving prompt feedback, and then inspecting and adapting your approach based on feedback.

Failure to Make Reasonable [Disability] Adjustments • A situation in which people with a disability can experience discrimination if their employer or organization does not make a reasonable adjustment. For example, refusing a parking space close to the office for an employee with mobility impairment because people in senior positions are the only employees with this privilege.

Female Empowerment • A process through which a woman's growing sense of self-worth strengthens her ability to determine personal choices and participate in the public sphere in a manner that creates social change that benefits herself and others.

Fight for $15 • An American political movement supporting the need to raise the minimum wage to $15 per hour.

Finishing school • A private school where young "ladies" from wealthy families are taught "proper" manners and behaviors before entry into upper-class society.

Flex program • A work schedule option that differs from the standard workweek.

Gender • A socially constructed concept of masculinity and femininity that was traditionally based on a binary system rather than the spectrum system that recognizes a full range of gender identities.

Glass ceiling • An oganizational hierarchy that prevents women and others from marginalized populations from achieving leadership positions.

Glass cliff • A tendency to promote women and others from marginalized populations when the chances of failure are highest, such as during an economic crisis.

Glass elevator • The phenomenon of men moving up the corporate ladder at a much quicker pace than their female counterparts.

Great Migration • The period of time between 1915 to 1970 when millions of African Americans moved from the southern region of the United States to urban areas in the north and west, seeking better opportunities away from the racial discrimination, Jim Crow laws, and violence in the South.

Harassment • Unwelcome conduct that is so frequent or severe that it objectively creates a hostile or offensive work environment or results in a negative employment action (such as being fired or demoted).

Heteronormativity • A view that promotes the idea of heterosexuality as the "normal," default, or preferred form of sexual orientation.

Historically disadvantaged • A person or population that has been socially, economically, or educationally disadvantaged over generations due to discriminatory laws or practices.

Identity • The concept, qualities, beliefs, and expressions that constitute a person (self identity) or group (a particular social category or social group).

Immigration Act of 1990 • Public Law 101 649 (Act of November 29, 1990), which increased the limits on legal immigration to the United States, revised all grounds for exclusion and deportation, authorized temporary protected status to "aliens" of designated countries, revised and established new nonimmigrant admission categories, revised and extended the visa waiver pilot program, and revised naturalization authority and requirements.

Implicit Bias • A form of bias that occurs automatically and unintentionally at an unconscious level and affects one's judgments, decisions, and behaviors (also known as nonconscious or unconscious bias).

Inclusion • Involvement, empowerment, and participation in which the inherent worth and dignity of each person is recognized and valued. An inclusive organization promotes and sustains a sense of belonging; it values, cultivates, and practices respect for the talents, beliefs, backgrounds, and ways of living of all members of its community.

Indirect Discrimination • A discriminatory action in which an otherwise neutral provision, criterion, or practice puts people from marginalized populations at a disadvantage.

Informal network • A person's business contacts, family, friends, and personal relationships and connections.

Ingroup bias • The tendency for groups to favor themselves by rewarding group members economically, socially, psychologically, and emotionally, which uplifts their group to the detriment of others.

Institutional racism • Discriminatory institutional practices – in organizations, schools, banks, and courts of law – that discriminate against marginalized racial groups in a systemic manner.

Intersecting inequalities • Overlapping identities and characteristics such as age, citizenship status, ethnicity, dis/ability, gender, sexual orientation, or socioeconomic status that result in multiple characteristics increasing the likelihood that people with multiple marginalized identities will be targeted for discrimination.

Intersectionality • The understanding that various forms of discrimination work to support and amplify each other.

Jim Crow laws • Laws passed in the South after the U.S. Civil War that segregated people by race in public places and otherwise discriminated against and disenfranchised Black and other non-White people. This system of segregation was enforced by law and customs to maintain White social dominance and resulted in the political and economic subjugation of African Americans from the late 1800s to the 1960s. Hispanic Americans experienced varying degrees of Jim Crow segregation in the Southwest during this same period.

Male bias • A preference for and promotion of males to the detriment or exclusion of females.

Male gaze • Actions or depictions of women by the dominant male culture that diminish, culturally subjugate, or sexually objectify women.

Marginalized • Diminished, excluded, ignored, or subjugated people, groups, societies, or communities.

Mentorship • A relationship in which a more experienced or knowledgeable person guides a less experienced or knowledgeable person. Mentors may be older or younger but must possess a certain amount of expertise that can be passed on to the person being mentored.

Microaggression • A subtle and often unintentional, yet offensive comment or action directed at a member of a nondominant group that reinforces a negative stereotype; e.g., "Tell me where you are from because you don't talk like a Black person."

Micromanage • A tendency to control every aspect of an activity, project, enterprise, or work performed by others.

Minority • The smaller portion of a group or population, although marginalized populations sometimes become a majority of the population over time. For example, White Anglo-Saxon students comprised the dominant group in public schools in the United States, but are now in the minority.

Misogyny • An intense hatred or dislike of girls, women, or femininity and the belittlement of women and characteristics considered to be feminine.

Objectification • The treatment or depiction of a person, usually a woman, as an object – typically a sexual object – rather than depicting or viewing her as a whole person.

Overt discrimination • A specific, observable, and negative action taken against a member or members of marginalized populations. This treatment also is referred to as "intentional discrimination."

Passive Resistance • A refusal to comply with power. For example, a political protester may choose to ignore a law-enforcement officer's verbal command to stand after being handcuffed while doing so in a manner that does not convey a threat to the officer or others; this passive resistance typically results in officers lifting the protester and delivering them to the squad car.

Patriarchy • A power structure that systematically elevates, empowers, and advances the standing of men while subjugating women.

Pay Discrimination • The act of determining wages based on a worker's race, color, religion, sex (including pregnancy, sexual orientation, or gender identity), national origin, age (40 or older), and disability or genetic information (including family medical history).

People of Color • A collective term for men and women of African, Asian, Hispanic, Latinx, and Native American backgrounds that differentiates these people from the collective "White" people of European ancestry.

Pregnancy Discrimination • Treating an applicant, employee, or former employee less favorably because of a current or past pregnancy, a potential or intended pregnancy, or a medical condition related to pregnancy, or childbirth. Pregnancy discrimination includes employment policies or practices that negatively affect women during their childbearing years even when pregnancy does not impact the operation of the business or diminish the capacity of the woman to perform her duties.

Prejudice • A preconceived judgment about a person or group of people that usually results in negative bias.

Quota • Fixed hiring and promotion rates based on race, sex, or other protected classifications. Judges sometimes assign quotas to employers who practice illegal employment discrimination.

Racial discrimination • Treating people in different manners based on their specific race. For example, in the Jim Crow South, racial discrimination resulted in laws that mandated separate public water fountains for Black and White people.

Racism • Prejudicial thoughts and discriminatory actions based on differences in a person's race or ethnicity.

Reasonable Accommodation • Reasonable adjustments or changes an employer must make in work schedules or work environments to enable employees with disabilities to perform their jobs; e.g., installing a ramp so that a person with limited mobility can reach a work station by navigating a wheel chair.

Retaliation • In the workplace, this refers to negative outcomes or behaviors in response to a person filing a complaint alleging discrimination, or serving as a witness for someone who filed a complaint; e.g., firing, demotion, or shunning.

Scapegoating • Casting blame, fault, or failure on innocent individuals or groups; e.g., blaming all female employees for the failure of an organization to receive grant funding.

Self actualization • A realization or fulfillment of one's talent and potentials through personal means.

Sex • A biological classification of male or female based on genetic or physiological features. Sex differs from gender, which can refer to a range of identities that may or may not be associated with the sex classification assigned at birth, and intersex people may have both male and female sex organs and characteristics.

Sexism • Prejudicial thoughts and discriminatory actions based on differences in sex or gender, usually directed at women by men.

Sexual harassment • Unwelcome sexual advances, requests for sexual favors, and other verbal or physical conduct of a sexual nature.

Sexual objectification • The treatment and perception of people – typically women – as sexual objects.

Sexual orientation • One's natural preference in sexual partners; a predilection for homosexuality, heterosexuality, or bisexuality.

Slavery • The act of one human being owning another human being. The American Slavery System, for example, enabled the kidnapping, transport, and sale of people from Africa and legally classified these enslaved people as chattel.

Stereotype • A blanket belief or expectation about members of certain groups that result in oversimplified opinions, prejudicial attitudes, or uncritical judgment about members of those groups. Stereotypes go beyond necessary and useful categorizations and generalizations and are typically negative, based on little information, and are highly generalized.

Stereotype Threat • The psychological threat felt when a person performs an action or is in a situation that aligns with a negative stereotype about their group.

Suffrage • Having the right to vote.

Tokenized • A practice in which a person, organization, or school, etc., makes an indifferent or symbolic effort to include members of a marginalized population in a effort to give the appearance that racial or gender inequality does not exist within its community. Tokenized people are sometimes expected to speak for their entire marginalized group and some communities make little or no effort to welcome or include the insights or experiences of these tokenized people.

Underrepresented • Inadequate representation of members of marginalized groups in the workforce or other settings. This term is used to describe the extent to which women, people of color, people with disabilities, and others are excluded from a group or workforce.

Unilateral communication • One-sided communication that a receiver is required to interpret and decode; e.g., a top-down statement of expectations or tasks from a manager or a micromanager that an employee must interpret as best they can becauses of a lack of bilaternal communication.

Upward mobility • The growth, movement, or increase in weath or status of an individual, social group, or class of people that leads to a position of higher status or power.

Wage theft • The denial of rightful wages or benefits that an employee is owed for their labor. One example is a restaurant requiring its employees to clock out when the restaurant closes but to continue cleaninng or otherwise working without pay. Another is assigning unattainable workloads to employees with the expectation that they perform additional labor without additional compensation.

Work-Life Balance • This term refers to the amount of priority an individual devotes to personal and professional activities, typically in environments in which an unequal focus on work can negatively impact social well-being or the employee's health.

Work-Life integration • This term references a state in which what a person does at work and outside of work (with family, friends, and their community) are driven by the same fundamental values and passions.

Section 3 • **Help and Information**

Directory of Support Organizations

GOVERNMENT ORGANIZATIONS

The Library of Congress (LOC)
Phone: 202-707-5000
Website: www.loc.gov

Millennium Challenge Corporation (MCC)
Phone: 202-521-3600
Website: www.mcc.gov

Office on Women's Health (OWH)
U.S. Department of Health and Human Services (HHS)
Toll-Free: 800-994-9662
Phone: 202-690-7650
Website: www.womenshealth.gov

Peace Corps Headquarters
Phone: 855-855-1961
Website: www.peacecorps.gov

The United States Agency for International Development (USAID)
Toll-Free: 800-996-7566
Phone: 202-712-0000
Website: www.usaid.gov

U.S. Department of Energy (DOE)
Phone: 202-586-5000
Website: www.energy.gov

U.S. Department of Health and Human Services (HHS)
Toll-Free: 877-696-6775
Website: www.hhs.gov

U.S. Department of Veterans Affairs (VA)
Toll-Free: 800-273-8255
Website: www.va.gov

U.S. Equal Employment Opportunity Commission (EEOC)
Phone: 202-663-4900
Website: www.eeoc.gov

Women's Bureau (WB)
U.S. Department of Labor (DOL)
Toll-Free: 866-487-2365
Website: www.dol.gov

PRIVATE ORGANIZATIONS

Alliance for Women in Media
Website: allwomeninmedia.org

American Association of University Women (AAUW)
Phone: 202-785-7700
Website: www.aauw.org

American Civil Liberties Union (ACLU)
Website: www.aclu.org

American Legion Auxiliary
Phone: 317-569-4500
Website: www.legion-aux.org

American Medical Women's Association
Website: www.amwa-doc.org

Asian Women in Business
Website: http://www.awib.org

Association for Professional Insurance Women
Website: www.apiw.org

Association for Women in Communications (AWC)
Phone: 417-886-8606
Website: www.womcom.org

Association for Women in Science (AWIS)
Phone:202-588-8175
Website: www.awis.org

Association of Women's Business Centers
Website: awbc.org

Business and Professional Women Foundation (BPW)
Phone: 202-293-1100
Website: bpwfoundation.org/rawalt-online-resource-center

CARE
Website: www.care.org

Catalyst
Phone: 212-514-7600
Website: www.catalyst.org

Center for Reproductive Rights
Website: reproductiverights.org

Chicago Abortion Fund (CAF)
Phone: 312-663-0336
Website: www.chicagoabortionfund.org

Commercial Real Estate Women (CREW)
Toll-free: 888-866-2739 (888-866-CREW)
Phone: 785-832-1808
Website: crewnetwork.org

Department for Professional Employees, AFL-CIO
Phone: 202-638-0320
Website: www.dpeaflcio.org

Dress for Success
Website: dressforsuccess.org

eWomen Network
Website: www.ewomennetwork.com

Financial Women's Association
Phone: 212-533-2141
Website: www.fwa.org

General Federation of Women's Clubs (GFWC)
Toll-free: 800-443-GFWC
Phone: 202-347-3168
Website: www.gfwc.org

Girls Who Code
Website: girlswhocode.com

In Her Shoes
Website: www.inhershoesmvmt.org

Institute for Women's Policy Research
Website: iwpr.org

Ladies Who Launch
Website: www.ladieswholaunch.org

Leadership Women
Website: leadership-women.org

Minority Business Development Agency
Website: www.mbda.gov

National Association for Female Executives (NAFE)
Website: www.workingmother.com/nafe

National Association for Women in Construction
Website: www.nawic.org

National Association for Women's Sales Professionals
Website: nawsp.org

National Council of Jewish Women (NCJW)
Phone: 202-296-2588
Website: www.ncjw.org

National Indigenous Women's Resource Center
Website: www.niwrc.org

National Organization for Women (NOW)
Phone: 202-628-8669 (628-8NOW)
Website: www.now.org

National Partnership for Women & Families
Phone: 202-986-2600
Website: www.nationalpartnership.org

National Women's Councils
Website: nationalwomenscouncil.org

National Women's Political Caucus (NWPC)
Phone: 202-785-1100
Website: www.nwpc.org

OWL
Toll-Free: 800-825-3695
Phone: 202-783-6686
Website: www.hotels-arizona.com/owl-nationalorg

Society of Women Engineers
Website: swe.org

Texas Business Women
Website: tbwconnect.com

UN Women
Phone: 646-781-4400
Website: www.unwomen.org

U.S. Small Business Administration, Office of Women's Business Ownership
Website: www.sba.gov

U.S. Women's Chamber of Commerce
Phone: 202-607-2488
Website: uswcc.org

Women Business Collaborative
Website: www.wbcollaborative.org

Women Creating Change (WCC)
Phone: 212-353-8070
Website: wccny.org

Women Employed
Website: womenemployed.org

Women in Government
Website: www.womeningovernment.org

Women's Diversity Network
Website: womensdiversitynetwork.org

Women's Institute for a Secure Retirement (WISER)
Phone: 202-393- 5452
Website: www.wiserwomen.org

Women's Sports Foundation
Website: www.womenssportsfoundation.org

Women in Technology International (WITI)®
Phone: 818-788-9484
Website: witi.com

Women in Trucking
Phone: 818-788-9484
Website: www.womenintrucking.org/join

Working for Women
Website: www.workingforwomen.org

Bibliography

References

Adams, Pat. "Five Fast Facts about Engineer Edith Clarke." US Department of Energy. March 10, 2015. https://www.energy.gov/articles/five-fast-facts-about-engineer-edith-clarke.

Addison-Lavelle, Laurie. 2016. "Millennial Women in Leadership: A New Generation of Women Still Facing Gender Inequalities in Business Leadership." Thesis. Pepperdine University.

Ali, S. S. 2016. "'Motherhood Penalty' Can Affect Women Who Never Even Have a Child." NBCNews. https://www.nbcnews.com/better/careers/motherhood-penalty-can-affect-women-who-never-even-have-child-n548511.

Alternate History. Fandom. "1925 American Revolution (From Sea to Shining Sea)." https://althistory.fandom.com/wiki/1925_American_Revolution_(From_Sea_to_Shining_Sea).

American Association for Access, Diversity, and Equity. "About Affirmative Action, Diversity, and Inclusion." https://www.aaaed.org/aaaed/About_Affirmative_Action__Diversity_and_Inclusion.asp.

—. "History of Affirmative Action." February 18, 2017. https://www.aaaed.org/aaaed/History_of_Affirmative_Action.asp.

American Chemical Society. Booklet. "Legacy of Rachel Carson's *Silent Spring*." October 26, 2012. https://www.acs.org/content/acs/en/education/whatischemistry/landmarks/rachel-carson-silent-spring.html.

American Civil Liberties Union. "Cases in Which Sandra Day O'Connor Cast the Decisive Vote." July 3, 2005. https://www.aclu.org/other/cases-which-sandra-day-oconnor-cast-decisive-vote.

American Council of Learned Societies. "Margaret Higgins Sanger." Dictionary of American Biography, Charles Scribner's Sons, 1988. Biography in Context, link.galegroup.com/apps/doc/BT2310004111/BIC1?u=tlc199095657&xid=7aecec55.

Anda, Robert F., V. I. Fleisher, Vincent J. Felitti, et al. "Childhood Abuse, Household Dysfunction, and Indicators of Impaired Worker Performance in Adulthood." *The Permanente Journal* 8(1) (2004), pp. 30–38. Retrieved from http://xnet.kp.org/permanentejournal/ winter04/childhood.pdf/.

Anderson, Ashlee. "Annie Oakley." National Women's History Museum. September 26, 2018. https://www.womenshistory.org/education-resources/biographies/annie-oakley.

Anthony, Carl. "Edith Wilson: The First Lady Who Became an Acting President - Without Being Elected," Biography, June 11, 2020. https://www.biography.com/news/edith-wilson-first-president-biography-facts.

Appelbaum, Lauren. "3,736 Women with Disabilities Lose Jobs in the U.S." RespectAbility. March 13, 2019. https://www.respectability.org/2019/03/women-disabilities-jobs-2019/.

Atomic Heritage Foundation. "The Radium Girls." April 25, 2017. tomicheritage.org/history/radium-girls.

Aurand, Andrew, Dan Emmanuel, Dan Threet, et al. *Out of Reach: The High Cost of Housing.* 2020. National Low Income Housing Coalition. https://reports.nlihc.org/sites/default/files/oor/OOR_BOOK_2020.pdf.

Autry, Brian, Chris Barr, and Christopher Young. "The Women's Army Corps at Chickamauga." National Park Service. https://www.nps.gov/articles/chickamaugawac.htm.

Aydlette, Larry. "What Were the Last Words Billie Jean King Said to Bobby Riggs?" *The Palm Beach Post*, October 2, 2017.

Bachman, R. "U.S. Women's Soccer Games Outearned Men's Games." June 17, 2019. *The Wall Street Journal*. https://www.wsj.com/articles/u-s-womens-soccer-games-out-earned-mens-games-11560765600.

Baker, Jean H. *Margaret Sanger: A Life of Passion.* New York: Hill and Wang, 2011.

Bansemer, Hattie C., and Gottlieb Bansemer, LNI: JJT, October 16, 1918; Confidential Correspondence, 1913–14; Office of Naval Intelligence; Records of the Chief of Naval Operations, Record Group (RG) 38. National Archives, Washington, D.C.

Baxter, K. "U.S. Women's Soccer Players Sue for Equal Treatment Just Months before World Cup." *The Los Angeles Times.* March 8, 2019. https://www.latimes.com/sports/soccer/la-sp-us-womens-soccer-lawsuit-20190308-story.html.

Bemus, Bethanee. "1917 National Women's Party Protest." *Smithsonian Magazine.* January 12, 2007. https://www.smithsonianmag.com/smithsonian-institution/scrap-suffrage-history-180961780/.

Bethune-Cookman University. "BCU News." December 8, 2020. https://cookman.edu/about_BCU/history/index.html.

Berenson, Barbara F. *Massachusetts in the Women Suffrage Movement.* Charleston, S.C.: The History Press, 2018.

Beyer, Kurt W. *Grace Hopper and the Invention of the Information Age.* Cambridge: MIT Press, 2009.

Biography.com Editors. "Gloria Steinem Biography." Biography. https://www.biography.com/activist/gloria-steinem.

—. "Grace Hopper." Biography. September 11, 2019. https://www.biography.com/scientist/grace-hopper.

Bisno, Adam. "Twenty-five Years of Women Aboard Combatant Vessels." U.S. Naval History and Heritage Command. https://www.history.navy.mil/content/history/nhhc/browse-by-topic/diversity/women-in-the-navy/women-in-combat.html.

Black, Frederick R. 1988. Charlestown Navy Yard, 1890–1973. *Cultural Resources Management Study* 20, Vol. I of III. U. S. National Park Service.

Black, Michelle C., Kathleen C. Basile, K. C., Matthew J. Breiding, et al. *National Intimate Partner and Sexual Violence Survey: 2010 Summary Report.* 2011. Retrieved from the Centers for Disease Control and Prevention. National Center for Injury Prevention and Control. http://www.cdc.gov/ViolencePrevention/pdf/NISVS_Report2010-a.pdf.

Blake, Brock. "Women Business Owners Still Face Difficulties in Obtaining Capital." *Forbes Magazine,* October 14, 2019. https://www.forbes.com/sites/brockblake/2019/10/14/women-business-capital/.

Blackman, Cally. "How the Suffragettes Used Fashion to Further Their Cause." *Stylist.* https://www.stylist.co.uk/fashion/suffragette-movement-fashion-clothes-what-did-the-suffragettes-wear/188043.

Blake Churchill, Lindsey. "*The Feminine Mystique.*" *Encyclopedia Britannica,* August 22, 2014. https://www.britannica.com/topic/The-Feminine-Mystique.

Blakemore, Erin. "Why Many Married Women Were Banned From Working during the Great Depression." A&E Television Network. March 5, 2019. Updated July 21, 2019. https://www.history.com/news/great-depression-married-women-employment.

Blazina, Carrie; Desilver, Drew. "A Record Number of Women Are Serving in the 117th Congress," Pew Research Center, January 15, 2021.

Bleiweis, R., Boesch, D., & Gaines, A. C. "The Basic Facts about Women in Poverty." Center for American Progress, August 3, 2020. https://www.americanprogress.org/issues/women/reports/2020/08/03/488536/basic-facts-women-poverty/.

Bose, Apurva. "History of Minimum Wage." BeBusinessed. January 21, 2017. https://bebusinessed.com/history/history-of-minimum-wage/.

Boston Daily Record. "Hub WAVE Vet in JFK Parade." January. 16, 1961, p. 13.

Boston Globe. "Bessie Edwards Post-Annual Bridge Party," April 23,1967, p. 79.

—. "Blanche Towle Obituary." Sept. 17, 1958, p. 11.

—. "Bunker Hill District." Sept. 11, 1923, p. 8.

—. "Charlestown Girl Made Yeoman in the Navy." May 16, 1917, p. 4.

—. "Endearing Young Charms." Sept. 17, 1958, p .11.

—. "Michael W. Collins Obituary." Oct. 7, 1956, p. 21.

—. "Mrs. Ryan, 70, of Brighton, A.L. Leader." August 23,1967, p. 79.

—. "Roxbury District." May 16, 1917, p. 6.

—. "Veterans Posts in Row at Charlestown." July 28,1929, p. 19.

—. "War Women Form Their First Post." July 9,1919, p. 4.

—. "Wed Hingham Instructor." Sept. 11, 1923, p. 8.

—. "Women's Legion Post Loses Charter." June 15, 1921 p. 1.

—. "Women's Legion Post May Remain." Feb. 19,1921, p. 6.

—. "Yeomen (F) Want to be Included in Bounty." May 26, 1919, p. 6.

Bread & Roses Heritage Committee. "The Strike That Started it All." April 6, 2018. https://www.breadandrosesheritage.org/strike.

British Broadcasting Corporation."*Roe v. Wade*: Trump Says Supreme Court Ruling on Abortion 'Possible.'" September 27, 2020. https://www.bbc.com/news/world-us-canada-54317894.

Brooks, Rebecca Beatrice. "Role of the Massachusetts Textile Mills in the Industrial Revolution." January 9, 2017. https://historyofmassachusetts.org/massachusetts-textile-mills/.

Brown, Laura. "Jane Fonda: The Interview." *Harper's Bazaar.* August 4, 2011. harpersbazaar.com/celebrity/latest/news/a769/jane-fonda-interview/.

Bundles, A'Lelia. "Madam C. J. Walker: American Businesswoman and Philanthropist." *Encyclopedia Brittanica.* https://www.britannica.com/biography/Madam-C-J-Walker.

—. The Economics Daily. "Employment Decreased in 355 of the 357 Largest U.S. Counties for Year Ended September 2020." https://www.bls.gov/opub/ted/2021/employment-decreased-in-355-of-the-357-largest-u-s-counties-for-year-ended-september-2020.htm.

Burch, Lauren M., Andrew C. Billings, and Matthew H. Zimmerman. "Comparing American Soccer Dialogues: Social Media Commentary Surrounding the 2014 US Men's and

2015 US Women's World Cup Teams," *Sport in Society* 21(7) (2018), 1047–62. DOI: 10.1080/17430437.2017.1284811.

Byer, Nina. "E. Noether's Discovery of the Deep Connection Between Symmetries and Conservation Laws." Israel Mathematical Conference Proceedings Vol. 12, 1999, The Heritage of Emmy Noether in Algebra, Geometry, and Physics, December 2-3, 1996.

Byerly, Victoria, 1986. *Hard Times Cotton Mill Girls: Personal Histories of Womanhood and Poverty in the South.* New York State School of Industrial and Labor Relations. Ithaca, New York: Cornell University.

Cable News Network. "Affirmative Action Fast Facts." November 12, 2013. https:www.cnn.com/2013/11/12/us/affirmative-action-fast-facts/index.html.

Cahn, Lauren. "12 Conspiracy Theories That Actually Turned Out to Be True." *Reader's Digest,* March 21, 2020. https://www.rd.com/list/conspiracy-theories-that-turned-out-to-be-true/.

—. "20 Things You Had No Idea Happened in 1920." *Reader's Digest,* December 5, 2019. https://www.rd.com/list/things-that-happened-1920/.

Caroli, Betty Boyd. "Eleanor Roosevelt." *Encyclopedia Britannica.* February 5, 2021. https://www.britannica.com/biography/Eleanor-Roosevelt.

Carroll, Berenice. 2012. "'Shut Down the Mills': Women, the Modern Strike, and Revolution." http://publici.ucimc.org/2012/03/shut-down-the-mills-women-the-modern-strike-and-revolution/.

Catalyst. "Infographic: The Double-Bind Dilemma for Women in Leadership." August 2, 2018. https://www.catalyst.org/research/infographic-the-double-bind-dilemma-for-women-in-leadership/.

—. "The Double-Bind Dilemma for Women in Leadership: Damned If You Do, Doomed If You Don't." June 15, 2007. https://www.catalyst.org/research/the-double-bind-dilemma-for-women-in-leadership-damned-if-you-do-doomed-if-you-dont/.

Cava, Michael. "Emmy Noether Google Doodle: Why Einstein Called Her a 'Creative Mathematical Genius.'" *The Washington Post.* March 23, 2015. https://www.washingtonpost.com/news/comic-riffs/wp/2015/03/23/emmy-noether-google-doodle-why-einstein-called-her-a-creative-mathematical-genius/.

Chappatta, Brian. "Citi Beats JPMorgan to Shatter Wall Street's Glass Ceiling." Employee Benefit Adviser. September 1, 2020. https://www.employeebenefitadviser.com/articles/citi-beats-jpmorgan-to-shatter-wall-streets-glass-ceiling.

Cheslak, Colleen. "Hedy Lamarr." National Women's History Museum. November 2017. https://www.womenshistory.org/education-resources/biographies/hedy-lamarr.

Chesler. Ellen. *Woman of Valor: Margaret Sanger and the Birth Control Movement in America.* New York: Simon and Schuster, 2007.

Chronicling America: Historic American Newspapers. "*New-York Tribune.* March 26, 1911, Image 1." March 26, 1911.

Coates, Patricia Walsh. *Margaret Sanger and the Origin of the Birth Control Movement, 1910–1930: The Concept of Women's Sexual Autonomy.* Lewiston, NY: Edwin Mellen Press, 2008.

Cobb, Elizabeth. *The Hello Girls: America's First Women Soldiers.* Cambridge, MA: Harvard University Press, 2017.

Colamosca, Anne. "Clare Boothe Luce, from Broadway to the Cold War." Jacobin, March 11, 2020.

Collins, Gail. *America's Women.* New York: Harper Perennial, 2007.

Collins, Jan Mackell. "The Tragic Real Life Story of Annie Oakley." Grunge, January 3, 2020. https://www.grunge.com/181925/the-tragic-real-life-story-of-annie-oakley/.

Conger, Cristen. "How Tupperware Works." How Stuff Works. https://people.howstuffworks.com/tupperware2.htm.

Congress.gov. "H.R.14752 - Equality Act." May 14, 1974.

Connley, Courtney. "Nearly 3 in 10 Native American Women Work a Front-line Job, But They're Far from Receiving Equal Pay." CNBC. October 1, 2020. https://www.cnbc.com/2020/10/01/native-american-women-are-still-far-from-receiving-equal-pay.html. 2021.

Cook, Paul W. Jr., and Thomas W. Collins, 1989. "The Plant Is Closed: What Now, Women? A Case Study of the Memphis Furniture Manufacturing Company." *Women in the South: An Anthropological Perspective*, edited by Holly F. Matthews. Southern Anthropological Society Proceedings, No. 22. (University of Georgia Press, Athens, GA), pp. 71–82.

Cooper, Cynthia. "Biography." https://cynthiacooper.com/.

Cornell University. "The 1911 Triangle Factory Fire." February 1, 2001. https://trianglefire.ilr.cornell.edu/.

Correia, Tricia. "Women, Millennials, and the Future Workplace: Empowering All Employees." Georgetown Institute for Women, Peace and Security, August 2017. https://giwps.georgetown.edu/wp-content/uploads/2017/08/Women-Millennials-and-the-Future-Workplace.

Covert, Bryce. "The Best Era for Working Women Was 20 Years Ago." *The New York Times*, September 2, 2017. https://www.nytimes.com/2017/09/02/opinion/sunday/working-women-decline-1990s.html.

Culture Plus Consulting. "Gender Bias at Work: The Assertiveness Double-Bind." Include-Empower. https://cultureplusconsulting.com/2018/03/10/gender-bias-work-assertiveness-double-bind/.

Dalli, Kristen. "Older Women Are Less Protected by Age Discrimination Laws Than Older Men." Consumer Affairs. https://www.consumeraffairs.com/news/older-women-are-less-protected-by-age-discrimination-laws-than-older-men-062220.html.

Daniel, Cletus E., "Introduction," in *Hard Times Cotton Mill Girls: Personal Histories of Womanhood and Poverty in the South* by Victoria Byerly. Ithaka, NY: ILR Press/New York State School of Industrial and Labor Relations, Cornell University, 1986.

Daughters of the American Revolution. "Fashioning the New Woman: 1890–1925." https://www.dar.org/museum/fashioning-new-woman-1890-1925-0.

Davenport, Coral. 2021."Fight over Deb Haaland, First Native American Cabinet Pick, Reflects Partisan Divide." *The New York Times*. February 22, 2021. https://www.nytimes.com/2021/02/22/climate/deb-haaland-interior.html.

DeLisi, M., A. Kosloski, M. Sweeny, et al. (2010). "Murder by Numbers: Monetary Costs Imposed by a Sample of Homicide Offenders." *Journal of Forensic Psychiatry and Psychology* 2(1), (2010) pp. 501–13. doi:10.1080/14789940903564388.

Direct Selling Association. MLM Industry. dsa.org/statistic-insights/factsheets.

Dixon-Fyle, Sundiatu, Kevin Dolan, Vivian Hunt, and Sara Prince. "Diversity Wins: How Inclusion Matters." *The McKinsey Report*. May 19, 2020. https://www.mckinsey.com/featured-insights/diversity-and-inclusion/diversity-wins-how-inclusion-matters.

Duhart, Detis. T. "National Crime Victimization Survey: Violence in the Workplace, 1993–99." (NCJ 190076). 2001. Retrieved from the U.S. Department of Justice, Office of Justice Programs, Bureau of Justice Statistics: http://bjs.ojp.usdoj.gov/content/pub/pdf/vw99.pdf.

Diao, Sophie. "Emmy Noether's 133rd Birthday." Google. March 23, 2015. https://www.google.com/doodles/emmy-noethers-133rd-birthday.

Divvy Research. "How Much of the Cost of Living Is Covered by Minimum Wage?" Blog. March 4, 2020. https://getdivvy.com/blog/minimum-wage-vs-living-wage/.

Dorenkamp, Angela G., John F. McClymer, Mary M. Moyniham, et al. *Images of Women in American Popular Culture*. New York: Harcourt Brace Jovanovich, 1985.

Duckworth, Tammy. Twitter Post. February,15, 2018, 10:29 AM. https://twitter.com/SenDuckworth/status/964160383677280256.

Dumenil, Lynn. *The Second Line of Defense: American Women and World War I*. Chapel Hill: University of North Carolina Press, 2017.

Ebbert, Jean, and Marie-Beth Hall. *The First, the Few, the Forgotten*. Annapolis, Md.: Naval Institute Press, 2002.

The Edit. "Innovation or Bust! The Surprising Story of New England's Textile Heyday." https://livetheedit.com/2020/04/new-england-textile-industry-history/.

Einstein, Albert. "The Late Emmy Noether." *The New York Times*. May 1, 1935. https://timesmachine.nytimes.com/timesmachine/1935/05/04/95502824.html.

Ekko. "10 Things You Didn't Know about Eleanor Roosevelt." Medium, November 8, 2015.

El Issa, Erin. "Women and Credit through the Decades: The 1990s." Nerdwallet, July 22, 2020. https://www.nerdwallet.com/article/credit-cards/women-credit-decades-90.

"*Eisenstadt v. Baird.*" Oyez. https://www.oyez.org/cases/1971/70-1.

Elliot, Danielle. "Google Doodle Honors Grace Hopper, 'First Lady of Software.'" CBS News. December 9, 2013. https://www.cbsnews.com/news/google-doodle-honors-grace-hopper-first-lady-of-software/.

Encyclopedia. "*Eisenstadt v. Baird* 405 U.S. 438 (1972)." Cengage. 1986. https://www.encyclopedia.com/politics/encyclopedias-almanacs-transcripts-and-maps/eisenstadt-v-baird-405-us-438-1972.

——. "Politics in the 1920s." *Encyclopedia*. Cengage. October 7, 2016. https://www.encyclopedia.com/history/encyclopedias-almanacs-transcripts-and-maps/politics-1920s.

——. "Women, Impact of the Great Depression On." Cengage. July 3, 2009. https://www.encyclopedia.com/economics/encyclopedias-almanacs-transcripts-and-maps/women-impact-great-depression.

Encyclopedia Britannica Editors. "Affirmative Action." Encyclopedia Britannica. May 18, 2020. https://www.britannica.com/topic/affirmative-action.

——. "Cobol." *Encyclopedia Britannica*. October 14, 2004. https://www.britannica.com/technology/COBOL.

——. "Politics in the 1920s." *Encyclopedia Britannica*. n.d. https://www.britannica.com/topic/Roaring-Twenties.

——. "*Roe v. Wade*." *Encyclopedia Britannica*. January 22, 2020. https://www.britannica.com/event/Roe-v-Wade/.

——. "Sandra Day O'Connor." *Encyclopedia Britannica*. n.d. https://www.britannica.com/biography/Sandra-Day-OConnor.

——. "Social Security Act." *Encyclopedia Britannica*. February 1, 2001. https://www.britannica.com/topic/Social-Security-Act-United-States-1935.

——. "Title IX." *Encyclopedia Britannica*. February 17, 2021. https://www.britannica.com/event/Title-IX.

—. "Women in the Workforce." *Encyclopedia Britannica*. n.d. https://www.britannica.com/topic/history-of-work-organization-648000/Women-in-the-workforce.

Enochs, Elizabeth. "7 Successful Women Who Overcame Being Fired." *Bustle*. September 20, 2016. https://www.bustle.com/articles/184778-7-successful-women-who-were-fired-dont-regret-it.

Eschner, Kat. "The Story of Brownie Wise, the Ingenious Marketer behind the Tupperware Party." *Smithsonian Magazine*. April 10, 2018. https://www.smithsonianmag.com/smithsonian-institution/story-brownie-wise-ingenious-marketer-behind-tupperware-party-180968658/.

Fairchild, Caroline. 2020. "The COVID-19 Job Market Is Leaving Millennial Women Behind." IWPR 2020, August 11. https://iwpr.org/media/press-hits/the-covid-19-job-market-is-leaving-millennial-women-behind/.

Fanzeres, Julie. "As Women Drop Out of the Labor Market, Moms Call for More Aid." Employee Benefit Adviser. February 24, 2021. https://www.employeebenefitadviser.com/articles/as-women-drop-out-of-labor-market-moms-call-for-more-aid.

Feldman, Lucy. "Head of the NYSE Stacey Cunningham Talks Changing History." *TIME magazine*. August 9, 2018. https://time.com/5362170/stacey-cunningham-nyse/.

Ferrise, Jennifer. "Jane Fonda on Her Biggest Regret – And How She Got Past It." *InStyle*. September 18, 2018. https://www.instyle.com/news/jane-fonda-activism-biggest-regret.

Field, Shivaune. "Hedy Lamarr: The Incredible Mind behind Secure Wifi, GPS and Bluetooth," *Forbes*, February 28, 2018. https://www.forbes.com/sites/shivaunefield/2018/02/28/hedy-lamarr-the-incredible-mind-behind-secure-wi-fi-gps-bluetooth/.

FindLaw. "*Meritor Savings Bank v. Vinson*." https://caselaw.findlaw.com/us-supreme-court/477/57.html.

—. "*Rostker v. Goldberg*." https://caselaw.findlaw.com/us-supreme-court/453/57.html.

Firer, Sarah. "Pinterest Pays $20 Million to End Discrimination Suit by Ex-COO." Employee Benefit Adviser. December 15, 2020. https://www.employeebenefitadviser.com/articles/pinterest-pays-20-million-to-end-discrimination-suit-by-ex-coo.

First Nations Development. "Twice Invisible: Understanding Rural Native America Report, 2017." https://usetinc.org/wp-content/uploads/bvenuti/WWS/2017/May%202017/May%208/Twice%20Invisible%20-%20Research%20Note.pdf.

Flood, Aoife. 2015."The Female Millennial: A New Era of Talent." PwC. Agnès Hussher. https://www.pwc.com/jg/en/publications/the-female-millennial-a-new-era-of-talent.html.

Fonda, Jane. *My Life So Far*. New York: Penguin: Random House, 2005.

Foner, Eric. "Reconstruction," National Park Service, August 11, 2017. https://www.nps.gov/articles/reconstruction.htm.

Foussianes, Chloe. "The True Story of *Ms. Magazine*, and What It Meant for Feminist Publishing." *Town and Country*. April 25, 2020. https://www.townandcountrymag.com/leisure/arts-and-culture/a32131889/gloria-steinem-ms-magazine-true-story/.

Fox News. "Jane Fonda Recalls Emotional, Private Moment with Distant Dad Henry." August 8, 2018. foxnews.com/entertainment/jane-fonda-recalls-emotional-private-moment-with-her-distant-dad-henry.

Fox, M. 2019. "The 'Motherhood Penalty' Is Real, and It Costs Women $16,000 a Year in Lost Wages." CNBC. https://www.cnbc.com/2019/03/25/the-motherhood-penalty-costs-women-16000-a-year-in-lost-wages.html.

Fratus, Matt. "Bessie Coleman: The Pioneering Stunt Aviator Who Became the World's First Female Black Civilian Pilot." Coffee or Die. Blog. February 9, 2021. https://coffeeordie.com/bessie-coleman/.

Frederickson, Mary, 1977. "The Southern Summer School for U.S. Workers." *Southern Exposure* 4: 70–75.

Frisk M, Donald. "American Labor in the 20th Century," U.S. Bureau of Labor Statistics, U.S. Department of Labor. January 30, 2003. https://www.bls.gov/opub/mlr/cwc/american-labor-in-the-20th-century.pd.

Garcia, Patricia." Jane Fonda's 1982 Workout Routine Is Still the Best Exercise Class Out There." *Vogue*. July 7, 2018. https://www.vogue.com/article/jane-fonda-workout-videos-health-aerobics-yoga-class-pass.

Gates, Melinda. "Fixing America's Broken Caregiving System Is Key to Rebuilding Our Economy." LinkedIn. Blog. May 11, 2020. https://www.linkedin.com/pulse/fixing-americas-broken-caregiving-system-key-rebuilding-melinda-gates/.

Gidlow, Liette. "Beyond 1920: The Legacies of Woman Suffrage." National Park Service. https://www.nps.gov/articles/beyond-1920-the-legacies-of-woman-suffrage.htm.

The Gilder Lehrman Institute of American History. "Herbert Hoover on the Great Depression and New Deal, 1931–1933." August 8, 2005. https://www.gilderlehrman.org/history-resources/spotlight-primary-source/herbert-hoover-great-depression-and-new-deal-1931%E2%80%931933.

Gilman, Charlotte Perkins. 1892. "The Yellow Wall-paper." *New England Magazine* (January 1892), pp. 647–56.

Goddard, Alexander. "Why Was the Minimum Wage First Established?" History News Network. n.d. https://historynewsnetwork.org/article/164635.

Gorman, E., & and Kay, F. "Women in the Legal Profession." *Annual Review of Law and Social Science* 4 (2008), pp. 299–332.

Govtrack.us. "H.R. 5452 (94th): Civil Rights Amendments." March 25, 1975.

Graham, Ciera. 2020. "Barriers and Biases: 4 Challenges Faced by Millennial Women Leaders." *The Seattle Times*. February 20, 2020. https://www.seattletimes.com/explore/careers/barriers-and-biases-4-challenges-faced-by-millennial-women-leaders/.

Granados, Jose A. Tapia; Roux, Ana V. Diez. "Life and Death during the Great Depression." Proceedings of the National Academy of Sciences of the United States of America, October 13, 2009.

Graves, L. 2020. "Women's Domestic Burden Just Got Heavier with the Coronavirus." *The Guardian*. https://www.theguardian.com/us-news/2020/mar/16/womens-coronavirus-domestic-burden.

Gray, Emma. "Eight Things Women Couldn't Do on the First Women's Equality Day in 1971 – and Six They Still Can't." 2014. *HuffPost*. August 2, 2014. https://www.huffpost.com/entry/womens-equality-day-things-women-couldnt-do-1971_n_5710075.

Green, Jeff. "Adobe Says Women Earn 99% as Much as Men in New Disclosure." Employee Benefit Adviser. December 4, 2020. https://www.employeebenefitadviser.com/articles/adobe-says-women-earn-99-as-much-as-men-in-new-disclosure.

Greene, Daniel, and Frank Newport. "American Public Opinion and the Holocaust." Gallup. April 23, 2018. https://news.gallup.com/opinion/polling-matters/232949/american-public-opinion-holocaust.aspx.

Greenspan, Jesse. "'Battle of the Sexes': When Billie Beat Bobby." History. A&E Television Networks. February 2, 2021. https://www.history.com/this-day-in-history/king-triumphs-in-battle-of-sexes.

—. "Workplace Gains Prompts Women to Set New 50% Representation Goal." Employee Benefit Adviser. January 20, 2021. https://www.employeebenefitadviser.com/articles/workplace-gains-prompt-women-to-set-new-50-representation-goal.

Guerrilla Girls. "Guerrilla Girls: Reinventing the 'F' Word: Feminism." https://www.guerrillagirls.com/about.

Guilder, George. 1865. "Women in the Work Force." *The Atlantic*. September 1986. https://www.theatlantic.com/magazine/archive/1986/09/women-in-the-work-force/304924/.

Harrell, Erika (2011). "Workplace Violence, 1993–2009: National Crime Victimization Survey and the Census of Fatal Occupational Injuries." (NCJ 233231). Retrieved from the U.S. Department of Justice. Office of Justice Programs. Bureau of Justice Statistics. http://bjs.ojp.usdoj.gov/content/pub/pdf/wv09.pdf.

Harrison, Bennett, and Andrew Sum. "The Theory of 'Dual' or Segmented Labor Markets." *Journal or Economic Issues* 13(3): pp. 131–38. https://doi.org/10.1080/00213624.1979.11503671.

Harrison, Cynthia. *On Account of Sex*: *The Politics of Women's Issues, 1945–1968*. Oakland: University of California Press, 1988.

Harvey, Brian. "Let's Talk About Mental Health and Millennials." Blue Cross Blue Shield. February 1, 2020. https://www.bcbs.com/smarter-better-healthcare/article/lets-talk-about-mental-health-and-millennials.

Hassan, Kamal, Monisha Varadan, and Claudia Zeisberger, "How the VC Pitch Process Is Failing Female Entrepreneurs." *Harvard Business Review*, January 13, 2020. https://hbr.org/2020/01/how-the-vc-pitch-process-is-failing-female-entrepreneurs.

Haverstock, Eliza."Female Founders Face Funding Hurdles amid the Pandemic." *PitchBook*. May 8, 2020. https://pitchbook.com/news/articles/female-founders-face-funding-hurdles-amid-the-pandemic.

Haynes, Suyin. "How America's 'First Female Cryptanalyst' Cracked the Code of Nazi Spies in World War II–and Never Lived to See the Credit." *TIME magazine*. January 11, 2021. https://time.com/5928583/elizebeth-friedman-codebreaker/.

Heise, L., M. Ellsberg, & M. Gottemoeller. 1999. "Population Reports: Ending Violence against Women." Issues in World Health, Series L, p. 1. Retrieved from VAWnet: National Online Resource Center on Violence Against Women: http://www.vawnet.org/Assoc_Files_VAWnet/PopulationReports.pdf.

Heisler, Gregory. "100 Women of the Year," *TIME magazine*. https://time.com/5793757/the-whistleblowers-100-women-of-the-year/.

Henricks, Nancy. 2018. *Popular Fads and Crazes through American History*. 2 volumes. Santa Barbara, California: ABC-CLIO, p. 526.

History.com Editors. "American Response to the Holocaust." History. A&E Television Networks. October 29, 2009. Updated August 21, 2018. https://www.history.com/topics/world-war-ii/american-response-to-the-holocaust.A&E

—."Controversial 'Coming Out' Episode of 'Ellen' Airs." This Day in History: April 30. A&E Television Networks. https://www.history.com/this-day-in-history/coming-out-episode-of-ellen.

—. "Crime in the Great Depression." History. A&E Television Networks. March 8, 2018. https://www.history.com/topics/great-depression/crime-in-the-great-depression.
—. "Dodd-Frank Act." History. A&E Television Networks. Original January 26, 2018. Update August 21, 2018. https://www.history.com/topics/21st-century/dodd-frank-act.
—. "Famous Firsts in Women's History." History. A&E Television Networks. https://www.history.com/topics/womens-history/famous-firsts-in-womens-history.
—. "First Enslaved Africans Arrive in Jamestown, Setting the Stage for Slavery in America." History. A&E Television Networks. August 13, 2019. https://www.history.com/this-day-in-history/first-african-slave-ship-arrives-jamestown-colony.
—. "Frances Perkins." History. A&E Television Networks. May 4, 2010. https://www.history.com/topics/womens-history/frances-perkins.
—. "Great Depression." History. A&E Television Networks. July 16, 2011. https://www.history.com/topics/great-depression.
—. "Industrial Revolution." History. A&E Television Networks. https://www.history.com/topics/industrial-revolution/the-industrial-revolition-video.
—. "Manhattan Project." History. A&E Television Networks. July 26, 2017. https://www.history.com/topics/world-war-ii/the-manhattan-project.
—. "Montgomery Bus Boycott." History. A&E Television Networks. January 27, 2021. https://www.history.com/topics/black-history/montgomery-bus-boycott.
—. "*Roe v. Wade*: Decision, Summary and Background." History. A&E Television Networks. March 27, 2018. https://www.history.com/topics/womens-rights/roe-v-wade.
—. "Sandra Day O'Connor." History. A&E Television Networks. August 21, 2018. https://www.history.com/topics/us-government/sandra-day-oconnor.
—. "Social Security Act." History. A&E Television Networks. January 26, 2018. https://www.history.com/topics/great-depression/social-security-act.
—. "Women's History Milestones: A Timeline." History. A&E Television Networks. https://www.history.com/topics/womens-history/womens-history-us-timeline.
History of American Women. "The Life of a Colonial Wife." 2008. https://www.womenhistoryblog.com/2008/05/life-of-colonial-wife.html.
HistoryRocket. "Women's Rights during Colonial America." http://www.historyrocket.com/American-History/colonial-america/Women-Rights-During-Colonial-America.html.
Holliday, Kenneth. "They Served: The 'Hello Girls' of WWI and Their Sixty-year Battle for Recognition," U.S. Department of Veteran Affairs, March 30, 2020. https://blogs.va.gov/VAntage/72875/they-served-the-hello-girls-of-wwi-and-their-sixty-year-battle-for-recognition/.
Holt, Andrew. "NYSE to Be Female-Led for the First Time." Thirty Percent Coalition, May 18, 2018. https://www.30percentcoalition.org/news/in-the-news/nyse-to-be-female-led-for-the-first-time.
Homer, Julia, and David Katz. "WorldCom Whistle-blower Cynthia Cooper." *CFO magazine*. February 1, 2008. https://www.cfo.com/human-capital-careers/2008/02/worldcom-whistle-blower-cynthia-cooper/.
Houlis, Annamarie. 2018. "I Face Ableism in the Workplace: What I Wish My Company Did Differently." Ladders. https://www.theladders.com/career-advice/i-face-ableism-in-the-workplace-and-heres-what-i-wish-my-company-did-differently.
Howard, Spencer. "The Economy Act of 1932." National Archive, July 29, 2020. https://hoover.blogs.archives.gov/2020/07/29/the-economy-act-of-1932/.

HuffPost News. "The Equality Act Turns 40." March 19, 2014. https://www.huffpost.com/entry/the-equality-act-turns-40_b_5352209.

Hunter, David H. "The 1975 Voting Rights Act and Language Minorities." *Catholic University Law Review*, 1976.

Hutchinson, Pamela. "Hedy Lamarr–the 1940s 'Bombshell' Who Helped Invent Wifi." *The Guardian*. March 8, 2018. https://www.theguardian.com/film/2018/mar/08/hedy-lamarr-1940s-bombshell-helped-invent-wifi-missile.

Hutchison, Peter. "Oprah Winfrey: Cultural Powerhouse and Trailblazing Billionaire." March 4, 2021. https://news.yahoo.com/oprah-winfrey-cultural-powerhouse-trailblazing-180756295.html.

Ibarra, Herminia, Robin J. Ely, and Deborah M. Kolb. "Women Rising: The Unseen Barriers." *Harvard Business Review* 91(1) (2013): 5. https://hbr.org/2013/09/women-rising-the-unseen-barriers.

Ideafinder. "Elias Silas Tupper." http://www.ideafinder.com/history/inventors/tupper.html

Indian Health Services. "History." https://www.ihs.gov/urban/history/.

Israrkahn. "Cultural and Social and Effects of the Great Depression on American Life." Lessons in History. https://medium.com/lessons-from-history/cultural-and-social-effects-of-the-great-depression-c3e5bf341e66

Jansen, Tanya. "How Employers Can Mitigate a Future Retirement Gap." Employee Benefit Adviser. June 15, 2020. https://www.employeebenefitadviser.com/news/how-companies-can-support-female-employees-as-they-return-to-work.

Jennings, Danielle. "Discovery Buys Majority Stake in OWN Network, Oprah to Remain CEO." Hello Beautiful. December 4, 2017. https://hellobeautiful.com/2970479/discovery-buys-majority-stake-in-own-network-oprah-to-remain-ceo/.

Jewkes, Rachel, P. Sen, and C. Garcia-Moreno. (2002). "Sexual Violence." In E. G. Krig, L. L. Dahlberg, J. A. Mercyet al. (eds.), World Report on Violence and Health, pp. 147–81. World Health Organization.

Joachim, David S. "Senate Republicans Block Bill on Equal Pay." *The New York Times*. April 9, 2014. https://www.nytimes.com/2014/04/10/us/politics/senate-republicans-block-bill-on-equal-pay.html.

Jones, Meg. "The 'Hello Girls' Documentary Celebrates WWI Female Telephone Operators." Military.com. February 12, 2018. https://www.military.com/off-duty/2018/02/12/hello-girls-documentary-celebrates-wwi-female-telephone-operators.html.

Joseph-Dezaiza, Gabriel. "Life's Work: An Interview with Jane Fonda." *Harvard Business Review* (March–April 2018). https://hbr.org/2018/03/lifes-work-an-interview-with-jane-fonda.

Jukes Morris, Sylvia. "Clare, in Love and War." *Vanity Fair*. July 2014. https://archive.vanityfair.com/article/2014/7/clare-in-love-and-war.

Kareem Nittle, Nadra. "How the Black Codes Limited African American Progress after the Civil War." History. A&E Television Networks. January 28, 2019. https://archive.vanityfair.com/article/2014/7/clare-in-love-and-war.

—. "The Black Codes and Why They Still Matter Today." ThoughtCo. December 21, 2020. https://www.thoughtco.com/the-black-codes-4125744.

Kary, Tiffany. "Kamala Harris Nomination Strengthens Workplace Diversity Conversations." Employee Benefit Adviser. August 13, 2020. https://www.employeebenefitadviser.com/articles/kamala-harris-is-something-you-cry-about-for-black-female-executives.

Katz, Esther. "The Editor as Public Authority: Interpreting Margaret Sanger." *The Public Historian* 17(1) (Winter, 1995), pp. 41–50.
Kelly J, Keith. "Oprah's Magazine Will Likely Cost Twice as Much in 2021." *New York Post*. August 25, 2020. https://nypost.com/2020/08/25/oprahs-magazine-will-likely-cost-twice-as-much-in-2021/.
Kelly, Kate. "Women Answered Call in World War I." America Comes Alive. October 25, 2018. https://www.worldwar1centennial.org/index.php/communicate/press-media/wwi-centennial-news/7082-women-answered-call-in-world-war-i.html.
Kelly, Katherine Feo. "Performing Prison: Dress, Modernity, and the Radical Suffrage Body." *Fashion Theory* 15:3, 299–321. https://doi.org/10.2752/175174111X13028583328801.
Kelly, Martin. "Top 10 New Deal Programs of the 1930s." ThoughtCo. April 7, 2020. https://www.thoughtco.com/top-new-deal-programs-104687.
Kenton, Will. "Affirmative Action." Investopedia. February 10, 2021. https://www.investopedia.com/terms/a/affirmative-action.asp.
Kiger, Patrick J. "How the Horrific Tragedy of the Triangle Shirtwaist Fire Led to Workplace Safety Laws." History. A&E Television Networks. March 25, 2019. https://www.history.com/news/triangle-shirtwaist-factory-fire-labor-safety-laws.
—. "Minimum Wage in America: A Timeline." History. A&E Television Networks. October 18, 2019. https://www.history.com/news/minimum-wage-america-timeline.
Kim, Whizy. "Coronavirus Is Already Impacting the Hiring Gap for Millennial Women." Refinery 29. June 1, 2020. https://www.refinery29.com/en-us/2020/06/9834826/unemployment-due-to-coronavirus-women-impact.
King, M. (2020). "Leaders, Stop Denying the Gender Inequity in Your Organization." *Harvard Business Review*. https://hbr.org/2020/06/leaders-stop-denying-the-gender-inequity-in-your-organization.
Kishan, Saijel. "California Lawmakers Approve Racial Quotas for Corporate Boards." Employee Benefit Adviser. September 2, 2020. https://www.employeebenefitadviser.com/articles/california-lawmakers-approve-racial-quotas-for-corporate-boards.
Kleiman, Kathy. 2018. "The Secret History of the ENIAC Women." Uploaded February 16, 2018. TedxBeaconStreet. Video. 13.42 min. https://www.youtube.com/watch?v=Zevt2blQyVs&ab_channel=TEDxTalk.
Klein, Christopher. "The Strike That Shook America." History. A&E Television Networks. September 3, 2012. https://www.history.com/news/the-strike-that-shook-america.
Konkel, Lindsey. "Life for the Average Family during the Great Depression." History. A&E Television Networks. April 19, 2018. https://www.history.com/news/life-for-the-average-family-during-the-great-depression.
Kosinski, Jessica. *Journal of Antiques and Collectibles*. Blog. https://journalofantiques.com/features/selling-from-the-comfort-of-your-own-home/.
Kreiswirth, Brian, and Anna-Marie Tabor. "What You Need to Know about the Equal Credit Opportunity Act and How It Can Help You: Why It Was Passed and What It Is." Consumer Financial Protection Bureau. October 31, 2016. https://www.consumerfinance.gov/about-us/blog/what-you-need-know-about-equal-credit-opportunity-act-and-how-it-can-help-you-why-it-was-passed-and-what-it/.
Kristofic, Jim. *Medicine Women: The Story of the First Native American Nursing School*. Albuquerque: University of New Mexico Press, 2019.

Kuadli, Jenifer. "32 Shocking Sexual Assault Statistics for 2021." Legal Jobs. Blog. February 26, 2021. https://legaljobs.io/blog/sexual-assault-statistics/.

Landrum, Sarah."Millennial Women: You Have So Much to Offer the Workplace." *Forbes Magazine*. December 22, 2017. https://www.forbes.com/sites/sarahlandrum/2017/12/22/millennial-women-you-have-so-much-to-offer-the-workplace/.

Latchison Mason, Deborah. "Biography of Mary Mcleod Bethune, Civil Rights Activist." ThoughtCo. June 3, 2019. https://www.thoughtco.com/mary-mcleod-bethune-1779881.

Law, Tara. "Virginia Just Became the 38th State to Pass the Equal Rights Amendment. Here's What to Know About the History of the ERA." *TIME magazine*. August 23, 2019.

Lawrimore, Stan. "For Native Americans, COVID-19 Is 'The Worst of Both Worlds at the Same Time.'" *The Harvard Gazette* (May 2020). https://news.harvard.edu/gazette/story/2020/05/the-impact-of-covid-19-on-native-american-communities/.

Learning to Give. "The Philanthropic Meaning of the #MeToo Movement." 2017. https://www.learningtogive.org/resources/philanthropic-meaning-metoo-movement.

Lee, Junghun (Jay), and Chihyung Ok. 2001. "Effects of Workplace Friendship on Employee Job Satisfaction, Organizational Citizenship Behavior, Turnover Intention, Absenteeism, and Task Performance." Scholars Work. https://scholarworks.umass.edu/cgi/viewcontent.cgi?article=1053&context=gradconf_hospitality.

Legal Information Institute. "Affirmative Action." n.d. https://www.law.cornell.edu/supct/cert/supreme_court_2013-2014_term_highlights/affirmative_action.

Letter from Augustine Lonergan (U.S. House of Representatives) to the Office of the Judge Advocate General, Navy Department, Oct. 6, 1919; Confidential Correspondence, 1913–24; Office of Naval Intelligence; RG 38: National Archives Building, Washington, D.C.

Levy, N. 2019. "Workplace Ableism Is a Problem for ADA Rights." OnLabor. https://onlabor.org/workplace-ableism-is-a-problem-for-ada-rights/.

Lewis Johnson, Jone. "Chien-Shiung Wu: A Pioneering Female Physicist." ThoughtCo. February 10, 2018. https://www.thoughtco.com/chien-shiung-wu-biography-3530366.

Lewis, Jone Johnson. "Emmy Noether, Mathematician." ThoughtCo. February 12, 2019. https://www.thoughtco.com/emmy-noether-biography-3530361.

—. "The 1912 Lawrence Textile Strike." ThoughtCo. February 5, 2019. https://www.thoughtco.com/1912-lawrence-textile-strike-3530831.

—. "Mary Church Terrell." ThoughtCo. December 15, 2018. https://www.thoughtco.com/mary-church-terrell-biography-3530557.

—. "A Short History of Women's Property Rights in the United States." ThoughtCo. July 13, 2019. https://www.thoughtco.com/property-rights-of-women-3529578.

LibCom. "A Selected Timeline of Women's Labor History." https://libcom.org/files/US-women-labour-history.pdf.

Library of Congress. "Detailed Chronology – National Woman's Party History." Women of Protest: Photographs from the Records of the National Woman's Party." https://www.loc.gov/static/collections/women-of-protest/images/detchron.pdf.

Linder, Doughlas O. "The Triangle Shirtwaist Factory Fire Trial: An Account." Famous Trials. March 1, 2003. https://www.famous-trials.com/trianglefire/964-home.

Lindeberg, Rafaela. "CEO Who Was Once a Man Brings Gender-Equality Outlook." Employee Benefit Adviser. November 23, 2020. https://www.employeebenefitadviser.com/articles/ceo-who-was-once-a-man-brings-gender-equality-outlook.

Lipnic, Victoria. "The State of Age Discrimination and Older Workers in the U.S. 50 Years after the Age Discrimination in Employment Act (ADEA)." U.S. Equal Employment Opportunity Commission (EEOC). June 2018. https://www.eeoc.gov/reports/state-age-discrimination-and-older-workers-us-50-years-after-age-discrimination-employment.

Liptak, Kevin. "The FBI Did Investigate Anita Hill's Accusation, and It Took 3 Days." CNN Politics. September 20, 2018. https://www.cnn.com/2018/09/19/politics/anita-hill-clarence-thomas-allegations-timeline.

Little Becky. "Details of Brutal First Slave Voyages Discovered." August 31, 2018 original, updated March 21, 2019. History.com. https://www.history.com/news/transatlantic-slave-first-ships-details.

Longley, Robert. "Edith Wilson: America's First Women President." ThoughtCo. June 3, 2019. https://www.thoughtco.com/edith-wilson-4146035.

Los Angeles Times. "Sandra Day O'Connor Has Surgery for Breast Cancer; Full Recovery Is Expected." October 23, 1988. https://www.latimes.com/archives/la-xpm-1988-10-23-mn-257-story.html.

Loubier, Andrea. "How Millennial Women and The Future of Work Are Charging Into 2018." *Forbes Magazine*, December 28, 2017. https://www.forbes.com/sites/andrealoubier/2017/12/28/millennial-women-and-the-future-of-work-charging-into-2018/.

The Lynching Sites Project of Memphis. "The People's Grocery Lynchings (Thomas Moss, Will Stewart, Calvin Mcdowell)." December 11, 2016. https://lynchingsitesmem.org/archives/photo-peoples-grocery.

Macias, Melba. "Senator Tammy Duckworth: An Advocate for Disability and Veterans' Rights." Enabling Devices. Blog. July 22, 2020. https://enablingdevices.com/blog/senator-tammy-duckworth-an-advocate-for-disability-and-veterans-rights/.

MacMillan, R. (2000). "Adolescent Victimization and Income Deficits in Adulthood: Rethinking the Costs of Criminal Violence from a Life-course Perspective." *Criminology* 38, pp. 553–88. doi:10.1111/j.1745-9125.2000.tb00899x.

Malmstrom, Malin, Jeaneth Johansson, and Joakim Wincent. "We Recorded VCs' Conversations and Analyzed How Differently They Talk About Female Entrepreneurs." *Harvard Business Review*. May 17, 2017. We Recorded VCs' Conversations and Analyzed How Differently They Talk About Female Entrepreneurs..

Marcus, Michael N. "1894: Women No Longer Owned by Men." The First Time (or the Last Time) When Things Changed in Society and Technology. Blog. August 23, 2007. https://4thefirsttime.blogspot.com/2007/08/1894-women-no-longer-owned-by-men.html.

Martin, Kali. "It's Your War, Too: Women in World War II." The National World War II Museum. March 13, 2020. https://www.nationalww2museum.org/war/articles/its-your-war-too-women-world-war-ii.

Martinuzzi, Elisa. 2020. "The Pandemic's Gender Bias Needs Urgent Fixing." Employee Benefit Adviser. May 18. https://www.employeebenefitadviser.com/articles/the-pandemics-gender-bias-needs-urgent-fixing.

Maryville University. "Understanding the Me Too Movement: A Sexual Harassment Awareness Guide." May 5, 2019. https://online.maryville.edu/blog/understanding-the-me-too-movement-a-sexual-harassment-awareness-guide/.

McGowan, Amanda. "First Lady of Physics' Chien-Shiung Wu Honored with US Postage Stamp." The World. February 11, 2021. https://www.pri.org/person/chien-shiung-wu.

McGreevy, Nora. "How Codebreaker Elizebeth Friedman Broke up a Nazi Spy Ring." *Smithsonian Magazine*. January 15, 2021. https://www.smithsonianmag.com/smart-news/new-pbs-film-tells-story-wwii-codebreaker-elizabeth-friedman-180976759/.

McKay, Dave. "What Is Cobol, and Why Do So Many Institutions Rely on It?" How to Geek. April 15, 2020. https://www.howtogeek.com/667596/what-is-cobol-and-why-do-so-many-institutions-rely-on-it/.

McKelway, A. J. *Child Wages in the Cotton Mills: Our Modern Feudalism*. National Child Labor Committee. Pamphlet No. 199. May 1913.

Mcmohan, Mary. "What Is the Order of the Coif?" *Wisegeek*. February 14, 2021. https://www.wise-geek.com/what-is-the-order-of-the-coif.htm.

Michals, Debra. "Margaret Sanger." National Women's History Museum. 2017. https://www.womenshistory.org/education-resources/biographies/margaret-sanger.

Michals, Debra. "Mary Church Terrell." National Women's History Museum. August 16, 2017. https://www.womenshistory.org/education-resources/biographies/mary-church-terrell.

Middleton-Keirn, Susan, and Jackie Howsden-Eller "Reconstructing Femininity: The Woman–Professional in the South" in Women in the South: An Anthropological Perspective, edited by Holly F. Matthews. Southern Anthropological Society Proceedings, No. 22. Athens, GA: University of Georgia Press,1989, pp. 57–70.

Mikel, Betsy. "One Really Good Reason Why Female Millennials Are So Ready to Quit Their Jobs." Inc.com. June 8, 2017. https://www.inc.com/betsy-mikel/millennial-women-really-want-to-quit-their-jobs-and-do-this-instead.html.

Miller, Rich. "U.S. Workers May Have to Switch Occupations Post Pandemic" Employee Benefit News. February 24, 2021. https://www.benefitnews.com/articles/workers-may-have-to-change-occupations-post-pandemic.

Milli, J., Huang, Y., Hartmann, H., & Hayes, J. (2017). "The Impact of Equal Pay on Poverty and the Economy." Institute for Women's Policy Research.

Milligan, Susan. "Stepping through History: A Timeline of Women's Rights from 1769 to the 2017 Women's March on Washington." *U.S. News and World Report*. January 20, 2017. https://www.usnews.com/news/the-report/articles/2017-01-20/timeline-the-womens-rights-movement-in-the-us.

Mitchell, Broadus, *The Rise of the Cotton Mills in the South*. Baltimore: Johns Hopkins University Press, 1921.

Mitchell, Damon. "The People's Grocery Lynching, Memphis, Tennessee," *JSTOR Daily*. January 24, 2018.

Monahan, Mary Agnes, Woman Yeoman 1st Class, List of Officers and Enlisted Men of the Regular Navy and the Naval Reserve Force Who Were Reported Dead or Missing during the Period 1917–19; Records of the Office of Naval Records and Library, RG 45; National Archives Building, Washington, D.C.

Moniuszko, Sara M., Maria Puente, and Veronica Bravo. "Ruth Bader Ginsburg Becomes the First Woman to Lie in State: Eight Other Strides She Made for Women." *USA Today*. September 24, 2020. https://www.usatoday.com/in-depth/life/2020/09/24/ruth-bader-ginsburg-8-things-she-did-womens-rights/3502065001/.

Monahan, Evelyn M., and Rosemary Neidel-Greenlee. *A Few Good Women: America's Military Women from World War I to the Wars in Afghanistan and Iraq*. New York: Knopf, 2010.

Moore, Kate. "The Forgotten Story Of The Radium Girls, Whose Deaths Saved Thousands Of Workers' Lives," Buzzfeed. May 5, 2017. vhttps://www.buzzfeed.com/authorkatemoore/the-light-that-does-not-lie.

Moore, Linda. "Events to Remember People's Grocery Lynching." Commercial Appeal. March 7, 2017. https://www.commercialappeal.com/story/news/local/2017/03/07/events-remember-peoples-grocery-lynching/98608166/.

Morrissey, Rasheed Malik, and Taryn Morrissey. "The COVID-19 Pandemic Is Forcing Millennial Mothers Out of the Workforce." Center for American Progress, August 12, 2020. https://www.americanprogress.org/issues/early-childhood/news/2020/08/12/489178/covid-19-pandemic-forcing-millennial-mothers-workforce/.

Muster Roll of the 1st Naval District ending September 30, 1918; Muster Rolls; Records of the Bureau of Navigation, RG 24; National Archives, Washington, D.C.

Myre, Greg. "100 Years On, The 'Hello Girls' Are Recognized For World War I Heroics." National Public Radio (NPR). November 9, 2018. https://www.npr.org/2018/11/09/659349910/100-years-on-the-hello-girls-are-recognized-for-world-war-i-heroics.

NaCo Brief: Summary of Legislative Action on Covid-10. Last updated January 13, 2021. https://penniur.upenn.edu/uploads/media/Summary_of_COVID_Legislation_Jan_2021.pdf.

Napikoski, Linda. "What Is the Feminine Mystique? The Idea behind Betty Friedan's Bestselling Book." ThoughtCo. September 3, 2018. https://www.thoughtco.com/what-is-the-feminine-mystique-3528925.

National Archives and Records Administration. "African Americans and the American Labor Movement." December 7, 2017. https://www.archives.gov/publications/prologue/1997/summer/american-labor-movement.html.

—. "The Story of the Female Yeomen during the First World War." https://www.archives.gov/publications/prologue/2006/fall/yeoman-f.html.

National Library of Medicine, National Institutes of Health. "[Dr.] Susan La Fesche Picotte." https://cfmedicine.nlm.nih.gov/physicians/biography_253.html.

National Library of Medicine, National Institutes of Health. "Confronting Violence: Advocates for Change," August 26, 2015. https://www.nlm.nih.gov/exhibition/confrontingviolence/index.html.

National Library of Science, National Insititutes of Health. "Dr. Anita Newcomb McGee." Changing the Face of Medicine series. https://cfmedicine.nlm.nih.gov/physicians/biography_216.html.

National Organization for Women (NOW). "Highlights." https://now.org/about/history/highlights/.

National Park Service. "Chickamauga and Chattanooga: Death Knell of the Confederacy." https://www.nps.gov/chch/index.htm.

—. "Alice Austen." 2021. https://www.nps.gov/gate/learn/historyculture/alice-austen.htm.

—. "[Dr.] Chien-Shiung Wu, the First Lady of Physics." January 23, 2020. https://www.nps.gov/people/dr-chien-shiung-wu-the-first-lady-of-physics.htm.

—. "First (and Only) Nursing School for Native Americans Established, 1932." 2021. https://www.nps.gov/orgs/1582/find/statelists/az/SageMemorial.pdf.

—. "Free a Marine to Fight: Women Marines in World War II." https://www.nps.gov/articles/womenmarinesworldwarii.htm.
—. "Ida B. Wells." https://www.nps.gov/people/idabwells.htm.
—. "Marie Louise Bottineau Baldwin." December 15, 2020. https://www.nps.gov/people/marie-louise-bottineau-baldwin.htm.
—. "Mary McLeod Bethune Council House." February 25, 2021. https://www.nps.gov/mamc/index.htm.
—. "1913 Woman Suffrage Procession." December 15, 2020. https://www.nps.gov/articles/woman-suffrage-procession1913.htm.
—. "The Politics of Dress." Democracy Limited Series. https://www.nps.gov/articles/democracy-limited-the-politics-of-dress.htm.
—. "The Politics of Respectability." Democracy Limited Series. https://www.nps.gov/articles/democracy-limited-the-politics-of-respectability.htm.
—. "Rosie the Riveter Memorial." 2021. https://www.nps.gov/rori/index.htm.
—. "Sage Memorial Hospital School of Nursing." https://www.nps.gov/orgs/1582/find/statelists/az/SageMemorial.pdf.
—. "Women Go to War." https://www.nps.gov/wwii/learn/historyculture/women-go-to-war.htm.
—. "Women in World War I." https://www.nps.gov/articles/women-in-world-war-i.htm.
—. "The WWII Home Front." https://www.nps.gov/articles/the-wwii-home-front.htm.
—. "Zitkala-Ša." https://www.nps.gov/people/zitkala-sa.htm.
National Museum of the Air Force. "WASP Created." January 9, 2009. Archived from the original on October 23, 2012. https://web.archive.org/web/20121023024148/http:/www.nationalmuseum.af.mil/factsheets/factsheet.asp.
—. "WASP Disbanded." January 9, 2009. Archived on October 14, 2012. https://web.archive.org/web/20121014045955/http:/www.nationalmuseum.af.mil/factsheets/factsheet.asp.
National Organization for Women (NOW). "Founding." https://now.org/about/history/founding-2/.
—. "Highlights." https://now.org/about/history/highlights/.
National Partnership. "History of the FMLA." https://www.nationalpartnership.org/our-work/economic-justice/history-of-the-fmla.html.
National Sexual Violence Resources Center. "Overview: Sexual Violence in the Workplace." https://www.nsvrc.org/sites/default/files/publications_nsvrc_overview_sexual-violence-workplace.pdf.
—. "Special Collection: Sexual Violence in the Military." 2011. Retrieved from VAWnet: National Online Resource Center on Violence Against Women. http://www.vawnet.org/specialcollections/SVMilitary.php.
National Security Agency. Central Security Service. "Elizebeth S. Friedman," February 1, 2002. https://www.nsa.gov/About-Us/Current-Leadership/Article-View/Article/1623028/elizebeth-s-friedman/.
National Whistleblower Center. "Coleen Rowley." https://www.whistleblowers.org/whistleblowers/sherron-watkins/.
—. "Cynthia Cooper." https://www.whistleblowers.org/whistleblowers/cynthia-cooper/.
—. "Sherron Watkins." https://www.whistleblowers.org/whistleblowers/sherron-watkins/.
National Women's Hall of Fame. "Ella Grasso." February 1, 2001. https://www.womenofthehall.org/inductee/ella-grasso/.

National Women's History Museum. "Gloria Steinem Handout No. 3." https://www.womenshistory.org/sites/default/files/document/2021-02/Gloria%20Steinem%20Lesson%20Handout%203.pdf.

—. "The Women of NASA." Exhibit. October 2, 2017. https://www.womenshistory.org/exhibits/women-nasa.

—. "The Women's Army Corps: Female Soldiers in WWII." Exhibit. August 26, 2020.

National Women's Law Center. "Equal Pay for Native American Women." https://nwlc.org/resources/equal-pay-for-native-women-2/.

National World War II Museum. "It's Your War, Too: Women in World War II." March 13, 2020. https://www.nationalww2museum.org/war/articles/its-your-war-too-women-world-war-ii.

Navajo Health Foundation. "Sage Memorial." https://sagememorial.com/.

Neumark, David, Ian Burn, and Patrick Button. "Is It Harder for Older Workers to Find Jobs? New and Improved Evidence from a Field Experiment." National Bureau of Economic Research. October 2015. Revised November 2017. http://www.nber.org/papers/w21669.

—. "Is It Harder for Older Workers to Find Jobs? New and Improved Evidence from a Field Experiment." *Journal of Political Economy* 127(20), pp. 922–70.

New England Historical Society. "Flashback Photo: The National Woman's Party Pickets the White House." https://www.newenglandhistoricalsociety.com/flashback-photo-national-womans-party-pickets-white-house/.

New York Historical Society. "Clare Boothe Luce – the Ambassador." May 10, 2018. https://blog.nyhistory.org/clare-boothe-luce-the-ambassador/.

New York Times. "Harvey Weinstein's Stunning Downfall: 23 Years in Prison." March 11, 2020. https://www.nytimes.com/2020/03/11/nyregion/harvey-weinstein-sentencing.html.

—. "Militants Demand a Special Session." March 11, 1919. *The New York Times*. https://timesmachine.nytimes.com/timesmachine/1919/03/11/97084088.pdf.

Neygorney, Adam. "'Cultural War' of 1992 Moves in from the Fringe." *The New York Times*. August 29, 2012. https://www.nytimes.com/2012/08/30/us/politics/from-the-fringe-in-1992-patrick-j-buchanans-words-now-seem-mainstream.html.

Nontoxicprint. "Painting with Radium: The Radium Girls." November 20, 2013. https://nontoxicprint.com/radiumgirls.htm.

New York University. "Biography of Margaret Sanger." The Margaret Sanger Papers Project. https://www.nyu.edu/projects/sanger/aboutms/index.php.

Norlian, Allison. "Workers with Disabilities Disproportionately Impacted by Covid-19 Pandemic." *Forbes magazine*. June 22, 2020. https://www.forbes.com/sites/allisonnorlian/2020/06/22/workers-with-disabilities-disproportionately-impacted-by-covid-19-pandemic/.

O-Brien, Alden. "Great Strides for the 'New Woman,' Suffrage, and Fashion." National Museum of American History. March 7, 2013. https://americanhistory.si.edu/blog/2013/03/guest-post-great-strides-for-the-new-woman-suffrage-and-fashion.html.

Office of the Director of National Intelligence. "NO FEAR Act (As Amended)." https://www.dni.gov/index.php/no-fear-act.

O-Gan, Patri. 2014. "Traveling for Suffrage, Part 4: Riding the Rails." National Museum of American History. March 24, 2014. https://americanhistory.si.edu/blog/2014/03/traveling-for-suffrage-part-4-riding-the-rails.html.

Omnigraphics. "Ada Deer." 2021.
—. "Addressing Discrimination Against Women in the Workplace with Affirmative Action." 2021.
—. "Anita Hill." 2021.
—. "Annie Oakley: A Different Way of Earning a Living." 2021.
—. "Army Nurse Corps." 2021.
—. "Army Nurse Corps Formed." 2021.
—. "The Bechdel Test: Sidebar." 2021.
—. 'Bessie Coleman." 2021.
—. "Betty Freidan's Groundbreaking Book *The Feminist Mystique* Launches Second-Wave Women's Movement." 2021.
—. "Bombshell Badass Jane Fonda." 2021.
—. "Bread and Roses Strike of 1912." 2021.
—. "Brownie Wise and the Tupperware® Party." 2021.
—. "Cadet Nurse Corps." 2021.
—. "Charlotte Perkins Gilman (1850–1933), a Woman Trapped by Her Time." 2021.
—. "Chien-Shiung Wu." 2021.
—. "Coast Guard SPARS." 2021.
,—. 'Congresswoman Geraldine Ferraro Chosen as Vice President on the Democratic Ticket." 2021.
—. "Cotton Mill Girls." 2021
—. "Deb Haaland." 2021.
—. "Dolores Huerta." 2021.
—. "The Double Bind: Likeability vs. Capability." 2021.
—. "Edith Clarke." 2021.
—. "Edith Wilson: America's First (Unofficial) President." 2021.
—. "*Eisenstadt v. Baird*." 2021.
—. "Ella T. Grasso." 2021.
—. "Emmy Noether: Invisible Genius." 2021.
—. "Environmental Scientist Rachel Carson's *Silent Spring*." 2021.
—. "Equity Act of 2019." 2021.
—. "Everyday Gender Bias – What Does It Look Like?" 2021.
—. "Fair Labor Standards and a Minimum Wage." 2021.
—. "First Lady Michelle Obama." 2021
—. "Frances Perkins: 'Architect of the New Deal.'" 2021.
—. "Gendered Career Paths and Self-Fulfilling Prophecies." 2021.
—. "Geraldine Ferraro Chosen as Walter Mondale's Running Mate." 2021.
—. "Gloria Steinem and the First National Magazine Owned, Produced, Written, Edited and Managed by Women for Women." 2021.
—. "The Great Depression and Women's Work." 2021.
—. "The Great Depression at a Glance." 2021.
—. "Guerrilla GIrls Expose Gender and Ethnic Bias in the Art World." 2021.
—. "Hedy Lamarr, Innovator Supreme." 2021.
—. "Helen Thomas." 2021
—. "Hidden Women of NACA and NASA." 2021.
—. "How to Advocate for the Economic Empowerment of Underrepresented Communities." 2021.

—. "The Impact of Discrimination on Economic Well-Being: Systemic Pay Disparity." 2021.
—. "The International Ladies' Garment Workers' Union (ILGWU)." 2021.
—. "Introduction to Part Two, Cultural Shifts and Sonic Booms, 1940–1969: Adaptability and Innovation." 2021.
—. "Introduction to Part Three, Revolution and Equality for All, 1970–1999: Living the Revolution." 2021.
—. "Introduction to Part Four, Diversity: the New Normal, 2000–2021." 2021.
—. "Introduction: Women Warriors,1940–1949.: 2021.
—. "Invisible Women Create Modern Computing: The ENIAC Women." 2021.
—. "Jeanette Rankin." 2021.
—. "*Johnson v. Transportation Agency*." 2021.
—. "Kamala Harris." 2021.
—. "1925 Labor Developments." 2021.
—. "Madam C. J. Walker." 2021.
—. "Maggie L. Walker." 2021.
—. "Margaret Sanger." 2021.
—. "Mary Church Turrell." 2021.
—. "Mary McLeod Bethune: Equalizing Education." 2021.
—. "May Chen Co-organizes the 1982 New York City Chinatown Strike." 2021.
—. "*Meritor Savings Bank v. Vinson*." 2021.
—. "Milestones for Women Prior to 1900." 2021.
—. "Military Ban on Women in Combat Lifted." 2021.
—. "Millennial Women in the Workplace." 2021.
—. "National Organization for Women (NOW) Founded, 1967." 2021.
—. "Native American Health in a Time of Scarcity." 2021.
—. "Navy Nurse Corps Formed." 2021.
—. "Navy Nurse Corps." 2021.
—. "A New President Addresses the Three Rs." 2021.
—. "1925 Labor Developments," 2021.
—. "NOW Member Shirley Chisholm Is First Black Woman Elected to the House." 2021.
—. ""Objectives of Affirmative Action." 2021.
—. "Overview: Women in the Workplace in America, 1900–1909." 2021.
—. "Overview: Women in the Workplace in America, 1910–1919." 2021.
—. "Overview: Women in the Workplace in America, 1920–1929." 2021.
—. "Overview: Women in the Workplace in America, 1930–1939." 2021.
—. "Overview: Women in the Workplace in America, 1950–1959." 2021.
—. "Overview: Women in the Workplace in America, 1960–1969." 2021.
—. "Overview: Women in the Workplace in America, 1970–1979." 2021.
—. "Overview: Women in the Workplace in America, 1980–1989." 2021.
—. "Overview: Women in the Workplace in America, 1990–1999." 2021.
—. "Overview: Women in the Workplace in America, 2010–2019." 2021.
—. "Overview: Women in the Workplace in America, 2020–2021." 2021
—. "Paterson Silk Strike of 1913." 2021.
—. "The Plight of the Radium Girls." 2021.
—. "President Clinton Signs Don't Ask, Don't Tell (DOMA) into Law." 2021.
—. "Rachel Levine." 2021.
—. "The Rise and Fall and Rise Again of Ellen DeGeneres." 2021.

—. "*Roe v. Wade* and Women's Reproductive RIghts." 2021.
—. "*Rostker v. Goldberg*." 2021.
—. "Section 213 of the Federal Economy Act: President Hoover's Lousy New Deal for Women." 2021
—. "Senate Majority Blocks Equal Pay for Women Workers." 2021.
—. "Senator Tammy Duckworth." 2021.
—. "Sexual Violence in the Workplace and the #MeToo Movement." 2021.
—. "Shirtwaist Workers Strike of 1909." 2021.
—. "Supreme Court Justice Ruth Bader Ginsburg." 2021.
—. "Supreme Court Justice Sandra Day O'Connor." 2021.
—. "The Silent Sentinels and Voting Rights." 2021.
—. "The Social Security Act of 1935." 2021.
—. "Standing Up for Fair Pay: The Lilly Ledbetter Fair Pay Act of 2009." 2021.
—. "Stacy Cunningham Named Head of the New York Stock Exchange." 2021.
—. "Tennis Great BIllie Jean King Wins the Battle of the Sexes." 2021.
—. "Trailblazer Hillary Rodham Clinton's Historic Run." 2021.
—. "Trailblazing Human-rights Advocate Eleanor Roosevelt." 2021.
—. "Trailblazing Talk-show Host and Media Mogul Oprah Winfrey." 2021.
—. "Triangle Shirtwaist Factory Fire of 1911." 2021.
—. "Two Steps Forward in the Long March to Full Inclusion." 2021.
—. "Uncredited Trailblazer: Elizebeth Smith Friedman: The Hero That History Nearly Forgot." 2021.
—. "*U.S. v. Virginia*: A Judicial Decision That Opened New Doors and Career Paths for Women." 2021.
—. "U.S. Women's Soccer Team." 2021.
—. "The United Nations Charter." 2021.
—. "The Whistleblowers." 2021.
—. "Woman's Suffrage: The Early Years." 2021.
—. "Women Accepted for Volunteer Emergency Service (WAVES)." 2021.
—. "Women Air Force Service Pilots (WASP)." 2021.
—. ""Women in a Changing Workforce." 2021.
—. "Women in Factories, An Introduction." 2021.
—. "Women Marines." 2021.
—. "Women Warriors, 1940–1949." 2021.
—. "Women with Disabilities Hit Hard by Pandemic Job Losses." 2021.
—. "Women's Auxiliary Corps (WAC)." 2021.
Oprah. "Oprah Winfrey's Official Biography." May 17, 2011. https://www.oprah.com/pressroom/oprah-winfreys-official-biography.
Ott, Tim. "How Billie Jean King Made Women's Sports History during the 'Battle of the Sexes.'" Biography. September 19, 2017. https://www.biography.com/news/battle-of-the-sexes-true-story-facts.
Owsley, Frank Lawrence. *Plain Folk of the Old South*. Baton Rouge: Louisiana State University Press, 1949.
Palczewski, Catherine H. "The 1919 Prison Special: Constituting White Women's Citizenship." *Quarterly Journal of Speech* 102:2, 107–32. https://doi.org/10.1080/00335630.2016.1154185.
Patch, Nathanial "The Story of the Female Yeomen during the First World War." *Prologue* 38:3, 2006. National Archives. https://www.archives.gov/publications/prologue/2006/fall/yeoman-f.html.

Paul, Alice. "Conversations with Alice Paul: Woman Suffrage and the Equal Rights Amendment: Interview by Amelia R. Fry, University of California,1976." http://content.cdlib.org/view?docId=kt6f59n89c&query=&brand=calisphere.

Paul, Kari. "Millennial Women Face New Mental Health Struggles in the Workplace." All Diversity IWE. https://alldiversity.com/articles/Millennial-women-face-new-mental-health-struggles-in-the-workplace.

PayScale. "Executive Summary. The State of the Gender Pay Gap 2020." https://www.payscale.com/compensation-today/2020/03/the-2020-gender-pay-gap-report-reveals-that-women-still-earn-less-for-equal-work.

Peters, M. "The Hidden Sexism in Workplace Language." BBC. March 30, 2017. https://www.bbc.com/worklife/article/20170329-the-hidden-sexism-in-workplace-language.

Picci, Aimee. "It's Been a Record 11 Years Since the Last Increase in U.S. Minimum Wage." Moneywatch. CBS News. https://www.cbsnews.com/news/minimum-wage-no-increases-11-years/.

Pickert, Reade. "Jobs Report Shows Record Unemployment, But Slow Wage Growth." Employee Benefit Adviser. January 10, 2020. https://www.employeebenefitadviser.com/articles/jobs-report-shows-record-unemployment-but-slow-wage-growth.

Place, Alyssa. "Black and Latinx Mothers Falling off the Career Track during COVID." Employee Benefit Adviser. February 12, 2021. https://www.employeebenefitadviser.com/news/black-and-latinx-mothers-falling-off-the-career-track-during-covid.

—. "Coronavirus Is Pushing the Gender Gap Even Wider for Working Mothers." Employee Benefit News. June 15, 2020. https://www.benefitnews.com/news/coronavirus-is-pushing-the-gender-gap-even-wider-for-working-moms.

—. "Employee Mental Health Is Improving but Benefits Are Still Needed." Employee Benefit Adviser. February 22, 2021. https://www.employeebenefitadviser.com/news/employee-mental-health-is-improving-but-benefits-are-still-needed.

—."The Top Tool for Retaining Your Female Workforce during COVID-19 Boosts Business and the Economy." Employee Benefit News. October 21, 2020. https://www.benefitnews.com/news/the-top-tool-for-retaining-your-female-workforce-during-covid-19.

—. "Why COVID-19 Has Been a 'Pressure Test' for Company Culture." Employee Benefit News. August 4, 2020. https://www.benefitnews.com/news/why-covid-19-has-been-a-pressure-test-for-company-culture.

—. "Why Keeping Women Employed during COVID-19 Boosts Business and the Economy." Employee Benefit News. September 9, 2020. https://www.benefitnews.com/news/women-leaving-the-workforce-could-cause-a-huge-burden-to-the-economy-and-your-business.

—. "Worker Burnout Is Soaring. Here's How to Reach Your Employees Before It's Too Late." Employee Benefit News. April 3, 2020. https://www.employeebenefitadviser.com/news/worker-burnout-is-soaring-heres-how-to-reach-your-employees-before-its-too-late.

—. "Yet Another Hurdle for Women at Work: Their Age." Employee Benefit News, February 24, 2021. https://www.benefitnews.com/news/age-is-another-hurdle-for-women-at-work.

Planned Parenthood Federation of America."Biography of Margaret Sanger." https://www.plannedparenthood.org/files/7513/9611/6635/Margaret_Sanger_Hero_1009.pdf.

—. "*Roe v. Wade*," https://www.plannedparenthood.org/planned-parenthood-western-pennsylvania/stay-informed/roe-v-wade.

Potter, Sharyn J., & Victoria L. Banyard. (2011). "The Victimization Experiences of Women in the Workforce: Moving Beyond Single Categories of Work or Violence." *Violence and Victims* 26, pp. 513–32. doi:10.1891/0886-6708.26.4.513.

Presidential Commission on the Assignment of Women in the Armed Forces. (1993) *Women in Combat: Report to the President*. McLean, Virginia: Brassey's.

Pruitt, Sarah. "How Anita Hill's Testimony Made America Cringe–and Change." History. A&E Television Networks. February 9, 2021. https://www.history.com/news/anita-hill-confirmation-hearings-impact.

—. "How Flappers of the Roaring Twenties Redefined Womanhood." History. A&E Television Networks. February 9, 2021. https://www.history.com/news/flappers-roaring-20s-women-empowerment.

Purmont E, Jon. "The Education of Ella Grasso." Connecticut History. January 8, 2021. https://www.ctexplored.org/the-education-of-ella-grasso/.

Rape, Abuse and Incest National Network. (RAINN). "Victims of Sexual Violence: Statistics." https://www.rainn.org/statistics/victims-sexual-violence.

Raymond. Adam K. "Politics May 7, 2019: A Brief Guide to the Joe Biden–Anita Hill Controversy," May 7, 2019. https://nymag.com/intelligencer/2019/05/guide-joe-biden-anita-hill-controversy.html.

Ren, Henry. "Pandemic Further Entrenches U.S. Gender Gap in Wage Bargaining." Employee Benefit Adviser, December 3, 2020. https://www.employeebenefitadviser.com/articles/pandemic-further-entrenches-u-s-gender-gap-in-wage-bargaining.

Renzulli, Karri Ann. "Closing the Gap: These 15 Jobs Have the Largest Pay Gaps between Men and Women." CNBC. March 27, 2019. https://www.cnbc.com/2019/03/27/glassdoor-15-jobs-with-the-biggest-gender-pay-gap.html/

Restaurant Opportunities Center United, Family Values @ Work, HERvotes Coalition, et al. National Association of Working Women. (2012). "Tipped over the Edge: Gender Inequity in the Restaurant Industry." Retrieved from http:// rocunited.org/files/2012/02/ROC_GenderInequity_F1-1.pdf.

Reuters Graphics. "Cobol Blues." April 10, 2017. http://fingfx.thomsonreuters.com/gfx/rngs/USA-BANKS-COBOL/010040KH18J/index.html.

Richard Nixon Presidential Library and Museum. "A Few Good Women: Advancing the Cause of Women in Government, 1969–74. Exhibit. June 15 to July 15, 2012. https://www.nixonlibrary.gov/few-good-women-advancing-cause-women-government-1969-74.

Rikleen, Lauren Stiller. "Older Women Are Being Forced Out of the Workforce." *Harvard Business Review*. March 10, 2016. https://hbr.org/2016/03/older-women-are-being-forced-out-of-the-workforce.

Robinson, Joanna. "Jane Fonda Regrets Hanoi Jane." *Vanity Fair*. January 19, 2015. vanityfair.com/hollywood/2015/01/jane-fona-regrets-hanoi-jane/jan01.

Rockeman, Olivia, Reade Pickert, and Catarine Saraiva. "The First Female Recession Threatens to Wipe Out Decades of Progress for U.S. Women." Employee Benefit Adviser, September 30, 2020. https://www.employeebenefitadviser.com/articles/the-first-female-recession-threatens-to-wipe-out-decades-of-progress-for-u-s-women.

Roosevelt, Franklin D. "Message to Congress on Establishing Minimum Wages and Maximum Hours Standards." May 24, 1937. https://teachingamericanhistory.org/library/document/message-to-congress-on-establishing-minimum-wages-and-maximum-hours/.

Rosenwald, Michael S. "The First Woman to Start a Bank – a Black Woman –Finally Gets Her Due in the Confederacy's Capital." *The Washington Post*. July 14, 2017. https://www.washingtonpost.com/news/retropolis/wp/2017/07/14/the-first-black-woman-to-start-a-bank-finally-gets-her-due-in-the-confederacys-capital/.

Roulo, Claudette "Defense Department Expands Women's Combat Role." American Forces Press Service. January 24, 2013. https://web.archive.org/web/20140412193528/http://www.defense.gov/news/newsarticle.aspx?id=119098#.

Rudin, Ken. "Geraldine Ferraro Broke a Barrier for Women, but Roadblocks Remain." North Country Public Radio. March 26, 2011. https://www.northcountrypublicradio.org/news/npr/134882628/geraldine-ferraro-broke-a-barrier-for-women-but-roadblocks-remain.

Ryskamp Alexis, Dani. "Biography of Eleanor Roosevelt, First Lady, Writer and Diplomat." ThoughtCo/ January 23, 2020.

Sahadi, J. (2019). "It's 2019 and Just One in Five C-Suite Executives Is a Woman." CNN Business. https://www.cnn.com/2019/10/15/success/gender-gap-women-at-work/index.html.

San Diego Supercomputer Center. "Emmy Noether: Creative Mathematical Genius." San Diego Supercomputer Center (SDSC), February 1, 2001. https://www.sdsc.edu/ScienceWomen/noether.html.

Sandberg, Sheryl, and Nell Scovell. "Lean In: For Graduates." *Lean In: For Graduates*. New York: Alfred A. Knopf, 2014.

Sands, Nicole. "How Oprah Winfrey Is Empowering Girls and Women around the World." *People magazine*, November 4, 2016.

Savage, M. (2020). "How COVID-19 Is Changing Women's Lives." British Broadcasting Corporation. https://www.bbc.com/worklife/article/20200630-how-covid-19-is-changing-womens-lives.

Schmitt, Eric, and Helene Cooper. "Promotions for Female Generals Were Delayed Over Fears of Trump's Reaction." *The New York Times*. February 17, 2021. https://www.nytimes.com/2021/02/17/us/politics/women-generals-promotions-trump.html.

Schneider, Gregory S. 2017. "Uncovered Boxes Shed Light on Maggie Lena Walker, an African American Icon and First Woman to Own a U.S. Bank." *The Washington Post*. March 26. https://www.washingtonpost.com/local/virginia-politics/over-boxes-from-the-last-century-an-eight-year-discussion-about-race-life-and-womanhood/2017/03/26/29eb0370-08db-11e7-b77c-0047d15a24e0_story.html.

Segers, Grace. "Here Are Some of the Questions Anita Hill Answered in 1991." CBS News. September, 19, 2018. https://www.cbsnews.com/news/here-are-some-of-the-questions-anita-hill-fielded-in-1991/.

Shutan Bruce. "How Data and Analytics Insulate Clients in MeToo Era." Employee Benefit Adviser. April 17, 2020. https://www.employeebenefitadviser.com/news/how-data-and-analytics-insulate-clients-in-metoo-era.

Siegel, D. I., & Abbott, A. A. (2007). "The Work Lives of the Low-income Welfare Poor." *Families in Society* 88, 401–12. doi:10.1606/1044-3894.3649.

Siew, Walden. "Views: New Class of Female Advisers Still Confronting the Same Challenge: Cracking the Glass Ceiling." Employee Benefit Adviser. June 26, 2020. https://www.employeebenefitadviser.com/opinion/new-class-of-female-advisers-still-confronting-old-challenge-cracking-the-glass-ceiling.

Simpson, Maddy. "How Companies Can Support Female Employees as They Return to Work." Employee Benefit Adviser. June 24, 2020. https://www.employeebenefitadviser.com/news/how-companies-can-support-female-employees-as-they-return-to-work.

Sisson, Patrick. "Sen. Duckworth: "'Offensive' Law Would Weaken Landmark ADA." Curbed. February 28, 2018. https://archive.curbed.com/2018/2/28/17060220/ada-disabled-rights-accessibility-senator-tammy-duckworth.

Slater, K. (2020). "The 'Glass Cliff': How Women and People of Color Are Set up to Fail in the Workplace." Today. https://www.today.com/tmrw/glass-cliff-why-women-people-color-are-often-set-fail-t189060.

Small, Lisa. [Professor Cunnea] *A Timeline of Women's Legal History in the United States and at Georgetown University*. 1988. http://wlh.law.stanford.edu/wp-content/uploads/2011/01/cunnea-timeline.pdf.

Smentkowski P, Brian. "Sandra Day O'Connor." *Encyclopedia Britannica*, March 22, 2021.

Smith, David D., Judith R. Rosenstein, and Margaret C. Nikolov. "The Different Words We Use to Describe Male and Female Leaders." *Harvard Business Review*. May 25, 2018. https://hbr.org/2018/05/the-different-words-we-use-to-describe-male-and-female-leaders.

Smith, Lillian E. *Killers of the Dream*. Original 1961, rev. ed. 1978. W.W. Norton: New York, 1978.

Southern Poverty Law Center. (2010). "Injustice on Our Plates: Immigrant Women in the U.S. Food Industry." Retrieved from http://www.splcenter.org/sites/default/files/downloads/publication/Injustice_on_Our_Plates.pdf.

Stanford University. "Law Professor Examines Interplay of Race and Gender in Anita Hill Case." News Release. February 3, 2021. https://news.stanford.edu/pr/93/930406Arc3336.html.

Statistica. "Number of Rape and Sexual Assault Victims in the United States in 2019, by Gender." https://www.statista.com/statistics/642458/rape-and-sexual-assault-victims-in-the-us-by-gender/.

Stegman, Stephanie. "By Paddle, By Wagon, By Car: Field Nursing on the Front Lines of Native American Health." https://ultimatehistoryproject.com/field-nurse-program.html.

Stevens, Doris. *Jailed for Freedom*. New York: Boni and Liveright, 1920.

Stillwell, Jadie. 2019. "That Time Jane Fonda Sculpted Abs to Save the Planet." Reprint of Jane Fonda Interview with Maura Moynihan, March 1984. *Interview*. November 13. https://www.interviewmagazine.com/culture/that-time-jane-fonda-sculpted-abs-to-save-the-planet.

Subject Hattie C. Bansemer, Section 1, New Haven, CT. July 15, 1918; Confidential Correspondence 1913–14; Office of Naval Intelligence; Records of the Chief of Naval Operations, Record Group (RG) 38; National Archives Building, Washington, D.C.

Surane, Jenny. "Citi's Female CEO Rose As Bank Faced Failings on Gender Equality." Employee Benefit Adviser. September 21, 2020. https://www.employeebenefitadviser.com/articles/citis-female-ceo-rose-as-bank-faced-failings-on-gender-equality.

Sutin, Angelina R., Stephan Yannick, Henry Carretta, et al, "Perceived Discrimination and Physical, Cognitive, and Emotional Health in Older Adulthood." *American Journal of Geriatric Psychiatry* 23(2), (February 2015), pp. 171–79.

Swaine, Michael R. "ENIAC Computer." *Encyclopedia Britannica*. https://www.britannica.com/technology/ENIAC. Last updated May 27, 2020.

Sweet, Joni. "History of Women in the Workplace." MSN.com. Article and slide show. https://www.msn.com/en-us/news/us/history-of-women-in-the-workplace/ss-BB17VQxX.

Tanenbaum, Sharon. 2011. "Jane Fonda Opens Up about Her Decades-Long Battle with Bulimia." *Everyday Health*. August 9. everydayhealth.com/eating-disorders/0809/jane-fonda-opens-up-about-her-decades-long-battle-with-bulimia.aspx.
Tanzi, Alex. "Women Closing the Pay Gap with Men, at Least When Newly Hired." Employee Benefit Adviser. September 4, 2020. https://www.employeebenefitadviser.com/articles/women-closing-the-pay-gap-with-men-at-least-when-newly-hired.
Tappe, Anneken, Clare Duffy, and Tai Yellin. "These 5 Charts Show the Pandemic's Devastating Effect on Working Women." Cable News Network. December 17, 2020. https://www.cnn.com/2020/12/17/economy/job-losses-women-pandemic/index.html.
Taylor, Bruce Lee. 1988. Presbyterians and *"The People": A History of Presbyterian Missions and Ministries to the Navajo*. (PhD diss., Union Theological Seminary in Virginia), p. 1,279.
Teaching American History. "Message to Congress on Establishing Minimum Wages and Maximum Hours." April 14, 2019. https://teachingamericanhistory.org/library/document/message-to-congress-on-establishing-minimum-wages-and-maximum-hours/.
Thomas, R. (2019). "Tech's Long Hours Are Discriminatory and Counterproductive." Medium. https://medium.com/s/story/techs-long-hours-are-discriminatory-counter-productive-17dc61071ed5.
Tjaden, P., & Thoennes, N. (2006). Extent, Nature, and Consequence of Rape Victimization: Findings from the National Violence Against Women Survey (NCJ 210346). Retrieved from https://www.ncjrs.gov/pdffiles1/nij/210346.pdf.
Toossi, Mitra, and Teresa L. Morisi. "Women in the Workforce before, during, and after the Great Recession." U.S. Bureau of Labor Statistics. U.S. Department of Labor. July 2017. https://www.bls.gov/spotlight/2017/women-in-the-workforce-before-during-and-after-the-great-recession/home.htm.
Trent, Ann. "The Effects of Industrialization on Women and Children." The Classroom, June 27, 2019. https://www.theclassroom.com/the-effects-of-industrialization-on-women-children-12084175.html.
Tsjeng, Zing. "The Chinese Madame Curie." *Cosmos Magazine*. March 14, 2018. https://cosmosmagazine.com/physics/forgotten-women-in-science-chien-shiung-wu/.
United Nations. "United Nations Charter." October 18, 2010. https://www.un.org/en/sections/un-charter/index.html.
United Nations News. "Women and the UN Charter." June 8, 2018. https://news.un.org/en/audio/2018/06/1011761.
United Nations Women. "Commission on the Status of Women." February 9, 2013. https://www.unwomen.org/en/csw.
U.S. Bureau of Labor Statistics. (2010). "American Time Use Survey: Table A-1." Retrieved from http://www.bls.gov/tus/tables/ a1_2010.pdf.
— "Latest Numbers." February 15, 2021. https://www.bls.gov/schedule/2021/02_sched_list.htm.
—. "The Life of American Workers in 1915." February 12, 2016. https://www.bls.gov/opub/mlr/2016/article/the-life-of-american-workers-in-1915.htm.
U.S Congress. House. Equity and Inclusion Enforcement Act of 2019. HR 2574. 116th Cong., 1st sess. Introduced to House May 8, 2010. Passed/agreed to in House September 16, 2020, https://www.congress/gov/bill/116fh-congress/house-bill/2574.

—. Resolution (to Accompany H.R.2574). H.R.1107, 117th Cong.,1st sess. Introduced to House September 14, 2020, https://www.congress.gov/bill/117th-congress/house-bill/1107.
—. Whistleblower Protection Enhancement Act of 2021. S,743. 112th Cong. 1st sess. Sponsored by Sena. Daniel K.Akaka. Became Law November 27, 2012. https://www.congress.gov/bill/112th-congress/senate-bill/743.
U.S. Congress. Senate. *A Resolution Honoring the Life and Legacy of Elizebeth Smith Friedman, Cryptanalyst*. 116th Sen., July 1, 2017. https://www.congress.gov/bill/116th-congress/senate-resolution/133/.
U. S. Department of Defense, Sexual Assault Prevention and Response. (2011). Department of Defense annual report of sexual assault in the military: Fiscal year 2010. Retrieved from http://www.sapr.mil/media/pdf/reports/DoD_Fiscal_Year_2010_Annual_Report_on_Sexual_Assault_in_the_Military.pdf.
U.S. Department of Energy. "Five Fast Facts about Scientist Rachel Carson." March 5, 2015. https://www.energy.gov/articles/five-fast-facts-about-scientist-rachel-carson.
U. S. Department of Health and Human Services, Centers for Disease Control and Prevention. (2003). "Costs of Intimate Partner Violence against Women in the United States." Retrieved from http://www.cdc.gov/ violenceprevention/pdf/IPVBook-a.pdf.
U.S. Department of the Interior. "Interior Secretary Kempthorne Designates 9 National Historic Landmarks in 9 States." January 16, 2009. https://web.archive.org/web/20090305040615/http://www.doi.gov/news/09_News_Releases/011609c.html.
U.S. Department of Justice. "The Voting Rights Act of 1965." https://www.justice.gov/crt/statutes-enforced-voting-section#vra.
U.S. Department of Justice. "Employment (Title I)." https://www.ada.gov/ada_title_I.htm.
—. Equal Credit Opportunity Act of 1974." https://www.justice.gov/crt/equal-credit-opportunity-act-3.
U.S. Department of Justice. "Sexual Assault." https://www.justice.gov/ovw/sexual-assault.
—. "Uniformed Services Employment and Reemployment Rights Act of 1994." https://www.justice.gov/crt-military/uniformed-services-employment-and-reemployment-rights-act-1994.
U.S. Department of Labor. Bureau of Labor Statistics. "Characteristics of Minimum Wage Workers, 2020." February 2021. https://www.bls.gov/opub/reports/minimum-wage/2020/pdf.
U.S. Department of Labor. "Equal Pay for Equal Work." https://www.dol.gov/agencies/oasam/centers-offices/civil-rights-center/internal/policies/equal-pay-for-equal-work.
—. "Family and Medical Leave Act." https://www.dol.gov/agencies/whd/fmla.
—. "History of Changes to the Minimum Wage Law." https://www.dol.gov/agencies/whd/minimum-wage/history.
U.S. Department of Labor. Office of the Assistant Secretary for Administration and Management. "The Genetic Information Nondiscrimination Act of 2008 (GINA)." https://www.dol.gov/agencies/oasam/centers-offices/civil-rights-center/statutes/genetic-information-nondiscrimination-act-of-2008/guidance.
U.S. Department of Labor. Women's Bureau. "100 Years of Working Women." https://www.dol.gov/agencies/wb/data/occupations-decades-100.
—. "Your Stories Series." https://www.dol.gov/agencies/wb/wb100/stories.
U.S. Department of State. "Biographies of the Secretaries of State: Hillary Rodham Clinton (1947–)." https://history.state.gov/departmenthistory/people/clinton-hillary-rodham.

U.S. Environmental Protections Agency. "Women in Radiation History: Chien-Shiung Wu." March 4, 2021. https://www.epa.gov/radtown/women-radiation-history-chien-shiung-wu.
U.S. Equal Employment Opportunity Commission."The Age Discrimination in Employment Act of 1967." https://www.eeoc.gov/statutes/age-discrimination-employment-act-1967.
——. "The Civil RIghts Act of 1991." https://www.eeoc.gov/statutes/civil-rights-act-1991.
——. "The Equal Pay Act of 1963 (EPA)." https://www.eeoc.gov/statutes/equal-pay-act-1963.
——. "Equal Pay Act of 1963 and Lilly Ledbetter Fair Pay Act of 2009." https://www.eeoc.gov/laws/guidance/equal-pay-act-1963-and-lilly-ledbetter-fair-pay-act-2009.
——. "Facts About Sexual Harassment." June 27, 2002. https://www.eeoc.gov/fact-sheet/facts-about-sexual-harassment.
——. "The Pregnancy Discrimination Act of 1978." https://www.eeoc.gov/statutes/pregnancy-discrimination-act-1978.
——. "Prohibited Employment Policies/Practices." September 8, 2009. https://www.eeoc.gov/prohibited-employment-policiespractices.
——. "The Rehabilitation Act of 1973." https://www.eeoc.gov/statutes/rehabilitation-act-1973.
——. "The Rehabilitation Act of 1973: Sections 501 and 505." https://www.eeoc.gov/statutes/rehabilitation-act-1973.
——. "The State of Age Discrimination and Older Workers in the U.S. Fifty Years after the Age Discrimination in Employment Act (ADEA)." https://www.eeoc.gov/reports/state-age-discrimination-and-older-workers-us-50-years-after-age-discrimination-employment.
——. "Title VI, Prohibition Against National Origin Discrimination Affecting Limited English Proficient Persons." https://www.archives.gov/eeo/laws/title-vi.html.
——. "Title VII of the Civil Rights Act of 1964." https://www.eeoc.gov/statutes/title-vii-civil-rights-act-1964.
U.S. Government Information. "Patient Protection and Affordable Care Act, Section 1557 (Nondiscrimination section)." https://www.govinfo.gov/content/pkg/BILLS-111hr3590enr/pdf/BILLS-111hr3590enr.pdf.
U.S. House of Representatives, Office of History, Art and Archives. "Constitutional Amendments and Major Civil Rights Acts of Congress Referenced in Black Americans in Congress." November 29, 2020. https://history.house.gov/Exhibitions-and-Publications/BAIC/Historical-Data/Constitutional-Amendments-and-Legislation/.
US. Indian Health Service. "Coronavirus (COVID-19)." https://www.ihs.gov/coronavirus/.
U.S. Library of Congress. "Women's Suffrage in the Progressive Era." February 2001. https://www.loc.gov/classroom-materials/united-states-history-primary-source-timeline/progressive-era-to-new-era-1900-1929/womens-suffrage-in-progressive-era/.
U. S. Merit Systems Protection Board. (1995). "Sexual Harassment in the Federal Workplace: Trends, Progress, Continuing Challenges." Retrieved from http://www.mspb.gov/netsearch/viewdocs.aspx?docnumber=253661& version=253948.
U.S. National Archives and Records Administration. "Woman Suffrage and the 19th Amendment." https://www.archives.gov/education/lessons/woman-suffrage.
U.S. National Park Service. "Alice Austen." https://www.nps.gov/gate/learn/historyculture/alice-austen.htm.
——. "Marie Louise Bottineau Baldwin." U.S. National Park Service. https://www.nps.gov/people/marie-louise-bottineau-baldwin.htm.

—. National Historical Landmark Nomination for Sage Memorial Hospital School of Nursing, Ganado Mission. NPS Form 10-900. https://home1.nps.gov/nhl/find/statelists/az/SageMemorial.pdf.

—. "National Woman's Party Protests during World War I." https://www.nps.gov/articles/national-womans-party-protests-world-war-i.htm.

—. "The Suffrage 'Prison Special' Tour of 1919." Democracy Limited Series. https://www.nps.gov/articles/series.htm?id=2DD55399-9218-B075-2AF1DAB34543A1CA.

—. "Symbols of the Women's Suffrage Movement." https://www.nps.gov/articles/symbols-of-the-women-s-suffrage-movement.htm.

—. "Telling All Americans' Stories: Introduction to Women's History." https://www.nps.gov/articles/taas-womenshistory-intro.htm.

—. "Women in World War I." https://www.nps.gov/articles/women-in-world-war-i.htm.

—. "Women Workers at the Boston Navy Yard during World War I." https://www.nps.gov/articles/women-workers-bny-wwi.htm.

—. "The WWII Home Front." U.S. https://www.nps.gov/articles/the-wwii-home-front.htm.

U.S. Navy. "Lenah H. Sutcliffe Higbee: The U.S. Navy's First Living Female Navy Cross Recipient." history.navy.mil/research/histories/biographies-list/bios-h/higbee-lenah-s.html.

U.S. Senate. "About Tammy. Duckworth Senate Biography." https://www.duckworth.senate.gov/about-tammy/biography.

University of Washington. "Hoovervilles and Homelessness." January 4, 2010. https://depts.washington.edu/depress/hooverville.shtml.

Visier Team. "Reduce Gender Bias Using Data-Driven Performance Reviews." 2020. /clarity/reduce-gender-bias-using-data-driven-performance-reviews/.

Vox Media. "7 Positive Changes That Have Come from the #MetooMovement." October 4, 2019. https://katherineclark.house.gov/in-the-news

Waller, Nikki. "Women in the Workplace: How Men and Women See the Workplace Differently." *The Wall Street Journal*. September 27 2016. http://graphics.wsj.com/how-men-and-women-see-the-workplace-differently//

Wamsley, L. "U.S. Women's Soccer Team Sues U.S. Soccer for Gender Discrimination." March 8, 2019. https://www.npr.org/2019/03/08/701522635/u-s-womens-soccer-team-sues-u-s-soccer-for-gender-discrimination.

—. "2020 Employee Well-Being Report." January 29, 2020. https://www.webmdhealthservices.com/campaign/2020-employee-well-being-report/.

Weiss, Suzannah. "4 Things Women Couldn't Do in 1990." Bustle. December 16, 2015. https://www.bustle.com/articles/129957-4-things-you-wont-believe-women-couldnt-do-in-1990.

Wendorf, Marcia. "The Radium Girls: Workers Who Painted with Radium and Suffered Radiation Exposure." Interesting Engineering. August 8, 2019. https://interestingengineering.com/the-radium-girls-workers-who-painted-with-radium-and-suffered-radiation-exposure.

Werft, Meghan. "In 1917 'Silent Sentinels' Protested for the Right to Vote." *Global Citizen*. January 10, 2017. https://www.globalcitizen.org/en/content/womens-march-white-house-protests-trump/.

Wething, Hilary. "Job Growth in the Great Recession Has Not Been Equal between Men and Women." Economic Policy Institute. August 26, 2014. https://www.epi.org/blog/job-growth-great-recession-equal-men-women/.

Whitehill, Steve. "The Problem Older Women Face in the Workplace." Anchor Business Brokers. June 25, 2019. https://anchorbusinessbrokers.com/the-problem-older-women-face-in-the-workplace/.

Wigington, Patti. "Geraldine Ferraro: First Female Democratic VP Candidate." ThoughtCo. July 18, 2019. https://www.thoughtco.com/geraldine-ferraro-4691713.

Wikipedia. "1913 Paterson Silk Strike." https://en.wikipedia.org/wiki/1913_Paterson_silk_strike. Last updated January 19, 2021.

—. "O, The Oprah Magazine." April 7, 2021.https://en.wikipedia.org/wiki/O,_The_Oprah_Magazine.

—. "Presidential Commission on the Status of Women." https://en.wikipedia.org/wiki/Presidential_Commission_on_the_Status_of_Women. Last updated December 11, 2020.

—. "*Roe v. Wade*." February 16, 2016. https://en.wikipedia.org/wiki/Roe_v._Wade/

—. "Sage Memorial Hospital School of Nursing." https://en.wikipedia.org/wiki/Sage_Memorial_Hospital_School_of_Nursing.

—. "SPARS." https://en.wikipedia.org/wiki/SPARS.

—. "U.S. Military Occupation Code." Last updated December 1, 2020. https://en.wikipedia.org/wiki/United_States_military_occupation_code.

Williams, Kathleen Broome. *Grace Hopper: Admiral of the Cyber Sea*. Annapolis: Naval Institute Press, 2004.

Wolfe, Molly. "This Day in History: National Organization for Women Was Founded." The White House. Obama Administration. June 30, 2015. https://obamawhitehouse.archives.gov/blog/2015/06/30/day-history-national-organization-women-was-founded.

Women and The American History. "Life Story: Mary Church Terrell (1863–1954)." March 8, 2021. https://wams.nyhistory.org/modernizing-america/woman-suffrage/mary-church-terrell//

Women's Center Youth and Family Services. "Sexual Assault Statistics." https://www.womenscenteryfs.org/index.php/get-info/sexual-assault/statistics/.

"Women's History Milestones: A Timeline." History. A&E Networks. February 26, 2019. https://www.history.com/topics/womens-history/womens-history-us-timeline.

Women's History of American Women Blog. "Plymouth Colony Women's Rights." https://www.womenhistoryblog.com/2007/09/plymouth-colony-womens-rights.html.

—. "Women Inventors–History of American Women." January 3, 2016. https://www.womenhistoryblog.com/2016/01/first-women-inventors.html.

World History Education "Major Achievements of Sandra Day O'Connor." https://www.worldhistoryedu.com/sandra-day-o-connor-biography-cases-achievements-and-facts/.

Yaffe, Alva. "A Hidden Chapter in the History Books: Who Were The Radium Girls?" History by Day. August 13, 2020. https://historybyday.com/pop-culture/a-hidden-chapter-in-the-history-books-who-were-the-radium-girls/#:~:text=The%20workers%20who%20were%20handling,items%20using%20the%20radium%20paint.

Yale University. "Biography of Grace Murray Hopper." August 16, 2017. https://president.yale.edu/biography-grace-murray-hopper.

Yang, J., Zhang, N., Miller, T. R., & LeHew, B. (2012). "Costs of Sexual Violence in Iowa." (2009). Retrieved from the University of Iowa College of Public Health: http://www.public-health.uiowa.edu/iprc/resources/Cost-SexualViolence-Iowa-FINAL.pdf.

Zilman, Claire. "Watch Anita Hill Get a Standing Ovation from Hundreds of Female Executives." Yahoo Finance. October 2, 2018. https://finance.yahoo.com/news/watch-anita-hill-standing-ovation-180918601.html.

Zinn Education Project. "Asian-Americans and Moments in People's History." https://www.zinnedproject.org/materials/asian-americans-and-moments-in-peoples-history/.

Image Attributions

PART ONE • 1900–1929

Chapter 1

Despite pressure to assimilate to White culture, Marie Louise Bottineau Baldwin braided her hair and wore tribal clothing for her government ID photo. (National Park Service, public domain)

Maggie L. Walker, whose parents were enslaved, was the first woman in the country to open a bank, c. 1919. (National Park Service, public domain)

Ida B. Wells was an African American civil-rights advocate, journalist, feminist, and American hero, c 1900. (National Park Service, public domain)

Chapter 2

African American women like Nannie Burroughs (far left, holding banner) were very involved in the suffrage movement with both mainstream and Black suffragist organizations, c.1905. (Library of Congress 93595951, public domain)

Woman suffrage marchers marched in white clothing. Although they were assaulted by angry and violent crowds, they continued to march in an effort to achieve enfranchisement and broader legal standing and freedom for women. (Library of Congress 20196v, public domain)

The Silent Sentinels protested in Lafayette Square – which is directly across the street from the White House – for nearly three years. (Library of Congress 000192, public domain)

Neither sleet nor sun nor rainy inaugurations nor threats of abuse deterred the Silent Sentinels from picketing for enfranchisement, and equal rights for women. In this image, the Sentinels are picketing President Wilson's second inauguration. (Library of Congress mnwp000293, public domain)

Silent Sentinels often addressed the president directly on their signage. (Library of Congress, public domain)

Silent Sentinel Helena Hill in her Occoquan workhouse jail cell. (Library of Congress ws00097, public domain)

Woman Suffrage Headquarters, Ohio (Library of Congress 97500065, public domain)

Headquarters of the National Association Opposed to Woman Suffrage (Shutterstock ID 242816995, by Everett Collection)

"Looking Backward" artwork by Laura E. Foster, c. 1912, published in *Life* magazine (August 22, 1912). This exemplary anti-suffrage artwork depicts a woman leaving behind love, marriage, children, and home for suffrage and loneliness. The message that women who had the vote would be miserable was common in anti-suffrage propaganda. (Library of Congress 2002716765, public domain)

Time spent in the Occoquan workhouse took its toll on even the strongest suffragists, as seen in this image of Dora Lewis upon her release. (Library of Congress mnwp160039, public domain)

Impassioned speeches were a highlight of the Prison Special tour, which drew huge crowds like this one in San Francisco, California. (Library of Congress 000247, public domain)

During the Prison Special tour, suffragists reenacted scenes from their time in the Occoquan prison workhouse. Here Pauline Adams demonstrates protests, such as hunger strikes, that she and her fellow inmates staged during meals. (Library of Congress 000068, public domain)

Suffragists in prison uniforms reenact scenes from their time imprisoned in the Occoquan workhouse. The uniform the suffragists were made to wear at Occoquan was rough and considered degrading to someone of their social standing. (Library of Congress mnwp000249, public domain)

A U.S. Navy yeoman (F) on submarine K-5 gazes through her binoculars. (National Archives 80-G-1025873, public domain)

Rear Admiral Victor Blue (left, center), chief of the Bureau of Navigation, inspects U.S. Navy yeomen (F) on the grounds of the Washington Monument in Washington, D.C., in 1918. (National Archives 19-1136, public domain)

Highly skilled bilingual switchboard operators in the Army Signal Corps were recruited by the Army and served in Chaumont, France, near the front lines – and sometimes in the trenches – during World War II. (Wikipedia Commons, United States Army Signal Corps, Photo SC-33446, public domain)

Grace Banker was chief operator for the first unit of the U.S. Army Signal Corps telephone operators that arrived in France in March 1918. The operators translated highly sensitive information about logistics, troop movements, and ammunition between major allied commanders. She was awarded the Army Distinguished Service Medal. (Wikipedia Commons, Malstrom Air Force Base, U.S. Air Force, public domain)

Pilot Bessie Coleman, 1923 (Wikimedia Commons, public domain)

Pilot Bessie Coleman and her plane,1922 (Wikimedia Commons, public domain)

Dr. Susan La Flesche Picotte, the first Native American woman in the United States to receive a medical degree, c. 1910 (National Library of Medicine, National Institutes of Health, public domain)

Survivors of the Triangle Shirtwaist Factory fire (Shutterstock ID 242301106, by Everett Collection)

Workers in the Bread and Roses Strike, 1912 (Wikimedia Commons, public domain)

Women work at their stations as supervisors monitor their productivity, c. 1915. (Shutterstock ID 24440520, by Everett Collection)

Chapter 3

One argument for woman suffrage, made popular by the song "She's Good Enough to Be Your Baby's Mother and She's Good Enough to Vote with You," was that it would improve women's ability to fulfill their socially acceptable roles as mothers and homemakers. (Library of Congress 2017562275, public domain)

Suffragists hold political placards with political-activist slogans in 1920. Signs read: Know Your Courts–Study Our Politicians, Liberty in Law, Law Makers Must Not Be Law Breakers, and Character in Candidates. (Shutterstock ID 755026417, by Everett Collection)

Suffragists formed the National League of Women Voters and concentrated their efforts on focused "get out the vote" campaigns ahead of elections. In this image, women from the League hold up signs that read "VOTE" on September 17, 1924. Millions of women did vote in 1920 and in 1924, but in a lower proportion than men. (Shutterstock 7555026393, by Everett Collection)

Despite giants in her field acknowledging Dr. Emmy Noether as the most significant female in the history of mathematics – Albert Einstein called her a "mathematical genius" – widespread gender discrimination at universities resulted in her only finding paid employment in the final few years of her life. (Department of Energy, public domain)

Mathematician and space scientist Katherine G. Johnson was one of the three students who first integrated West Virginia University. She was hired by NACA in 1953 and worked in the racially segregated West Area Computing Unit of the Langley Research Center until 1958, when NASA took the reins and abolished racial segregation. Johnson overcame the cultural barriers of race and gender to progress from mathematical calculations to computing experimental flight and ground-test data. This photo is taken of her working at the Research Center in 1962. Johnson is featured in the 2016 nonfiction book *Hidden Figures: The American Dream and the Untold Story of the Black Women Who Helped Win the Space Race* and as one of three protagonists in the film adaptation *Hidden Figures*. Young people interested in science, technology, engineering, and mathematics (STEM) consider her a role model. (Langley Research Center, NASA, NASA photographer Bob Nye, public domain)

Dorothy Vaughan was the first Black female supervisor at NACA and she worked on an IBM machine. She supervised Black human computers who were sequestered in the segregated West Area Computing Unit at the Langley Research Center from 1943 to 1958, when NASA took the reins and abolished racial segregation. Vaughan is featured in the 2016 nonfiction book *Hidden Figures: The American Dream and the Untold Story of the Black Women Who Helped Win the Space Race* and as one of three protagonists in the film adaptation *Hidden Figures*. She was inducted into the Langley Hall of Honor on June 1, 2017. (NASA on the Commons, public domain)

Mathematician and aerospace engineer Mary Jackson, a former math teacher, was hired as a research mathematician, or human computer, for NACA in 1951. She was the first African American engineer at NASA and is featured in the 2016 nonfiction book *Hidden Figures: The American Dream and the Untold Story of the Black Women Who Helped Win the Space Race* and as one of three protagonists in the film adaptation *Hidden Figures.* She worked in the segregated West Area Computer Unit until 1958, when she transitioned to the Transonic Aerodynamic Branch, where this photo was taken on June 2, 1977. Jackson retired from NASA in 1985 and was posthumously awarded the Congressional Gold Medal. In 2021, NASA also named its D.C. Headquarters after her. (Langley Research Center, NASA, public domain)

Mathematician, space scientist, and diversity advocate Jeanette Scissum joined NASA's Marshall Space Flight Center in Alabama in 1964 after earning bachelor's and master's degrees in mathematics from Alabama A&M University. She was the first African American mathematician to be hired by the Marshall Center. Scissum published the NASA report "Survey of Solar Cycle Prediction Models" in 1967. This report put forward techniques for improved forecasting of the sunspot cycle. She worked as a space scientist in the Marshall Space Environment Branch in the mid-1970s, and later led activities in the Marshall Atmospheric, Magnetospheric, and Plasmas in Space project. Over the course of her 39-year career at NASA, Scissum held positions across the agency, including stints at the Goddard Space Flight Center in Maryland, at NASA Headquarters in Washington, D.C., and with the Space Shuttle Program. (Photographer, NASA/Marshall Space Flight Center, public domain)

Human computers calculating test data from the Ames 16-foot wind tunnel, Ames Research Center, Moffett Field, California, at the southernmost end of San Francisco Bay. The human computers were responsible for making aerodynamic calculations that were critical to NASA's research and mission success. (NACA, public domain)

Young women workers at the Bureau of Aeronautics in a typing contest, April 15, 1926 (Shutterstock ID 755026384, by Everett Collection)

Electrical engineer Kitty Joyner is believed to be the first female NACA engineer as well as the first female engineer to graduate from the University of Virginia – but she had to sue the University before they agreed to admit her to its formerly all-male engineering school. Joyner rose to the level of a NASA branch head. (Langley Research Center, NASA / Photographer, NACA Langley, public domain)

Annie Oakley, 1885 (Wikimedia Commons, public domain)

Chapter 4

Graduates of the Sage Memorial Hospital School of Nursing, c. 1935. This accredited school eventually attracted not only Native American students but also women from other marginalized groups. As the first and only nursing school for Native Americans, Sage Memorial was a landmark institution in changing White attitudes about the abilities of Native American people. (National Archives, public domain)

U.S. Patent No. 2,292,387 for a "Secret Communication System" invented by Hedy Kiesler Markey (Hedy Lamarr) and George Antheil. The pair invented the earliest known form of a telecommunications technique called "frequency hopping." The secret system used a piano roll to manipulate radio frequencies, making it impossible for classified messages and radio-guided torpedoes to be intercepted. Years later, the invention had a global impact on everyday communications. (Wikimedia Commons, public domain)

PART TWO • CULTURAL SHIFTS AND SONIC BOOMS, 1940–1969

Chapter 5

A munitions worker tightens nose plugs on 500-pound aerial bombs, c. 1943. (Shutterstock 249573385, by Everett Collection)

Two Daytona Beach, Florida, housewives weld in an aircraft-construction class during World War II. Both have sons in the military, April 1942. (Shutterstock ID 244393786, by Everett Collection)

On the home front and waiting in line for rationed sugar (Office for Emergency Management, Office of War Information, National Archives, public domain via Wikimedia Commons)

Poster promoting rationing on the home front during World War II (Wikimedia Commons, public domain)

Mary Lasker with President Harry S. Truman and Lucile Petry. When U.S. Public Health Service established the Division of Nurse Education, Surgeon General Thomas Parran appointed Lucile Petry, RN, as the head of the Cadet Nurse Corps, making her the first woman to head a major division of the U.S. Public Health Service. (U.S. National Library of Medicine digital collection 101449665, public domain)

Recruiting poster for the Cadet Nurse Corps (US Army, public domain)

The Cadet Nurse Corps was open to all, regardless of race, ethnicity or marital status. Though women of color were still underrepresented among Cadet Nurses, the common curriculum ensured that all underrepresented populations received the same training. Also, schools of nursing that discriminated against African American or other marginalized populations were at risk of losing federal funding if they continued this practice. Pictured left to right are Cadet Nurses Elizabeth Carroll, Hortense Ashe, Merdine Thompson, and Elizabeth Martin. All sat for the Ohio State Board Examinations in December of 1944. (National Archives, public domain)

Lenah H. Sutcliffe Higbee, c. 1916, was the first chief of the Navy Nurse Corps and for her wartime efforts was awarded the Navy Cross, an award second only to the Medal of Honor. A U.S. Navy destroyer was also named in her honor. Three other nurses from the Navy Corps received the Navy Cross posthumously. (U.S. Navy, public domain)

WAVES apprentice Seaman Frances Bates inspects a Grumman Wildcat engine as part of her training at the U.S. Naval Training School (WR) Bronx, New York. (National Archives, public domain)

From left: WAFS pilots Nancy Batson, Cornelia Fort, Evelyn Sharp, Barbara J. Erickson, and Gertrude Meserve, a flight instructor who taught hundreds of students at Harvard and MIT, March 7th, 1943. When the War Department floated the idea of recruiting female pilots to meet domestic aviation needs, General Hap Arnold, Chief of the U.S. Army Air Corps, declared the idea "utterly unfeasible" and asserted that women are just too "high strung" to fly airplanes. First Lady Eleanor Roosevelt intervened and the Women's Auxiliary Ferrying Squadron (WAFS) unit was created. The WAFS team consisted of 28 commercially licensed pilots who operated under the leadership of Nancy Harkness Love. WAFS pilots initially transported military trainers and flew light aircraft from factories to domestic bases. When the WAFS unit merged with the new Women Airforce Service Pilots (WASP) unit, however, their duties expanded significantly. (National Museum of the U.S. Air Force, public domain)

A WASP pilot, sometimes referred to as a "Fly Girl," circa 1943. The Women Airforce Service Pilots (WASP) pilots ferried military personnel trainers and flew light aircraft from factories to domestic bases, but also delivered bombers, fighter planes, and transport planes as well. All told, 1,070 women pilots completed WASP training and served as pilots during the war. These pioneering women paved the way for modern U.S. Air Force women pilots. (National Archives, public domain)

Women's Army Corps soldiers assigned to the Eighth Air Force in England operate Teletype machines during World War II. (U.S. Department of Defense, public domain)

Private First Class Priscilla Goodrich (left) and Private Elaine Munsinger (right) of the Wrench and Hammer Brigade break down an airplane engine in the Assembly and Repair department at Marine Corps Air Station Cherry Point, North Carolina, c. 1943. (U.S. Marine Corps Archives, public domain)

The experiments of Columbia University physicists (left to right) Chien-Shiung Wu, Y. K. Lee, and L. W. Mo confirmed the theory of conservation of vector current. In the experiments, which took several months to complete, proton beams from Columbia's Van de Graaff accelerator were transmitted through pipes to strike a 2 mm. Boron target at the entrance to a spectrometer chamber. (Wikimedia Commons, public domain)

Programmers Betty Jennings (left) and Frances Bilas (right) operating the ENIAC's main control panel, c.1945–1947. (Wikimedia Commons, U.S. Army, public domain)

First Lady Eleanor Roosevelt addressing the Democratic National Convention on July 18, 1940, in Chicago. (Wikimedia Commons from the Franklin Delano Roosevelt Presidential Library, public domain)

Chapter 6

Biologist working in a lab (Shutterstock ID1686294913, by Arunporn Thanapotivirat)

Tupperware® party, 1950s (Wikimedia Commons, Tupperware Corporation, public domain)

Chapter 7

A student chemist conducting research in the lab. (Shutterstock ID 1217200690, by H. Ko)

Luci Baines Johnson, Mary Wilson, and Dolores Huerta at the Summit on Race in America at the LBJ Presidential Library on April 8, 2019. Huerta, a Presidential Medal of Freedom recipient, cofounded the United Farm Workers of America with Cesar Chavez in the 1960s and has spent decades advocating for laborers, women and children. (Wikimedia commons, public domain)

PART THREE • REVOLUTION AND EQUALITY FOR ALL, 1970–1999

Chapter 8

Shirley Chisholm (D-NY), the first Black woman elected to the U.S. House of Representatives, announcing her candidacy in 1972. (Library of Congress ds.07135, public domain)

American tennis great Billie Jean King, 1978 (©Lynn Gilbert 1978, New York, Wikimedia Commons, licensed under the Creative Commons Attribution-Share Alike 4.0 International license)

Gloria Steinem at a news conference, Women's Action Alliance, January 12, 1972. (Library of Congress, public domain)

Chapter 9

Sandra Day O'Connor, first female Associate Justice of the Supreme Court of the United States (Library of Congress, public domain)

President Barack Obama awards the 2013 Presidential Medal of Freedom to Oprah Winfrey during a ceremony in the East Room of the White House, November 20, 2013. (Official White House photography by Lawrence Jackson 2013, public domain)

Hollywood starlet Jane Fonda in 1963 (Wikimedia Commons, publicity photo of Jane Fonda for the film Sunday in New York, public domain)

Jane Fonda at a political rally in 1975 (Wikimedia Commons, Dutch National Archives, The Hague, Fotocollectie Algemeen Nederlands Persbureau (ANeFo), 1945–1989, Nummer toegang 2.24.01.05 Bestanddeelnummer 927-6990, public domain)

Chapter 10

President Jimmy Carter with Ruth Bader Ginsburg at Reception for women federal judges, October 3, 1980. (National Archives, public domain)

PART FOUR • DIVERSITY: THE NEW NORMAL, 2020–2021

Chapter 11

CEO in a meeting with her staff (Shutterstock ID 1043108527, by fizkes)

First Lady Michelle Obama, Official Portrait (White House, public domain)

U.S. Senator Tammy Duckworth of Illinois wearing a Chicago Cubs cap on Capitol Hill, October 7, 2015. (Wikimedia Commons, public domain)

Chapter 12

Secretary of State Hillary Rodham Clinton, September 28, 2010 (U.S. Department of State in Washington, D.C., public domain)

The American #MeToo Movement (Wikimedia Commons, by Donna Rotunno)

Chapter 13

During the pandemic, working women with children have either left their jobs or are trying to work from home while parenting, handling the bulk of the housework, and ensuring that their children are keeping up with their online classes. (Shutterstock ID 1703893741, by Przemek Klos)

Kamala Harris, May 12, 2017 (Wikimedia Commons, United States Congress, official Senate portrait of Senator Kamala Harris of California, public domain)

Contributors

ABOUT EDITORIAL DIRECTOR

Angela Williams, M.F.A., is an editorial director, visual artist, typographer, and writer who has produced, written, and curated a wide range of award-winning content for archival collections, museums, and academic and trade publishers. She graduated at the top of her M.F.A. class. Angela directed publishing programs in the Triangle area of North Carolina before moving to the Greater Detroit area to focus on content aggregation for reference and educational markets. She serves as a board member and volunteer ally for an organization whose programming is based on the premise that developing meaningful relationships across socioeconomic lines can have a dramatic impact on the efficacy rate of moving families out of poverty. As Editorial Director at Omnigraphics, she manages the diversity collection and a series of reference books.

ABOUT CONTRIBUTING EDITOR

Heather McDonough is a library resource specialist and is initiating her editorial and writing work with this important Omnigraphics title. She has extensive experience in sales and customer success capacities within publishing and is looking to further her impact with insightful editorial contribution on key topics. Heather is an advent hiker, rescues and fosters dogs, and is a leading volunteer in her community.

ABOUT CONTRIBUTING WRITERS

Jamie Maniloff, M.A. in Applied Communication, is a recognized leader across academic, corporate and non-profit organizations. Jamie has worked with Brené Brown to become a certified Dare to Lead Facilitator, is a two-time scholarship recipient from The Cardoner Institute for Contemplative Leadership and is a content strategy professional specializing in structuring data-driven, multi-channel customer lifecycle and digital shopping programs for businesses, including Fortune 500 companies. Jamie graduated at the top of her Master's class from Indiana University–Purdue University Indianapolis, and is involved with a variety of committees including Together Digital Detroit, The American Alpine Club, and the Association of National Advertisers (ANA), where she participates in conversations around Relationship Marketing and the #SeeHerInSports initiative, which is focused on increasing the visibility and portrayal of women in sports.

Sue Maniloff is a seasoned professional who has been working within publishing, aggregation and education technology for decades. Her background includes global content acquisition for the first to market library discovery service, along with developing a winning business strategy for an early stage EdTech startup that leveraged machine learning applications for taxonomy curation. She has expertise in building relationships and developing publishing strategies that complete collections and fulfill gaps, best serving the needs of students and library patrons. As VP Business Development at Omnigraphics, she publishes nonfiction and reference content for schools and libraries.

Nonjabulo Mlangeni, M.A., is an experienced journalist, editor, and technical writer, with work appearing in books, magazines, newspapers, and industry newsletters. She has provided editorial direction and copyediting on content written for the academic, professional, public library, global nonprofits, and NGO market sectors. Her deep understanding and knowledge of discrimination and diversity and inclusion issues is woven in throughout this title. Nonjabulo holds a M.A. in African American Studies from UCLA.

Madhavi Murali, B.Sc. is an experienced content creator who has provided writing services to various clients and websites. She has also provided editorial direction for several reference resources spanning the areas of health and culture. She works as a consultant editor in a reference publishing company focused on providing high-quality content to library and education markets.

Index

Index

Page numbers in *italics* indicate a table or illustration.

E

M

N

O

P

Q

R

S

T

Z